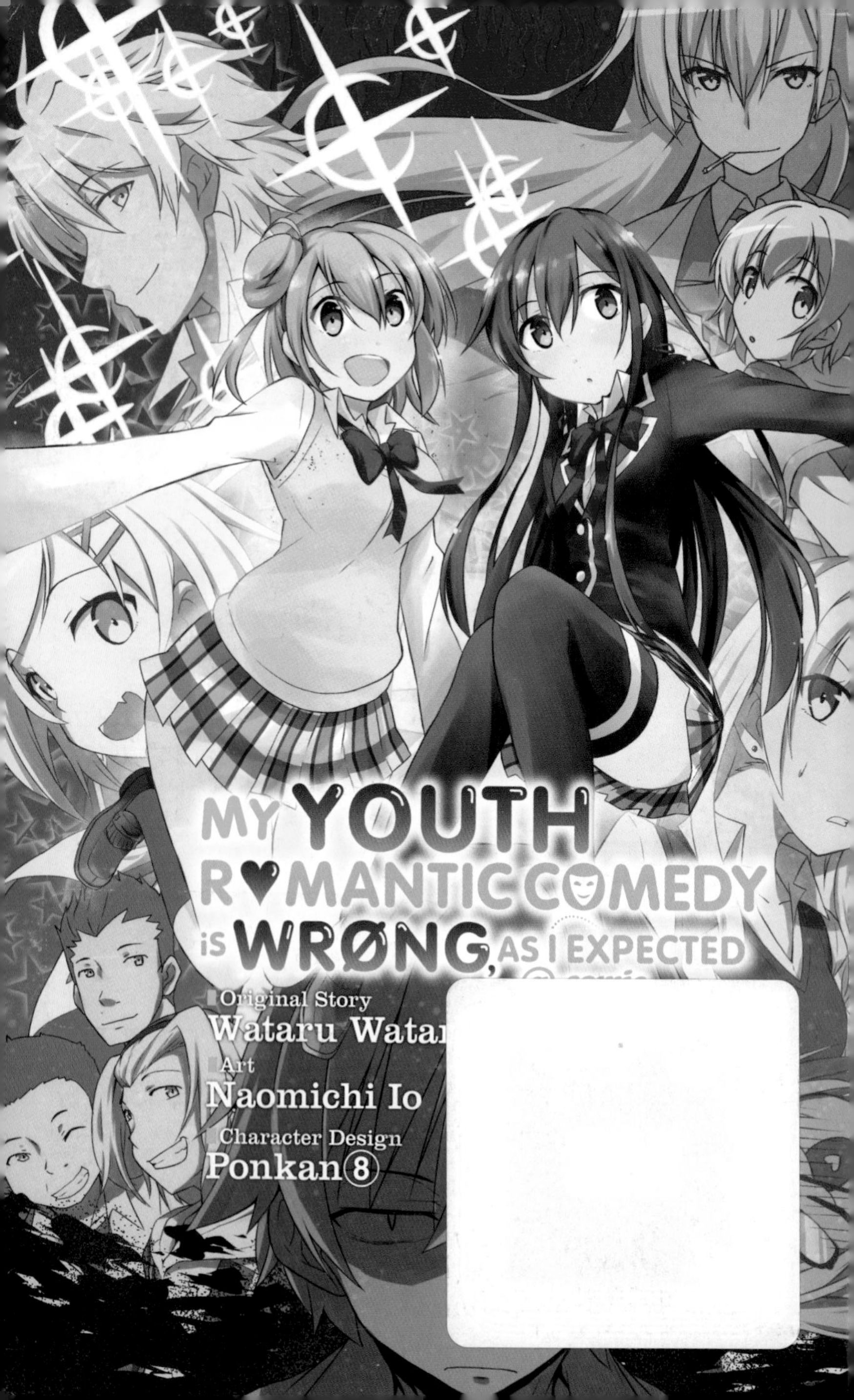
MY YOUTH
ROMANTIC COMEDY
IS WRONG, AS I EXPECTED
Original Story
Wataru Watar
Art
Naomichi Io
Character Design
Ponkan 8

MY YOUTH ROMANTIC COMEDY IS WRONG, AS I EXPECTED @COMIC

CHARACTERS + STORY SO FAR

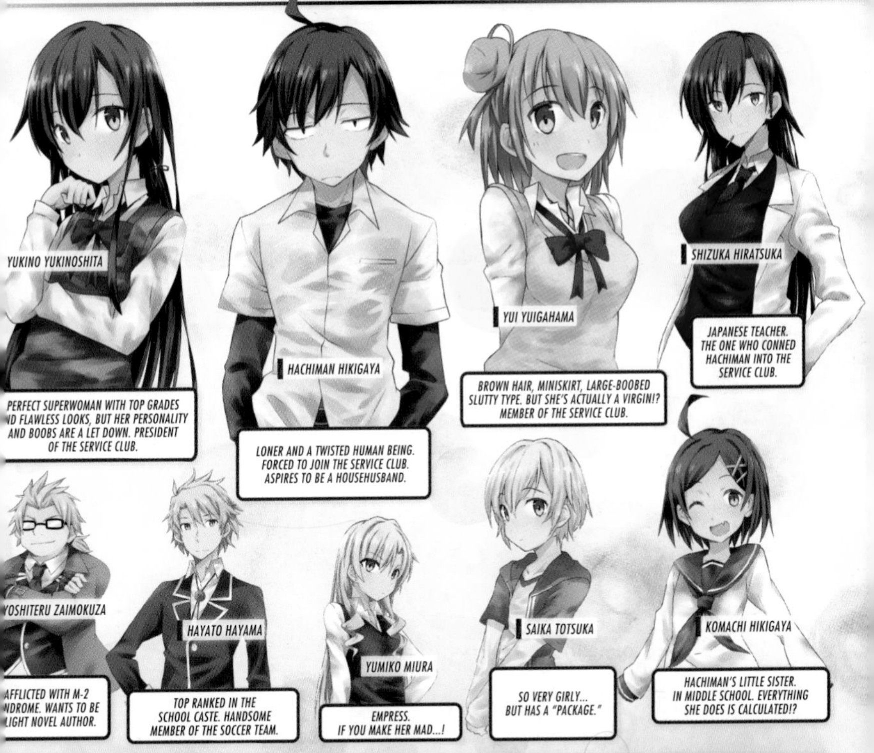

YUKINO YUKINOSHITA
PERFECT SUPERWOMAN WITH TOP GRADES ND FLAWLESS LOOKS, BUT HER PERSONALITY AND BOOBS ARE A LET DOWN. PRESIDENT OF THE SERVICE CLUB.
HACHIMAN HIKIGAYA
LONER AND A TWISTED HUMAN BEING. FORCED TO JOIN THE SERVICE CLUB. ASPIRES TO BE A HOUSEHUSBAND.
YUI YUIGAHAMA
BROWN HAIR, MINISKIRT, LARGE-BOOBED SLUTTY TYPE. BUT SHE'S ACTUALLY A VIRGIN!? MEMBER OF THE SERVICE CLUB.
SHIZUKA HIRATSUKA
JAPANESE TEACHER. THE ONE WHO CONNED HACHIMAN INTO THE SERVICE CLUB.
YOSHITERU ZAIMOKUZA
AFFLICTED WITH M-2 NDROME. WANTS TO BE LIGHT NOVEL AUTHOR.
HAYATO HAYAMA
TOP RANKED IN THE SCHOOL CASTE. HANDSOME MEMBER OF THE SOCCER TEAM.
YUMIKO MIURA
EMPRESS. IF YOU MAKE HER MAD...!
SAIKA TOTSUKA
SO VERY GIRLY... BUT HAS A "PACKAGE."
KOMACHI HIKIGAYA
HACHIMAN'S LITTLE SISTER. IN MIDDLE SCHOOL. EVERYTHING SHE DOES IS CALCULATED!?

MY STORY

Y NAME IS HACHIMAN HIKIGAYA. I'M A SECOND-YEAR AT SOUBU HIGH SCHOOL IN CHIBA CITY. OUR GUIDANCE COUNSELOR, HIRATSUKA-SENSEI, NNOUNCED THAT SHE'D CORRECT MY "TWISTED LONER PERSONALITY" AND FORCED ME INTO JOINING A MYSTERIOUS CLUB CALLED THE "SERVICE CLUB." ERE, I MET YUKINO YUKINOSHITA, A BEAUTIFUL GIRL WITH TOP GRADES, AND YUI YUIGAHAMA, WHO SCORES HIGH IN SLUT QUOTIENT. AND THAT'S HEN ALL THE EEK-EEK TEE-HEE-HEE SCHOOL HIJINKS BEGIN! ...YEAH, NO, MY LIFE AT SCHOOL IS AS DISAPPOINTING AS ALWAYS, BUT AT THE VERY AST I DON'T HATE IT ANYMORE...MAYBE. WELL, THAT'S HOW IT IS.

CONTENTS

MADE IN COOPERATION WITH THE CHIBA CITY LOCATION SERVICE

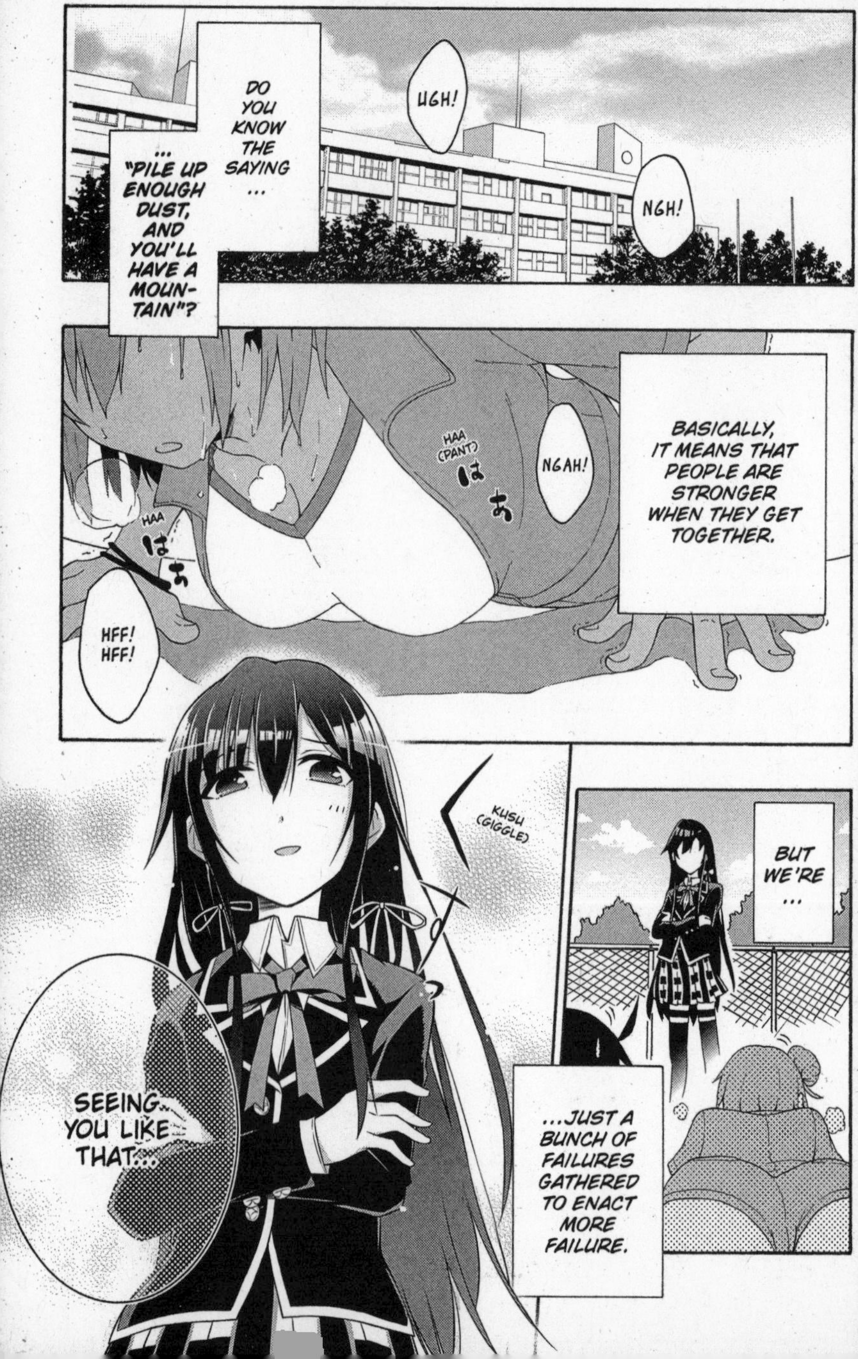
UGH!
NGH!
DO YOU KNOW THE SAYING ...
... "PILE UP ENOUGH DUST, AND YOU'LL HAVE A MOUN-TAIN"?
BASICALLY, IT MEANS THAT PEOPLE ARE STRONGER WHEN THEY GET TOGETHER.
NGAH!
HAA (PANT) はあ
HAA はあ
HFF! HFF!
BUT WE'RE ...
...JUST A BUNCH OF FAILURES GATHERED TO ENACT MORE FAILURE.
KUSU (GIGGLE)
SEEING YOU LIKE THAT...

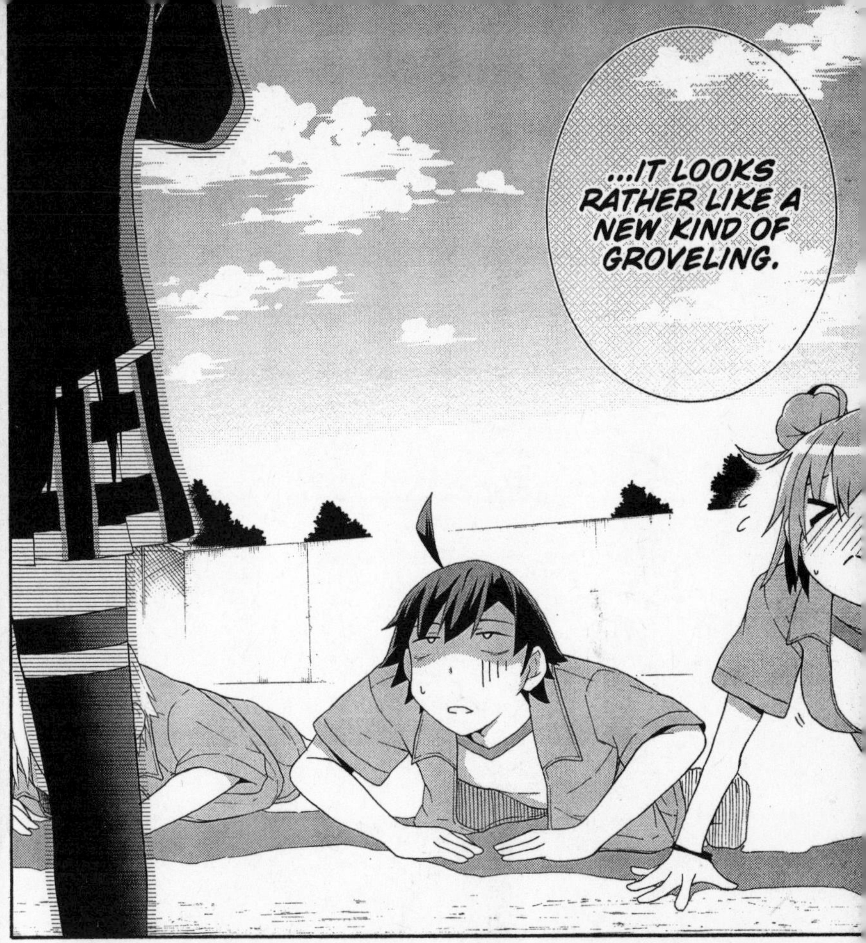
...IT LOOKS RATHER LIKE A NEW KIND OF GROVELING.
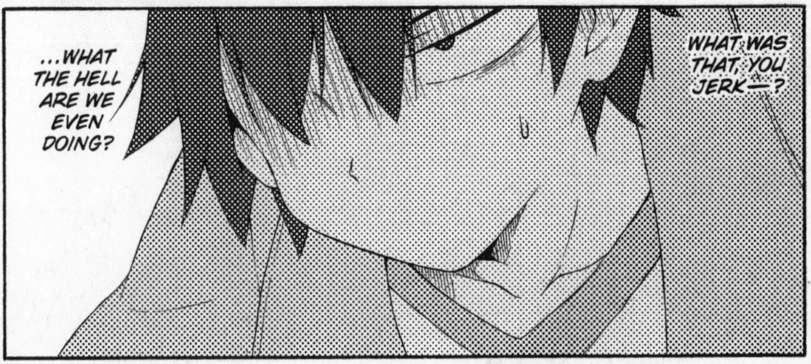
WHAT WAS THAT, YOU JERK—?
...WHAT THE HELL ARE WE EVEN DOING?

CHAPTER 6 ··· BUT SAIKA TOTSUKA HAS A "PACKAGE."

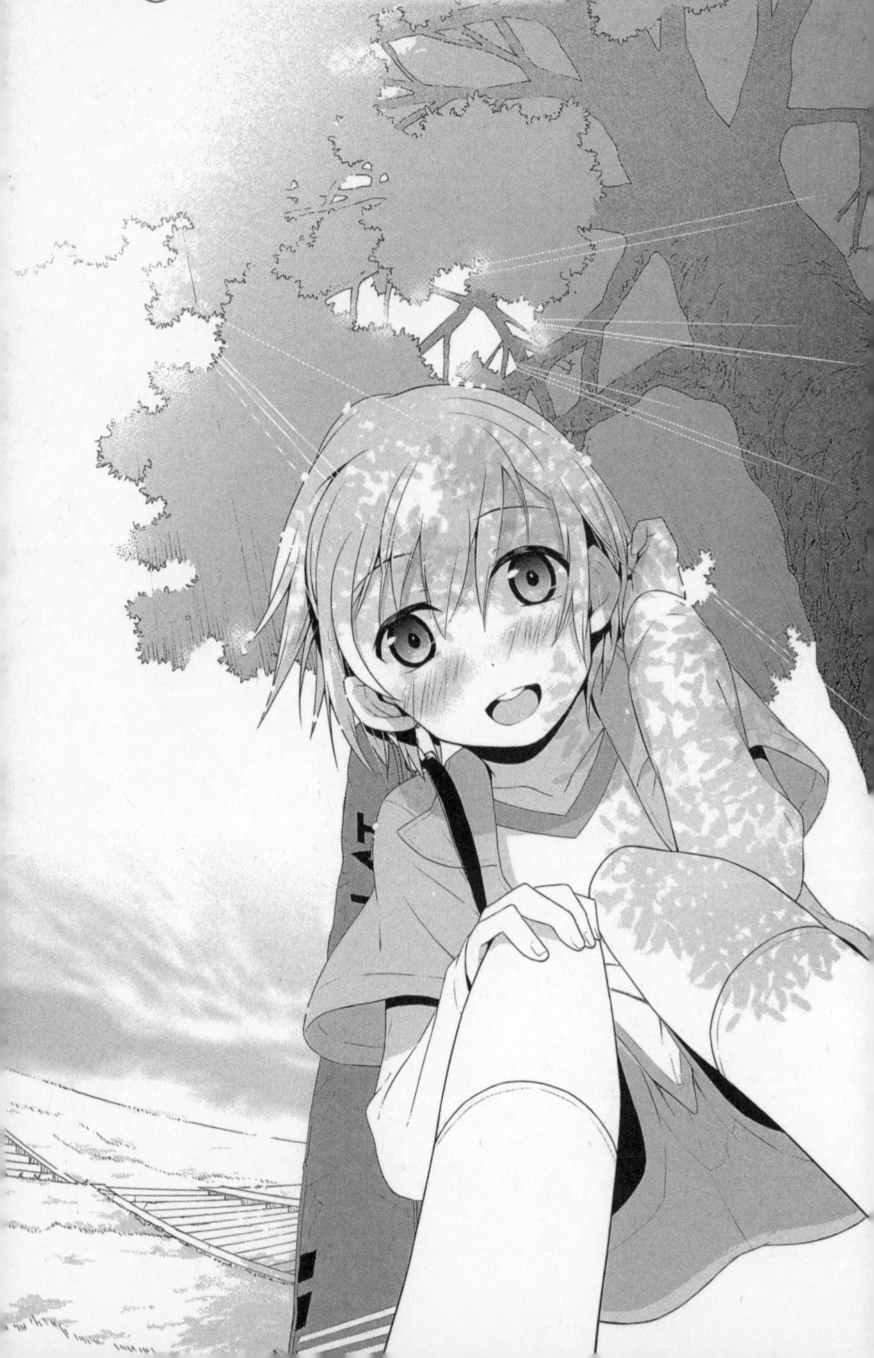

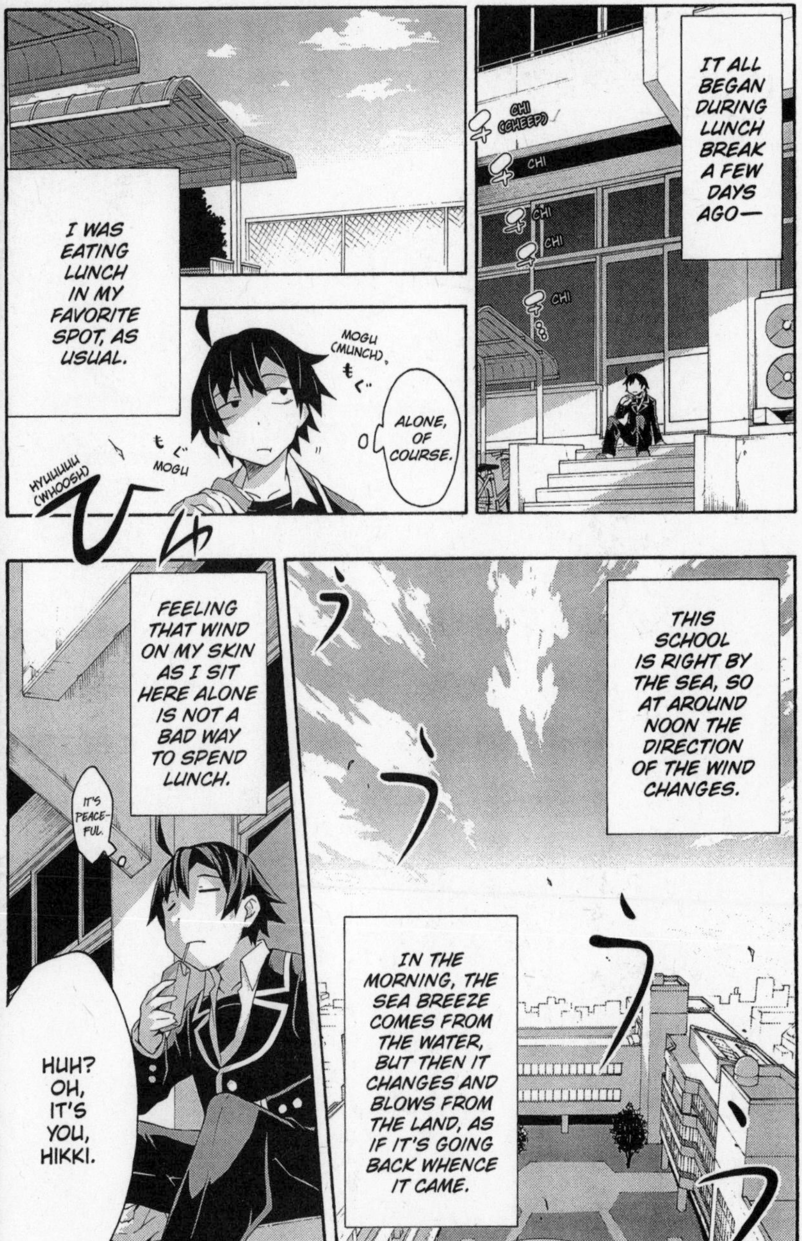
IT ALL BEGAN DURING LUNCH BREAK A FEW DAYS AGO—
CHI (CHEEP)
CHI
CHI
CHI
CHI
I WAS EATING LUNCH IN MY FAVORITE SPOT, AS USUAL.
MOGU (MUNCH)
ALONE, OF COURSE.
MOGU
HYUUUUU (WHOOSH)
THIS SCHOOL IS RIGHT BY THE SEA, SO AT AROUND NOON THE DIRECTION OF THE WIND CHANGES.
IN THE MORNING, THE SEA BREEZE COMES FROM THE WATER, BUT THEN IT CHANGES AND BLOWS FROM THE LAND, AS IF IT'S GOING BACK WHENCE IT CAME.
FEELING THAT WIND ON MY SKIN AS I SIT HERE ALONE IS NOT A BAD WAY TO SPEND LUNCH.
IT'S PEACEFUL.
HUH? OH, IT'S YOU, HIKKI.

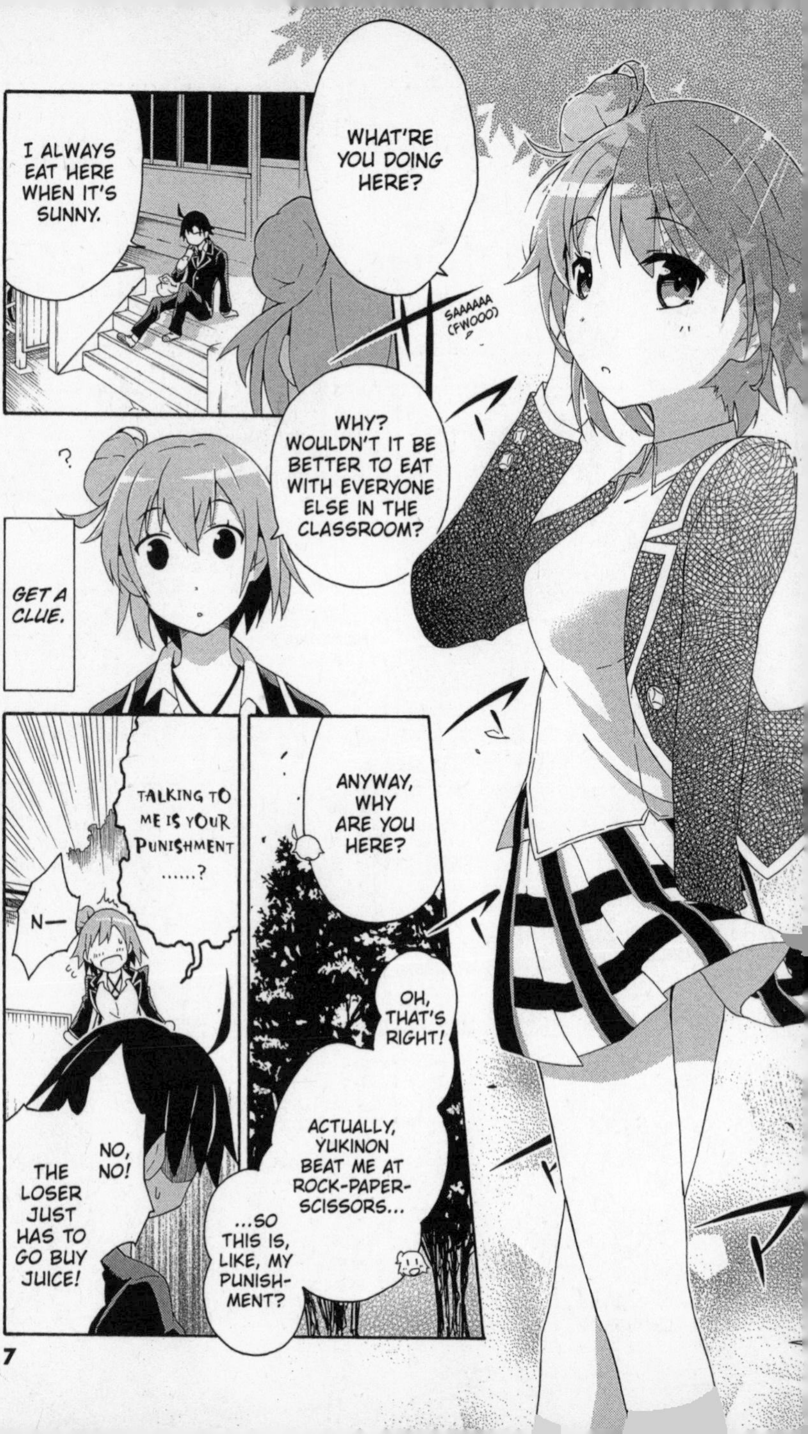

WHAT'RE YOU DOING HERE?
SAAAAAA (FWOOO)
I ALWAYS EAT HERE WHEN IT'S SUNNY.
WHY? WOULDN'T IT BE BETTER TO EAT WITH EVERYONE ELSE IN THE CLASSROOM?
?
GET A CLUE.
ANYWAY, WHY ARE YOU HERE?
OH, THAT'S RIGHT!
ACTUALLY, YUKINON BEAT ME AT ROCK-PAPER-SCISSORS...
...SO THIS IS, LIKE, MY PUNISHMENT?
TALKING TO ME IS YOUR PUNISHMENT ......?
N—
NO, NO!
THE LOSER JUST HAS TO GO BUY JUICE!

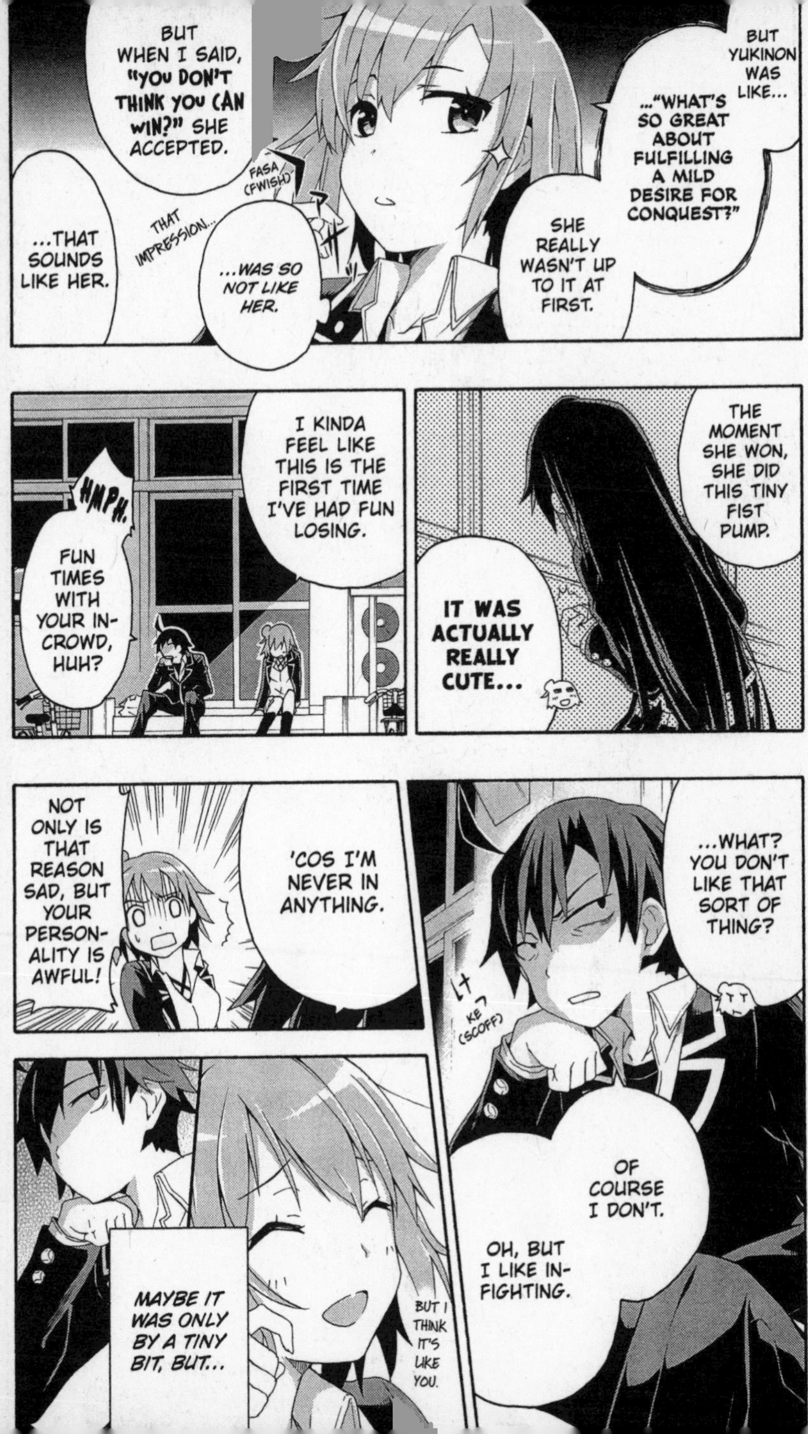
BUT YUKINON WAS LIKE...
..."WHAT'S SO GREAT ABOUT FULFILLING A MILD DESIRE FOR CONQUEST?"
SHE REALLY WASN'T UP TO IT AT FIRST.
BUT WHEN I SAID, "YOU DON'T THINK YOU CAN WIN?" SHE ACCEPTED.
FASA (FWISH)
THAT IMPRESSION...
...WAS SO NOT LIKE HER.
...THAT SOUNDS LIKE HER.
THE MOMENT SHE WON, SHE DID THIS TINY FIST PUMP.
IT WAS ACTUALLY REALLY CUTE...
I KINDA FEEL LIKE THIS IS THE FIRST TIME I'VE HAD FUN LOSING.
HMPH.
FUN TIMES WITH YOUR IN-CROWD, HUH?
...WHAT? YOU DON'T LIKE THAT SORT OF THING?
KE (SCOFF)
OF COURSE I DON'T.
OH, BUT I LIKE IN-FIGHTING.
'COS I'M NEVER IN ANYTHING.
NOT ONLY IS THAT REASON SAD, BUT YOUR PERSON-ALITY IS AWFUL!
BUT I THINK IT'S LIKE YOU.
MAYBE IT WAS ONLY BY A TINY BIT, BUT...

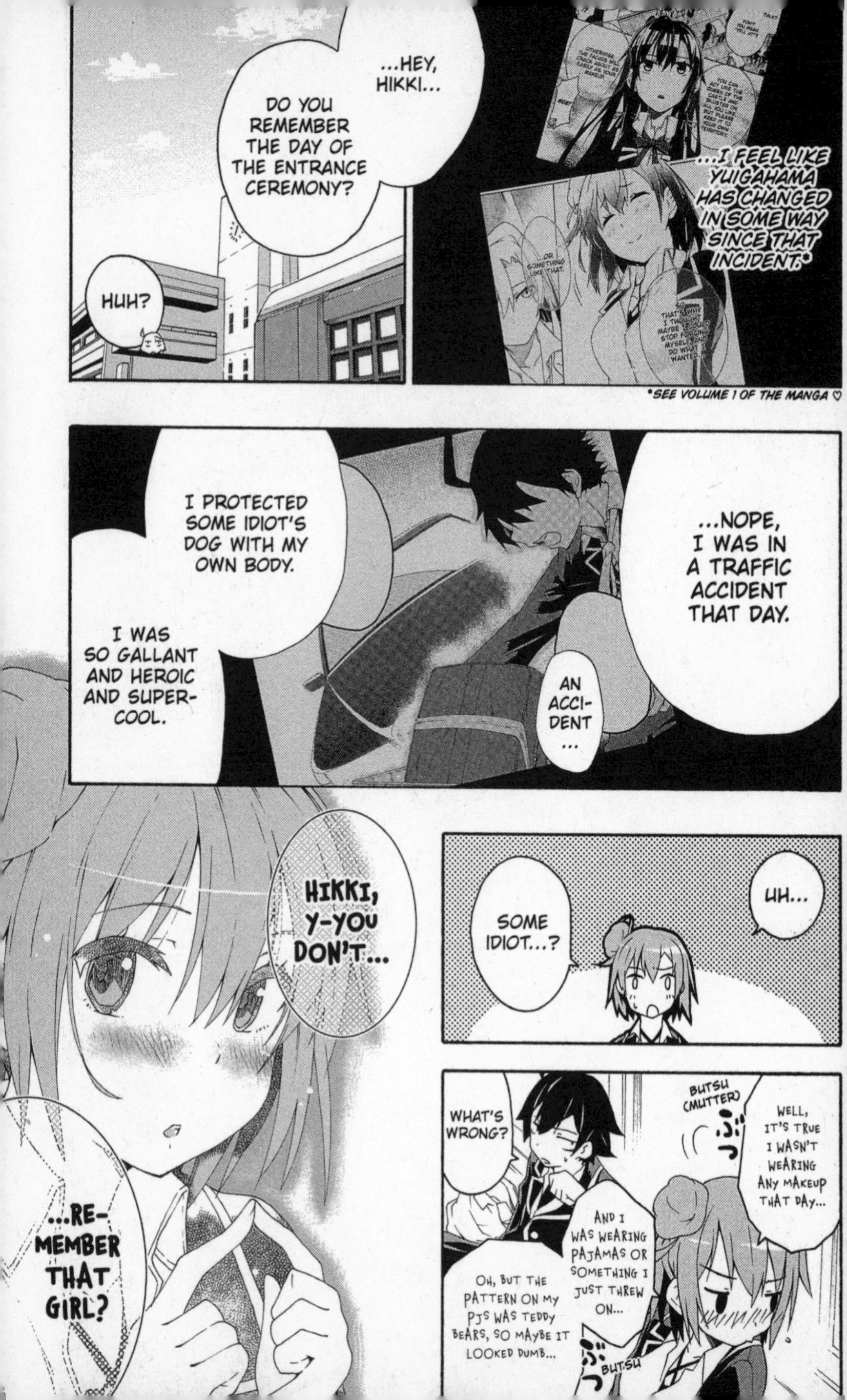
...I FEEL LIKE YUIGAHAMA HAS CHANGED IN SOME WAY SINCE THAT INCIDENT.*
...HEY, HIKKI...
DO YOU REMEMBER THE DAY OF THE ENTRANCE CEREMONY?
HUH?
...NOPE, I WAS IN A TRAFFIC ACCIDENT THAT DAY.
AN ACCI-DENT...
I PROTECTED SOME IDIOT'S DOG WITH MY OWN BODY.
I WAS SO GALLANT AND HEROIC AND SUPER-COOL.
UH...
SOME IDIOT...?
BUTSU (MUTTER)
WELL, IT'S TRUE I WASN'T WEARING ANY MAKEUP THAT DAY...
AND I WAS WEARING PAJAMAS OR SOMETHING I JUST THREW ON...
OH, BUT THE PATTERN ON MY PJS WAS TEDDY BEARS, SO MAYBE IT LOOKED DUMB...
BUTSU
WHAT'S WRONG?
HIKKI, Y-YOU DON'T...
...RE-MEMBER THAT GIRL?
*SEE VOLUME 1 OF THE MANGA ♡

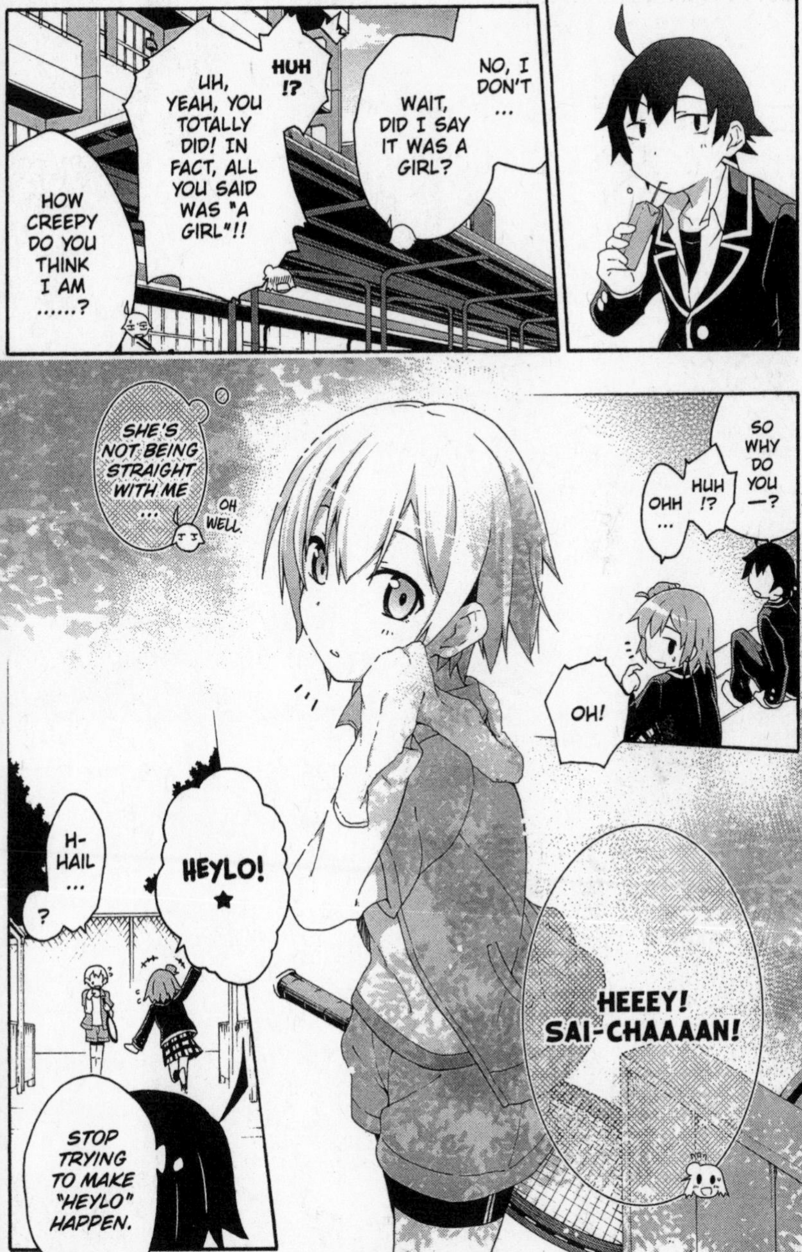
NO, I DON'T ...
WAIT, DID I SAY IT WAS A GIRL?
HUH !?
UH, YEAH, YOU TOTALLY DID! IN FACT, ALL YOU SAID WAS "A GIRL"!!
HOW CREEPY DO YOU THINK I AM ......?
SO WHY DO YOU—?
HUH !?
OHH ...
OH!
SHE'S NOT BEING STRAIGHT WITH ME ...
OH WELL.
HEEEY! SAI-CHAAAAN!
HEYLO! ★
H-HAIL ... ?
STOP TRYING TO MAKE "HEYLO" HAPPEN.

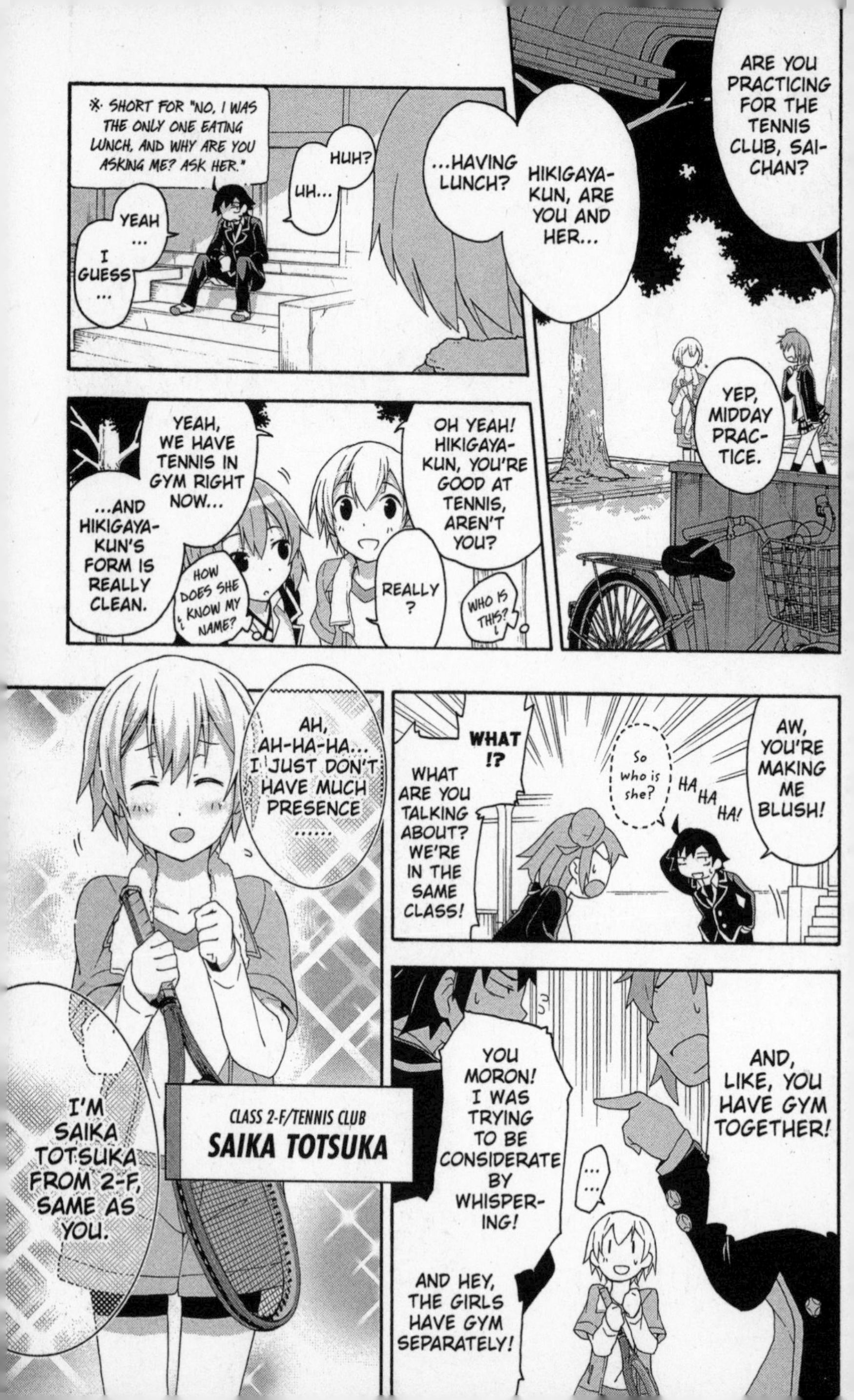

ARE YOU PRACTICING FOR THE TENNIS CLUB, SAI-CHAN?
YEP, MIDDAY PRAC-TICE.
HIKIGAYA-KUN, ARE YOU AND HER...
...HAVING LUNCH?
HUH?
UH...
YEAH... I GUESS...
※ SHORT FOR "NO, I WAS THE ONLY ONE EATING LUNCH, AND WHY ARE YOU ASKING ME? ASK HER."
OH YEAH! HIKIGAYA-KUN, YOU'RE GOOD AT TENNIS, AREN'T YOU?
WHO IS THIS?
REALLY?
YEAH, WE HAVE TENNIS IN GYM RIGHT NOW...
...AND HIKIGAYA-KUN'S FORM IS REALLY CLEAN.
HOW DOES SHE KNOW MY NAME?
AW, YOU'RE MAKING ME BLUSH!
HA HA HA!
So who is she?
WHAT!?
WHAT ARE YOU TALKING ABOUT? WE'RE IN THE SAME CLASS!
AND, LIKE, YOU HAVE GYM TOGETHER!
YOU MORON! I WAS TRYING TO BE CONSIDERATE BY WHISPER-ING!
......
AND HEY, THE GIRLS HAVE GYM SEPARATELY!
AH, AH-HA-HA... I JUST DON'T HAVE MUCH PRESENCE......
I'M SAIKA TOTSUKA FROM 2-F, SAME AS YOU.
CLASS 2-F/TENNIS CLUB
SAIKA TOTSUKA

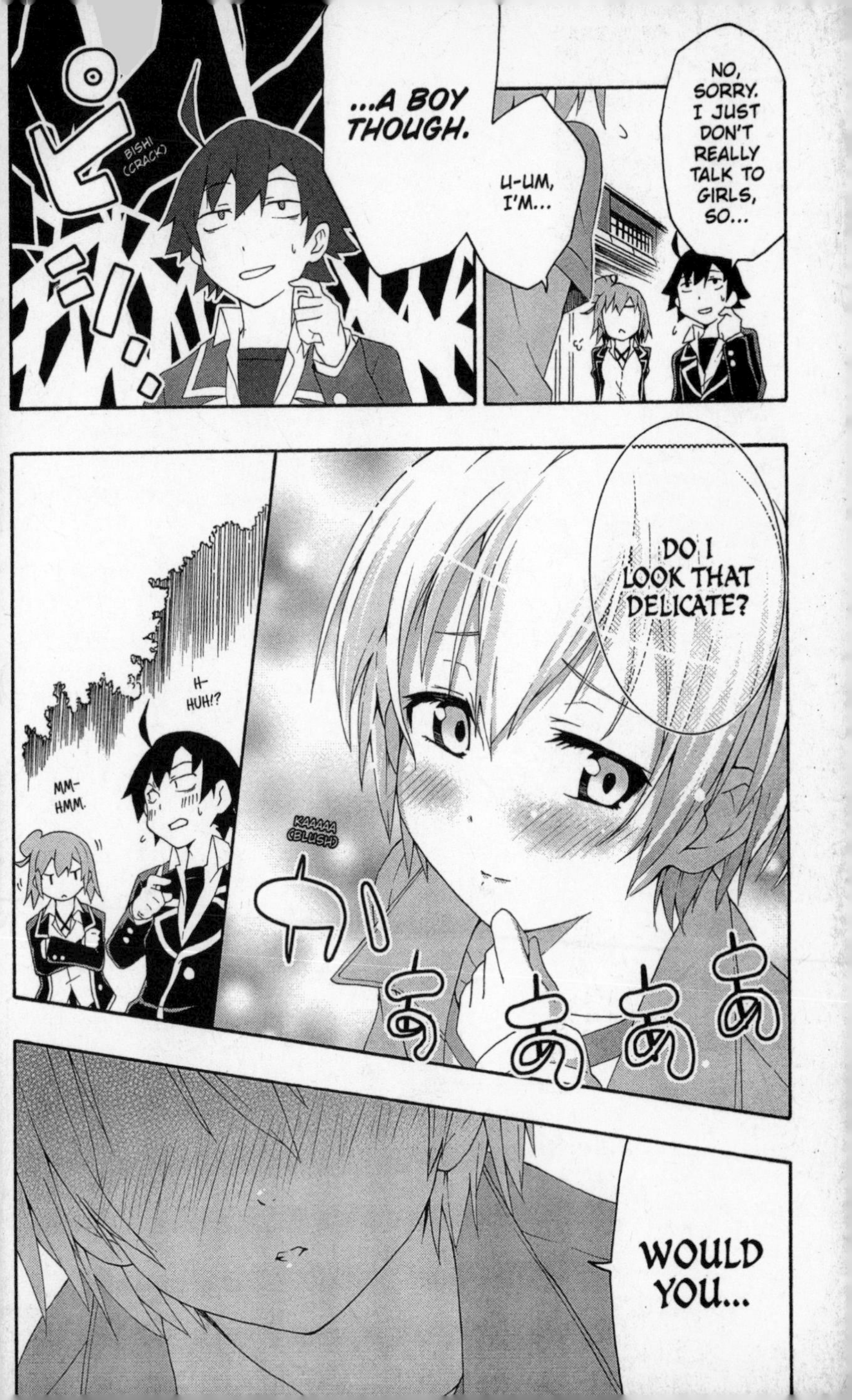

NO, SORRY. I JUST DON'T REALLY TALK TO GIRLS, SO...
U-UM, I'M...
...A BOY THOUGH.
BISHI (CRACK)
DO I LOOK THAT DELICATE?
KAAAAA (BLUSH)
H-HUH!?
MM-HMM.
WOULD YOU...

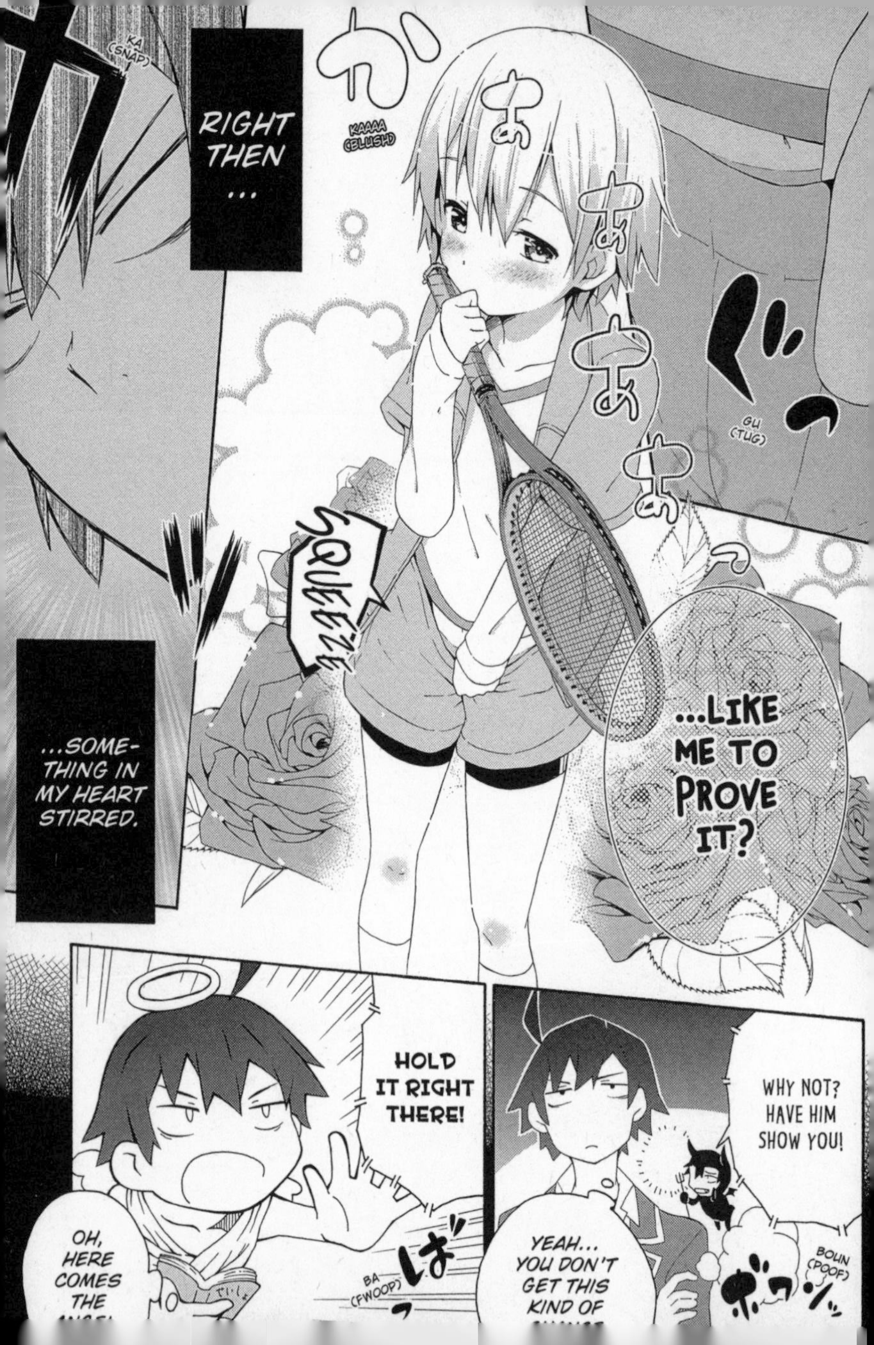
KAAAA (BLUSH)
GU (TUG)
SQUEEZE
...LIKE ME TO PROVE IT?
KA (SNAP)
RIGHT THEN ...
...SOME-THING IN MY HEART STIRRED.
WHY NOT? HAVE HIM SHOW YOU!
BOUN (POOF)
YEAH... YOU DON'T GET THIS KIND OF
HOLD IT RIGHT THERE!
BA (FWOOP)
OH, HERE COMES THE

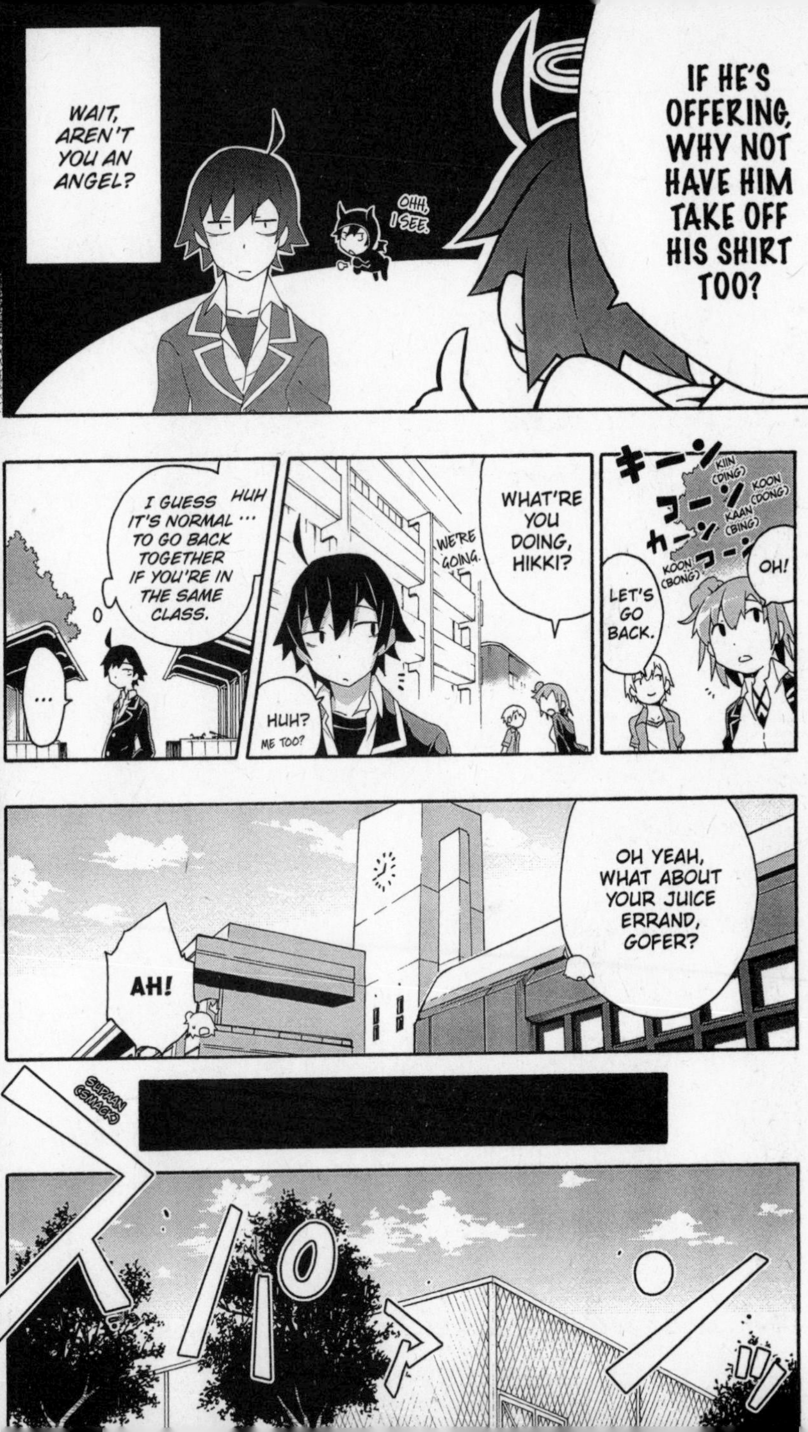
IF HE'S OFFERING, WHY NOT HAVE HIM TAKE OFF HIS SHIRT TOO?
OHH, I SEE.
WAIT, AREN'T YOU AN ANGEL?
KIIN (DING)
KOON (DONG)
KAAN (BING)
KOON (BONG)
OH!
LET'S GO BACK.
WHAT'RE YOU DOING, HIKKI?
WE'RE GOING.
HUH? ME TOO?
HUH ...
I GUESS IT'S NORMAL TO GO BACK TOGETHER IF YOU'RE IN THE SAME CLASS.
...
OH YEAH, WHAT ABOUT YOUR JUICE ERRAND, GOFER?
AH!
[redacted]
SUPAAN (SMACK)

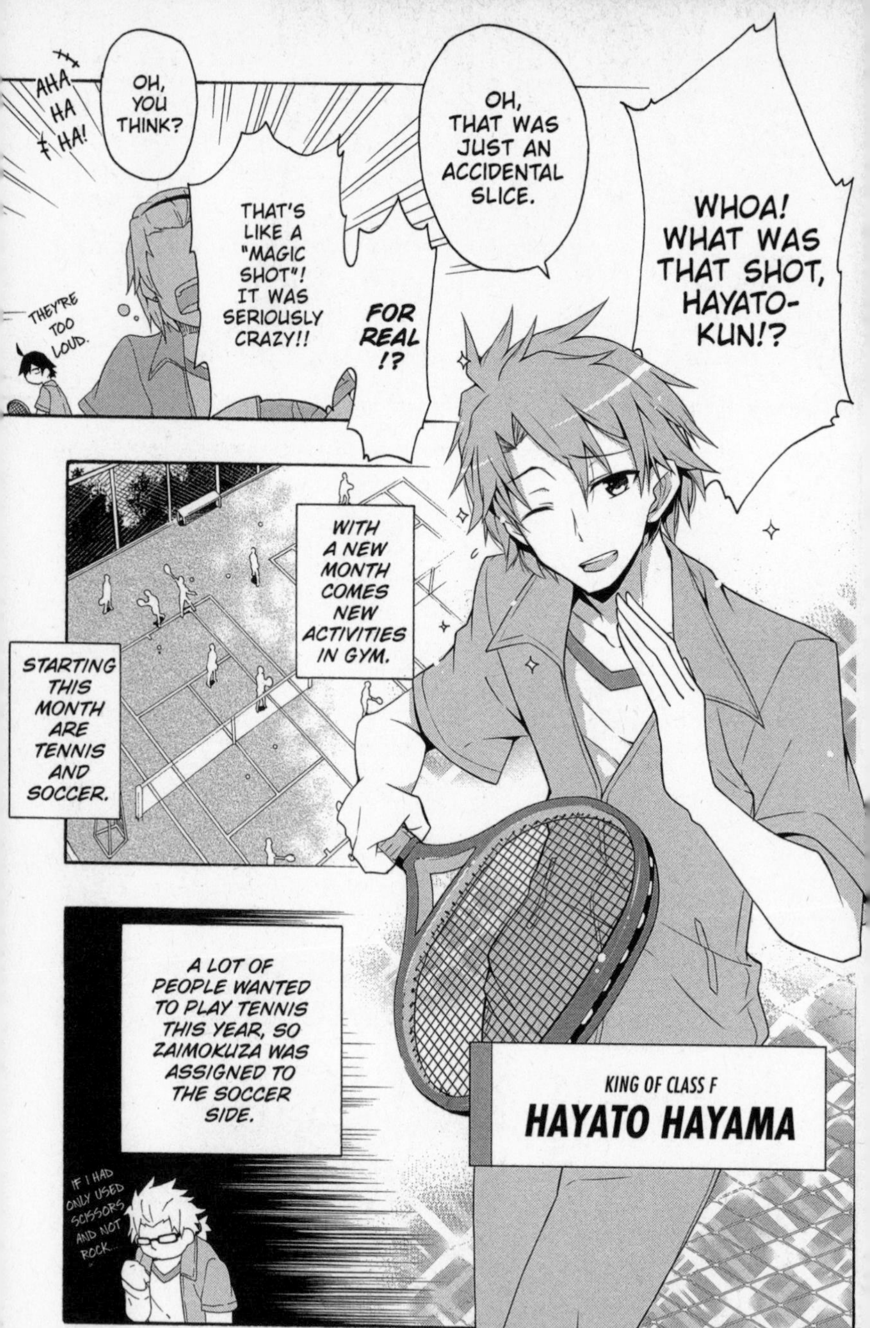
WHOA! WHAT WAS THAT SHOT, HAYATO-KUN!?
OH, THAT WAS JUST AN ACCIDENTAL SLICE.
FOR REAL!?
THAT'S LIKE A "MAGIC SHOT"! IT WAS SERIOUSLY CRAZY!!
OH, YOU THINK?
AHAHA HA HA!
THEY'RE TOO LOUD.
KING OF CLASS F
HAYATO HAYAMA
WITH A NEW MONTH COMES NEW ACTIVITIES IN GYM.
STARTING THIS MONTH ARE TENNIS AND SOCCER.
A LOT OF PEOPLE WANTED TO PLAY TENNIS THIS YEAR, SO ZAIMOKUZA WAS ASSIGNED TO THE SOCCER SIDE.
IF I HAD ONLY USED SCISSORS AND NOT ROCK...

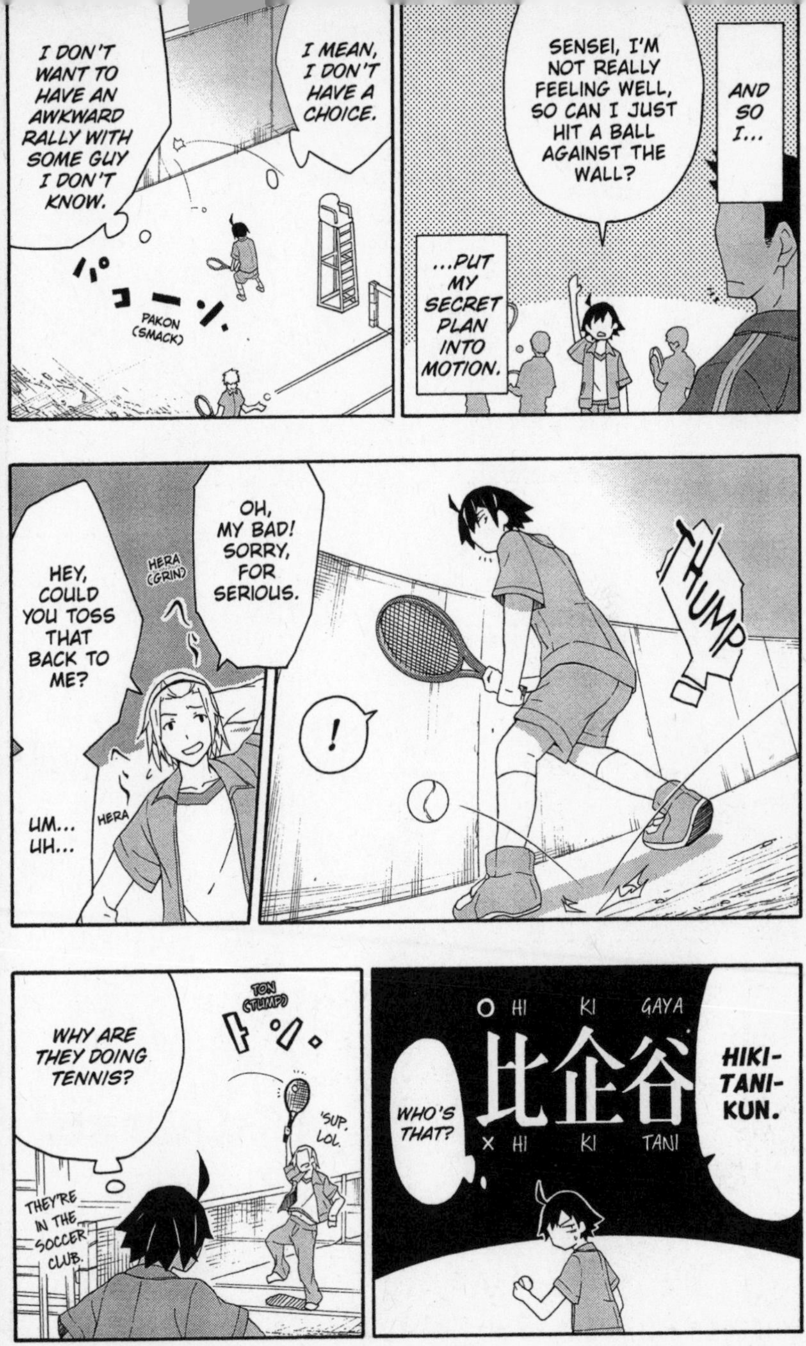
AND SO I...
SENSEI, I'M NOT REALLY FEELING WELL, SO CAN I JUST HIT A BALL AGAINST THE WALL?
...PUT MY SECRET PLAN INTO MOTION.
I MEAN, I DON'T HAVE A CHOICE.
I DON'T WANT TO HAVE AN AWKWARD RALLY WITH SOME GUY I DON'T KNOW.
パコーン。
PAKON (SMACK)
THUMP
!
OH, MY BAD! SORRY, FOR SERIOUS.
HERA (GRIN)
へら
HEY, COULD YOU TOSS THAT BACK TO ME?
UM... UH...
HERA
HIKI-TANI-KUN.
O HI KI GAYA
比企谷
× HI KI TANI
WHO'S THAT?
TON (TUMP)
トン。
WHY ARE THEY DOING TENNIS?
'SUP, LOL.
THEY'RE IN THE SOCCER CLUB.

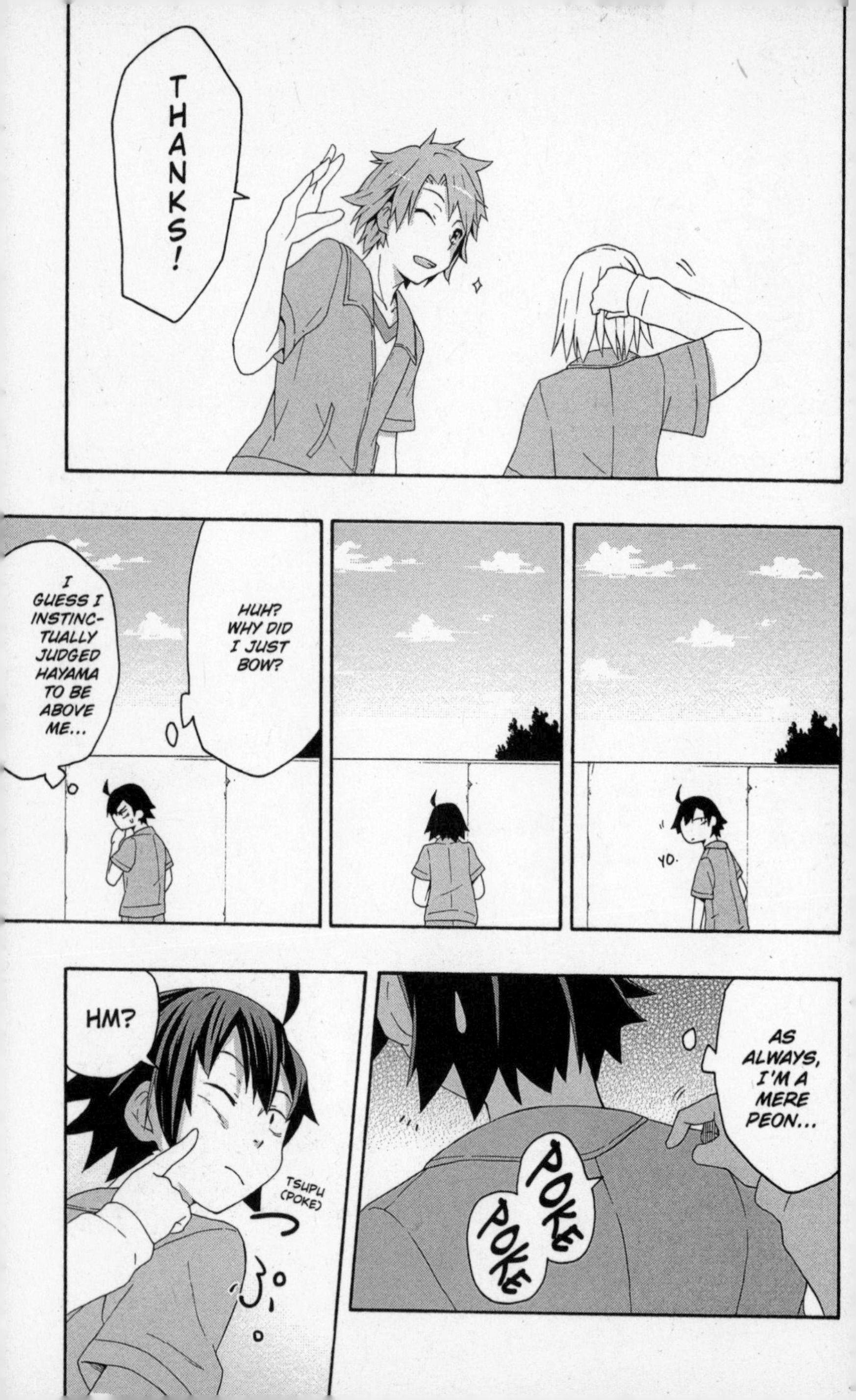
THANKS!
YO.
HUH? WHY DID I JUST BOW?
I GUESS I INSTINCTUALLY JUDGED HAYAMA TO BE ABOVE ME...
AS ALWAYS, I'M A MERE PEON...
POKE POKE
HM?
TSUPU (POKE)

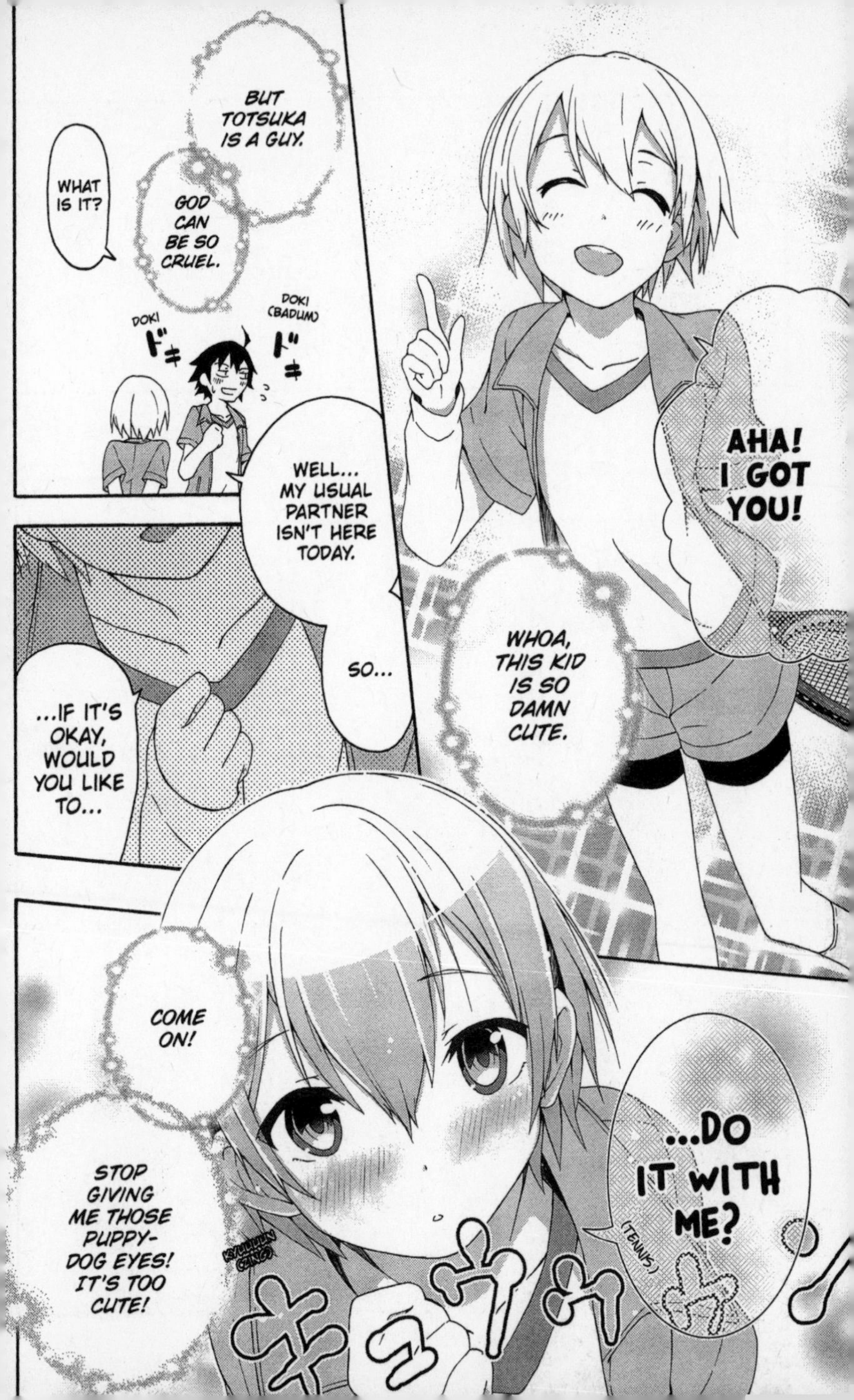
AHA! I GOT YOU!
WHOA, THIS KID IS SO DAMN CUTE.
BUT TOTSUKA IS A GUY.
GOD CAN BE SO CRUEL.
WHAT IS IT?
DOKI (BADUM)
DOKI
WELL... MY USUAL PARTNER ISN'T HERE TODAY.
SO...
...IF IT'S OKAY, WOULD YOU LIKE TO...
...DO IT WITH ME?
(TENNIS)
COME ON!
STOP GIVING ME THOSE PUPPY-DOG EYES! IT'S TOO CUTE!
KYUUUN (ZING)

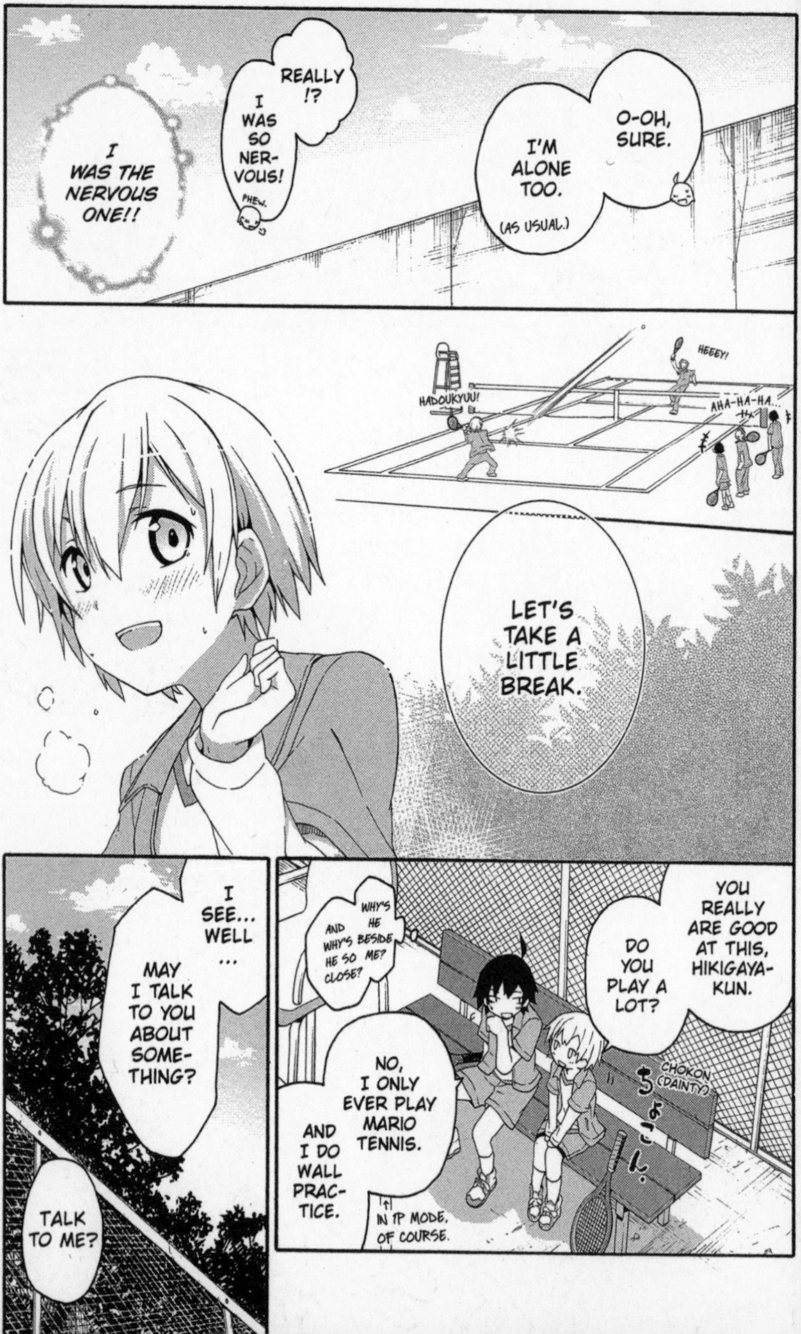
O-OH, SURE.
I'M ALONE TOO.
(AS USUAL.)
REALLY!?
I WAS SO NERVOUS!
PHEW.
I WAS THE NERVOUS ONE!!
HEEEY!
AHA-HA-HA...
HADOUKYUU!
LET'S TAKE A LITTLE BREAK.
YOU REALLY ARE GOOD AT THIS, HIKIGAYA-KUN.
DO YOU PLAY A LOT?
CHOKON (DAINTY)
WHY'S HE BESIDE ME?
AND WHY'S HE SO CLOSE?
NO, I ONLY EVER PLAY MARIO TENNIS.
AND I DO WALL PRACTICE.
↑ IN 1P MODE, OF COURSE.
I SEE... WELL...
MAY I TALK TO YOU ABOUT SOMETHING?
TALK TO ME?

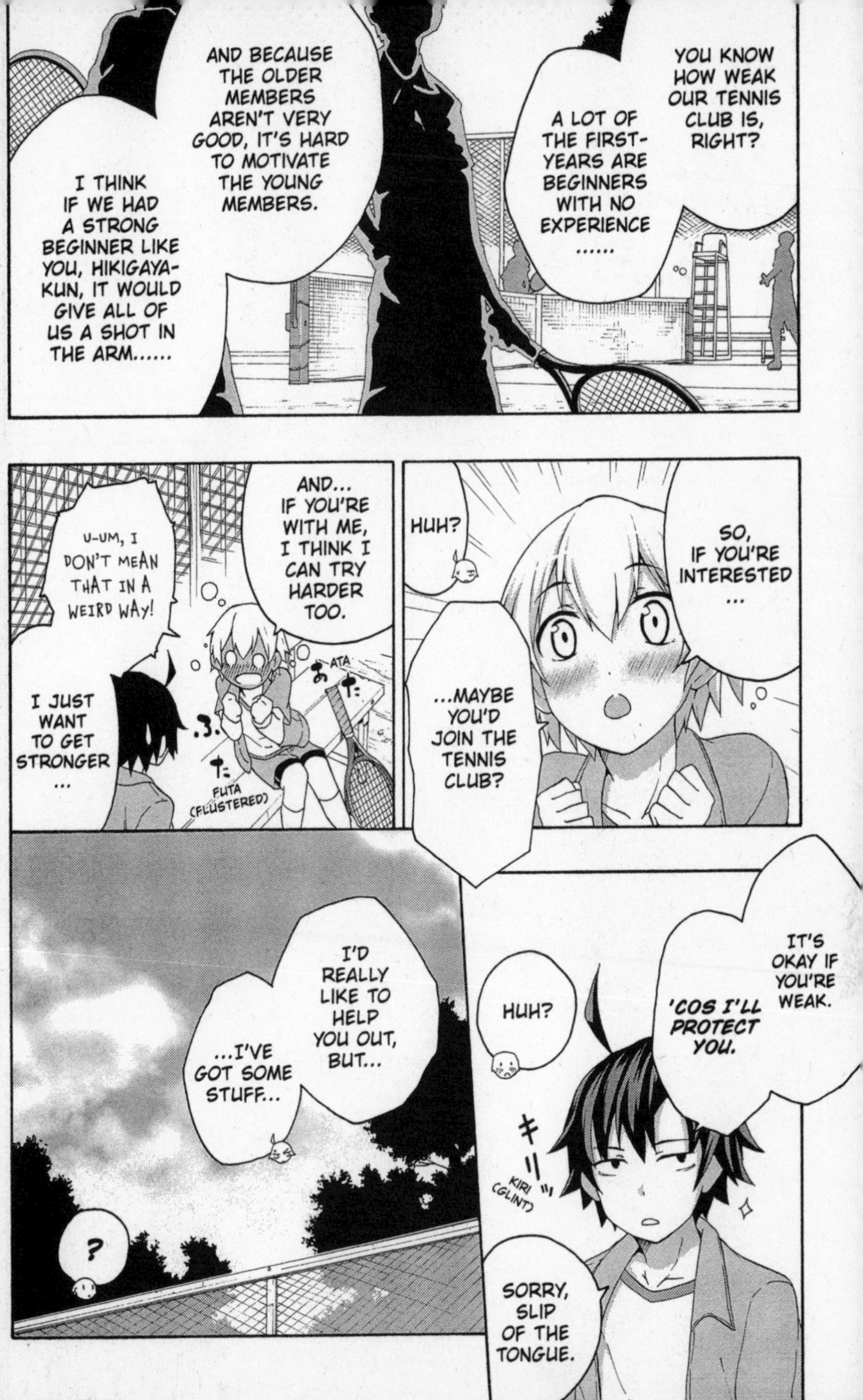
YOU KNOW HOW WEAK OUR TENNIS CLUB IS, RIGHT?
A LOT OF THE FIRST-YEARS ARE BEGINNERS WITH NO EXPERIENCE ......
AND BECAUSE THE OLDER MEMBERS AREN'T VERY GOOD, IT'S HARD TO MOTIVATE THE YOUNG MEMBERS.
I THINK IF WE HAD A STRONG BEGINNER LIKE YOU, HIKIGAYA-KUN, IT WOULD GIVE ALL OF US A SHOT IN THE ARM......
SO, IF YOU'RE INTERESTED ...
HUH?
...MAYBE YOU'D JOIN THE TENNIS CLUB?
AND... IF YOU'RE WITH ME, I THINK I CAN TRY HARDER TOO.
ATA
U-UM, I DON'T MEAN THAT IN A WEIRD WAY!
FUTA (FLUSTERED)
I JUST WANT TO GET STRONGER ...
IT'S OKAY IF YOU'RE WEAK.
'COS I'LL PROTECT YOU.
HUH?
KIRI (GLINT)
SORRY, SLIP OF THE TONGUE.
I'D REALLY LIKE TO HELP YOU OUT, BUT...
...I'VE GOT SOME STUFF...
?

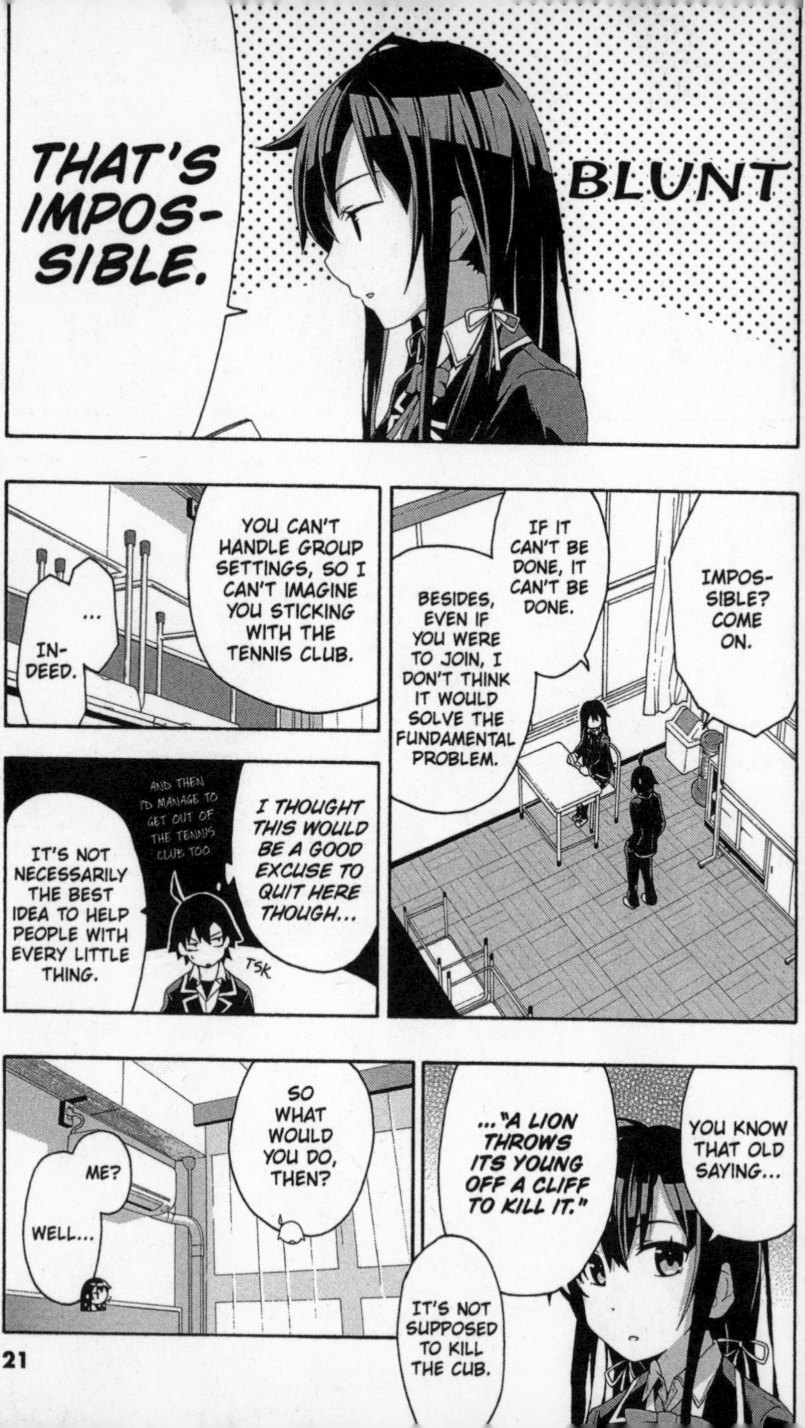
BLUNT
THAT'S IMPOSSIBLE.
IMPOSSIBLE? COME ON.
IF IT CAN'T BE DONE, IT CAN'T BE DONE.
BESIDES, EVEN IF YOU WERE TO JOIN, I DON'T THINK IT WOULD SOLVE THE FUNDAMENTAL PROBLEM.
YOU CAN'T HANDLE GROUP SETTINGS, SO I CAN'T IMAGINE YOU STICKING WITH THE TENNIS CLUB.
... INDEED.
I THOUGHT THIS WOULD BE A GOOD EXCUSE TO QUIT HERE THOUGH...
AND THEN I'D MANAGE TO GET OUT OF THE TENNIS CLUB TOO
TSK
IT'S NOT NECESSARILY THE BEST IDEA TO HELP PEOPLE WITH EVERY LITTLE THING.
YOU KNOW THAT OLD SAYING...
..."A LION THROWS ITS YOUNG OFF A CLIFF TO KILL IT."
IT'S NOT SUPPOSED TO KILL THE CUB.
SO WHAT WOULD YOU DO, THEN?
ME?
WELL...

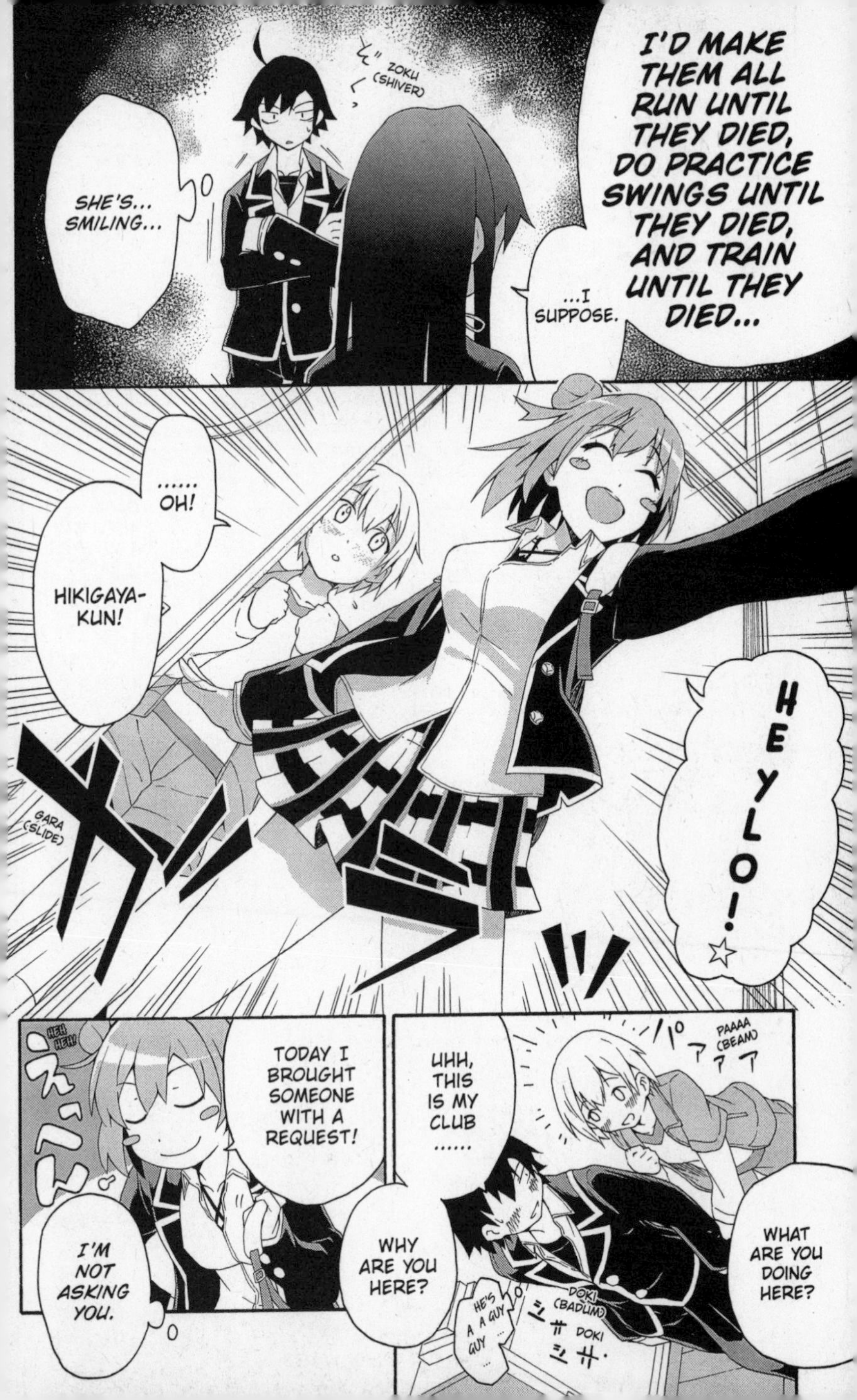
I'D MAKE THEM ALL RUN UNTIL THEY DIED, DO PRACTICE SWINGS UNTIL THEY DIED, AND TRAIN UNTIL THEY DIED...
...I SUPPOSE.
ZOKU (SHIVER)
SHE'S... SMILING...
HEYLO!☆
GARA (SLIDE)
......OH!
HIKIGAYA-KUN!
PAAAA (BEAM)
UHH, THIS IS MY CLUB ......
WHAT ARE YOU DOING HERE?
DOKI (BADUM) DOKI
HE'S A GUY ... A GUY ...
WHY ARE YOU HERE?
HEH HEH!
TODAY I BROUGHT SOMEONE WITH A REQUEST!
I'M NOT ASKING YOU.

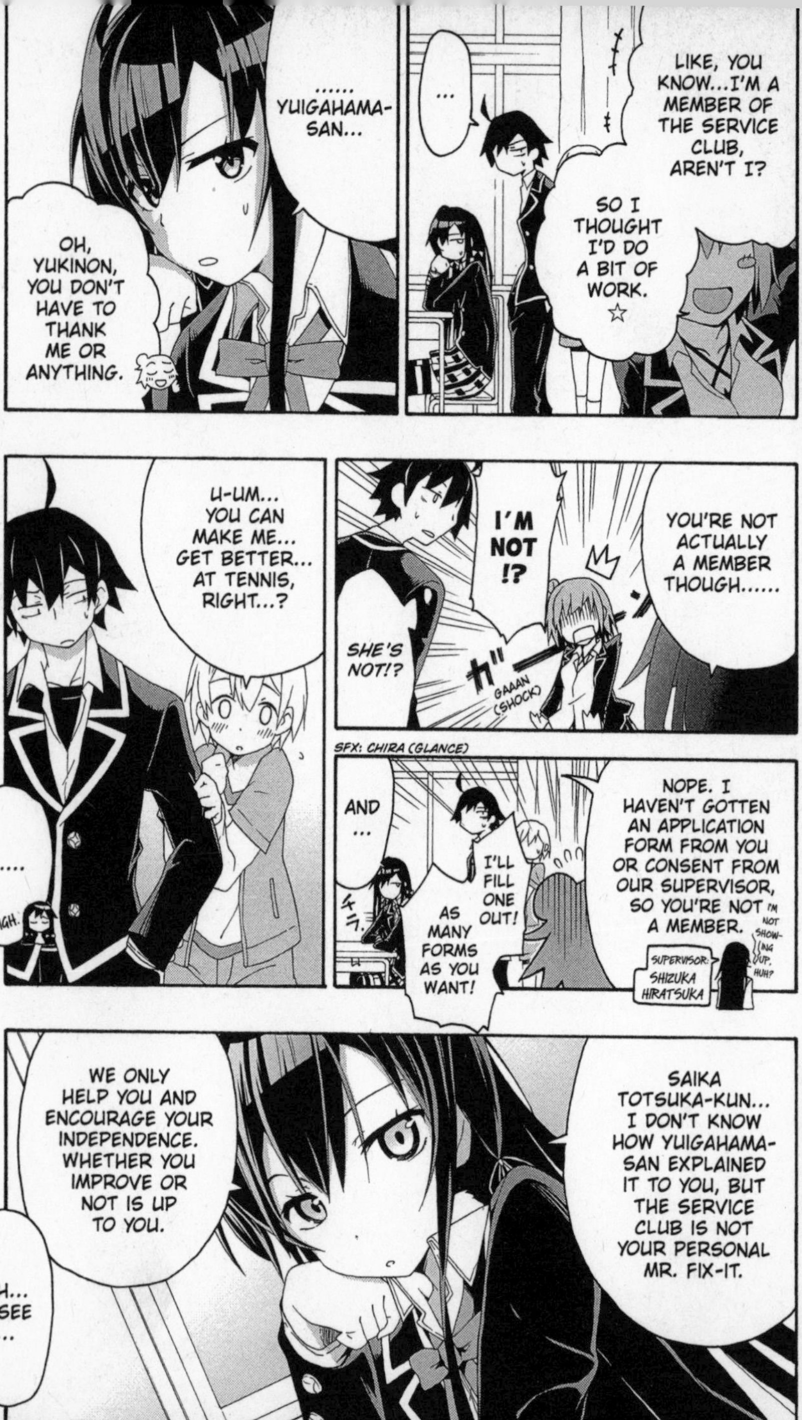
LIKE, YOU KNOW...I'M A MEMBER OF THE SERVICE CLUB, AREN'T I?
SO I THOUGHT I'D DO A BIT OF WORK. ☆
...
...... YUIGAHAMA-SAN...
OH, YUKINON, YOU DON'T HAVE TO THANK ME OR ANYTHING.
YOU'RE NOT ACTUALLY A MEMBER THOUGH......
I'M NOT!?
SHE'S NOT!?
GAAAN (SHOCK)
SFX: CHIRA (GLANCE)
NOPE. I HAVEN'T GOTTEN AN APPLICATION FORM FROM YOU OR CONSENT FROM OUR SUPERVISOR, SO YOU'RE NOT A MEMBER.
I'M NOT SHOWING UP, HUH?
SUPERVISOR: SHIZUKA HIRATSUKA
I'LL FILL ONE OUT!
AS MANY FORMS AS YOU WANT!
AND ...
U-UM... YOU CAN MAKE ME... GET BETTER... AT TENNIS, RIGHT...?
......
SIGH.
SAIKA TOTSUKA-KUN... I DON'T KNOW HOW YUIGAHAMA-SAN EXPLAINED IT TO YOU, BUT THE SERVICE CLUB IS NOT YOUR PERSONAL MR. FIX-IT.
WE ONLY HELP YOU AND ENCOURAGE YOUR INDEPENDENCE. WHETHER YOU IMPROVE OR NOT IS UP TO YOU.
OH... I SEE ...

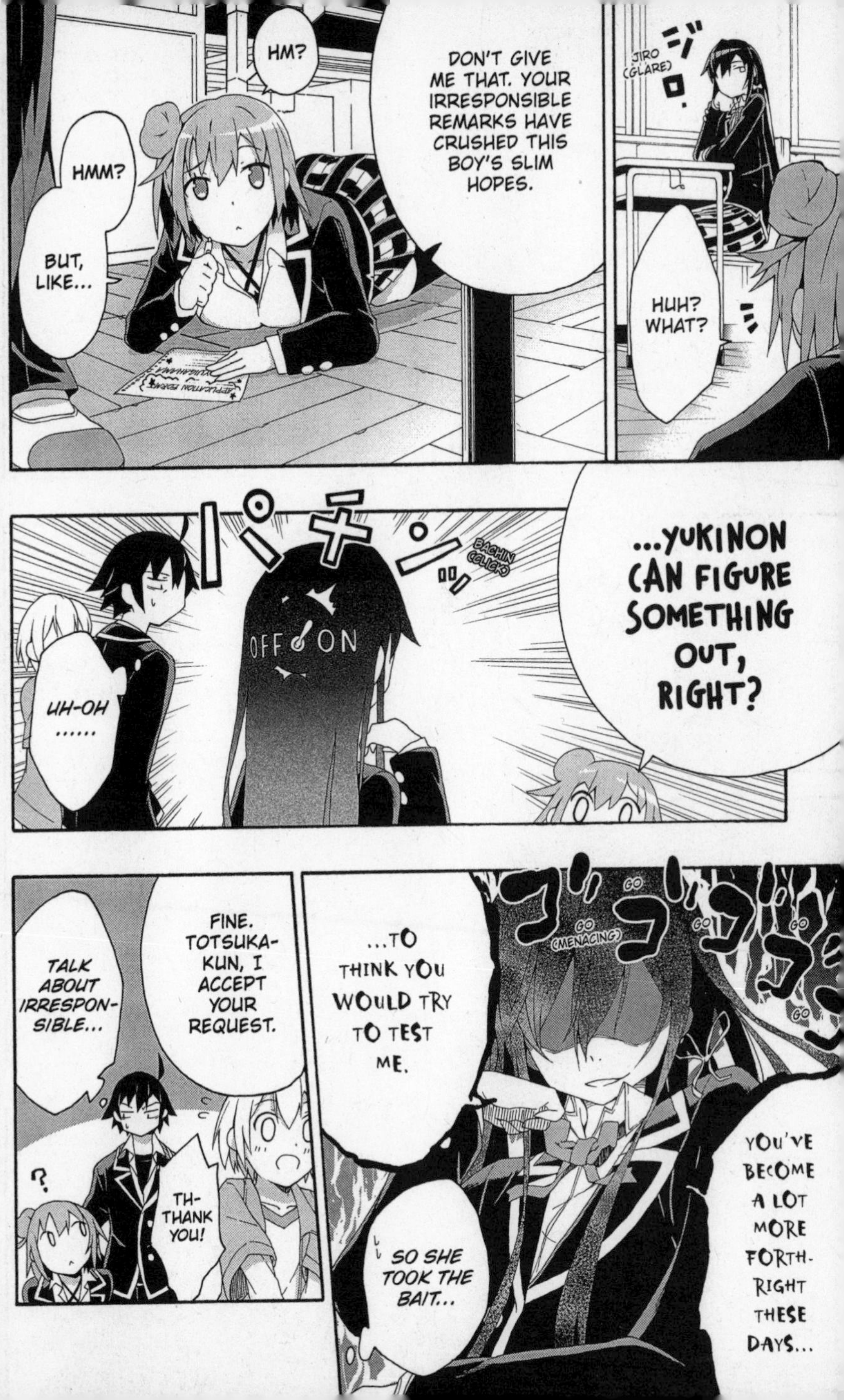
JIRO (GLARE)
HUH? WHAT?
DON'T GIVE ME THAT. YOUR IRRESPONSIBLE REMARKS HAVE CRUSHED THIS BOY'S SLIM HOPES.
HM?
HMM?
BUT, LIKE...
...YUKINON CAN FIGURE SOMETHING OUT, RIGHT?
BACHIN (CLICK)
OFF ON
UH-OH ......
GO GO (MENACING) GO GO GO
YOU'VE BECOME A LOT MORE FORTHRIGHT THESE DAYS...
...TO THINK YOU WOULD TRY TO TEST ME.
SO SHE TOOK THE BAIT...
FINE. TOTSUKA-KUN, I ACCEPT YOUR REQUEST.
TALK ABOUT IRRESPONSIBLE...
TH-THANK YOU!
?

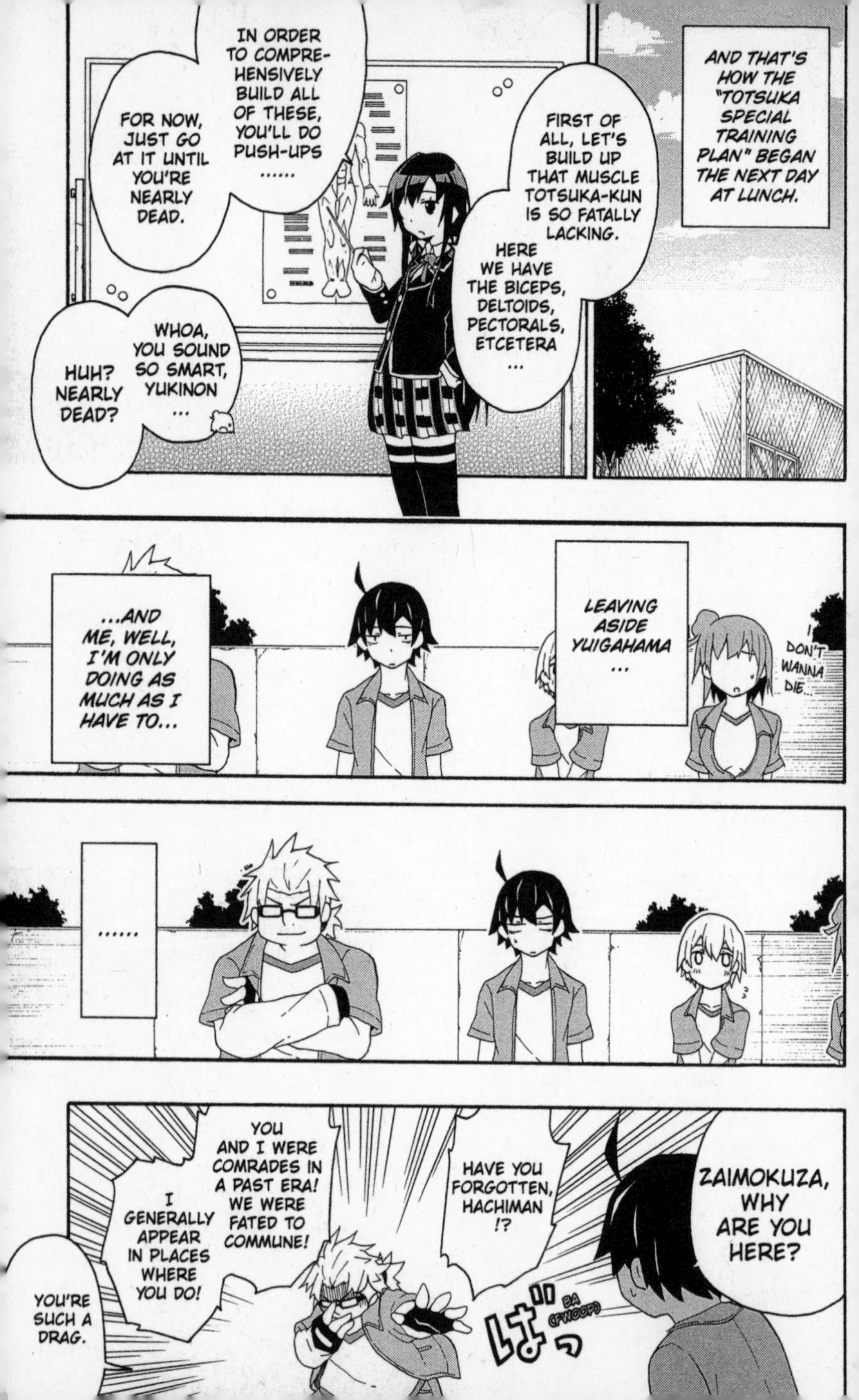
AND THAT'S HOW THE "TOTSUKA SPECIAL TRAINING PLAN" BEGAN THE NEXT DAY AT LUNCH.
FIRST OF ALL, LET'S BUILD UP THAT MUSCLE TOTSUKA-KUN IS SO FATALLY LACKING.
HERE WE HAVE THE BICEPS, DELTOIDS, PECTORALS, ETCETERA ...
IN ORDER TO COMPRE-HENSIVELY BUILD ALL OF THESE, YOU'LL DO PUSH-UPS ......
FOR NOW, JUST GO AT IT UNTIL YOU'RE NEARLY DEAD.
WHOA, YOU SOUND SO SMART, YUKINON ...
HUH? NEARLY DEAD?
I DON'T WANNA DIE...
LEAVING ASIDE YUIGAHAMA ...
...AND ME, WELL, I'M ONLY DOING AS MUCH AS I HAVE TO...
......
ZAIMOKUZA, WHY ARE YOU HERE?
BA (FWOOP)
HAVE YOU FORGOTTEN, HACHIMAN !?
YOU AND I WERE COMRADES IN A PAST ERA! WE WERE FATED TO COMMUNE!
I GENERALLY APPEAR IN PLACES WHERE YOU DO!
YOU'RE SUCH A DRAG.

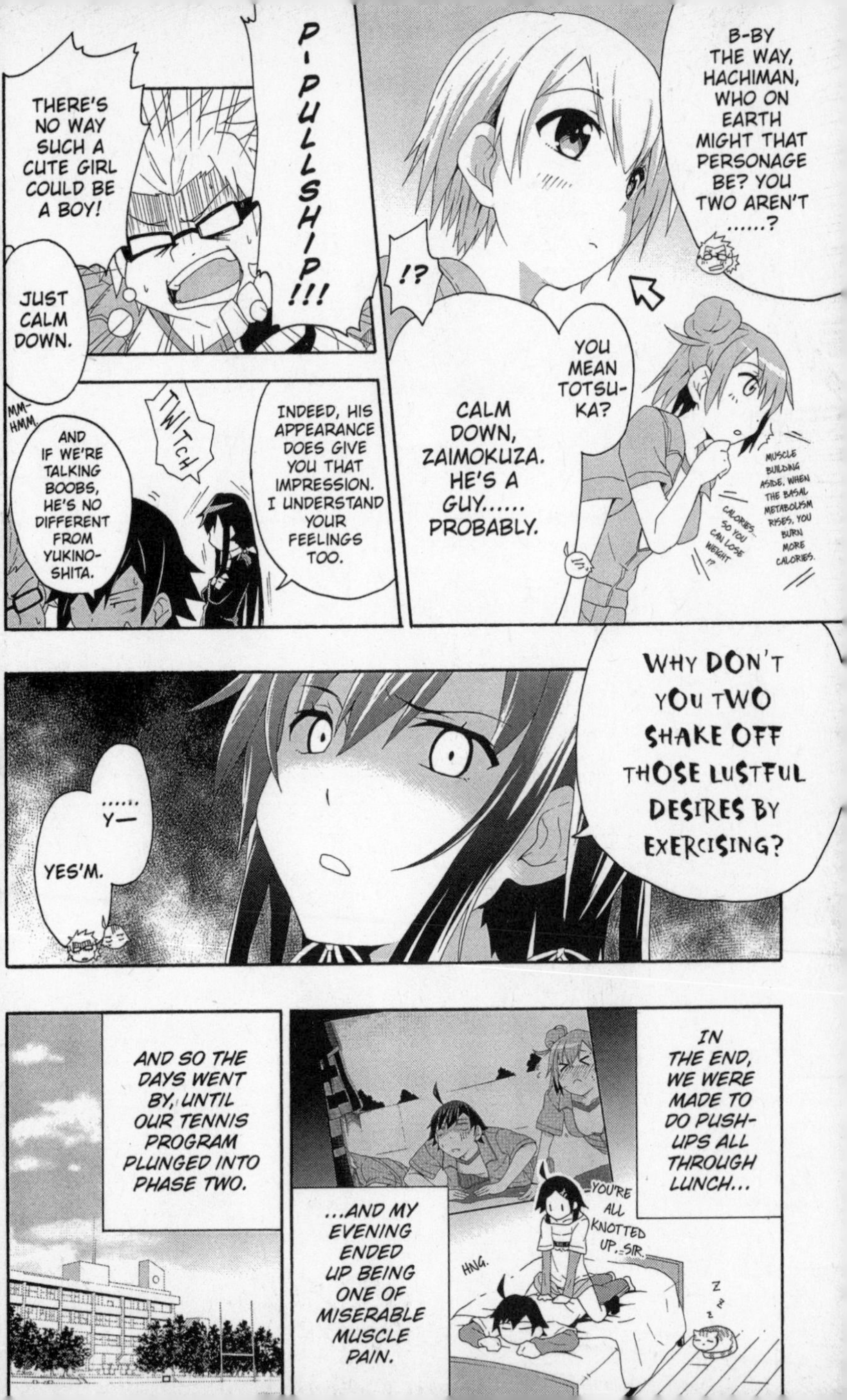
B-BY THE WAY, HACHIMAN, WHO ON EARTH MIGHT THAT PERSONAGE BE? YOU TWO AREN'T ......?
!?
YOU MEAN TOTSUKA?
CALM DOWN, ZAIMOKUZA. HE'S A GUY...... PROBABLY.
MUSCLE BUILDING ASIDE, WHEN THE BASAL METABOLISM RISES, YOU BURN MORE CALORIES.
CALORIES... SO YOU CAN LOSE WEIGHT !?
P-PULLSHIP!!!
THERE'S NO WAY SUCH A CUTE GIRL COULD BE A BOY!
JUST CALM DOWN.
TWITCH
INDEED, HIS APPEARANCE DOES GIVE YOU THAT IMPRESSION. I UNDERSTAND YOUR FEELINGS TOO.
AND IF WE'RE TALKING BOOBS, HE'S NO DIFFERENT FROM YUKINO-SHITA.
MM-HMM.
WHY DON'T YOU TWO SHAKE OFF THOSE LUSTFUL DESIRES BY EXERCISING?
...... Y— YES'M.
IN THE END, WE WERE MADE TO DO PUSH-UPS ALL THROUGH LUNCH...
YOU'RE ALL KNOTTED UP, SIR.
HNG.
Z Z Z
...AND MY EVENING ENDED UP BEING ONE OF MISERABLE MUSCLE PAIN.
AND SO THE DAYS WENT BY, UNTIL OUR TENNIS PROGRAM PLUNGED INTO PHASE TWO.

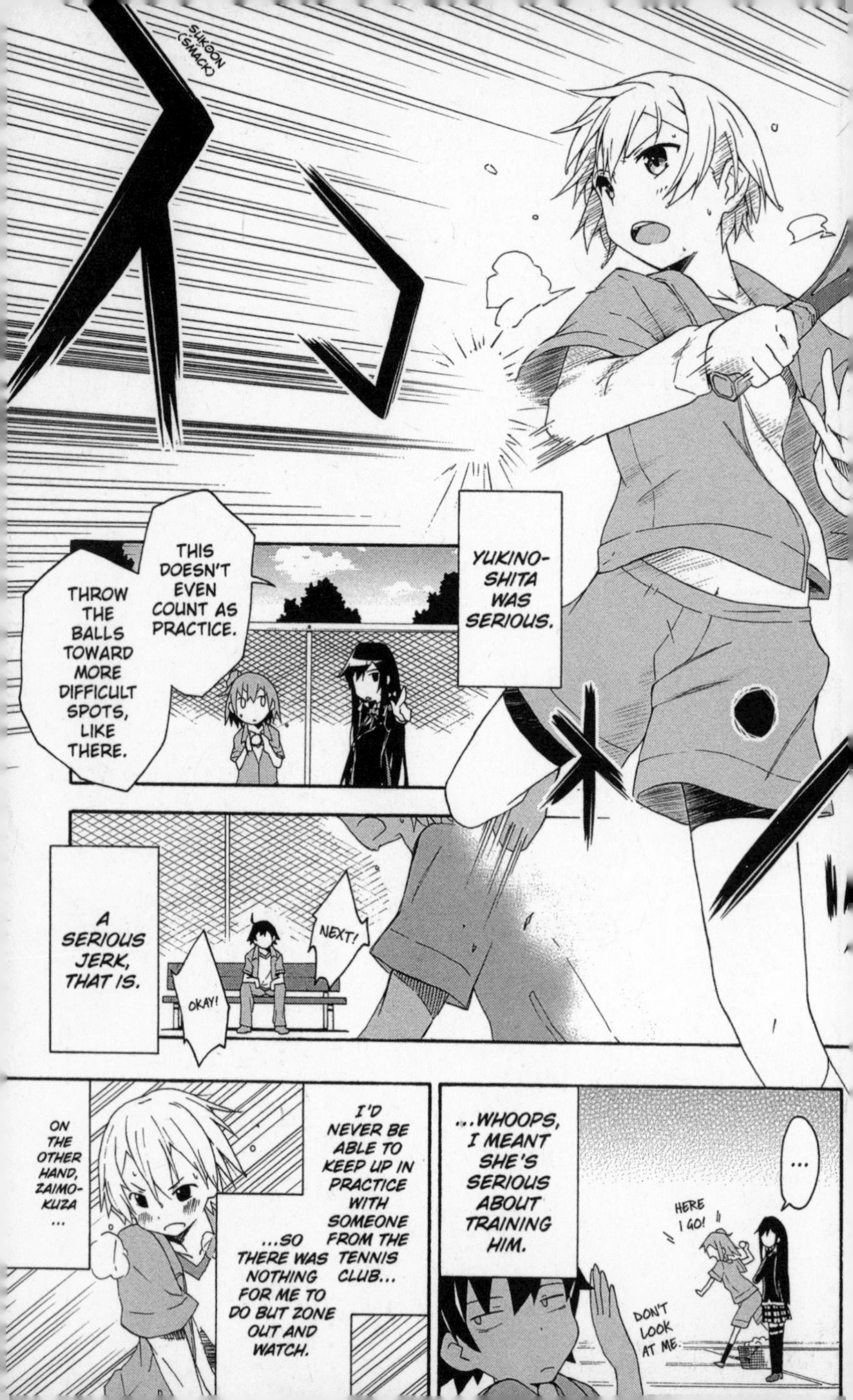
SUKOON (SMACK)
YUKINO-SHITA WAS SERIOUS.
THIS DOESN'T EVEN COUNT AS PRACTICE.
THROW THE BALLS TOWARD MORE DIFFICULT SPOTS, LIKE THERE.
NEXT!
OKAY!
A SERIOUS JERK, THAT IS.
...
HERE I GO!
...WHOOPS, I MEANT SHE'S SERIOUS ABOUT TRAINING HIM.
DON'T LOOK AT ME.
I'D NEVER BE ABLE TO KEEP UP IN PRACTICE WITH SOMEONE FROM THE TENNIS CLUB...
...SO THERE WAS NOTHING FOR ME TO DO BUT ZONE OUT AND WATCH.
ON THE OTHER HAND, ZAIMOKUZA ...

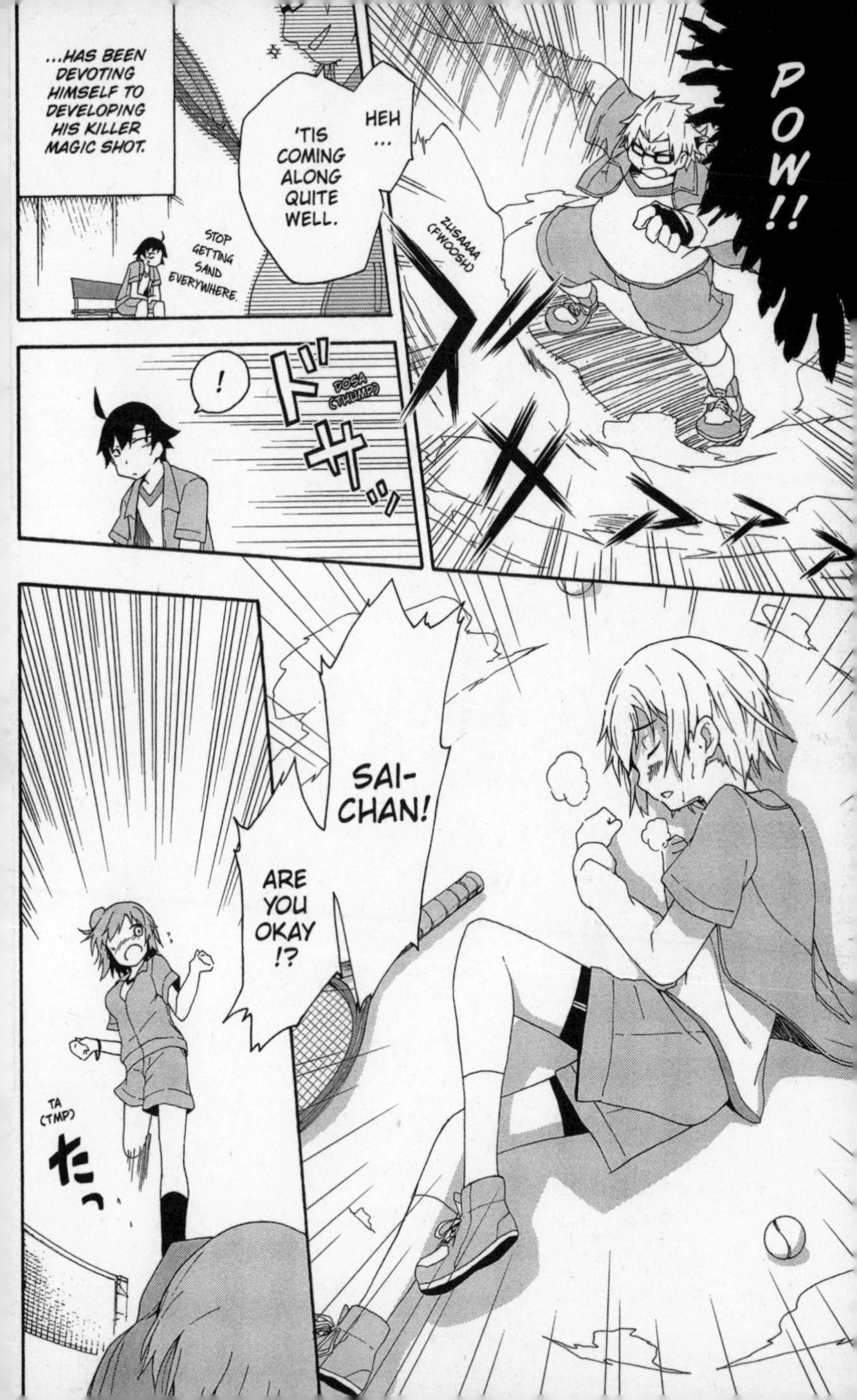
POW!!
ZUSAAAA (FWOOSH)
...HAS BEEN DEVOTING HIMSELF TO DEVELOPING HIS KILLER MAGIC SHOT.
HEH ... 'TIS COMING ALONG QUITE WELL.
STOP GETTING SAND EVERYWHERE.
!
ドサッ
DOSA (THUMP)
SAI-CHAN!
ARE YOU OKAY !?
たっ
TA (TMP)

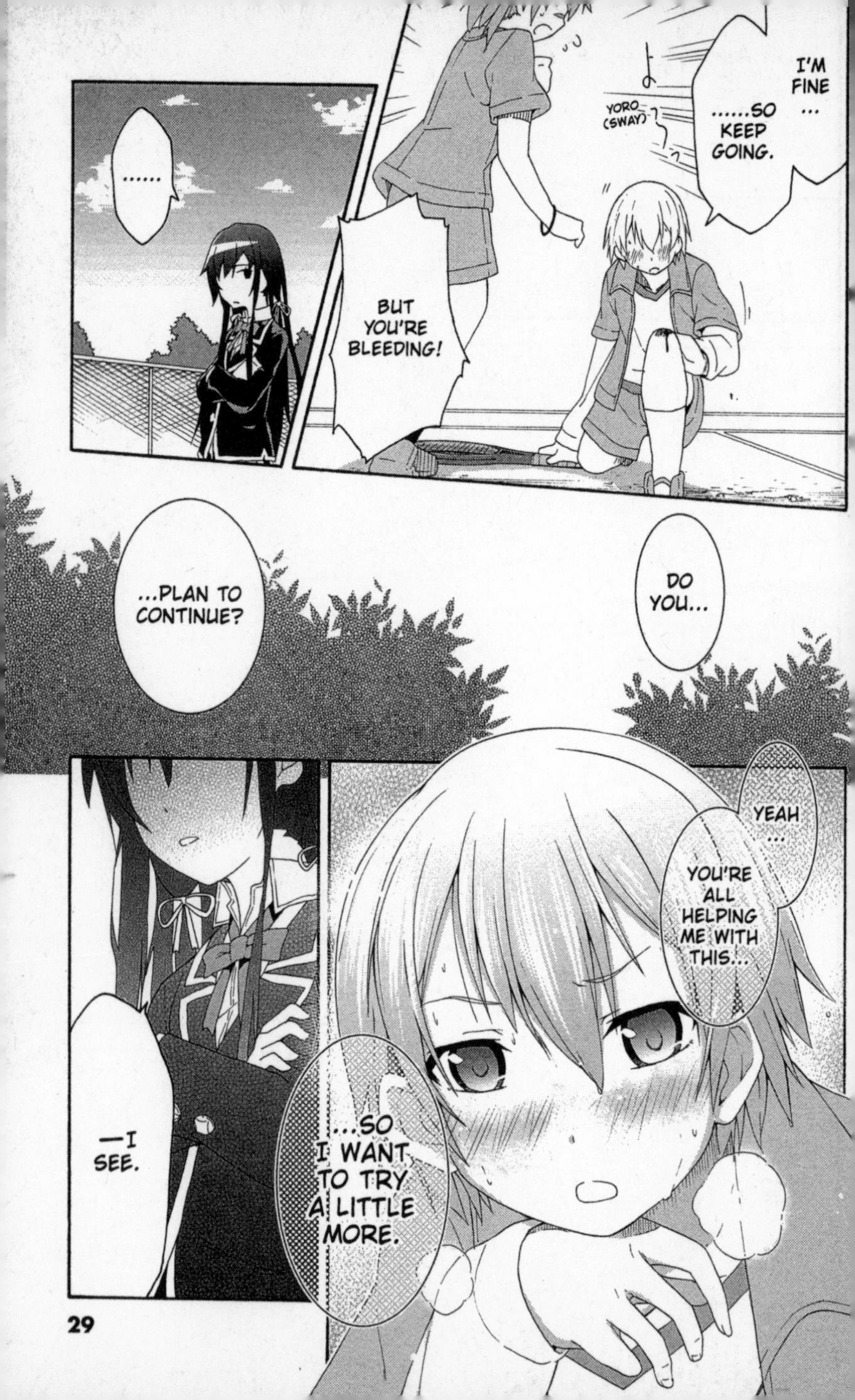
I'M FINE ... .SO KEEP GOING.
YORO (SWAY)
BUT YOU'RE BLEEDING!
......
DO YOU...
...PLAN TO CONTINUE?
YEAH ...
YOU'RE ALL HELPING ME WITH THIS...
...SO I WANT TO TRY A LITTLE MORE.
—I SEE.

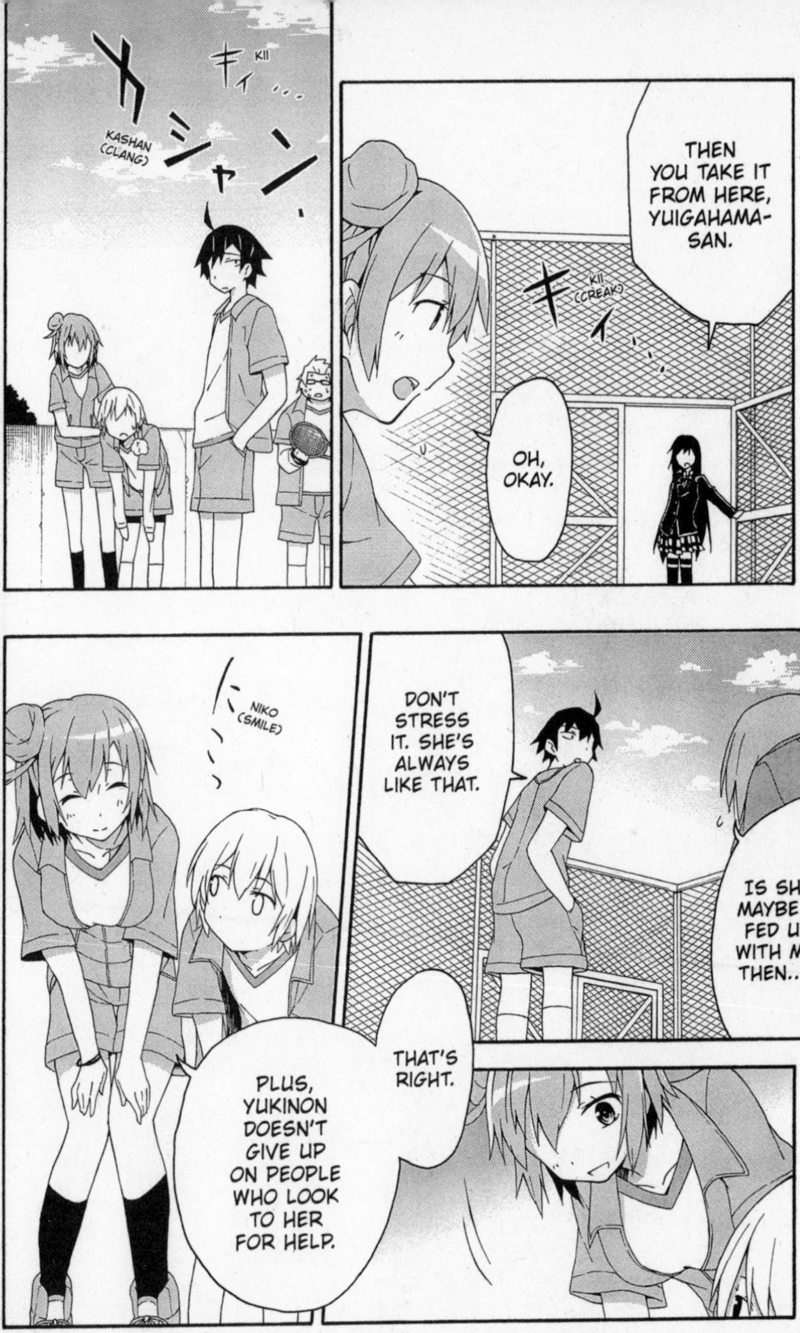
THEN YOU TAKE IT FROM HERE, YUIGAHAMA-SAN.
KII (CREAK)
OH, OKAY.
KII
KASHAN (CLANG)
IS SHE MAYBE... FED UP WITH ME, THEN...?
DON'T STRESS IT. SHE'S ALWAYS LIKE THAT.
THAT'S RIGHT.
NIKO (SMILE)
PLUS, YUKINON DOESN'T GIVE UP ON PEOPLE WHO LOOK TO HER FOR HELP.

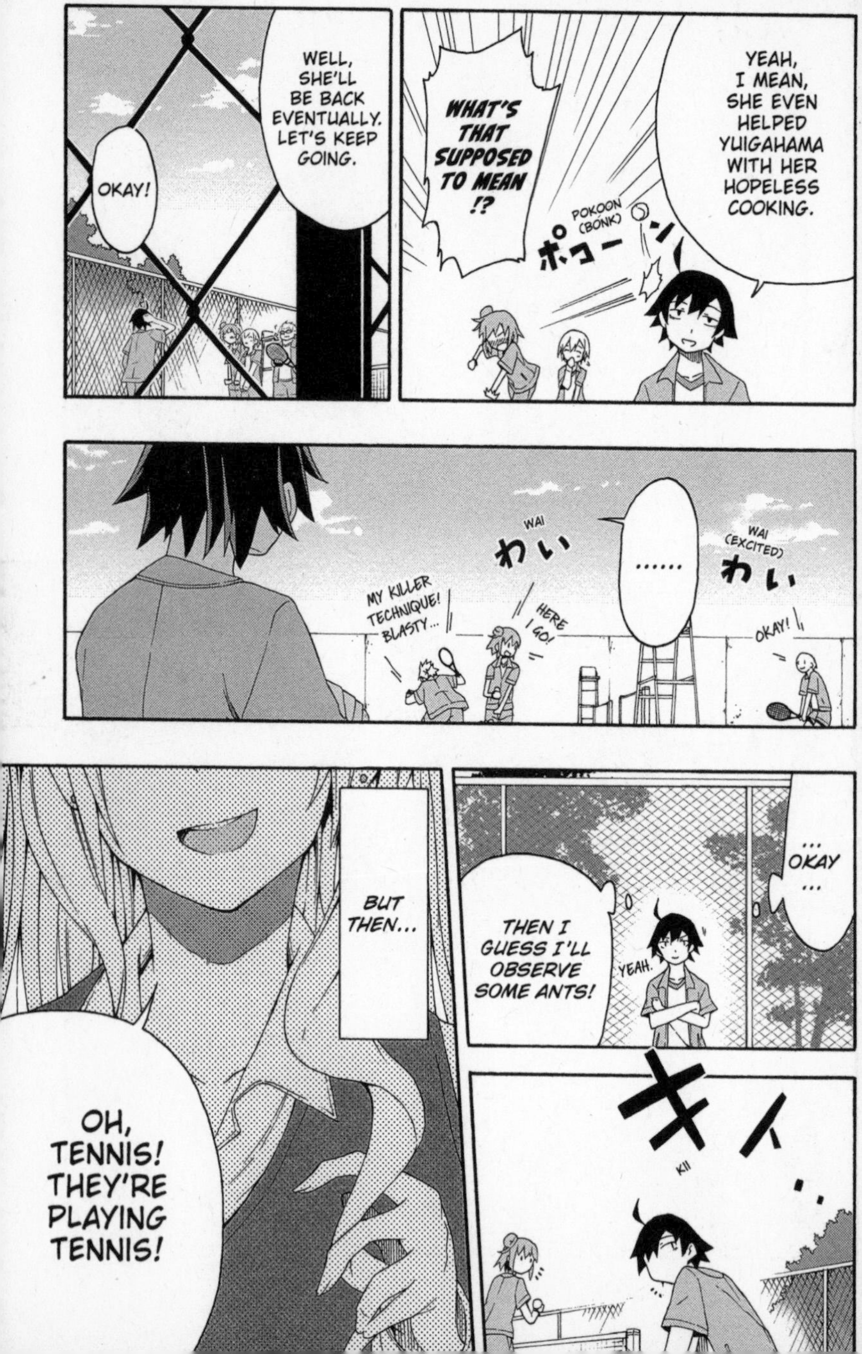
YEAH, I MEAN, SHE EVEN HELPED YUIGAHAMA WITH HER HOPELESS COOKING.
WHAT'S THAT SUPPOSED TO MEAN !?
ポコーン
POKOON (BONK)
WELL, SHE'LL BE BACK EVENTUALLY. LET'S KEEP GOING.
OKAY!
......
わい
WAI (EXCITED)
OKAY!
HERE I GO!
わい
WAI
MY KILLER TECHNIQUE! BLASTY...
... OKAY ...
THEN I GUESS I'LL OBSERVE SOME ANTS!
YEAH.
キィ
KII
BUT THEN...
OH, TENNIS! THEY'RE PLAYING TENNIS!

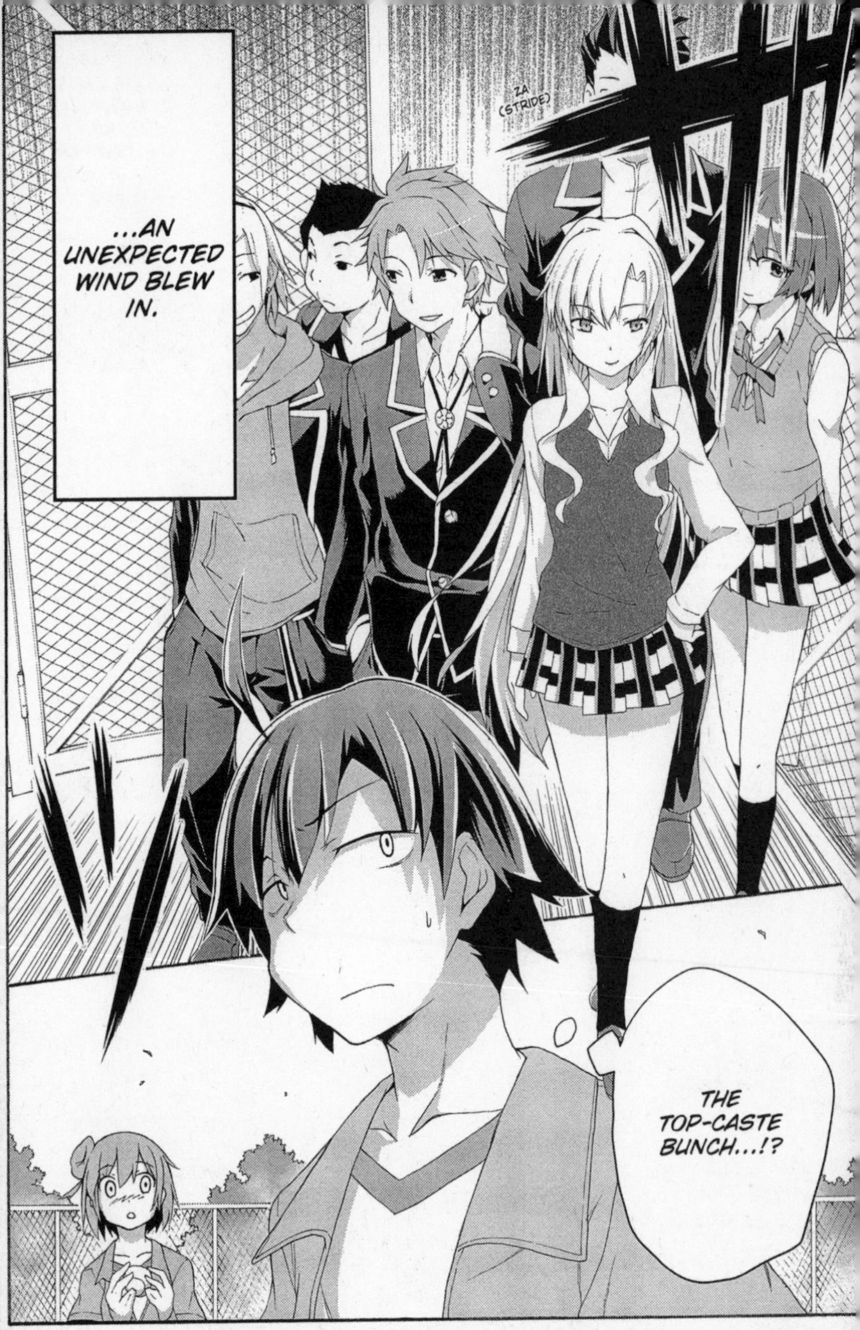
ZA (STRIDE)
...AN UNEXPECTED WIND BLEW IN.
THE TOP-CASTE BUNCH...!?

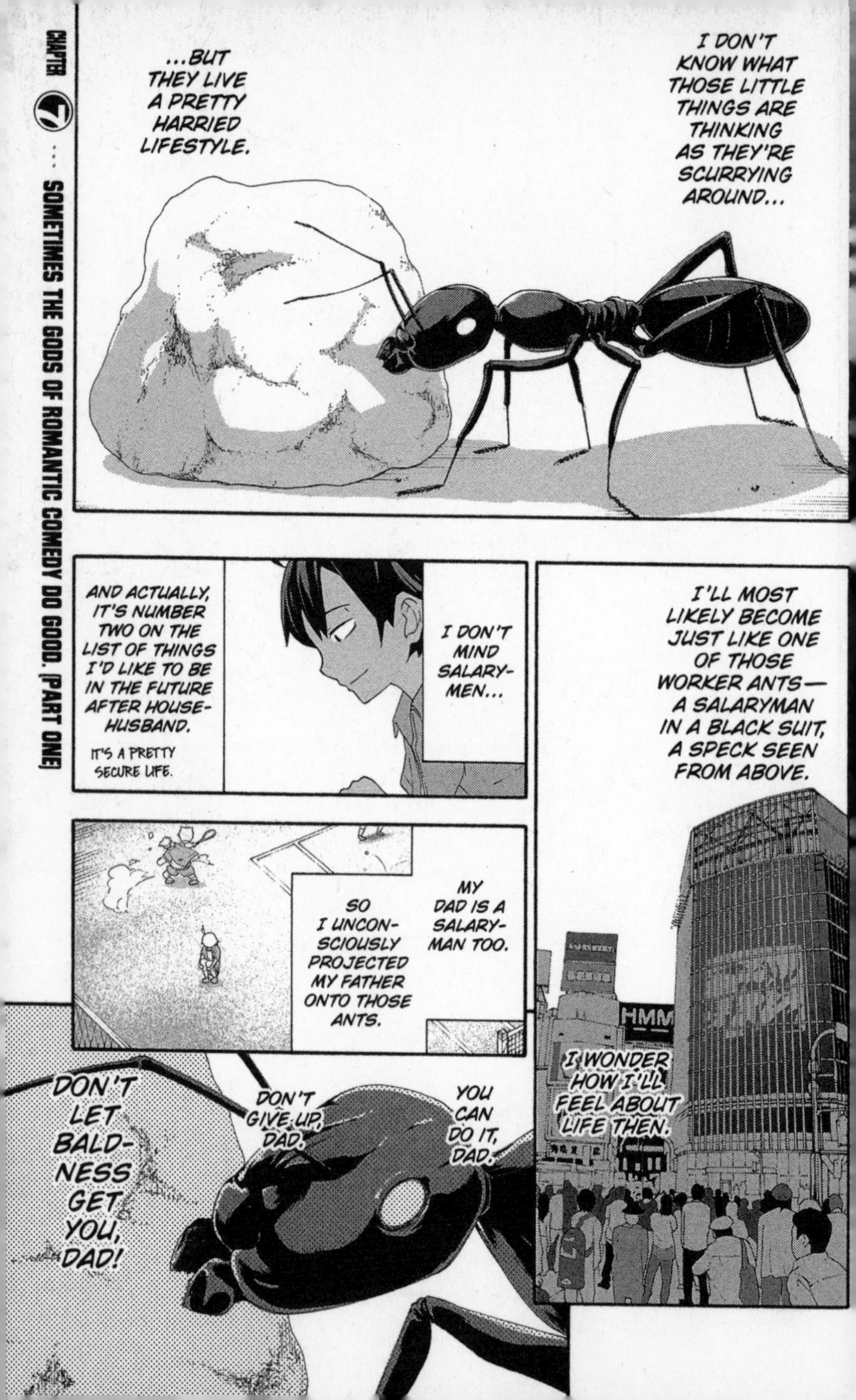
I DON'T KNOW WHAT THOSE LITTLE THINGS ARE THINKING AS THEY'RE SCURRYING AROUND...
...BUT THEY LIVE A PRETTY HARRIED LIFESTYLE.
I'LL MOST LIKELY BECOME JUST LIKE ONE OF THOSE WORKER ANTS—A SALARYMAN IN A BLACK SUIT, A SPECK SEEN FROM ABOVE.
I WONDER HOW I'LL FEEL ABOUT LIFE THEN.
I DON'T MIND SALARYMEN...
AND ACTUALLY, IT'S NUMBER TWO ON THE LIST OF THINGS I'D LIKE TO BE IN THE FUTURE AFTER HOUSEHUSBAND.
IT'S A PRETTY SECURE LIFE.
MY DAD IS A SALARYMAN TOO.
SO I UNCONSCIOUSLY PROJECTED MY FATHER ONTO THOSE ANTS.
YOU CAN DO IT, DAD.
DON'T GIVE UP, DAD.
DON'T LET BALDNESS GET YOU, DAD!

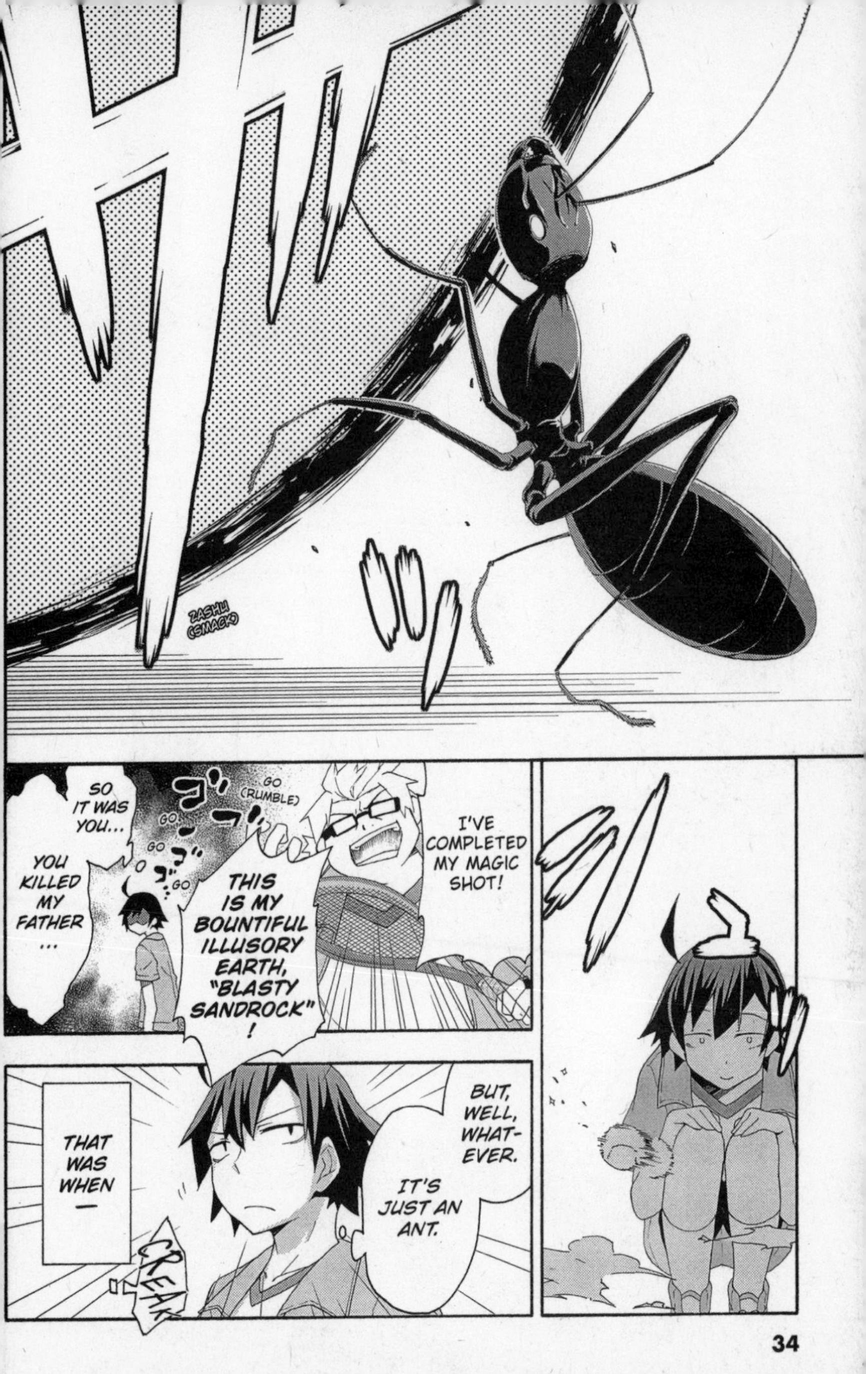
ZASHU (SMACK)
I'VE COMPLETED MY MAGIC SHOT!
GO (RUMBLE)
THIS IS MY BOUNTIFUL ILLUSORY EARTH, "BLASTY SANDROCK"!
SO IT WAS YOU...
GO GO GO GO
YOU KILLED MY FATHER...
BUT, WELL, WHATEVER.
IT'S JUST AN ANT.
CREAK
THAT WAS WHEN—

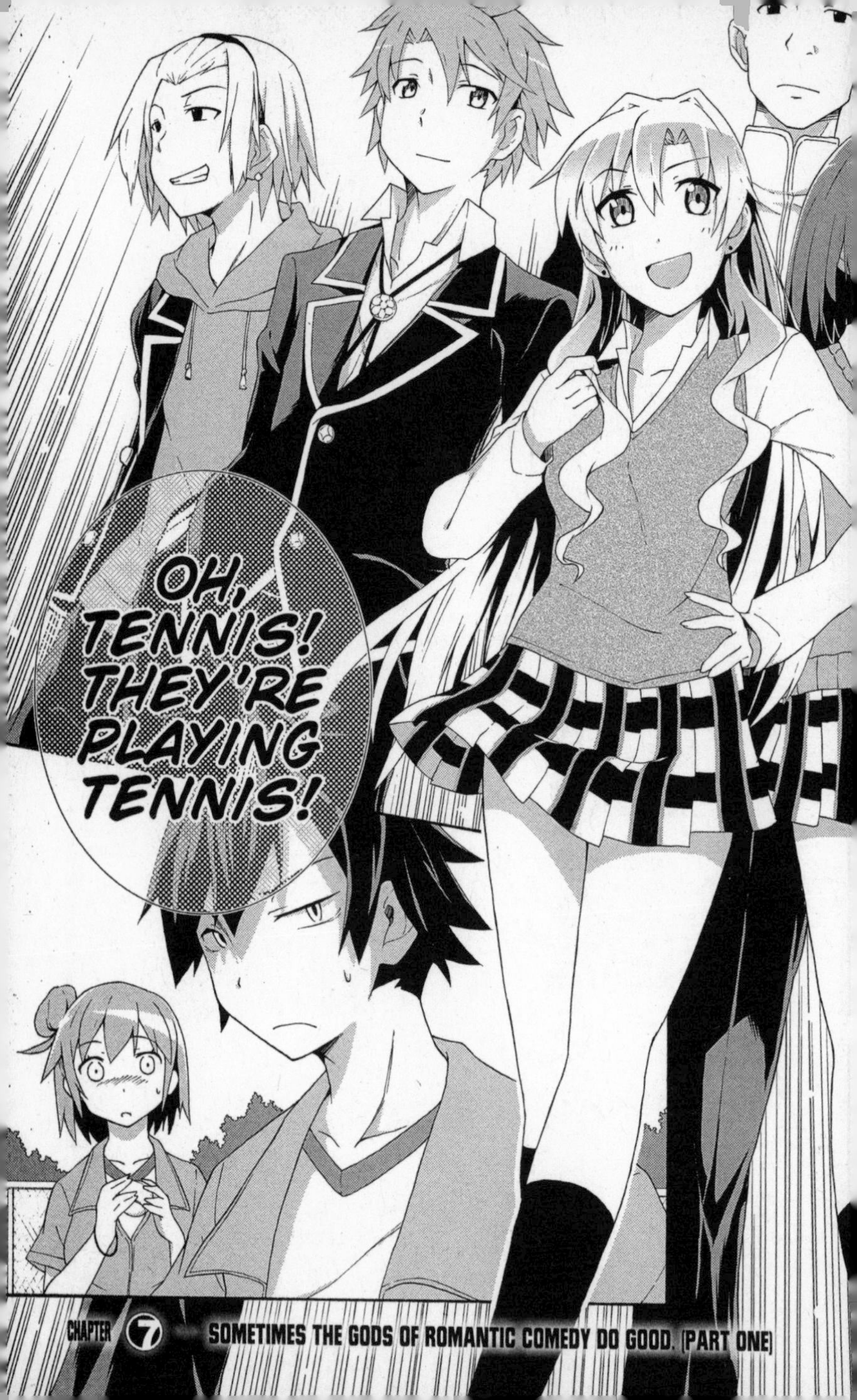
OH, TENNIS! THEY'RE PLAYING TENNIS!

CHAPTER 7 SOMETIMES THE GODS OF ROMANTIC COMEDY DO GOOD. (PART ONE)

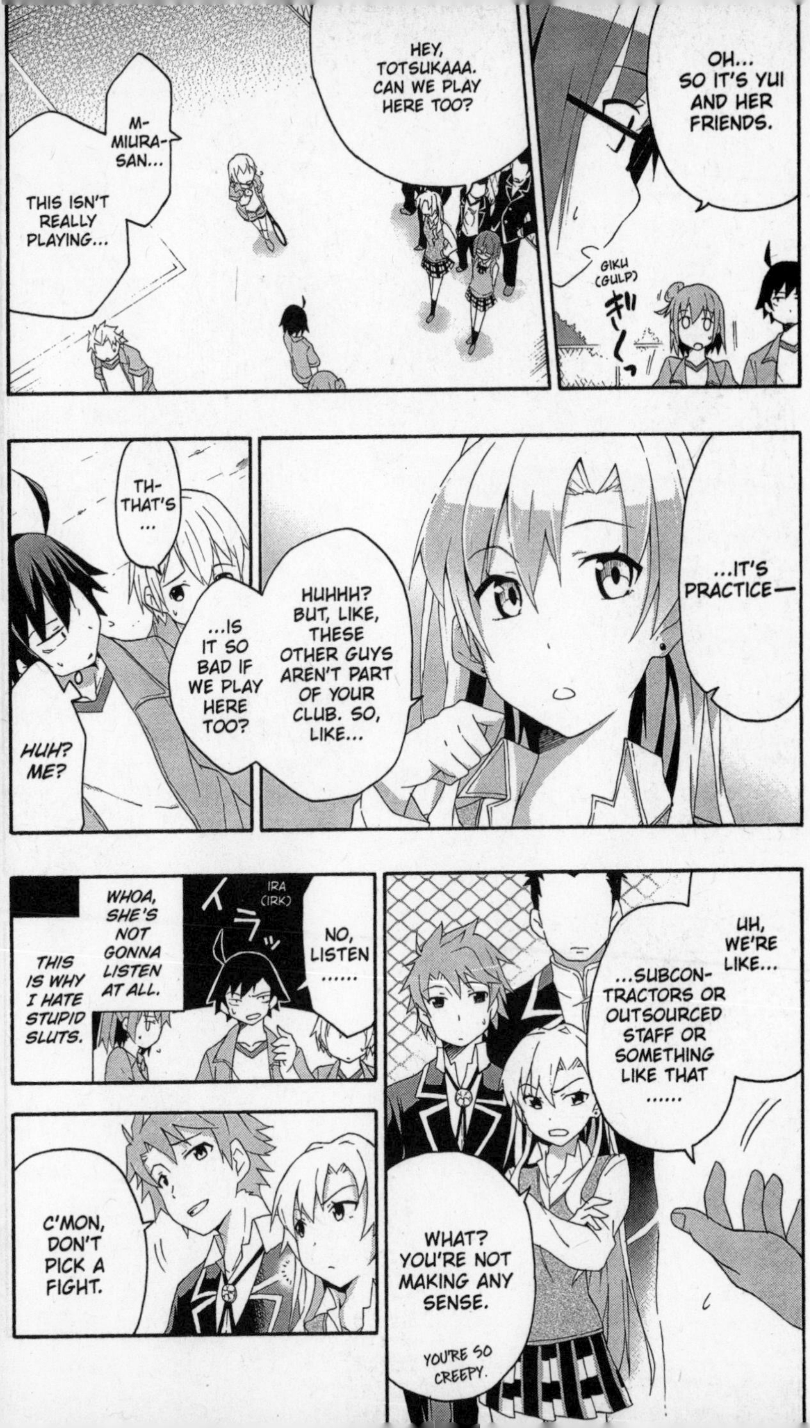
OH... SO IT'S YUI AND HER FRIENDS.
GIKU (GULP)
ぎくっ
HEY, TOTSUKAAA. CAN WE PLAY HERE TOO?
M-MIURA-SAN...
THIS ISN'T REALLY PLAYING...
...IT'S PRACTICE—
HUHHH? BUT, LIKE, THESE OTHER GUYS AREN'T PART OF YOUR CLUB. SO, LIKE...
...IS IT SO BAD IF WE PLAY HERE TOO?
TH-THAT'S...
HUH? ME?
UH, WE'RE LIKE...
...SUBCONTRACTORS OR OUTSOURCED STAFF OR SOMETHING LIKE THAT......
WHAT? YOU'RE NOT MAKING ANY SENSE.
YOU'RE SO CREEPY.
NO, LISTEN......
IRA (IRK)
イラッ
WHOA, SHE'S NOT GONNA LISTEN AT ALL.
THIS IS WHY I HATE STUPID SLUTS.
C'MON, DON'T PICK A FIGHT.

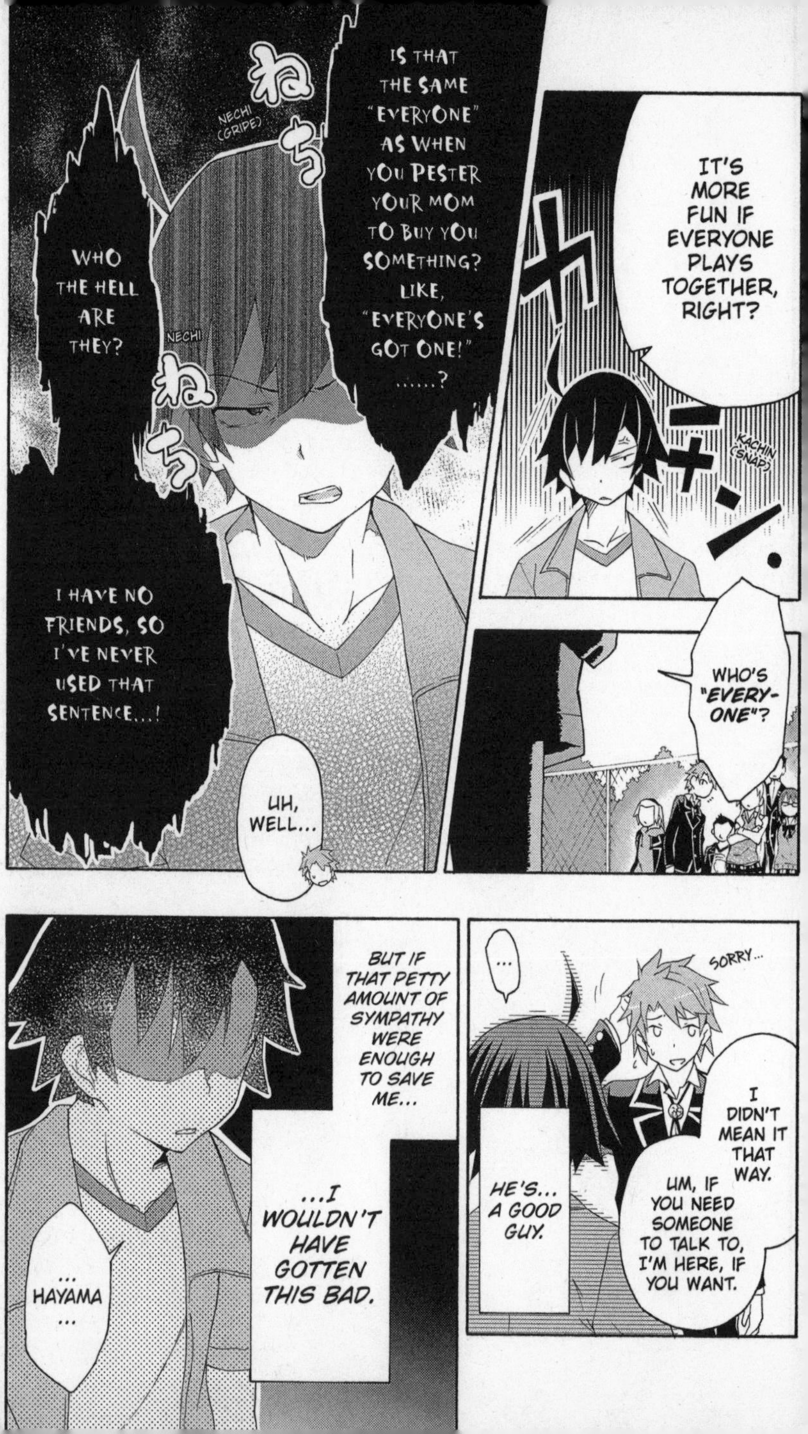
IT'S MORE FUN IF EVERYONE PLAYS TOGETHER, RIGHT?
KACHIN (SNAP)
WHO'S "EVERYONE"?
IS THAT THE SAME "EVERYONE" AS WHEN YOU PESTER YOUR MOM TO BUY YOU SOMETHING? LIKE, "EVERYONE'S GOT ONE!" ......?
ねち
NECHI (GRIPE)
WHO THE HELL ARE THEY?
NECHI
ねち
I HAVE NO FRIENDS, SO I'VE NEVER USED THAT SENTENCE...!
UH, WELL...
...
SORRY...
I DIDN'T MEAN IT THAT WAY.
UM, IF YOU NEED SOMEONE TO TALK TO, I'M HERE, IF YOU WANT.
HE'S... A GOOD GUY.
BUT IF THAT PETTY AMOUNT OF SYMPATHY WERE ENOUGH TO SAVE ME...
...I WOULDN'T HAVE GOTTEN THIS BAD.
... HAYAMA ...

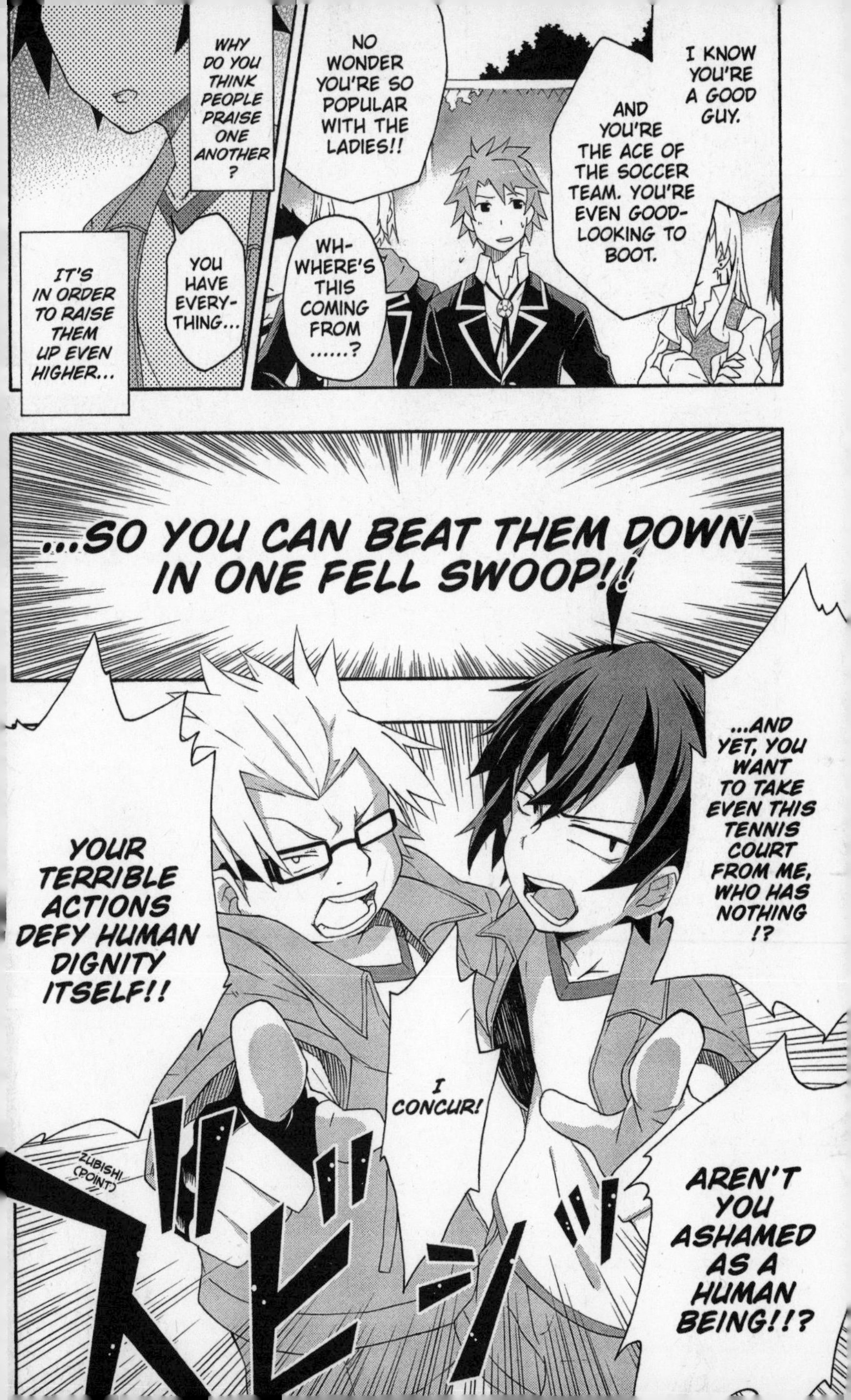
I KNOW YOU'RE A GOOD GUY.
AND YOU'RE THE ACE OF THE SOCCER TEAM. YOU'RE EVEN GOOD-LOOKING TO BOOT.
NO WONDER YOU'RE SO POPULAR WITH THE LADIES!!
WH-WHERE'S THIS COMING FROM ......?
WHY DO YOU THINK PEOPLE PRAISE ONE ANOTHER?
YOU HAVE EVERYTHING...
IT'S IN ORDER TO RAISE THEM UP EVEN HIGHER...
...SO YOU CAN BEAT THEM DOWN IN ONE FELL SWOOP!!
...AND YET, YOU WANT TO TAKE EVEN THIS TENNIS COURT FROM ME, WHO HAS NOTHING!?
AREN'T YOU ASHAMED AS A HUMAN BEING!!?
I CONCUR!
YOUR TERRIBLE ACTIONS DEFY HUMAN DIGNITY ITSELF!!
ZUBISHI (POINT)

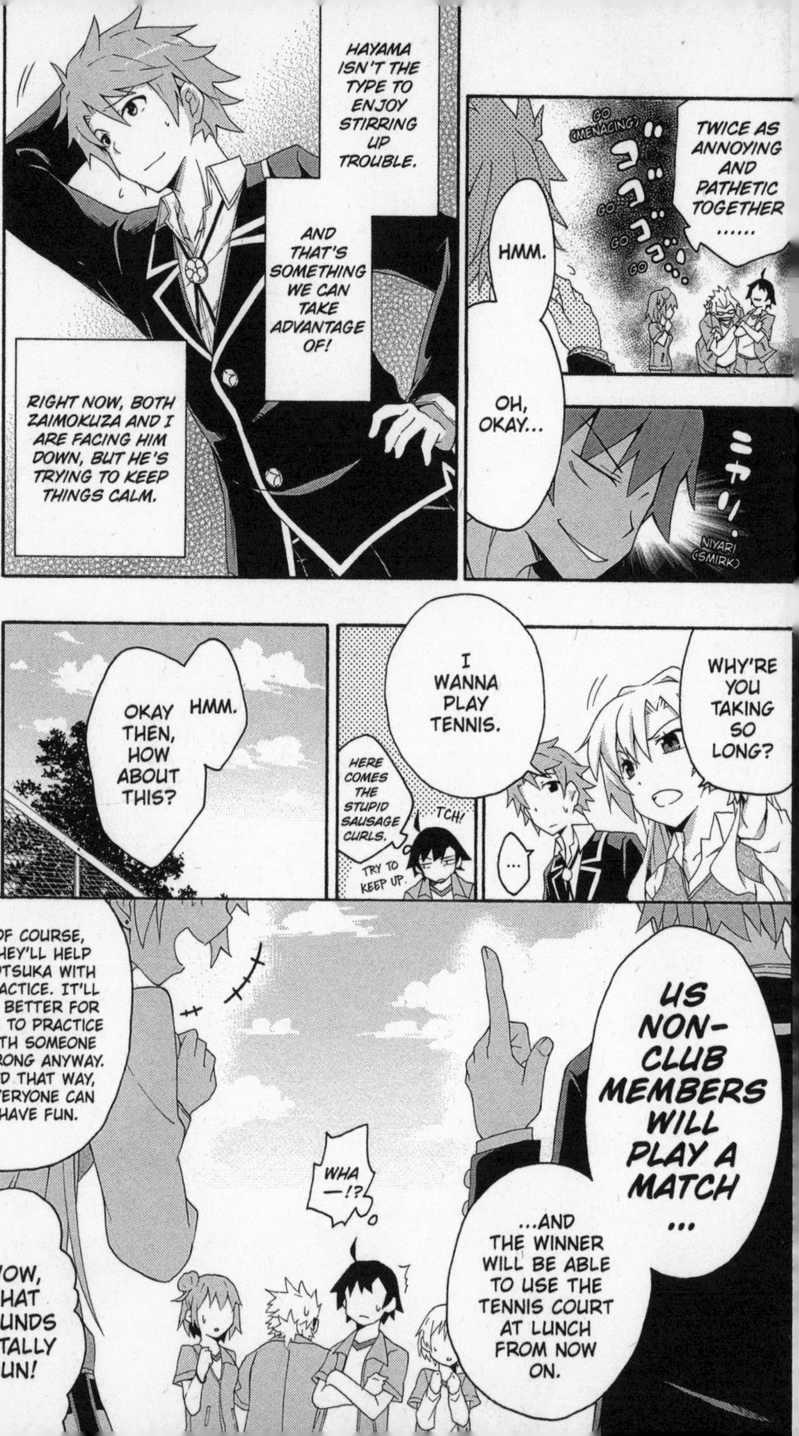
TWICE AS ANNOYING AND PATHETIC TOGETHER......
GO (MENACING)
GO
GO
GO
HMM.
OH, OKAY...
NIYARI (SMIRK)
HAYAMA ISN'T THE TYPE TO ENJOY STIRRING UP TROUBLE.
AND THAT'S SOMETHING WE CAN TAKE ADVANTAGE OF!
RIGHT NOW, BOTH ZAIMOKUZA AND I ARE FACING HIM DOWN, BUT HE'S TRYING TO KEEP THINGS CALM.
WHY'RE YOU TAKING SO LONG?
...
I WANNA PLAY TENNIS.
TCH!
HERE COMES THE STUPID SAUSAGE CURLS.
TRY TO KEEP UP.
HMM.
OKAY THEN, HOW ABOUT THIS?
US NON-CLUB MEMBERS WILL PLAY A MATCH...
...AND THE WINNER WILL BE ABLE TO USE THE TENNIS COURT AT LUNCH FROM NOW ON.
OF COURSE, THEY'LL HELP TOTSUKA WITH PRACTICE. IT'LL BE BETTER FOR HIM TO PRACTICE WITH SOMEONE STRONG ANYWAY. AND THAT WAY, EVERYONE CAN HAVE FUN.
WHA—!?
WOW, THAT SOUNDS TOTALLY FUN!

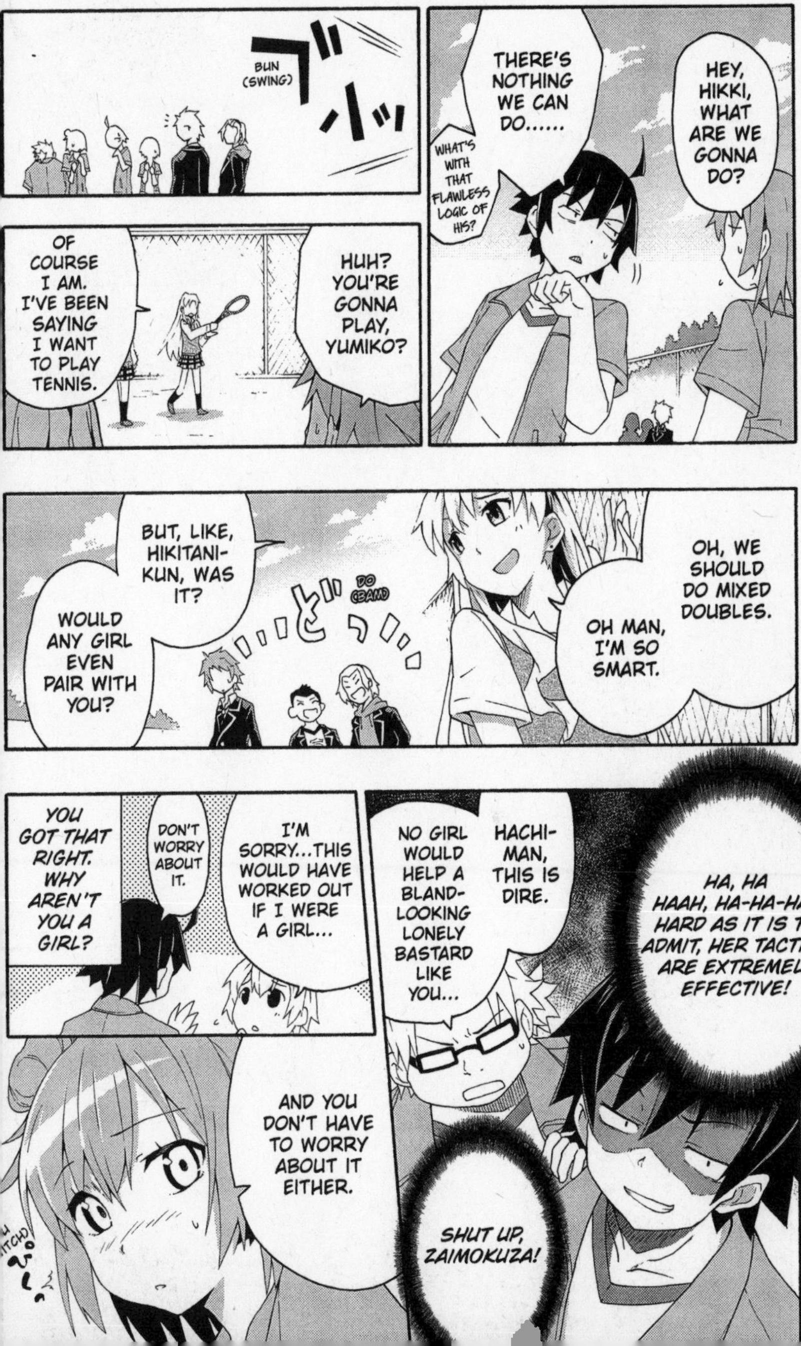
HEY, HIKKI, WHAT ARE WE GONNA DO?
THERE'S NOTHING WE CAN DO......
WHAT'S WITH THAT FLAWLESS LOGIC OF HIS?
BUN (SWING)
HUH? YOU'RE GONNA PLAY, YUMIKO?
OF COURSE I AM. I'VE BEEN SAYING I WANT TO PLAY TENNIS.
OH, WE SHOULD DO MIXED DOUBLES.
OH MAN, I'M SO SMART.
DO (BAM)
BUT, LIKE, HIKITANI-KUN, WAS IT?
WOULD ANY GIRL EVEN PAIR WITH YOU?
HA, HA HAAH, HA-HA-HA-HARD AS IT IS TO ADMIT, HER TACTICS ARE EXTREMELY EFFECTIVE!
HACHI-MAN, THIS IS DIRE.
NO GIRL WOULD HELP A BLAND-LOOKING LONELY BASTARD LIKE YOU...
I'M SORRY...THIS WOULD HAVE WORKED OUT IF I WERE A GIRL...
DON'T WORRY ABOUT IT.
YOU GOT THAT RIGHT. WHY AREN'T YOU A GIRL?
AND YOU DON'T HAVE TO WORRY ABOUT IT EITHER.
SHUT UP, ZAIMOKUZA!

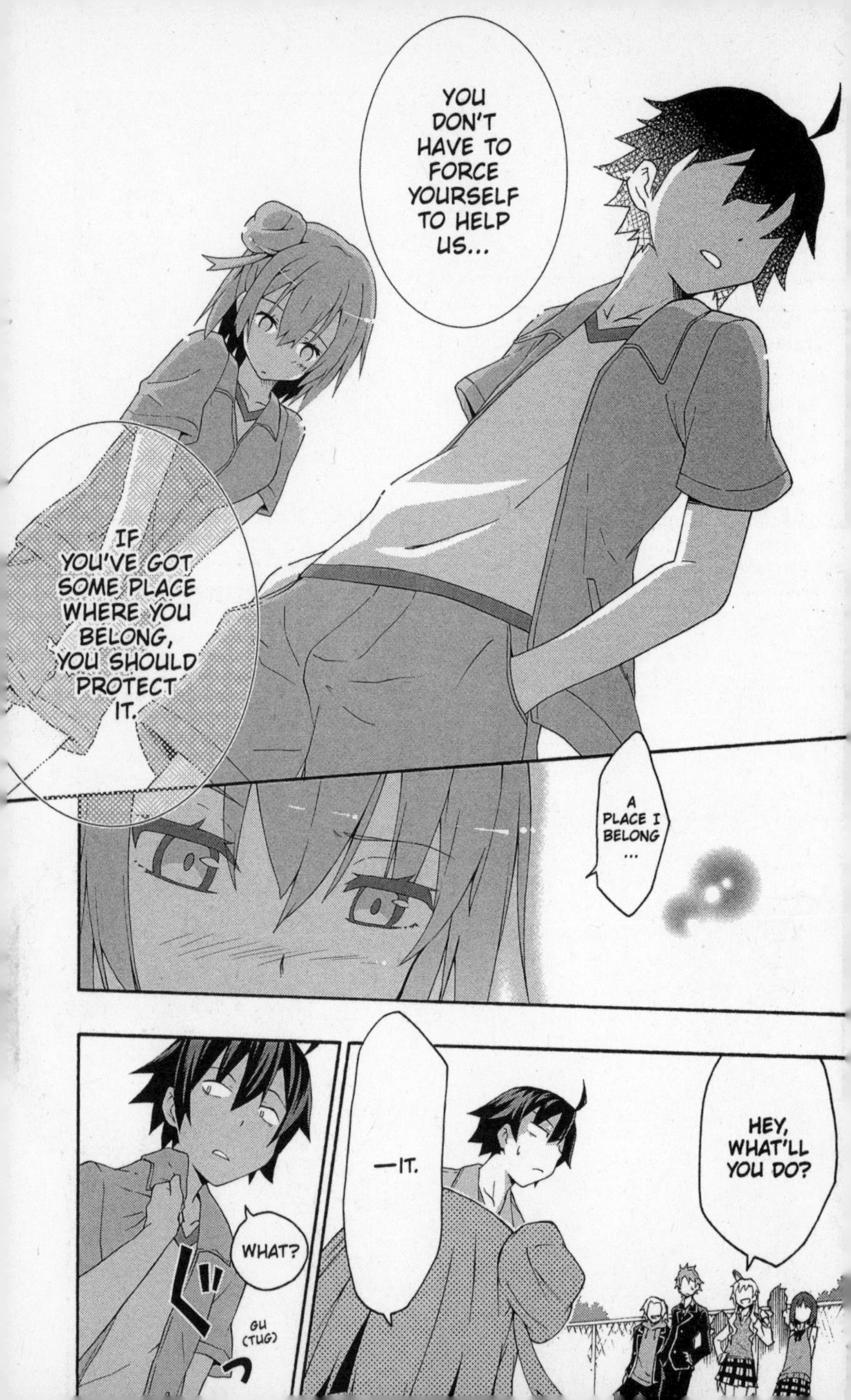
YOU DON'T HAVE TO FORCE YOURSELF TO HELP US...
IF YOU'VE GOT SOME PLACE WHERE YOU BELONG, YOU SHOULD PROTECT IT.
A PLACE I BELONG...
HEY, WHAT'LL YOU DO?
—IT.
WHAT?
GU (TUG)

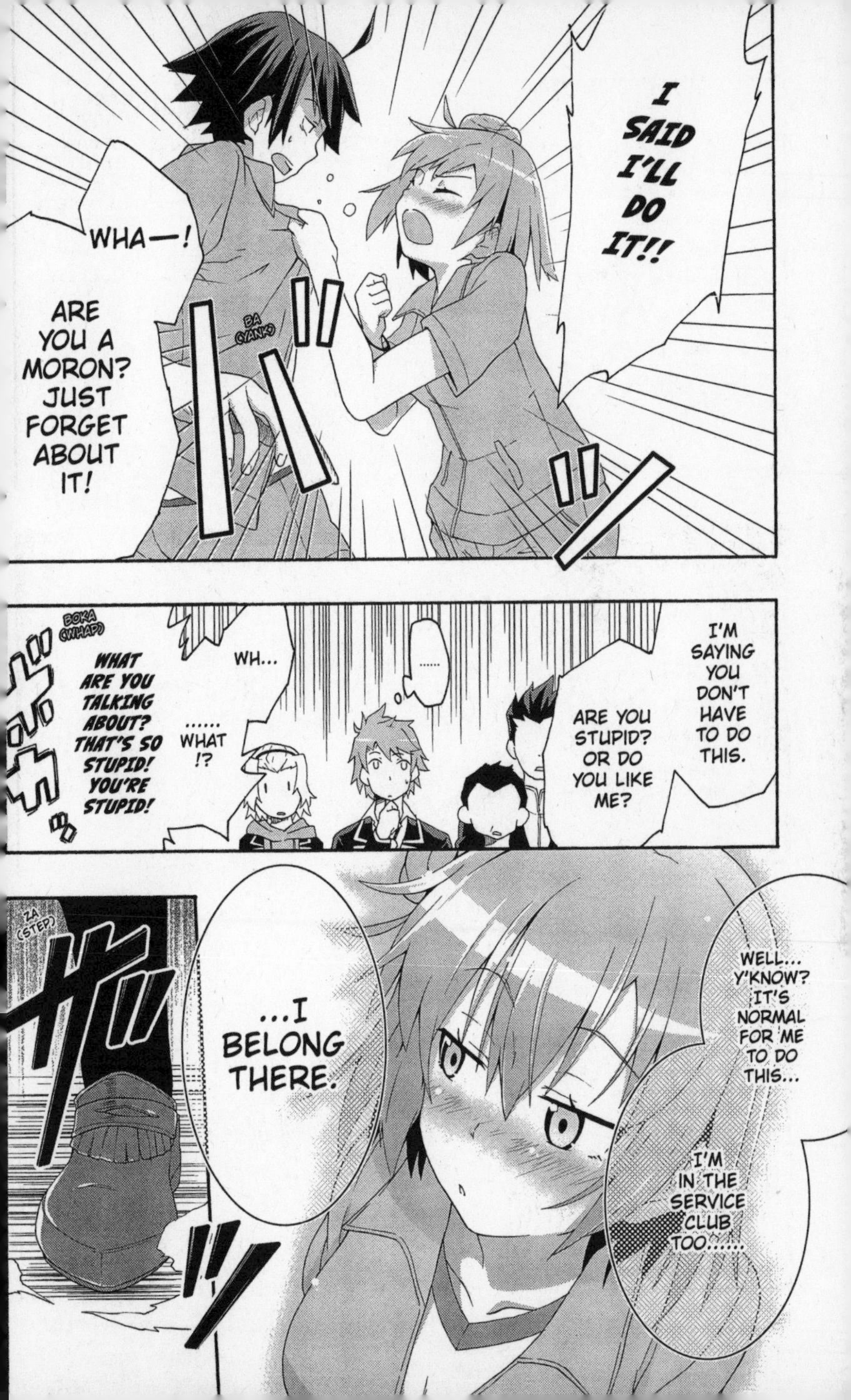
I SAID I'LL DO IT!!
WHA—!
BA (YANK)
ARE YOU A MORON? JUST FORGET ABOUT IT!
I'M SAYING YOU DON'T HAVE TO DO THIS.
ARE YOU STUPID? OR DO YOU LIKE ME?
......
WH...
......WHAT!?
WHAT ARE YOU TALKING ABOUT? THAT'S SO STUPID! YOU'RE STUPID!
BOKA (WHAP)
WELL... Y'KNOW? IT'S NORMAL FOR ME TO DO THIS...
I'M IN THE SERVICE CLUB TOO......
...I BELONG THERE.
ZA (STEP)

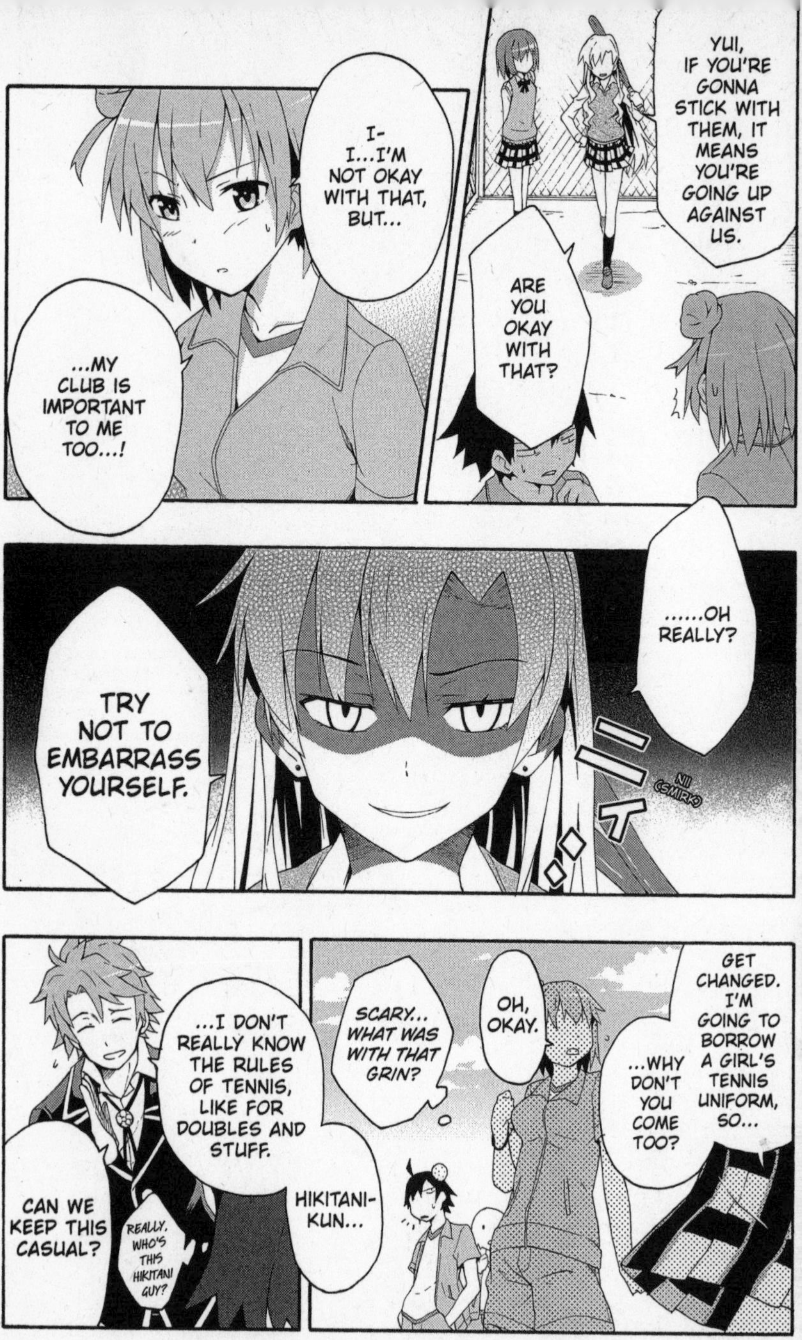
YUI, IF YOU'RE GONNA STICK WITH THEM, IT MEANS YOU'RE GOING UP AGAINST US.
ARE YOU OKAY WITH THAT?
I- I...I'M NOT OKAY WITH THAT, BUT...
...MY CLUB IS IMPORTANT TO ME TOO...!
......OH REALLY?
NII (SMIRK)
TRY NOT TO EMBARRASS YOURSELF.
GET CHANGED. I'M GOING TO BORROW A GIRL'S TENNIS UNIFORM, SO...
...WHY DON'T YOU COME TOO?
OH, OKAY.
SCARY... WHAT WAS WITH THAT GRIN?
...I DON'T REALLY KNOW THE RULES OF TENNIS, LIKE FOR DOUBLES AND STUFF.
HIKITANI-KUN...
CAN WE KEEP THIS CASUAL?
REALLY. WHO'S THIS HIKITANI GUY?

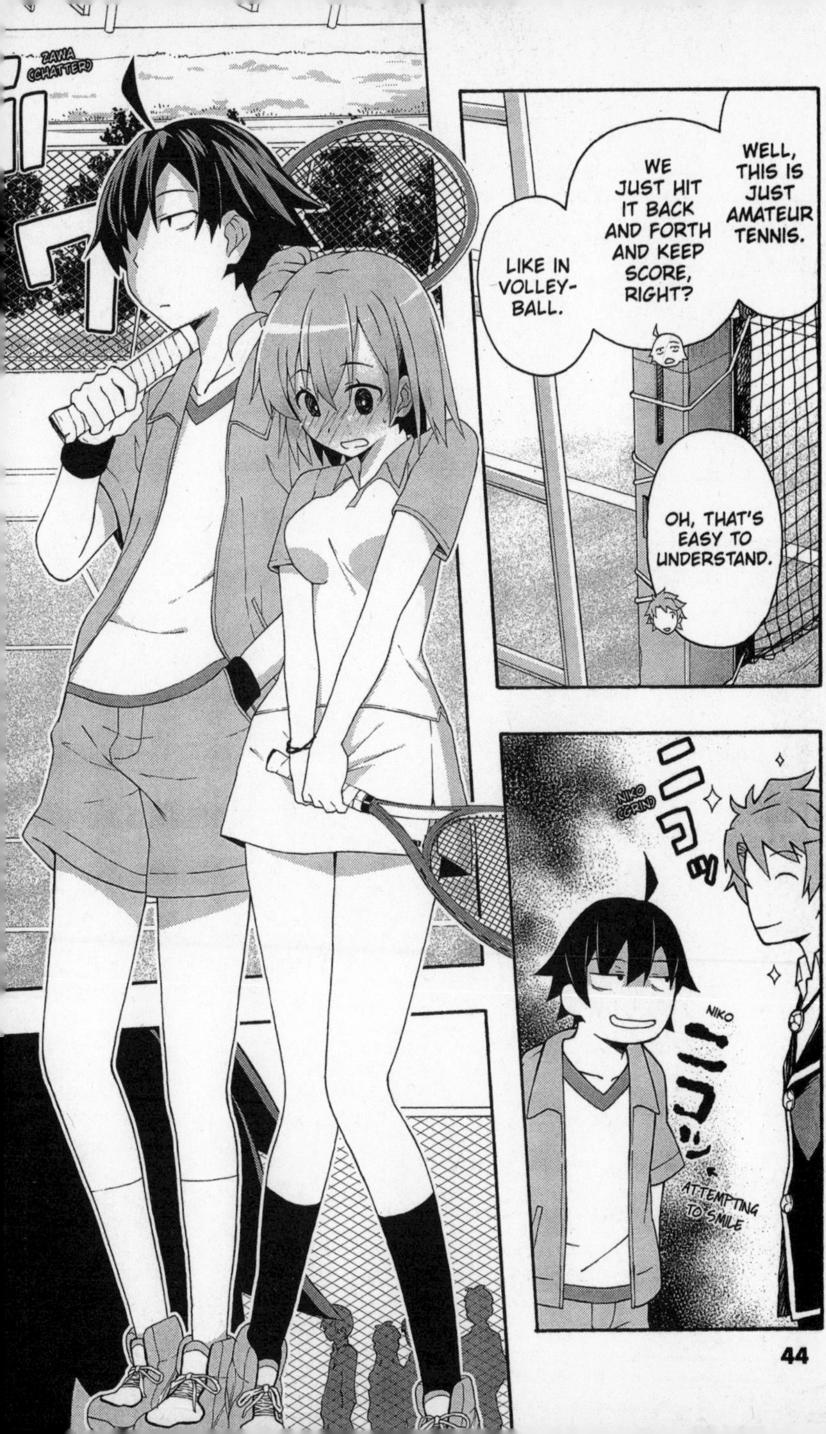
WELL, THIS IS JUST AMATEUR TENNIS.
WE JUST HIT IT BACK AND FORTH AND KEEP SCORE, RIGHT?
LIKE IN VOLLEY-BALL.
OH, THAT'S EASY TO UNDERSTAND.
NIKO (GRIN)
NIKO
ATTEMPTING TO SMILE
ZAWA (CHATTER)

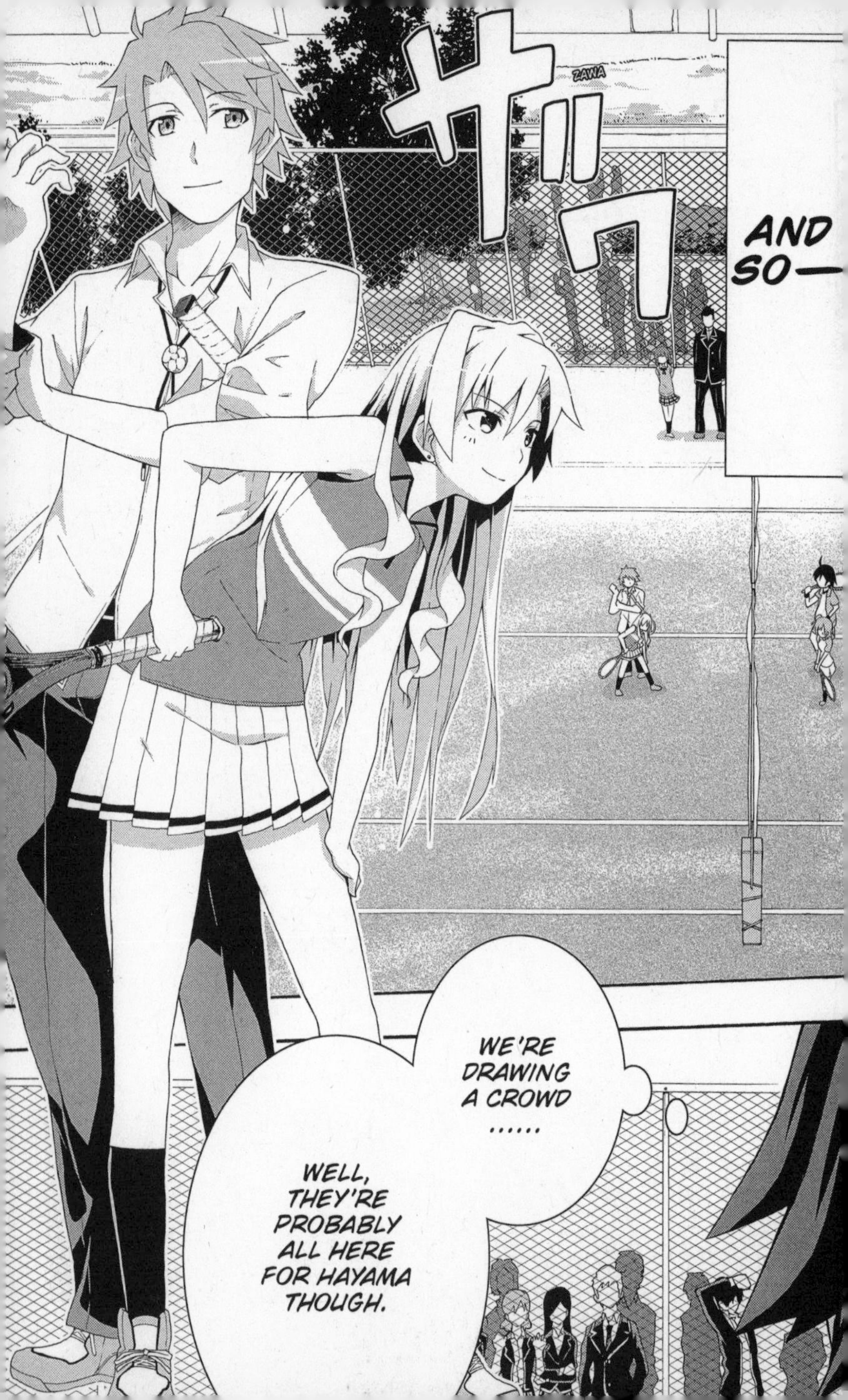
AND SO—
ザワ
ZAWA
WE'RE DRAWING A CROWD ......
WELL, THEY'RE PROBABLY ALL HERE FOR HAYAMA THOUGH.

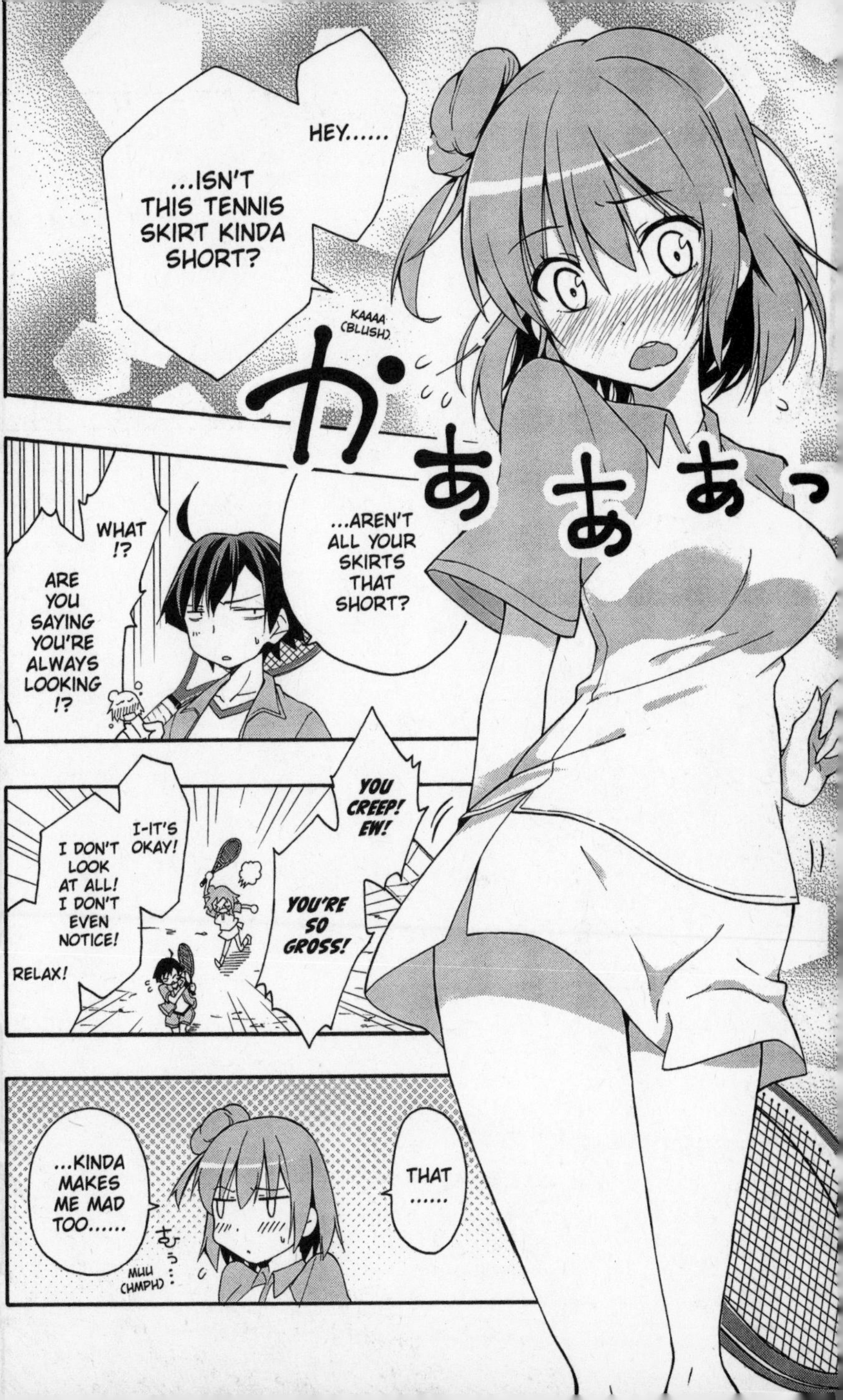
HEY......
...ISN'T THIS TENNIS SKIRT KINDA SHORT?
KAAAA (BLUSH)
があああっ
...AREN'T ALL YOUR SKIRTS THAT SHORT?
WHAT !?
ARE YOU SAYING YOU'RE ALWAYS LOOKING !?
YOU CREEP! EW!
YOU'RE SO GROSS!
I-IT'S OKAY!
I DON'T LOOK AT ALL! I DON'T EVEN NOTICE!
RELAX!
THAT ......
...KINDA MAKES ME MAD TOO......
むぅ…
MUU (HMPH)

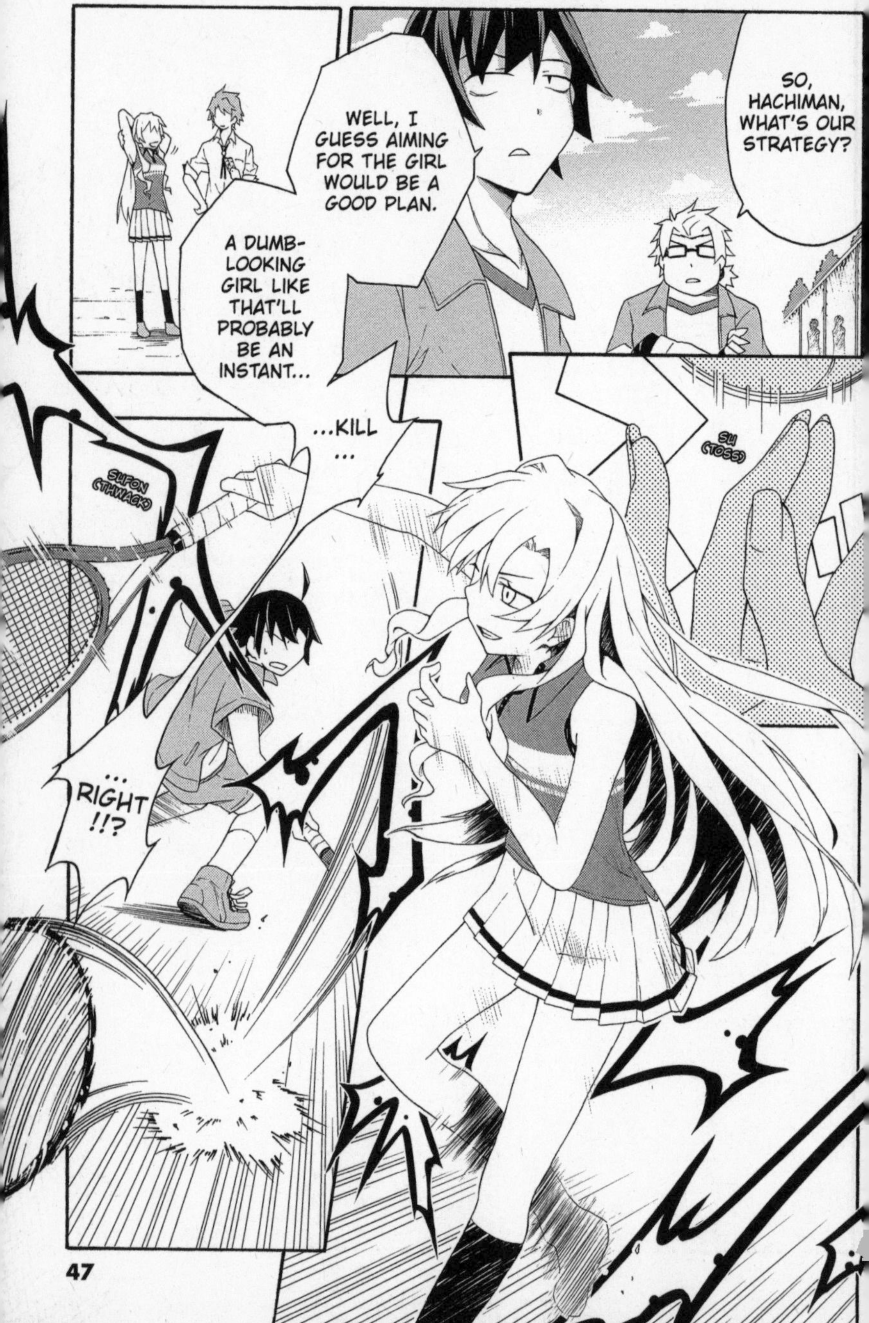
SO, HACHIMAN, WHAT'S OUR STRATEGY?
WELL, I GUESS AIMING FOR THE GIRL WOULD BE A GOOD PLAN.
A DUMB-LOOKING GIRL LIKE THAT'LL PROBABLY BE AN INSTANT...
SU (TOSS)
...KILL ...
SUFON (THWACK)
... RIGHT !!?

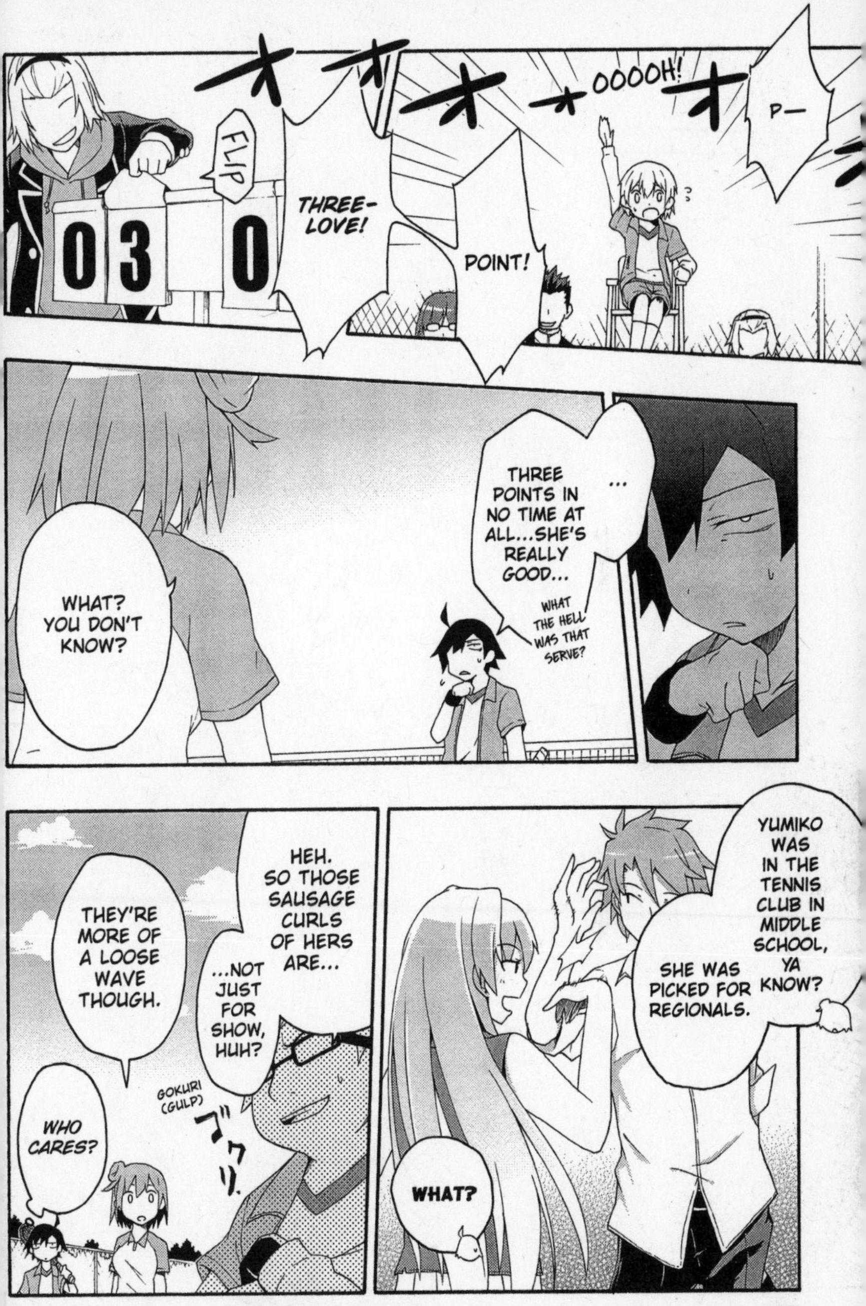
OOOOH!
P—
POINT!
FLIP
THREE-LOVE!
...
THREE POINTS IN NO TIME AT ALL...SHE'S REALLY GOOD...
WHAT THE HELL WAS THAT SERVE?
WHAT? YOU DON'T KNOW?
YUMIKO WAS IN THE TENNIS CLUB IN MIDDLE SCHOOL, YA KNOW?
SHE WAS PICKED FOR REGIONALS.
WHAT?
HEH. SO THOSE SAUSAGE CURLS OF HERS ARE...
...NOT JUST FOR SHOW, HUH?
GOKURI (GULP)
THEY'RE MORE OF A LOOSE WAVE THOUGH.
WHO CARES?

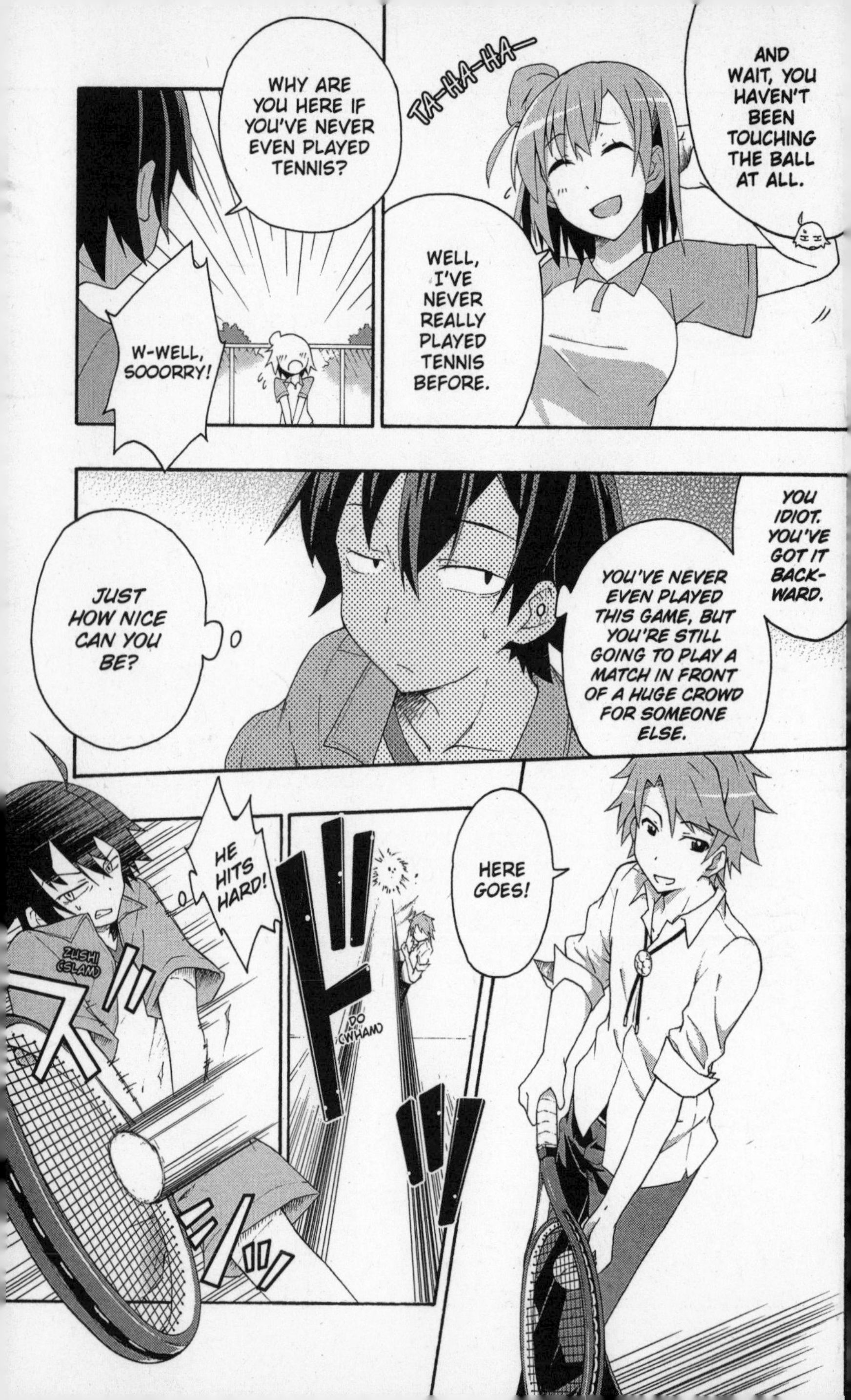
AND WAIT, YOU HAVEN'T BEEN TOUCHING THE BALL AT ALL.
TA-HA-HA—
WELL, I'VE NEVER REALLY PLAYED TENNIS BEFORE.
WHY ARE YOU HERE IF YOU'VE NEVER EVEN PLAYED TENNIS?
W-WELL, SOOORRY!
YOU IDIOT. YOU'VE GOT IT BACKWARD.
YOU'VE NEVER EVEN PLAYED THIS GAME, BUT YOU'RE STILL GOING TO PLAY A MATCH IN FRONT OF A HUGE CROWD FOR SOMEONE ELSE.
JUST HOW NICE CAN YOU BE?
HERE GOES!
DO (WHAM)
HE HITS HARD!
ZUSHI (SLAM)

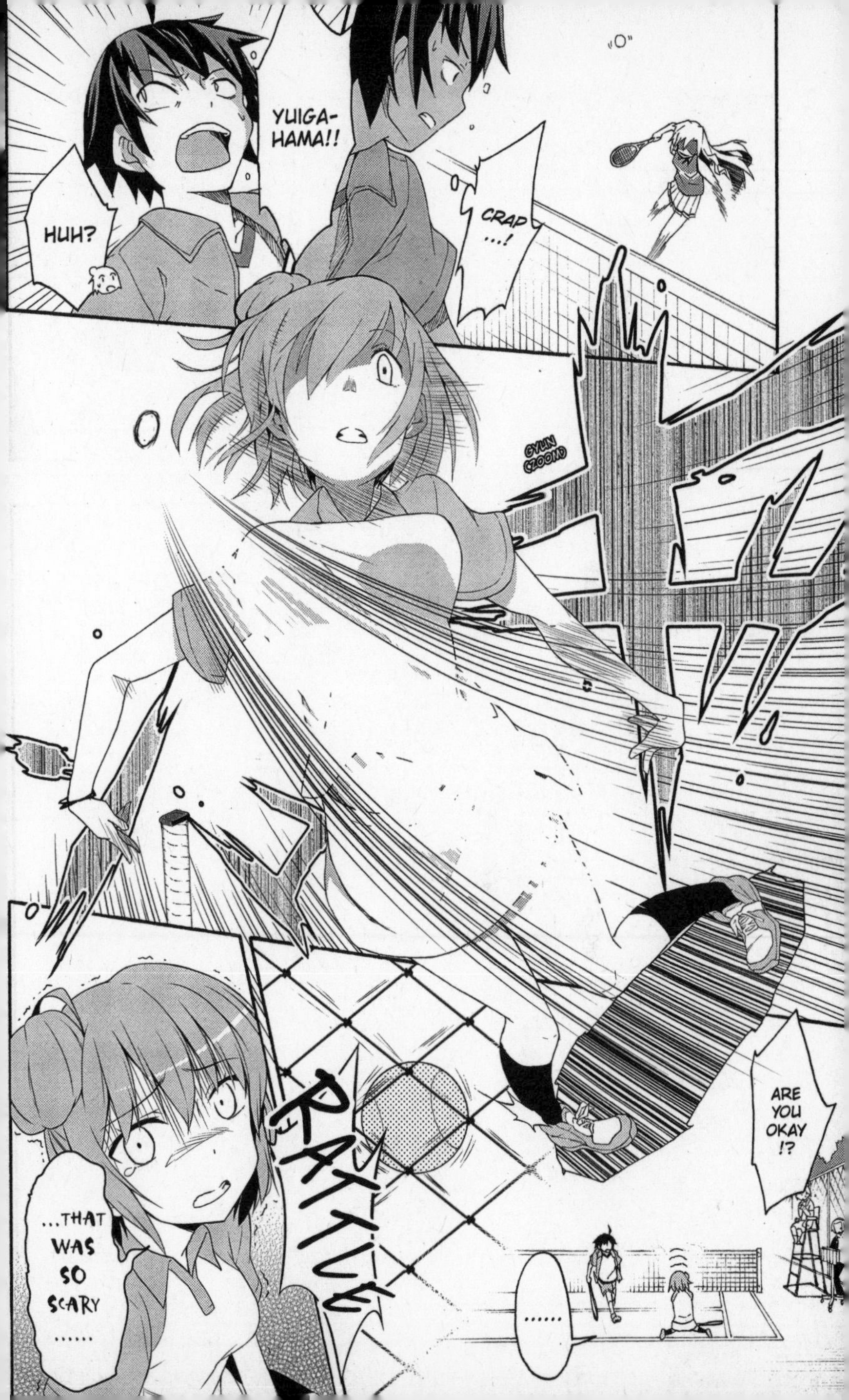
CRAP ...!
YUIGA-HAMA!!
HUH?
GYUN (ZOOM)
ARE YOU OKAY !?
......
RATTLE
...THAT WAS SO SCARY ......

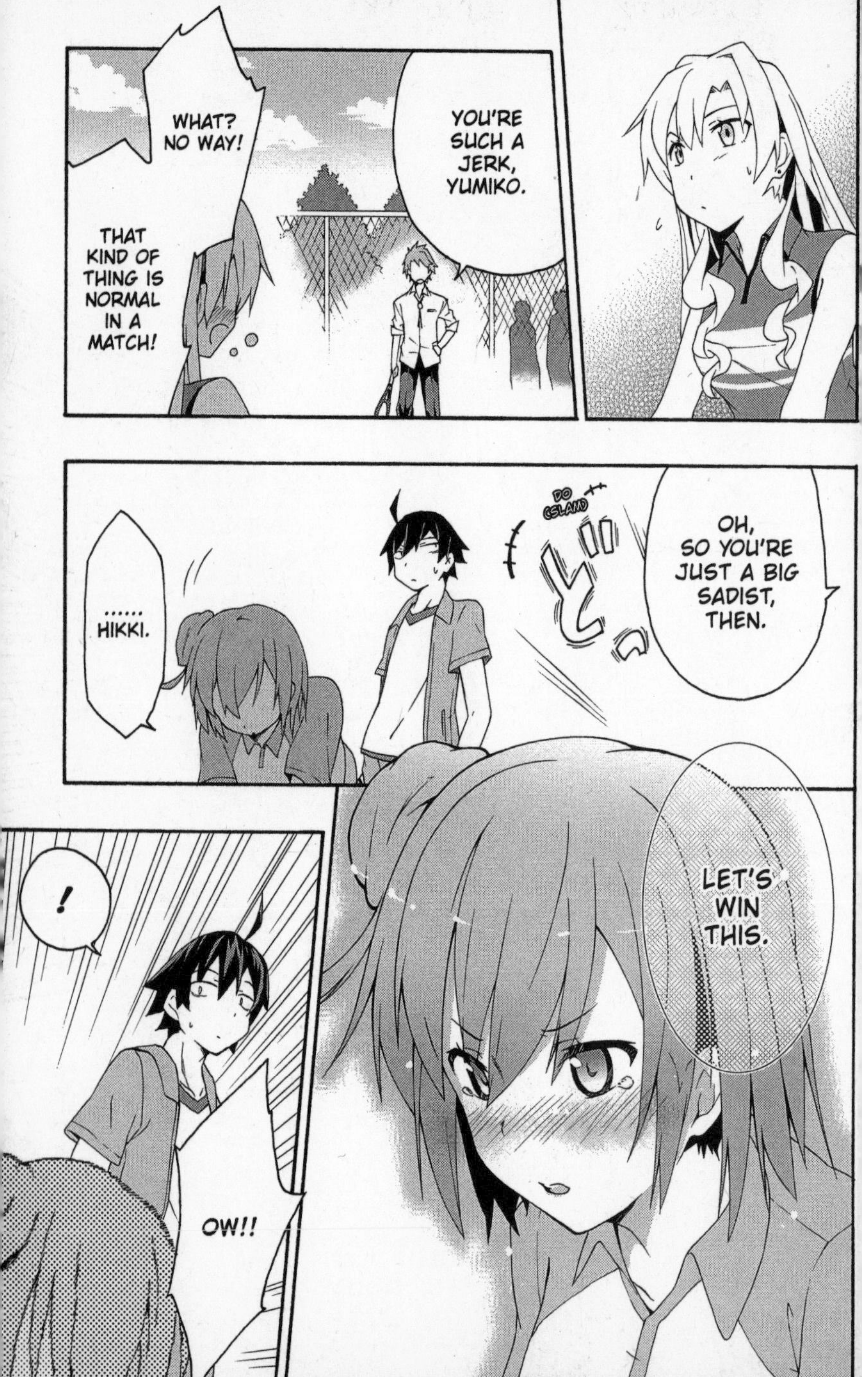
YOU'RE SUCH A JERK, YUMIKO.
WHAT? NO WAY!
THAT KIND OF THING IS NORMAL IN A MATCH!
OH, SO YOU'RE JUST A BIG SADIST, THEN.
DO (SLAM)
...... HIKKI.
LET'S WIN THIS.
!
OW!!

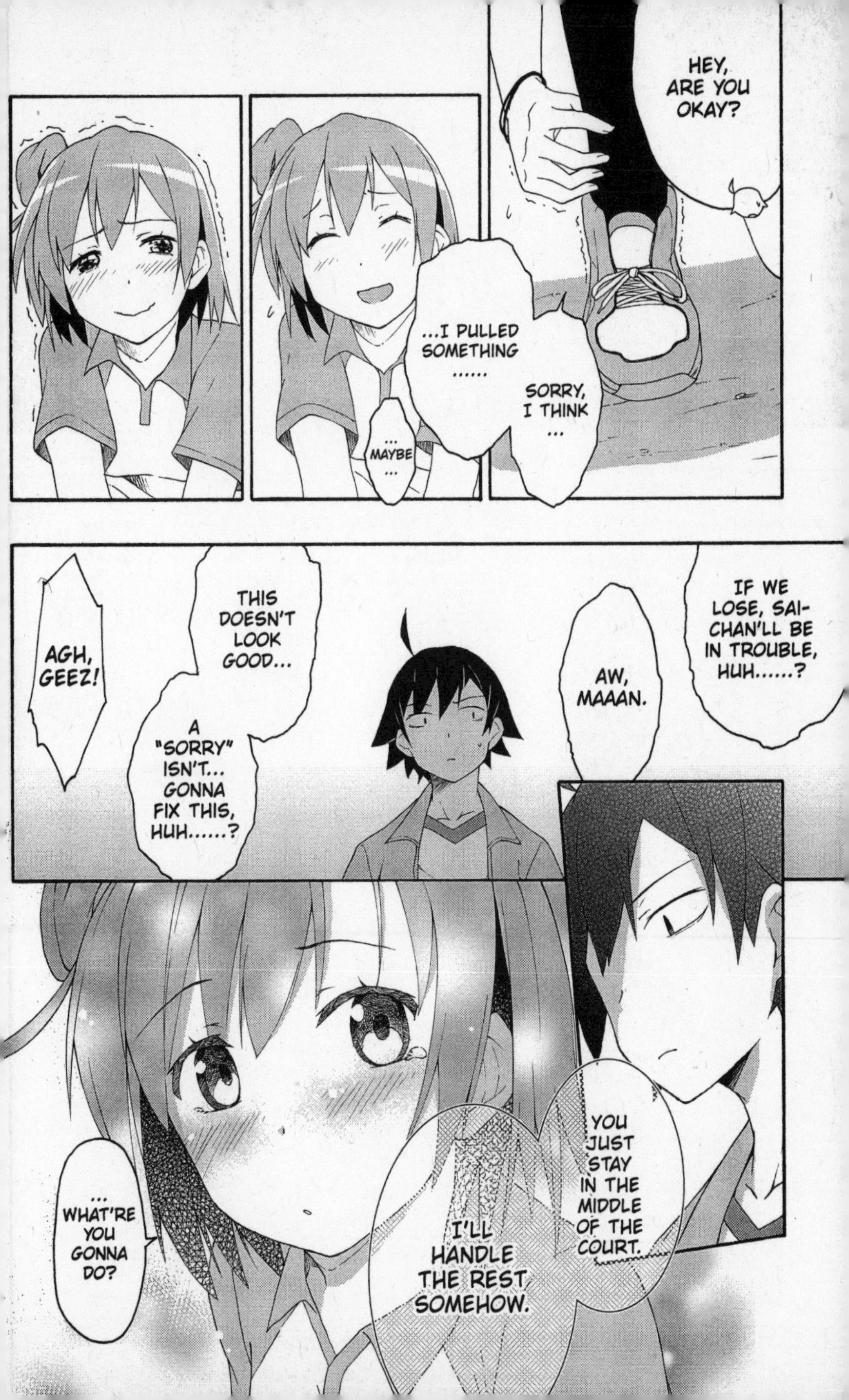
HEY, ARE YOU OKAY?
SORRY, I THINK ...
...I PULLED SOMETHING ......
... MAYBE ...
IF WE LOSE, SAI-CHAN'LL BE IN TROUBLE, HUH......?
AW, MAAAN.
THIS DOESN'T LOOK GOOD...
A "SORRY" ISN'T... GONNA FIX THIS, HUH......?
AGH, GEEZ!
YOU JUST STAY IN THE MIDDLE OF THE COURT.
I'LL HANDLE THE REST SOMEHOW.
...WHAT'RE YOU GONNA DO?

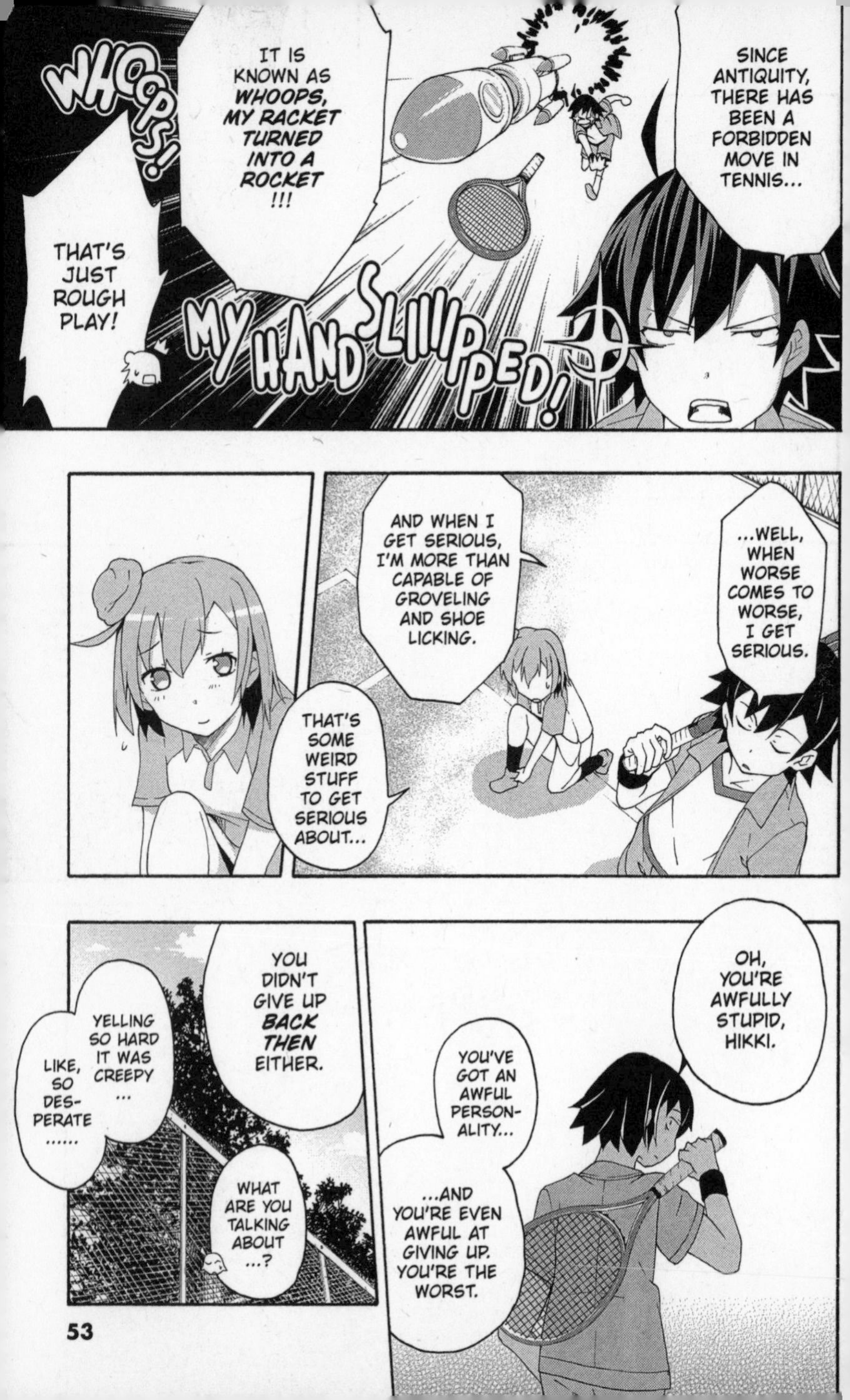
SINCE ANTIQUITY, THERE HAS BEEN A FORBIDDEN MOVE IN TENNIS...
MY HAND SLIIIIPPED!
IT IS KNOWN AS *WHOOPS, MY RACKET TURNED INTO A ROCKET* !!!
WHOOPS!
THAT'S JUST ROUGH PLAY!
...WELL, WHEN WORSE COMES TO WORSE, I GET SERIOUS.
AND WHEN I GET SERIOUS, I'M MORE THAN CAPABLE OF GROVELING AND SHOE LICKING.
THAT'S SOME WEIRD STUFF TO GET SERIOUS ABOUT...
OH, YOU'RE AWFULLY STUPID, HIKKI.
YOU'VE GOT AN AWFUL PERSONALITY...
...AND YOU'RE EVEN AWFUL AT GIVING UP. YOU'RE THE WORST.
YOU DIDN'T GIVE UP *BACK THEN* EITHER.
YELLING SO HARD IT WAS CREEPY...
LIKE, SO DESPERATE......
WHAT ARE YOU TALKING ABOUT...?

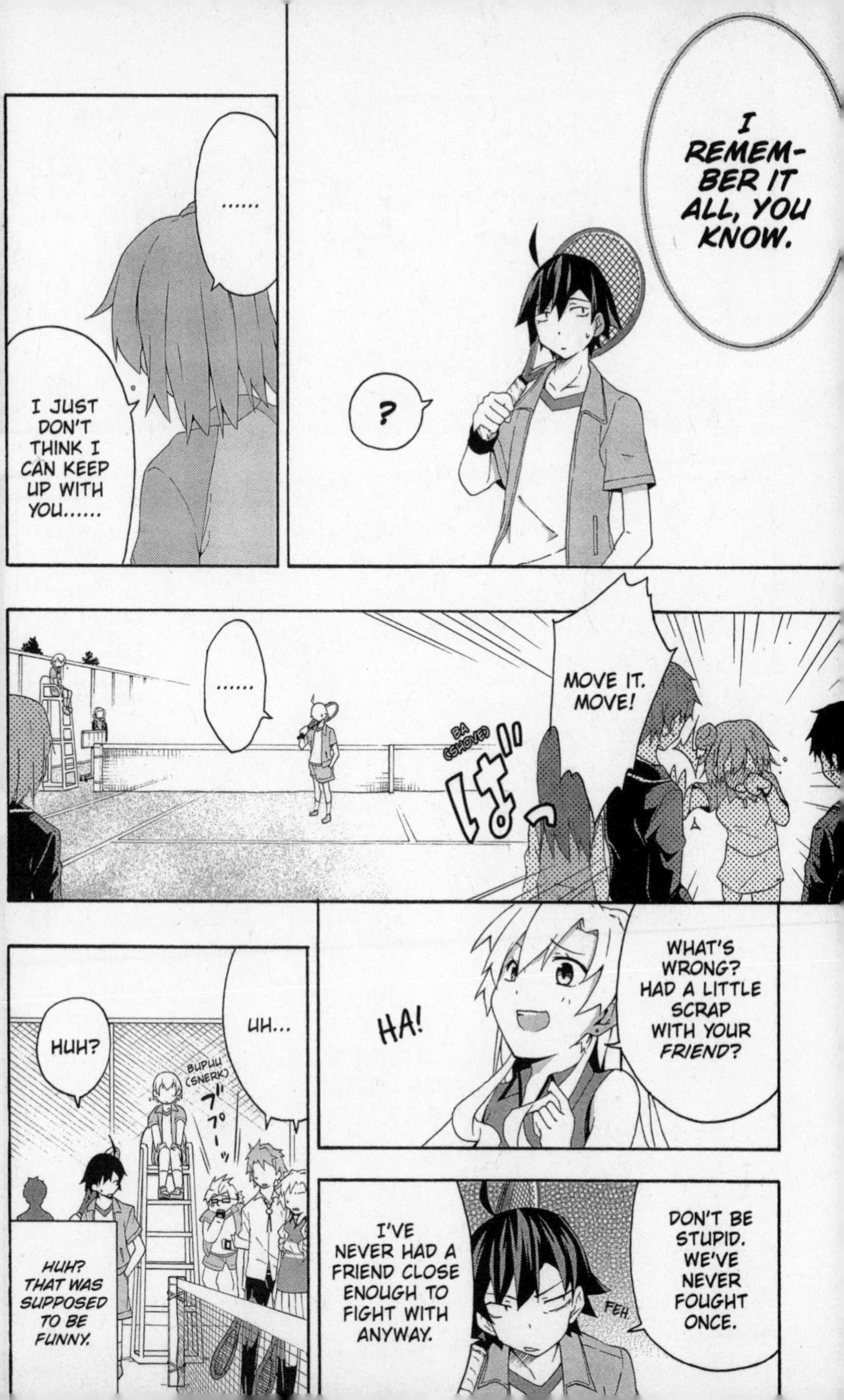
I REMEMBER IT ALL, YOU KNOW.
?
......
I JUST DON'T THINK I CAN KEEP UP WITH YOU......
MOVE IT. MOVE!
BA (SHOVE)
......
WHAT'S WRONG? HAD A LITTLE SCRAP WITH YOUR FRIEND?
HA!
DON'T BE STUPID. WE'VE NEVER FOUGHT ONCE.
FEH
I'VE NEVER HAD A FRIEND CLOSE ENOUGH TO FIGHT WITH ANYWAY.
UH...
HUH?
BUPUU (SNERK)
HUH? THAT WAS SUPPOSED TO BE FUNNY.

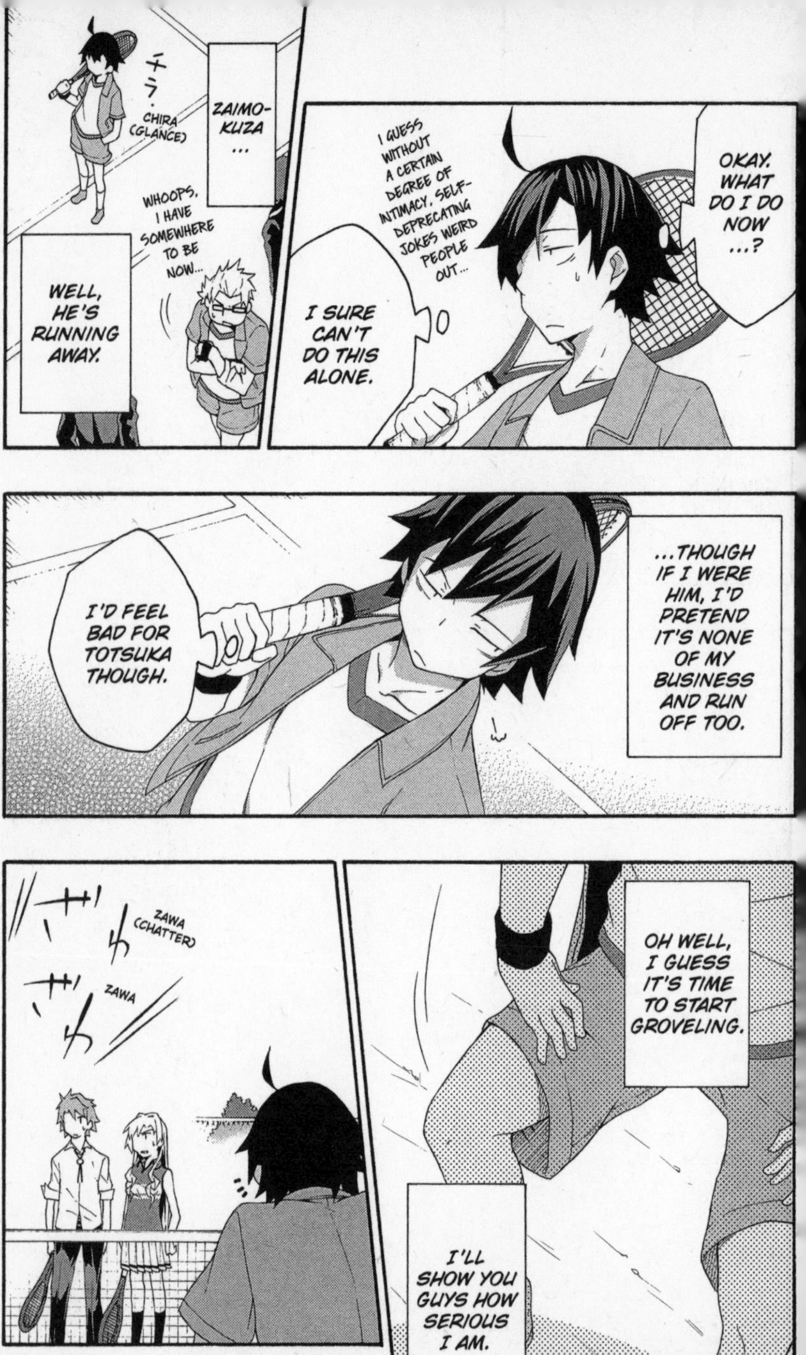
OKAY. WHAT DO I DO NOW ...?
I SURE CAN'T DO THIS ALONE.
I GUESS WITHOUT A CERTAIN DEGREE OF INTIMACY, SELF-DEPRECATING JOKES WEIRD PEOPLE OUT...
ZAIMOKUZA ...
チラ・
CHIRA (GLANCE)
WHOOPS, I HAVE SOMEWHERE TO BE NOW...
WELL, HE'S RUNNING AWAY.
...THOUGH IF I WERE HIM, I'D PRETEND IT'S NONE OF MY BUSINESS AND RUN OFF TOO.
I'D FEEL BAD FOR TOTSUKA THOUGH.
OH WELL, I GUESS IT'S TIME TO START GROVELING.
I'LL SHOW YOU GUYS HOW SERIOUS I AM.
ZAWA (CHATTER)
ZAWA

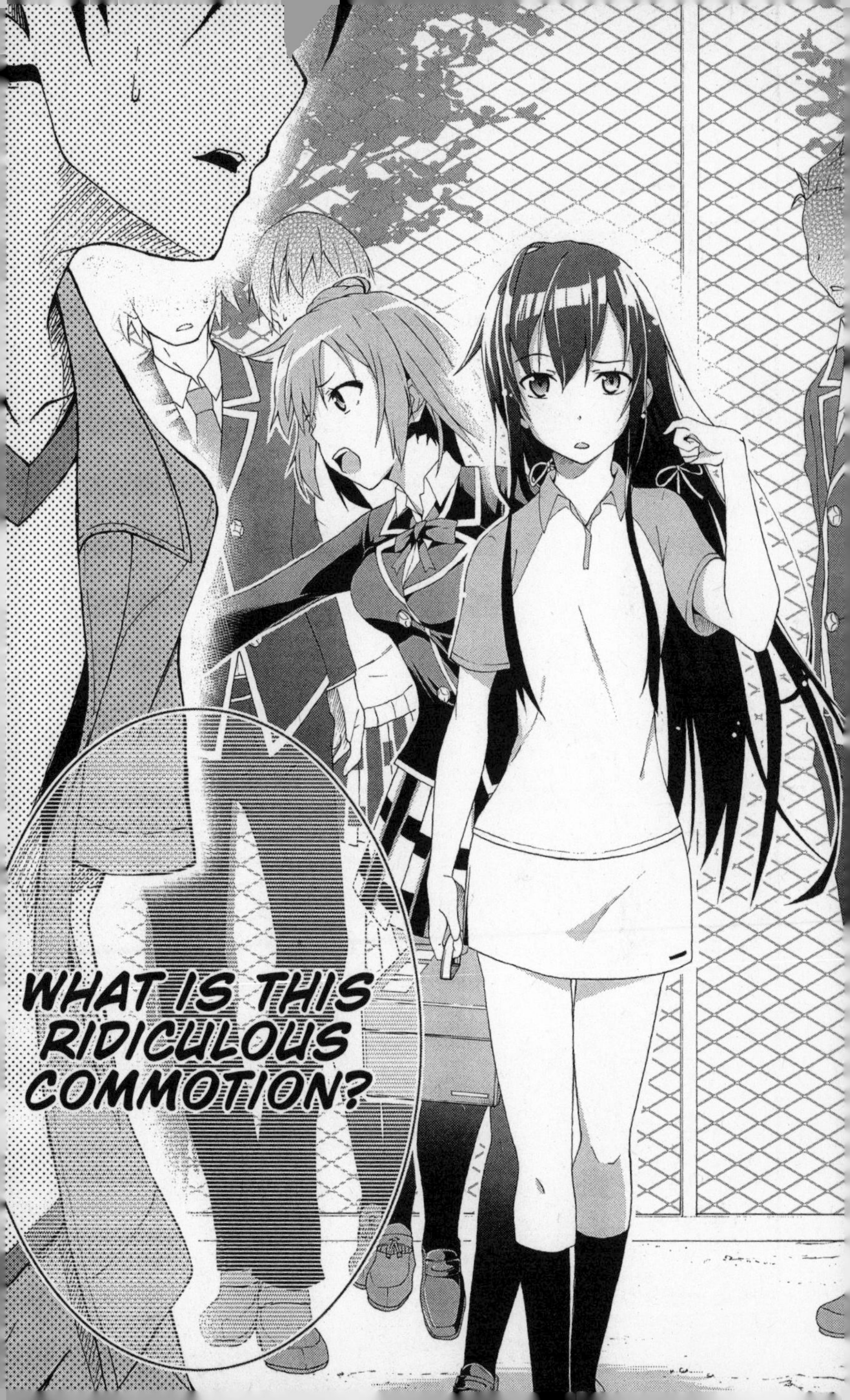
WHAT IS THIS RIDICULOUS COMMOTION?

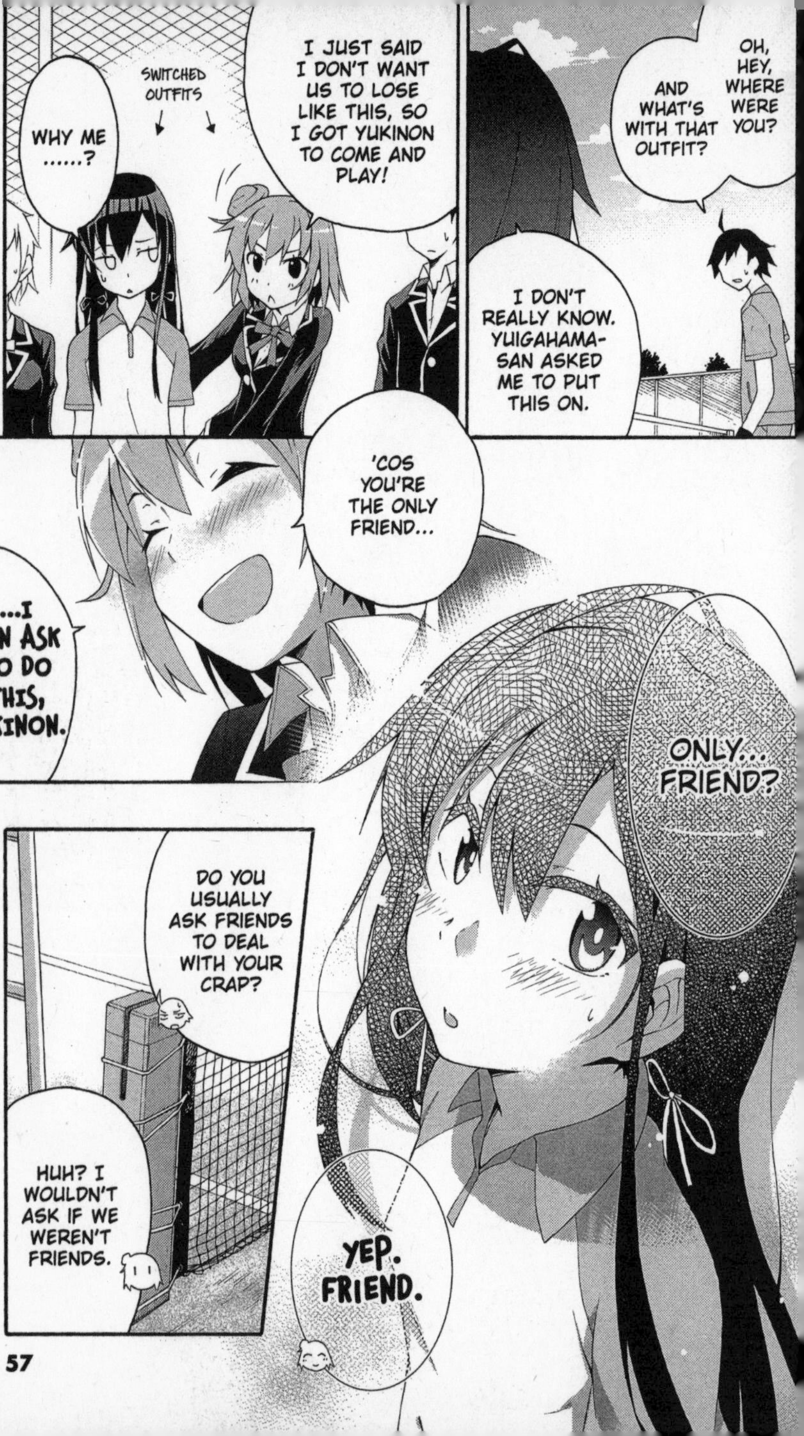
OH, HEY, WHERE WERE YOU?
AND WHAT'S WITH THAT OUTFIT?
I DON'T REALLY KNOW. YUIGAHAMA-SAN ASKED ME TO PUT THIS ON.
I JUST SAID I DON'T WANT US TO LOSE LIKE THIS, SO I GOT YUKINON TO COME AND PLAY!
SWITCHED OUTFITS
WHY ME ......?
'COS YOU'RE THE ONLY FRIEND...
...I CAN ASK TO DO THIS, YUKINON.
ONLY... FRIEND?
DO YOU USUALLY ASK FRIENDS TO DEAL WITH YOUR CRAP?
HUH? I WOULDN'T ASK IF WE WEREN'T FRIENDS.
YEP. FRIEND.

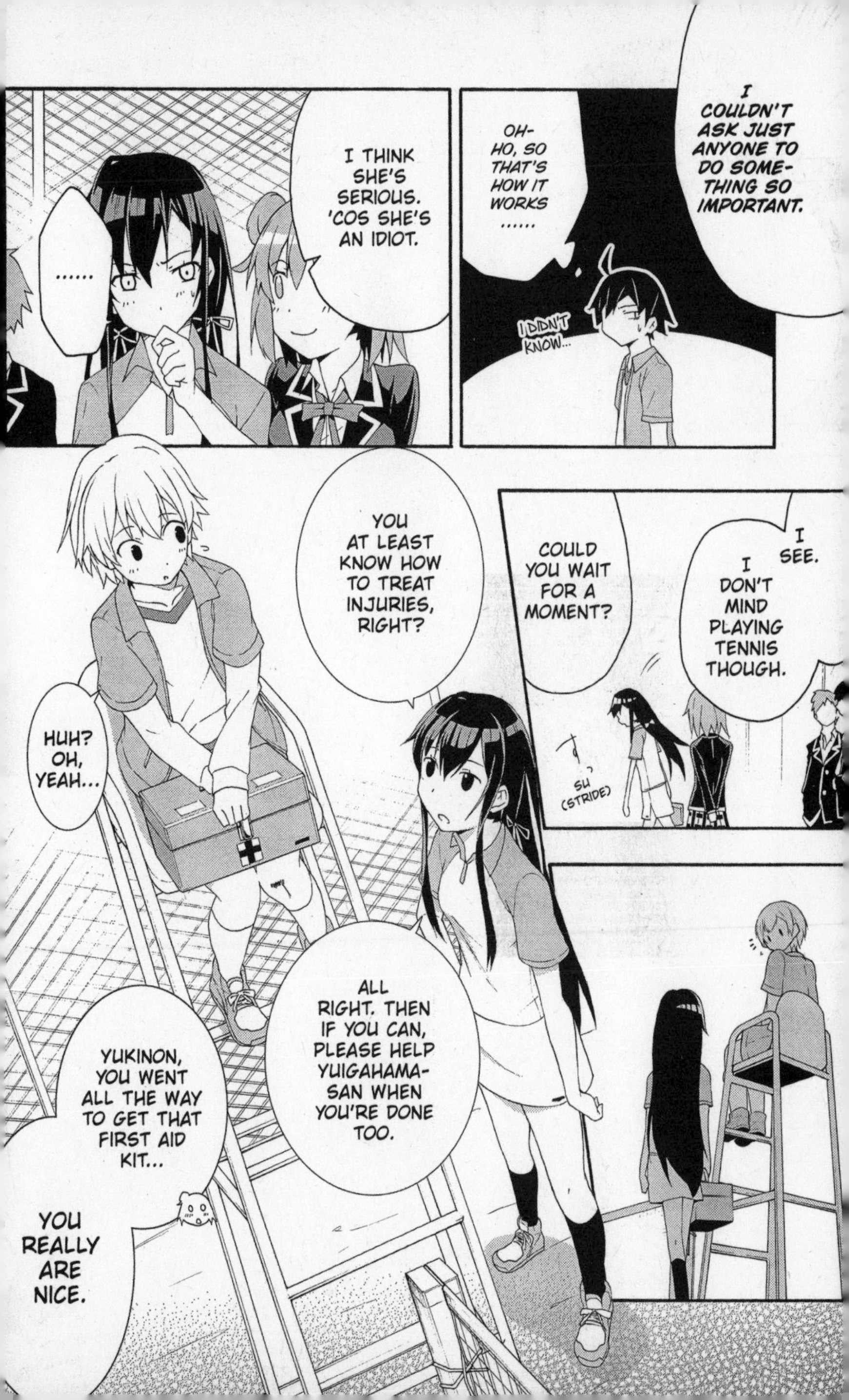
I COULDN'T ASK JUST ANYONE TO DO SOMETHING SO IMPORTANT.
OH-HO, SO THAT'S HOW IT WORKS ......
I DIDN'T KNOW...
I THINK SHE'S SERIOUS. 'COS SHE'S AN IDIOT.
......
I SEE.
I DON'T MIND PLAYING TENNIS THOUGH.
COULD YOU WAIT FOR A MOMENT?
SU (STRIDE)
YOU AT LEAST KNOW HOW TO TREAT INJURIES, RIGHT?
HUH? OH, YEAH...
ALL RIGHT. THEN IF YOU CAN, PLEASE HELP YUIGAHAMA-SAN WHEN YOU'RE DONE TOO.
YUKINON, YOU WENT ALL THE WAY TO GET THAT FIRST AID KIT...
YOU REALLY ARE NICE.

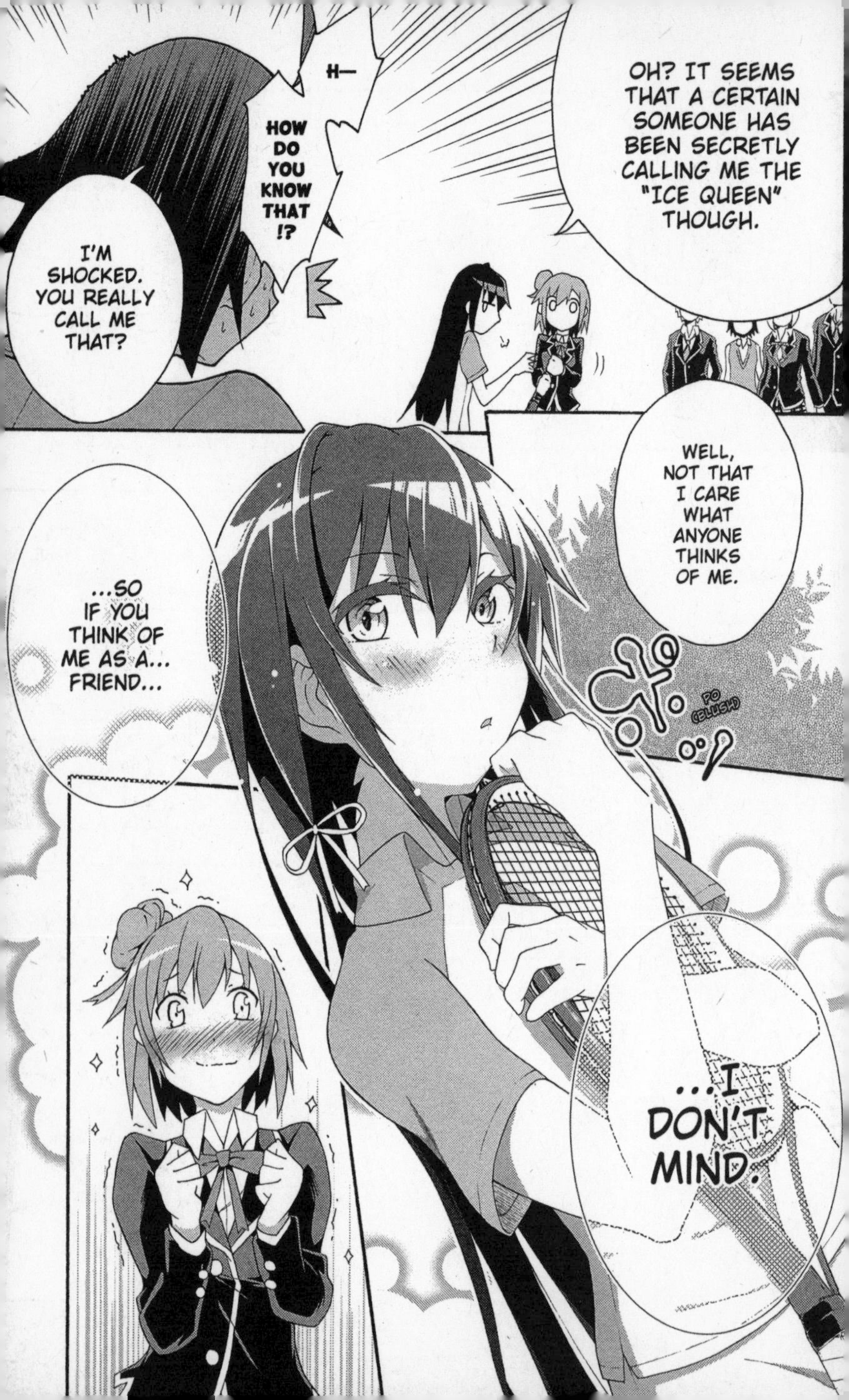

OH? IT SEEMS THAT A CERTAIN SOMEONE HAS BEEN SECRETLY CALLING ME THE "ICE QUEEN" THOUGH.
H—
HOW DO YOU KNOW THAT!?
I'M SHOCKED. YOU REALLY CALL ME THAT?
WELL, NOT THAT I CARE WHAT ANYONE THINKS OF ME.
PO (BLUSH)
...SO IF YOU THINK OF ME AS A... FRIEND...
...I DON'T MIND.

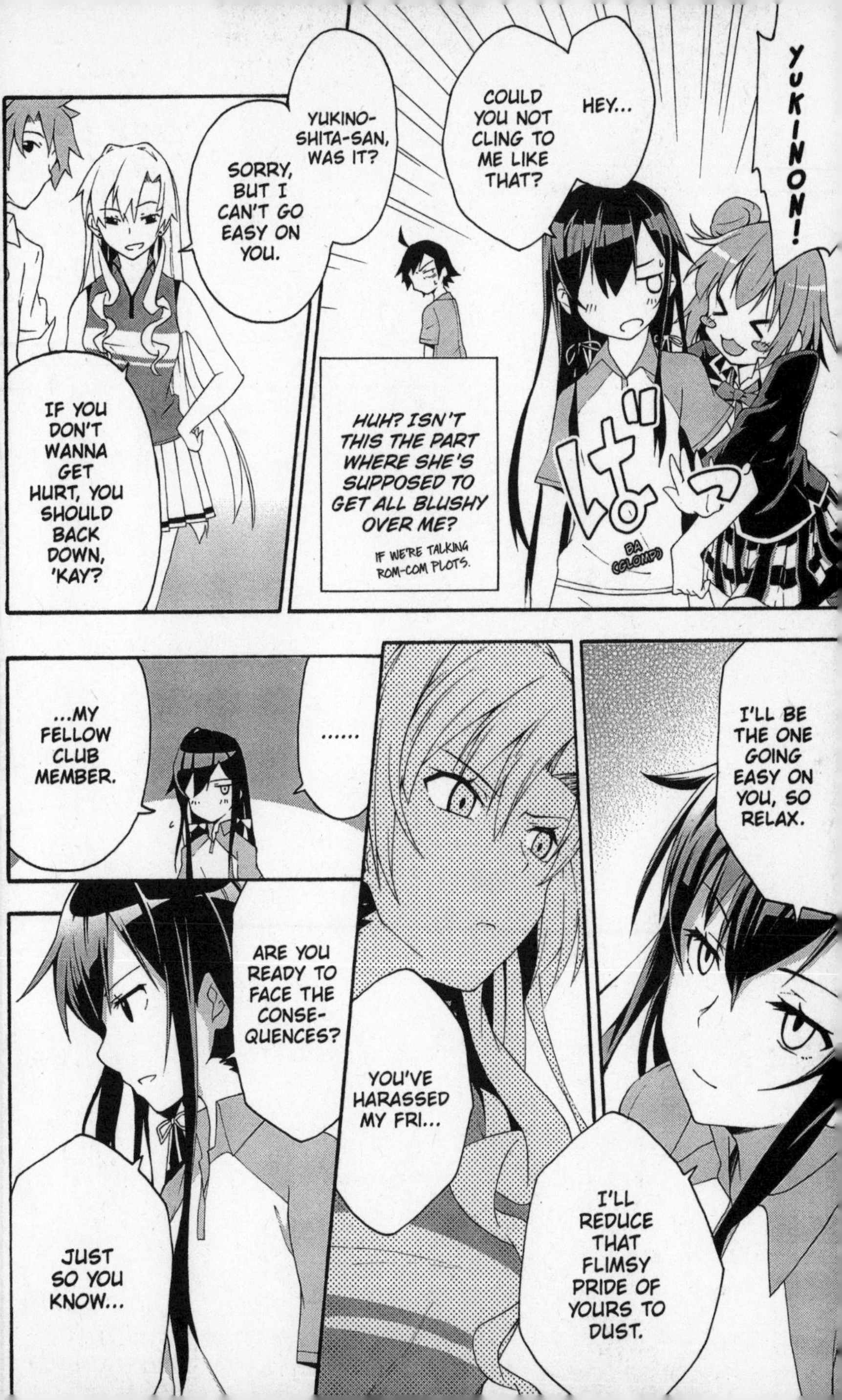
YUKINON!
HEY...
COULD YOU NOT CLING TO ME LIKE THAT?
BA (GLOMP)
HUH? ISN'T THIS THE PART WHERE SHE'S SUPPOSED TO GET ALL BLUSHY OVER ME?
IF WE'RE TALKING ROM-COM PLOTS.
YUKINO-SHITA-SAN, WAS IT?
SORRY, BUT I CAN'T GO EASY ON YOU.
IF YOU DON'T WANNA GET HURT, YOU SHOULD BACK DOWN, 'KAY?
I'LL BE THE ONE GOING EASY ON YOU, SO RELAX.
I'LL REDUCE THAT FLIMSY PRIDE OF YOURS TO DUST.
YOU'VE HARASSED MY FRI...
......
...MY FELLOW CLUB MEMBER.
ARE YOU READY TO FACE THE CONSE-QUENCES?
JUST SO YOU KNOW...

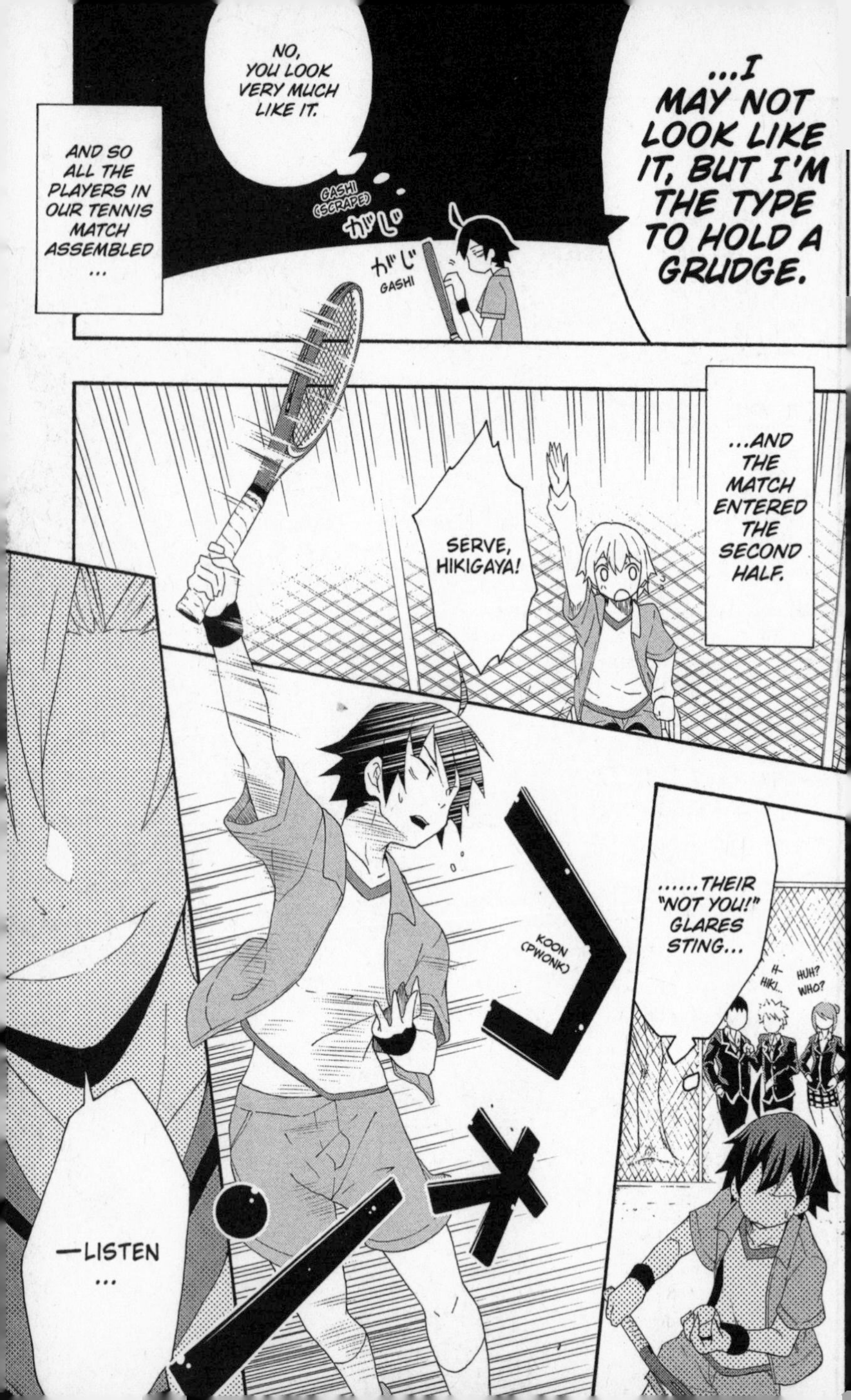
...I MAY NOT LOOK LIKE IT, BUT I'M THE TYPE TO HOLD A GRUDGE.
NO, YOU LOOK VERY MUCH LIKE IT.
GASHI (SCRAPE) がじ
がじ GASHI
AND SO ALL THE PLAYERS IN OUR TENNIS MATCH ASSEMBLED ...
...AND THE MATCH ENTERED THE SECOND HALF.
SERVE, HIKIGAYA!
......THEIR "NOT YOU!" GLARES STING...
H-HIKI...
HUH? WHO?
KOON (PWONK)
—LISTEN ...

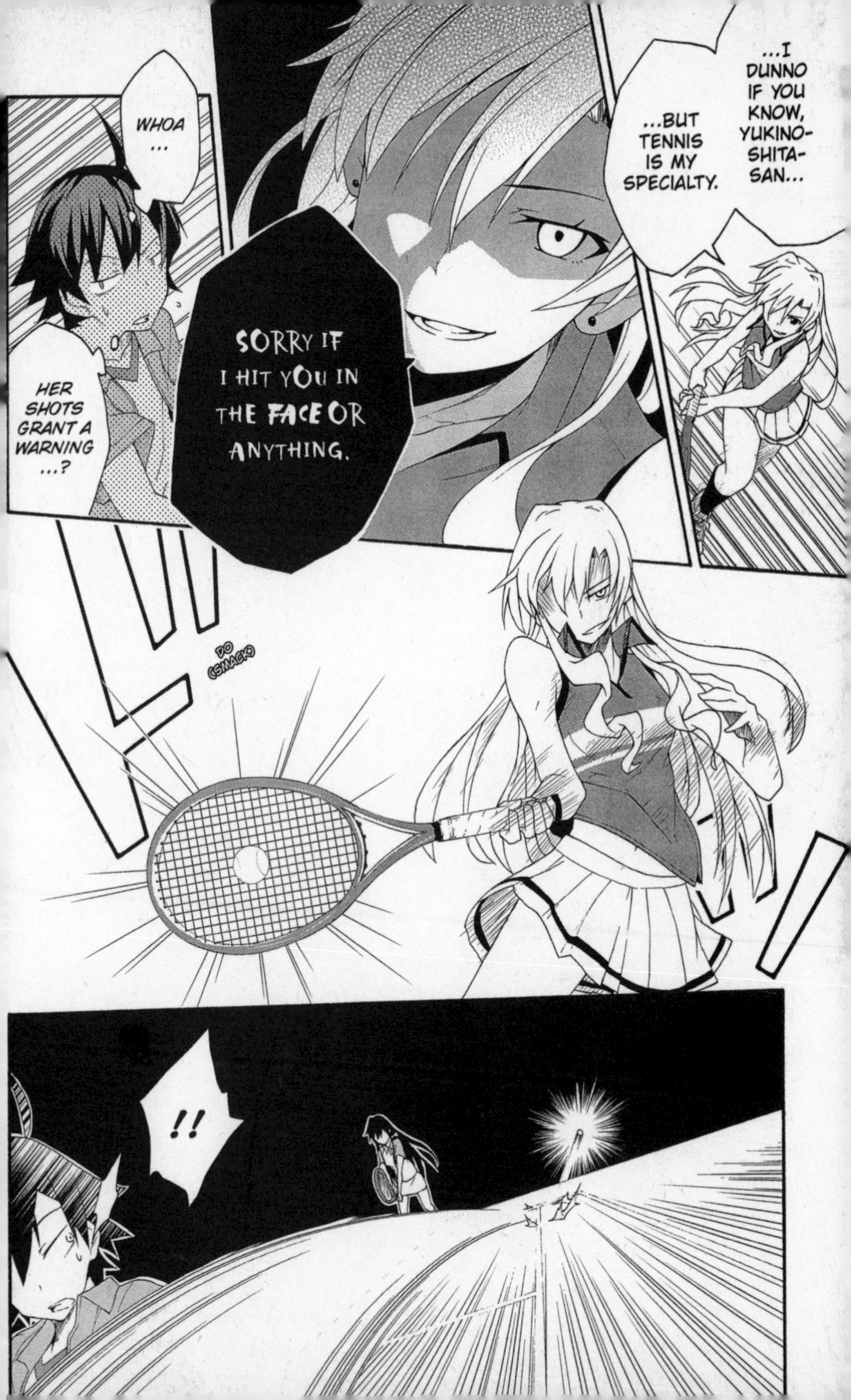
...I DUNNO IF YOU KNOW, YUKINO-SHITA-SAN...
...BUT TENNIS IS MY SPECIALTY.
SORRY IF I HIT YOU IN THE FACE OR ANYTHING.
WHOA...
HER SHOTS GRANT A WARNING...?
DO (SMACK)
!!

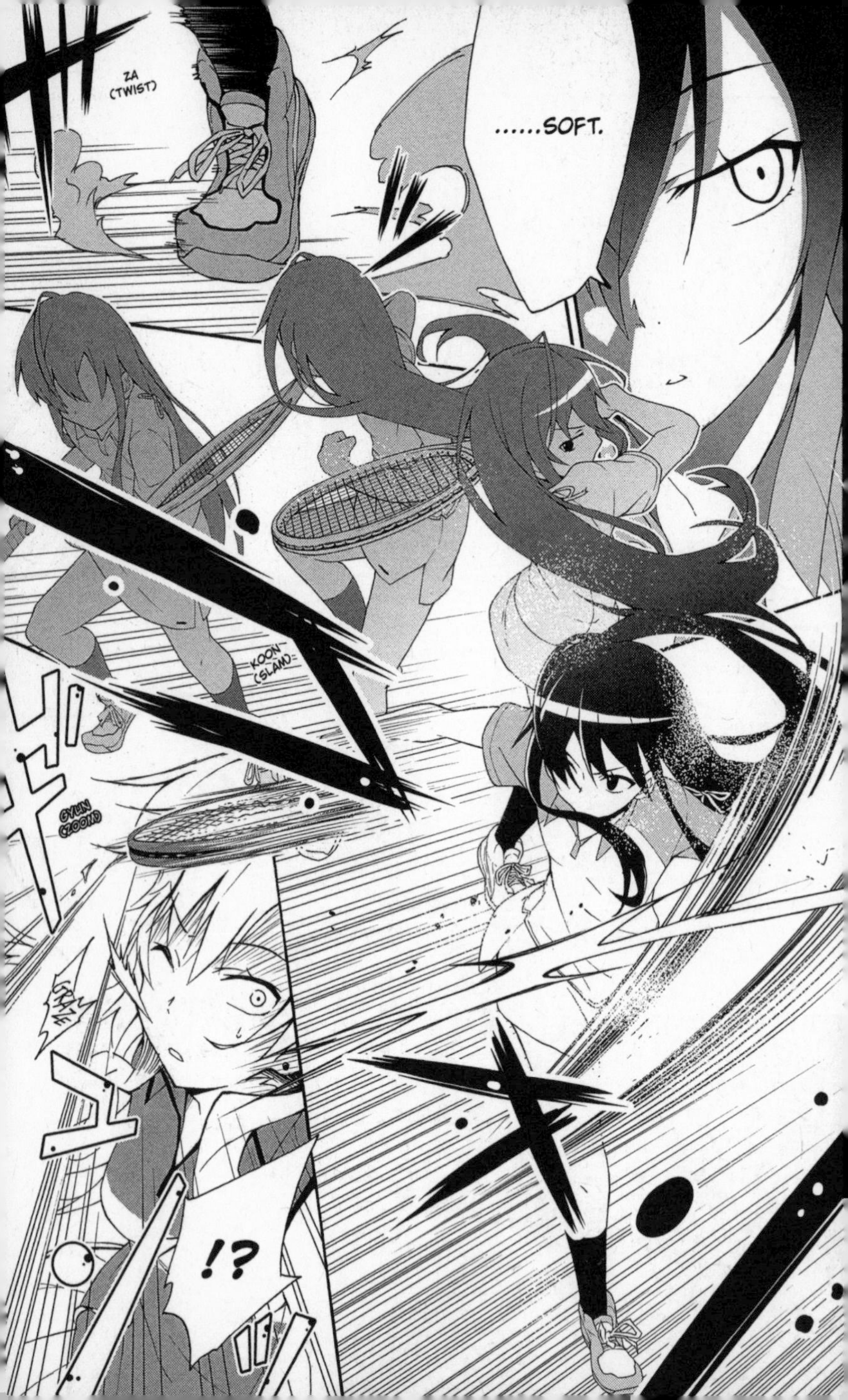
......SOFT.
ZA (TWIST)
KOON (SLAM)
GYUN (ZOOM)
GRAZE
!?

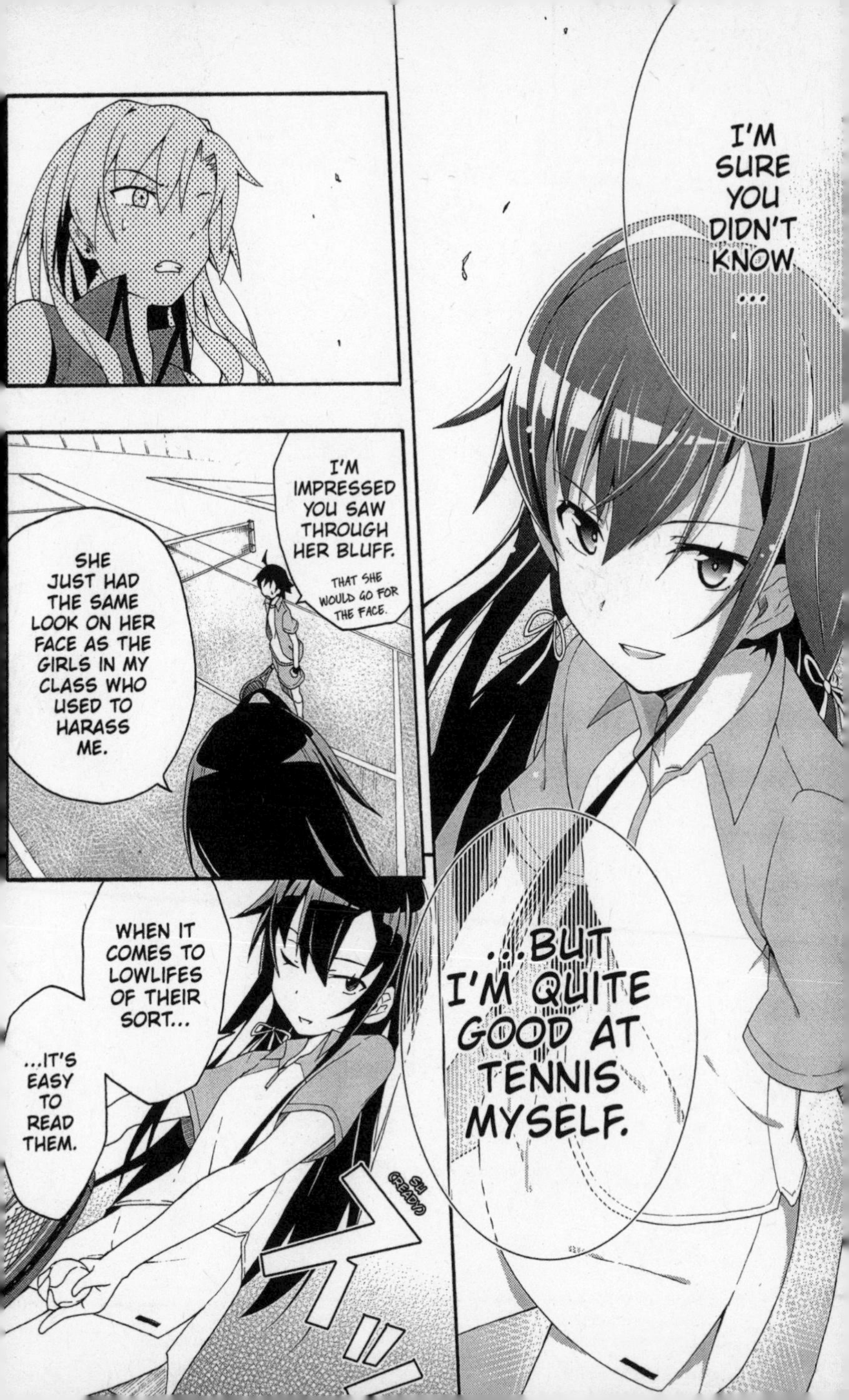
I'M SURE YOU DIDN'T KNOW...
...BUT I'M QUITE GOOD AT TENNIS MYSELF.
I'M IMPRESSED YOU SAW THROUGH HER BLUFF.
THAT SHE WOULD GO FOR THE FACE.
SHE JUST HAD THE SAME LOOK ON HER FACE AS THE GIRLS IN MY CLASS WHO USED TO HARASS ME.
WHEN IT COMES TO LOWLIFES OF THEIR SORT...
...IT'S EASY TO READ THEM.
SU (READY)

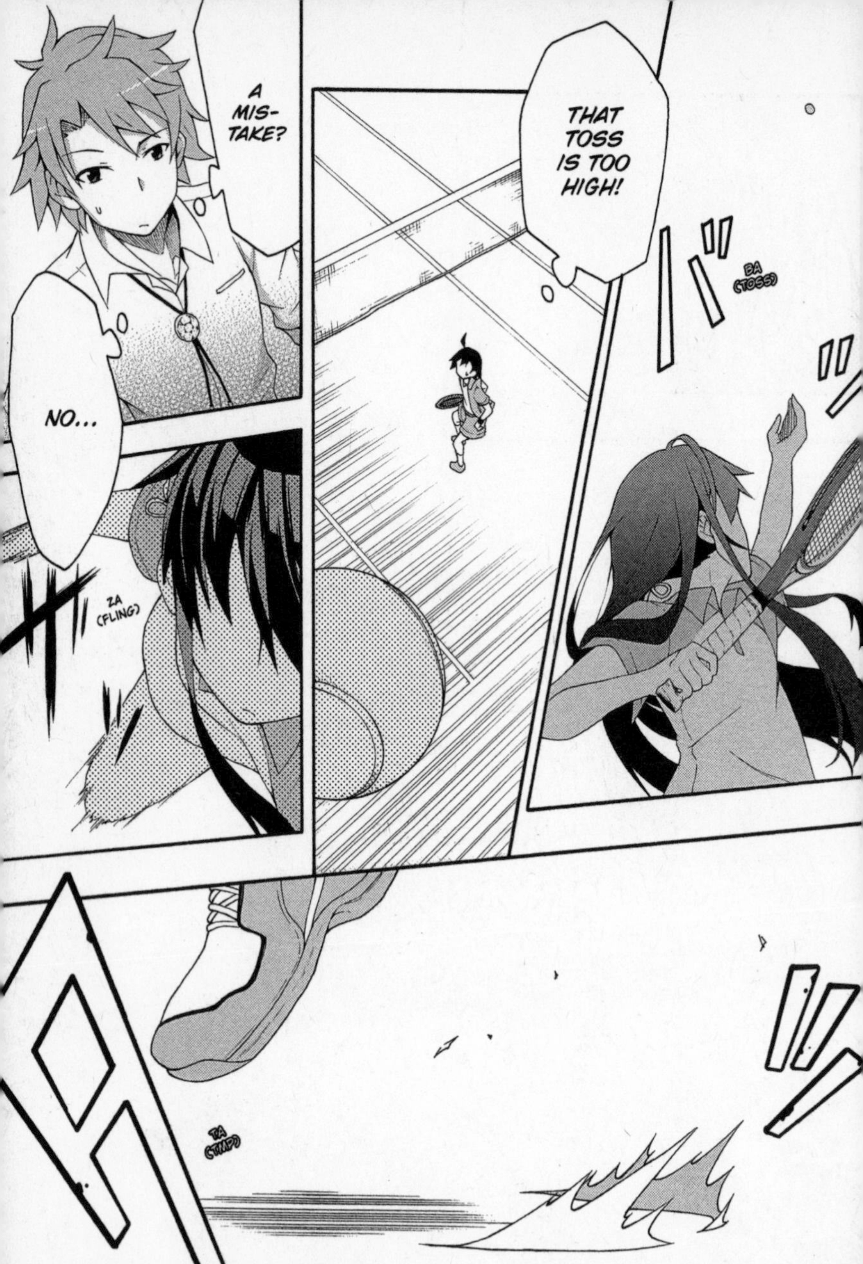
THAT TOSS IS TOO HIGH!
BA (TOSS)
A MIS-TAKE?
NO...
ZA (FLING)
TA (TMP)

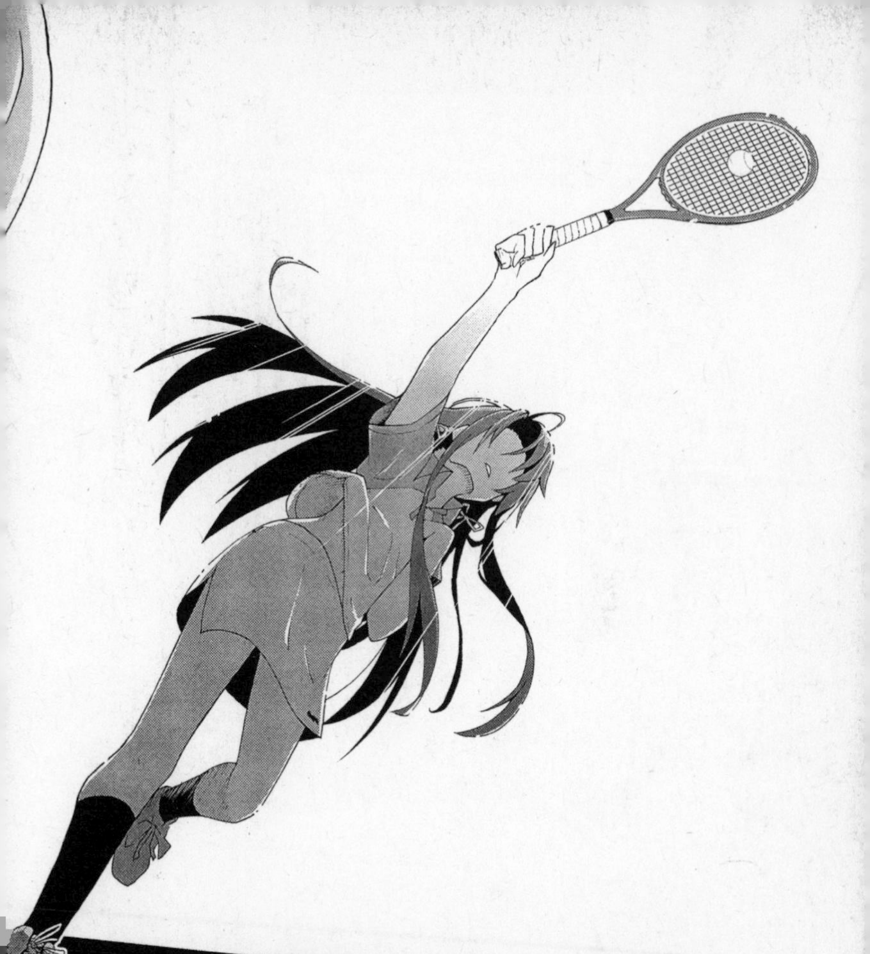

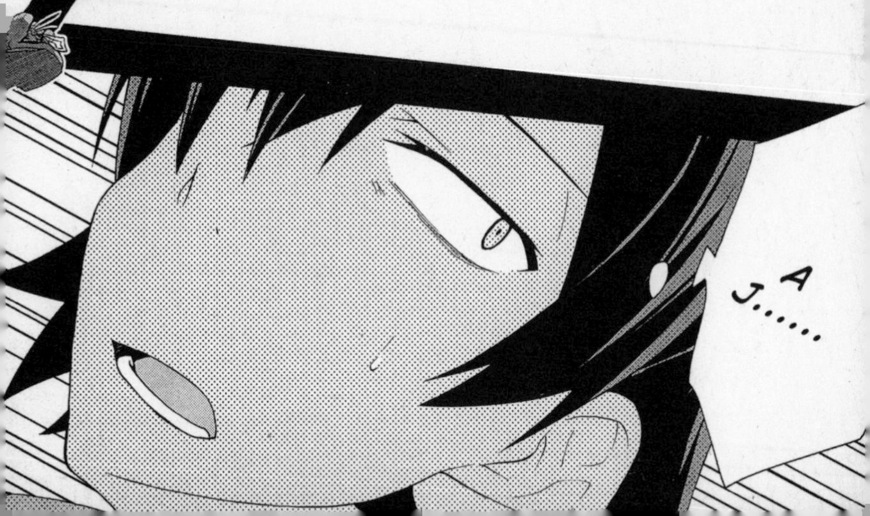
AJ......

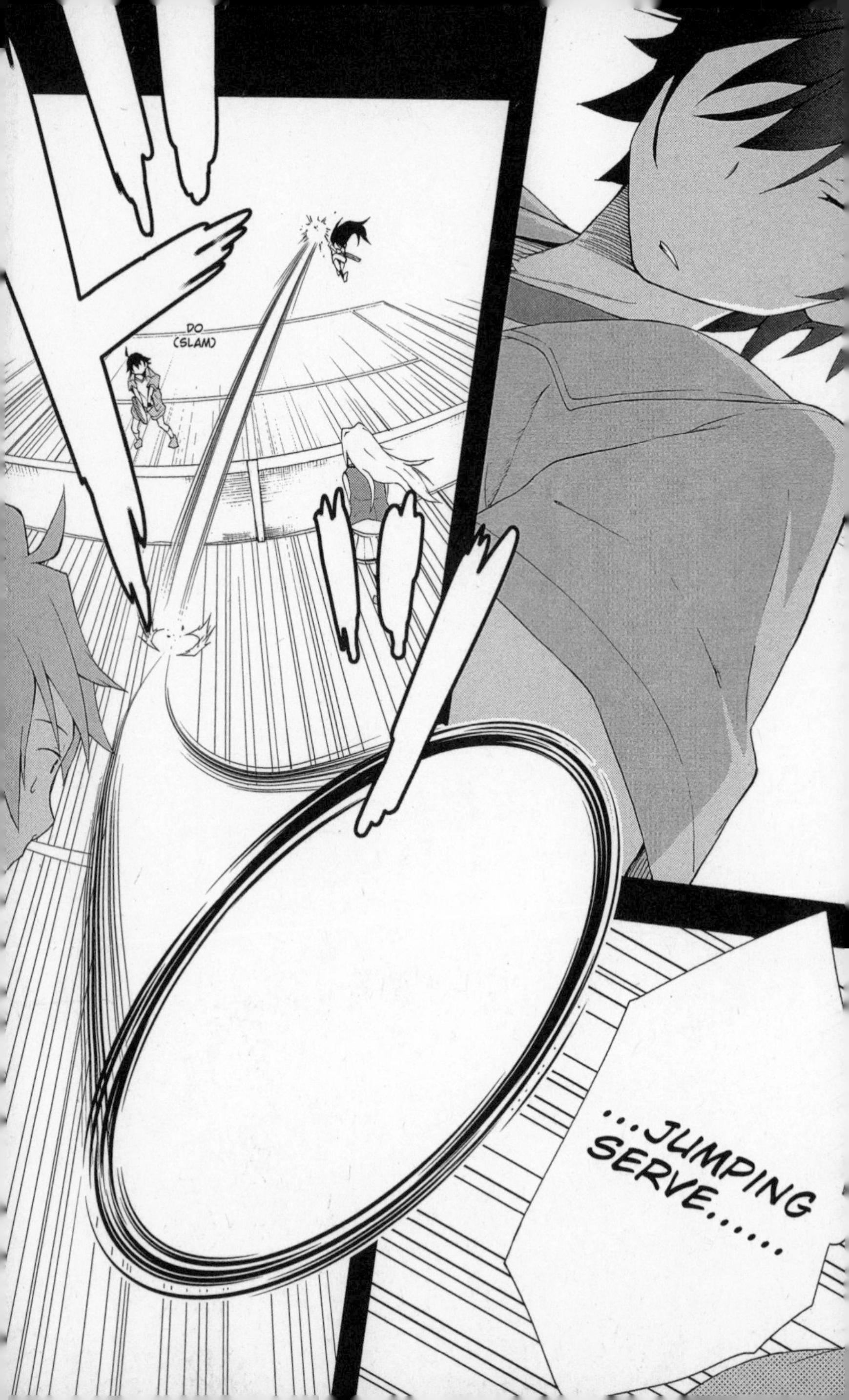
...JUMPING SERVE......
DO
(SLAM)

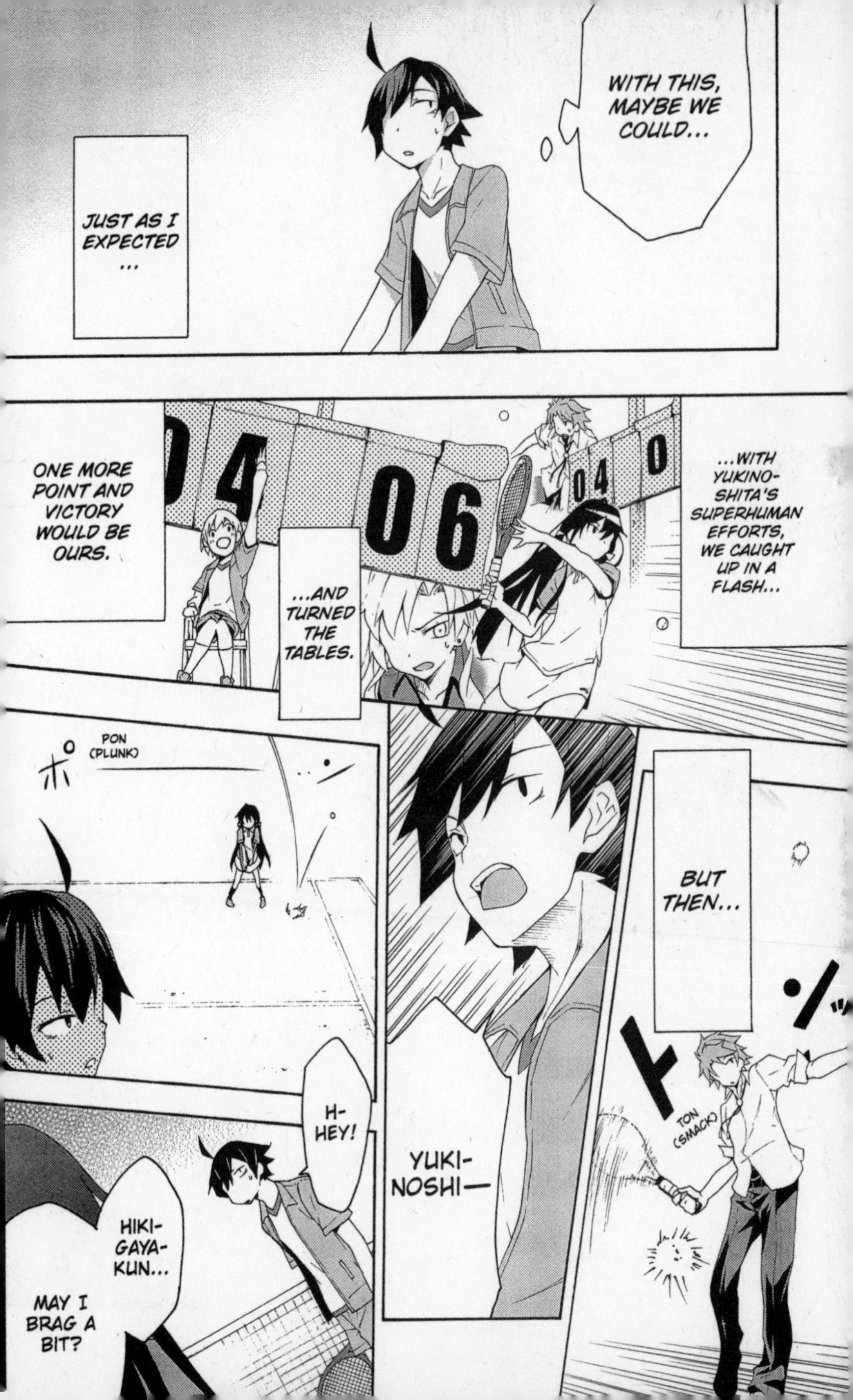
WITH THIS, MAYBE WE COULD...
JUST AS I EXPECTED ...
...WITH YUKINO-SHITA'S SUPERHUMAN EFFORTS, WE CAUGHT UP IN A FLASH...
...AND TURNED THE TABLES.
ONE MORE POINT AND VICTORY WOULD BE OURS.
BUT THEN...
TON (SMACK)
YUKI-NOSHI—
PON (PLUNK)
H-HEY!
HIKI-GAYA-KUN...
MAY I BRAG A BIT?

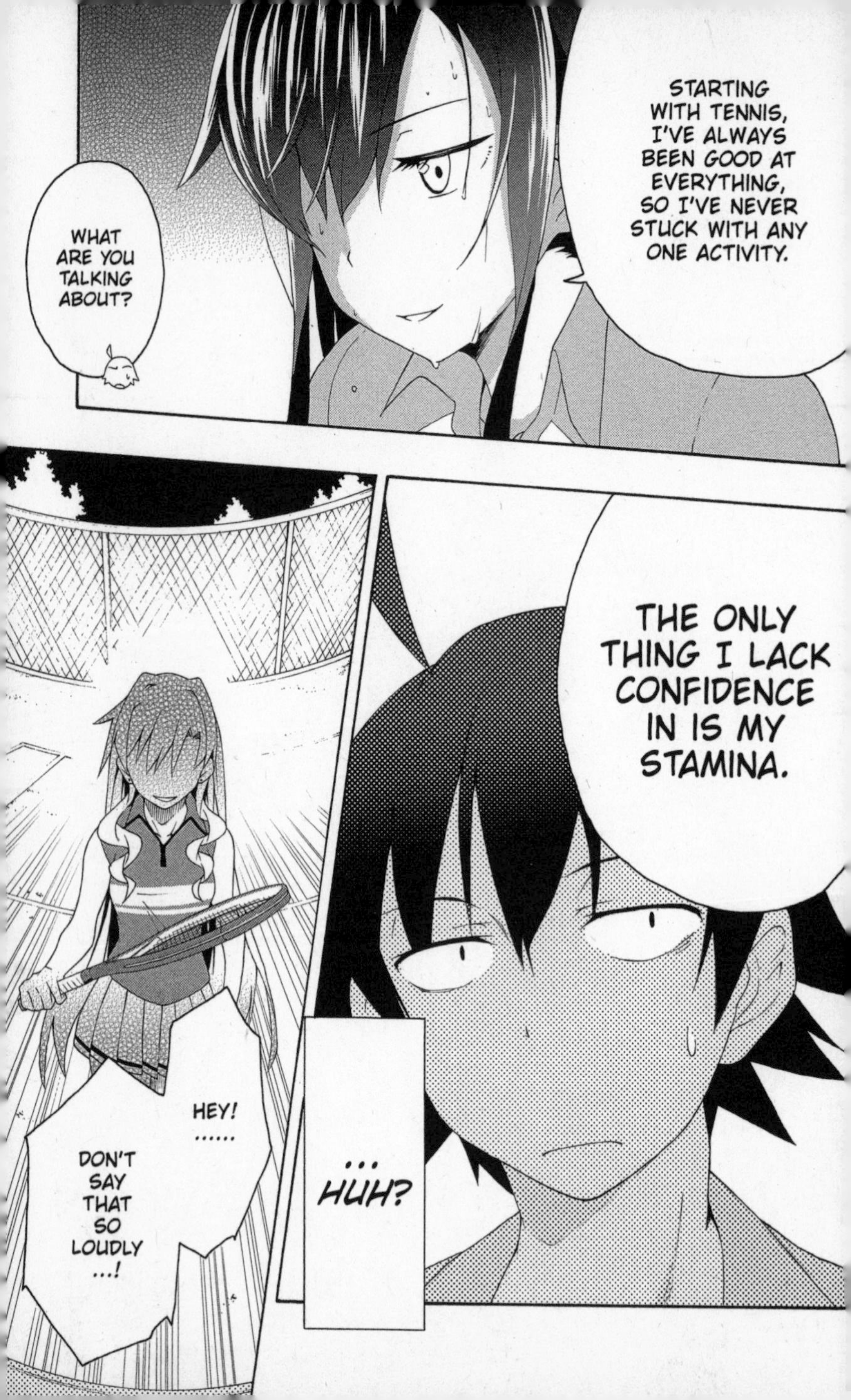
STARTING WITH TENNIS, I'VE ALWAYS BEEN GOOD AT EVERYTHING, SO I'VE NEVER STUCK WITH ANY ONE ACTIVITY.
WHAT ARE YOU TALKING ABOUT?
THE ONLY THING I LACK CONFIDENCE IN IS MY STAMINA.
...HUH?
HEY! ......
DON'T SAY THAT SO LOUDLY ...!

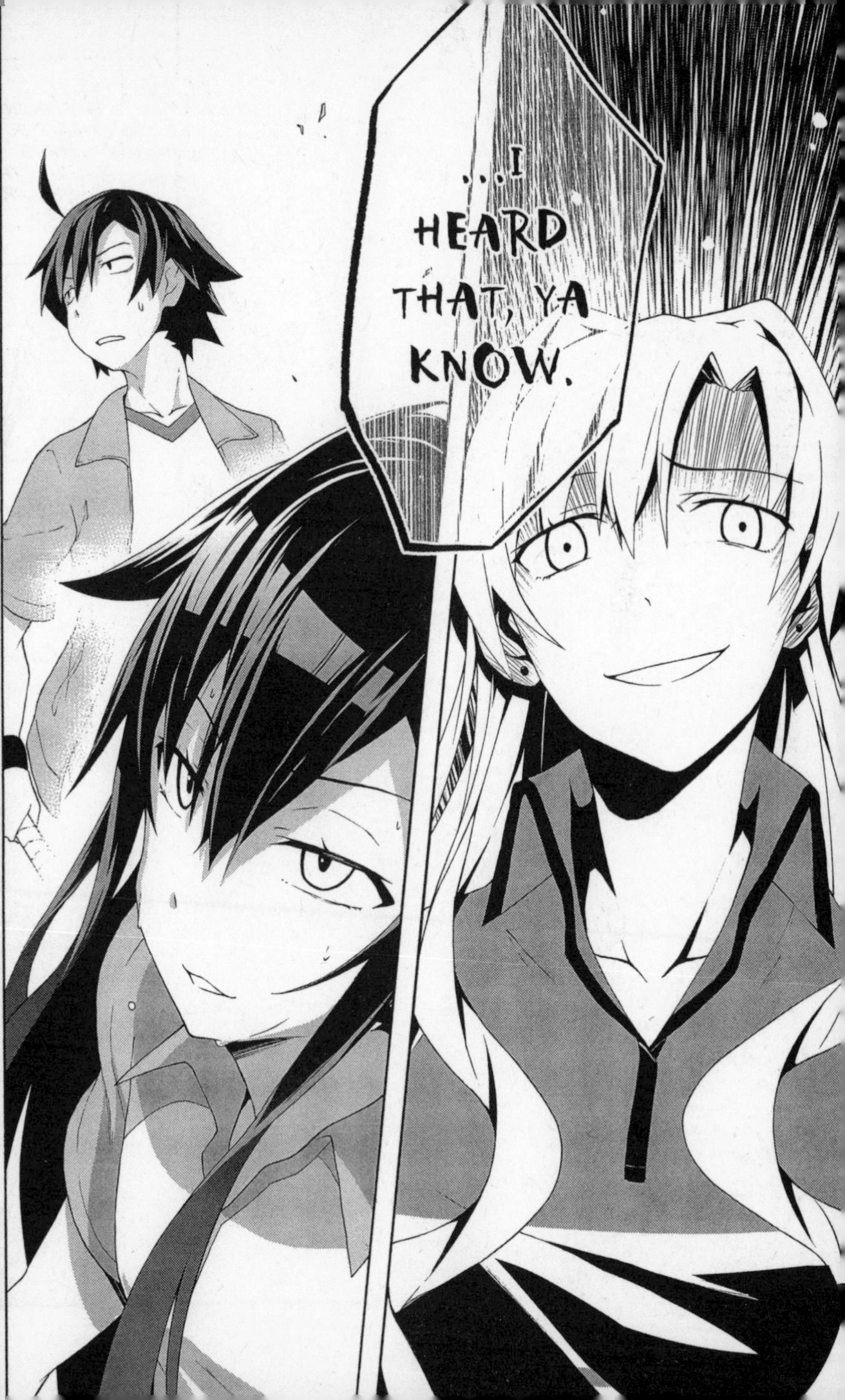
...I HEARD THAT, YA KNOW.

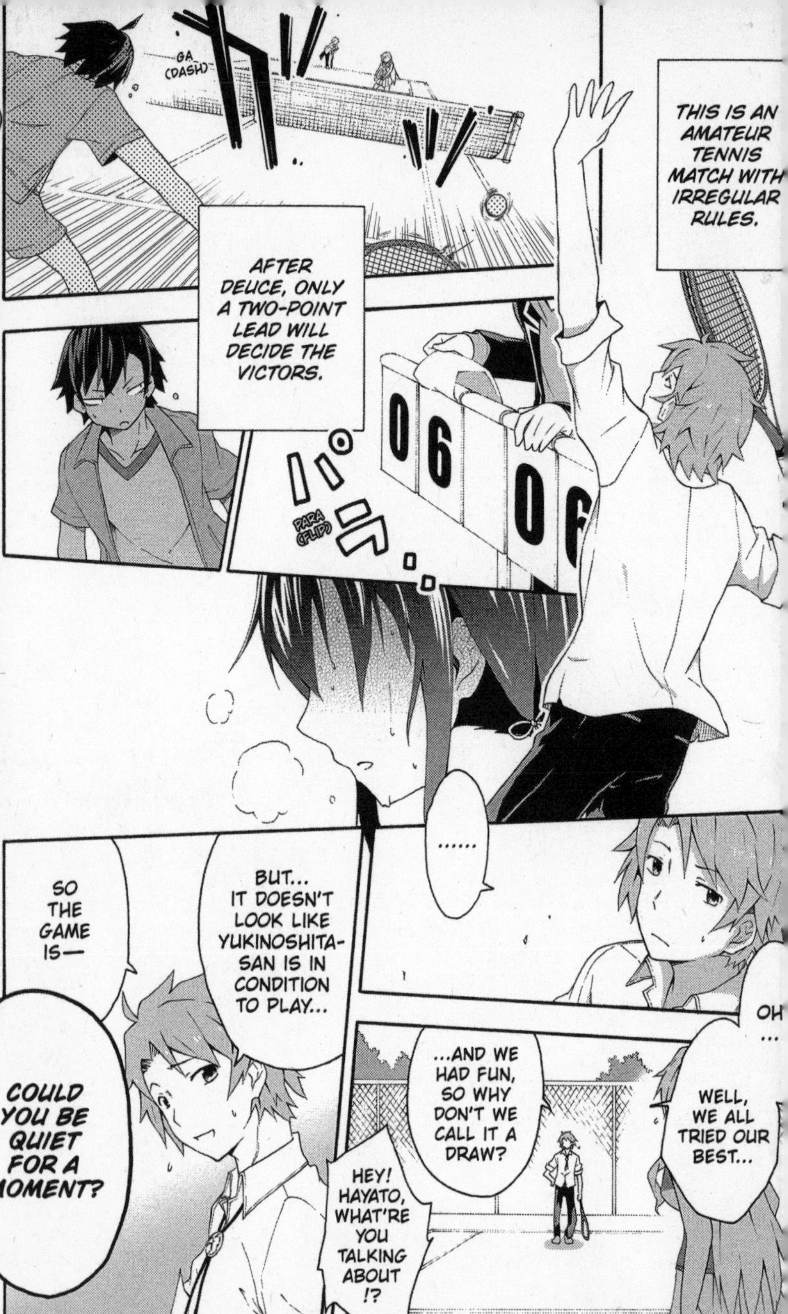
THIS IS AN AMATEUR TENNIS MATCH WITH IRREGULAR RULES.
GA (DASH)
AFTER DEUCE, ONLY A TWO-POINT LEAD WILL DECIDE THE VICTORS.
06 06
PARA (FLIP)
......
OH...
WELL, WE ALL TRIED OUR BEST...
...AND WE HAD FUN, SO WHY DON'T WE CALL IT A DRAW?
HEY! HAYATO, WHAT'RE YOU TALKING ABOUT!?
SO THE GAME IS—
BUT... IT DOESN'T LOOK LIKE YUKINOSHITA-SAN IS IN CONDITION TO PLAY...
COULD YOU BE QUIET FOR A MOMENT?

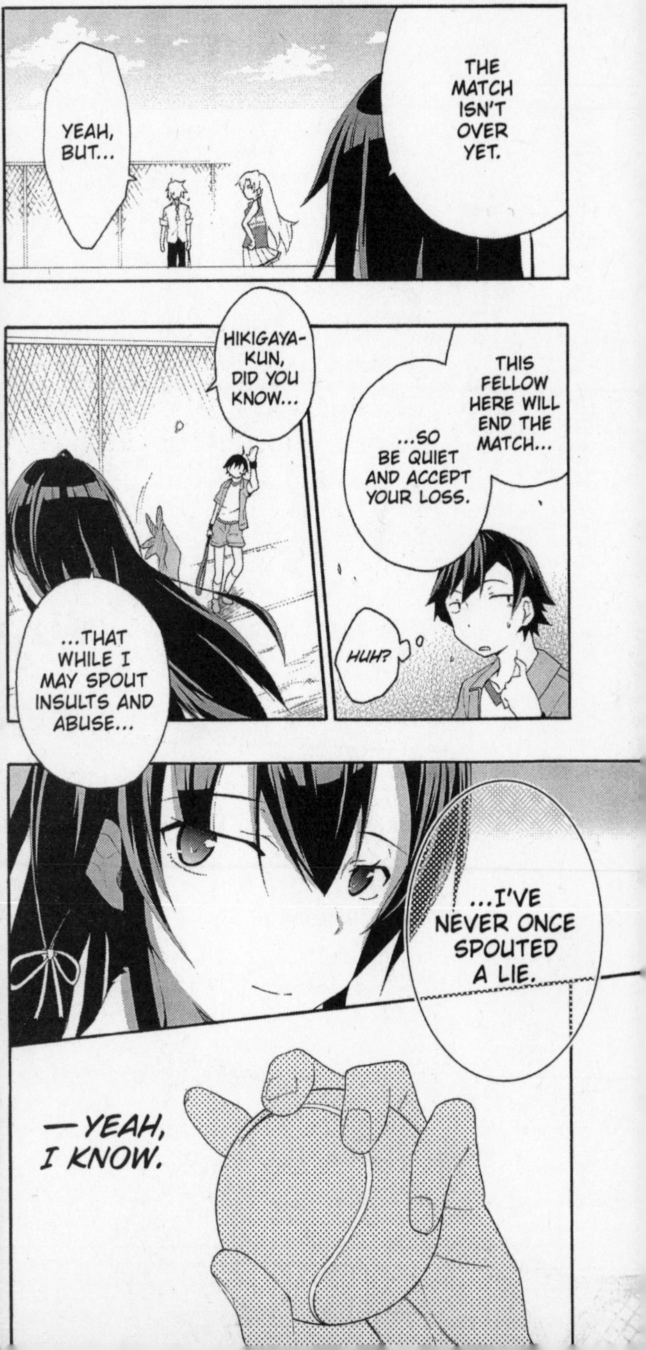
THE MATCH ISN'T OVER YET.
YEAH, BUT...
THIS FELLOW HERE WILL END THE MATCH...
...SO BE QUIET AND ACCEPT YOUR LOSS.
HUH?
HIKIGAYA-KUN, DID YOU KNOW...
...THAT WHILE I MAY SPOUT INSULTS AND ABUSE...
...I'VE NEVER ONCE SPOUTED A LIE.
—YEAH, I KNOW.

THE ONLY LIARS HERE ARE ME AND THEM.

CHAPTER 8 ··· SOMETIMES THE GODS OF ROMANTIC COMEDY DO GOOD. (PART TWO)

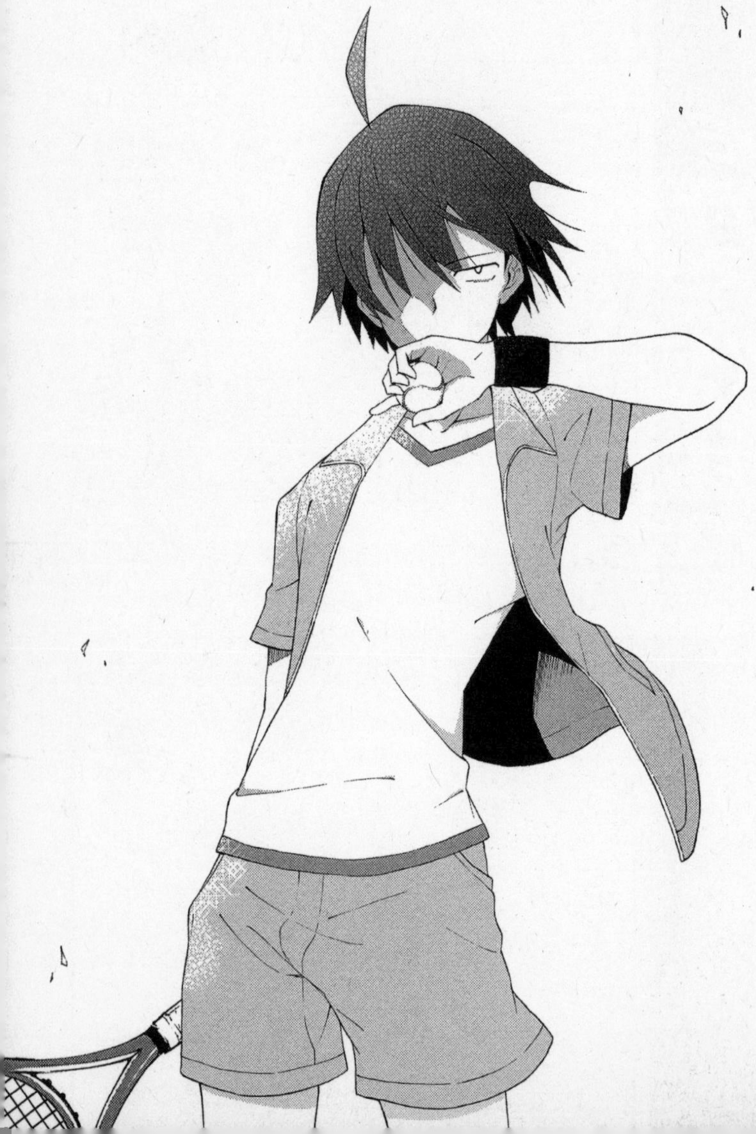

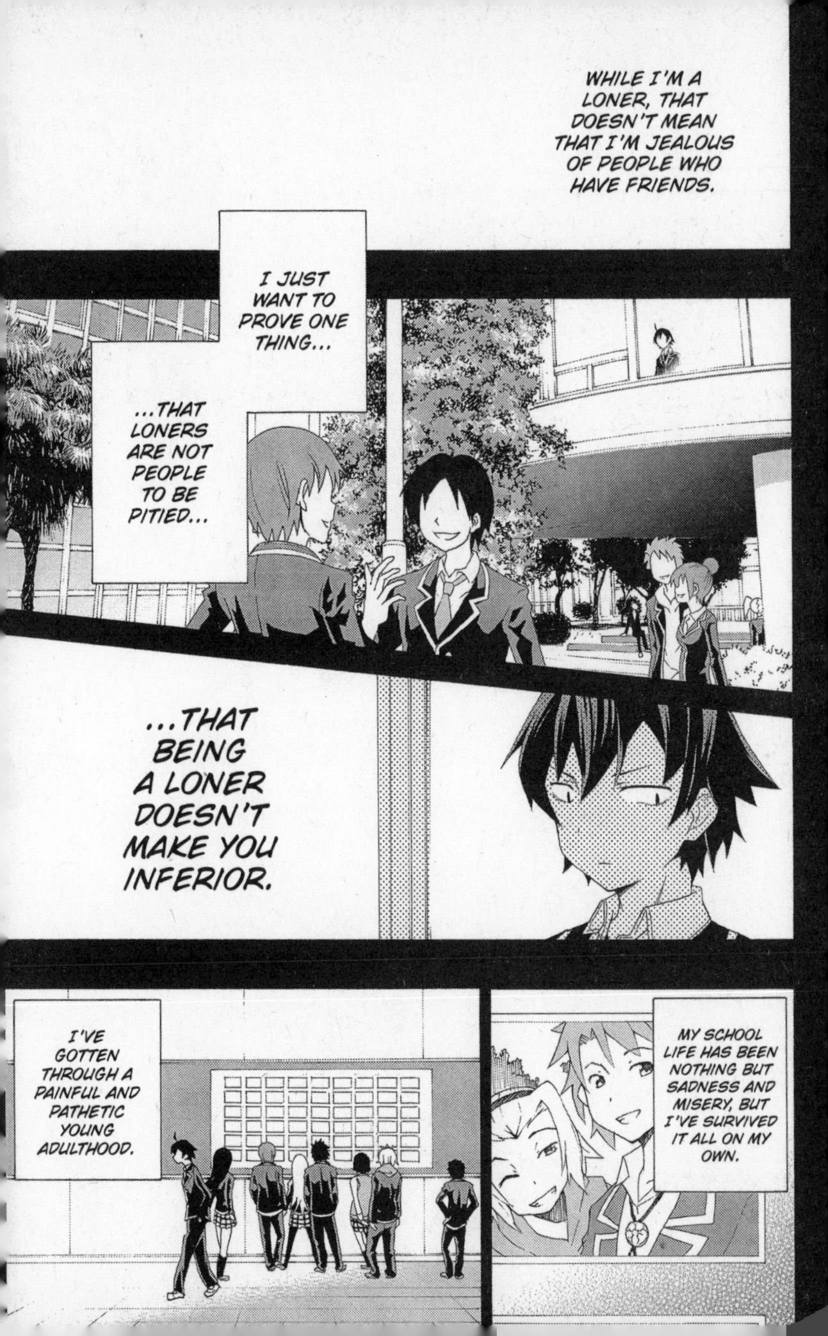
WHILE I'M A LONER, THAT DOESN'T MEAN THAT I'M JEALOUS OF PEOPLE WHO HAVE FRIENDS.
I JUST WANT TO PROVE ONE THING...
...THAT LONERS ARE NOT PEOPLE TO BE PITIED...
...THAT BEING A LONER DOESN'T MAKE YOU INFERIOR.
MY SCHOOL LIFE HAS BEEN NOTHING BUT SADNESS AND MISERY, BUT I'VE SURVIVED IT ALL ON MY OWN.
I'VE GOTTEN THROUGH A PAINFUL AND PATHETIC YOUNG ADULTHOOD.

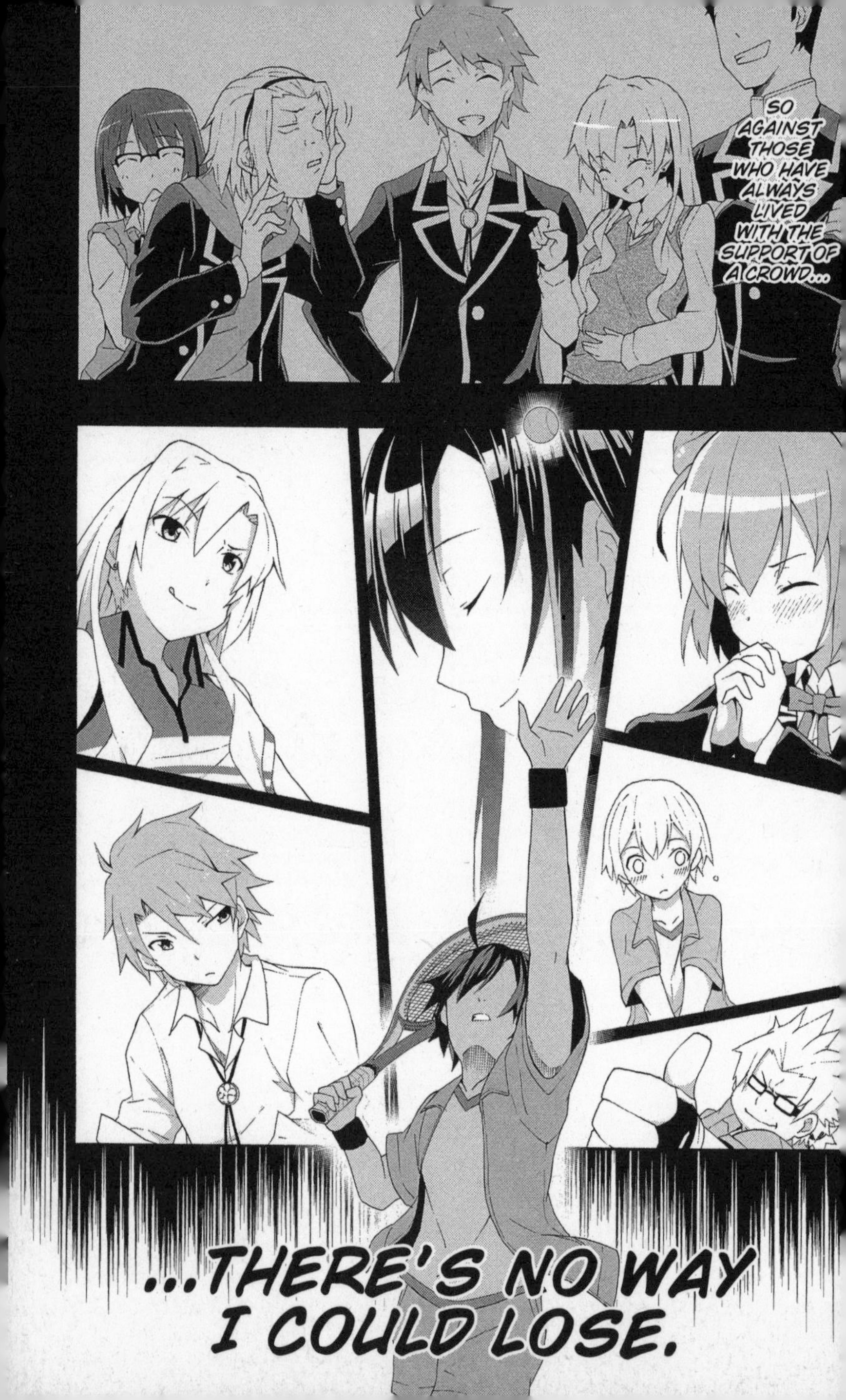
SO AGAINST THOSE WHO HAVE ALWAYS LIVED WITH THE SUPPORT OF A CROWD...
...THERE'S NO WAY I COULD LOSE.

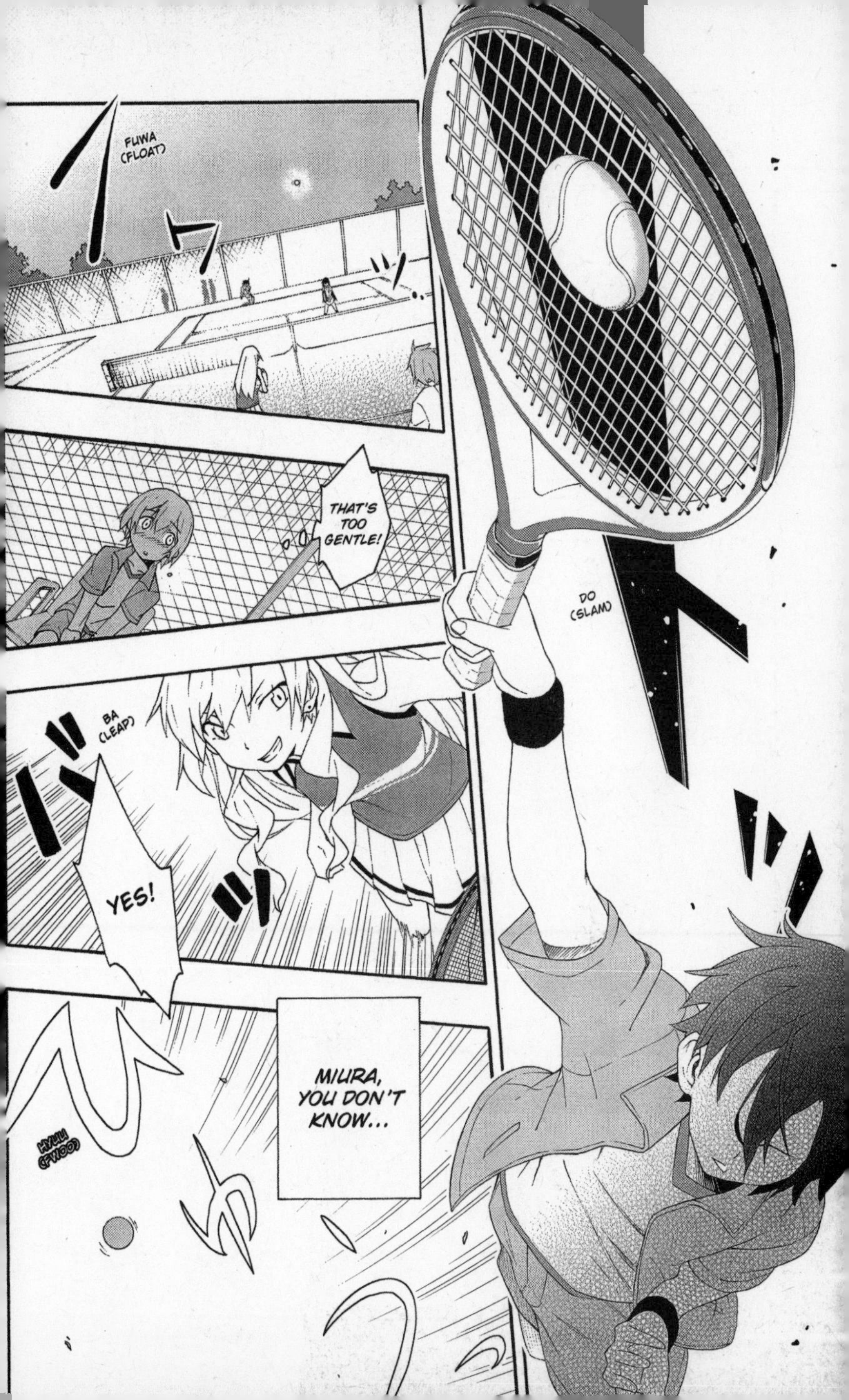

FUWA (FLOAT)
THAT'S TOO GENTLE!
BA (LEAP)
YES!
DO (SLAM)
MIURA, YOU DON'T KNOW...
HYUU (FWOO)

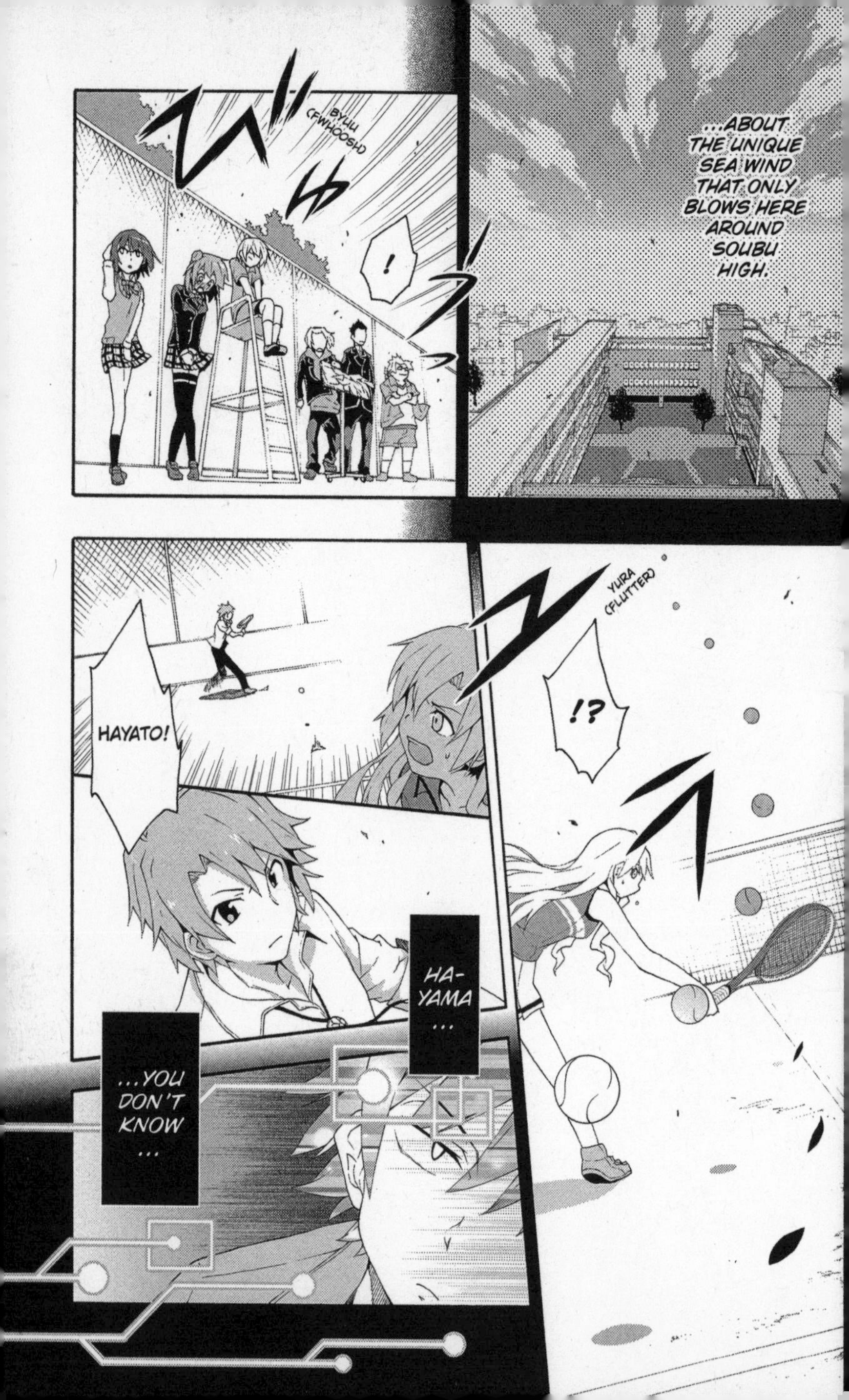
...ABOUT THE UNIQUE SEA WIND THAT ONLY BLOWS HERE AROUND SOUBU HIGH.
BYUU (FWHOOSH)
!
YURA (FLUTTER)
!?
HAYATO!
HA-YAMA...
...YOU DON'T KNOW...

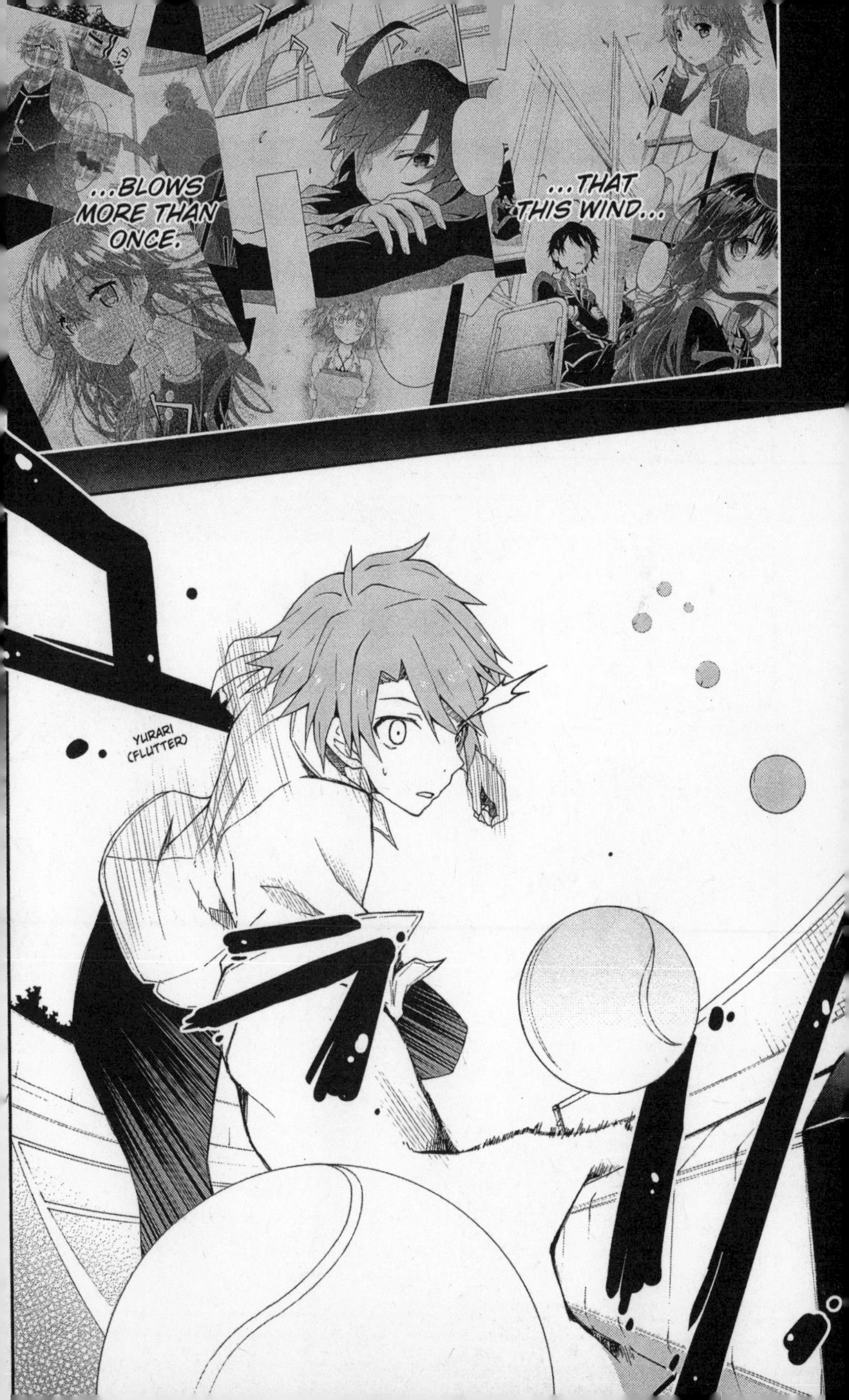
...THAT THIS WIND...
...BLOWS MORE THAN ONCE.
YURARI (FLUTTER)

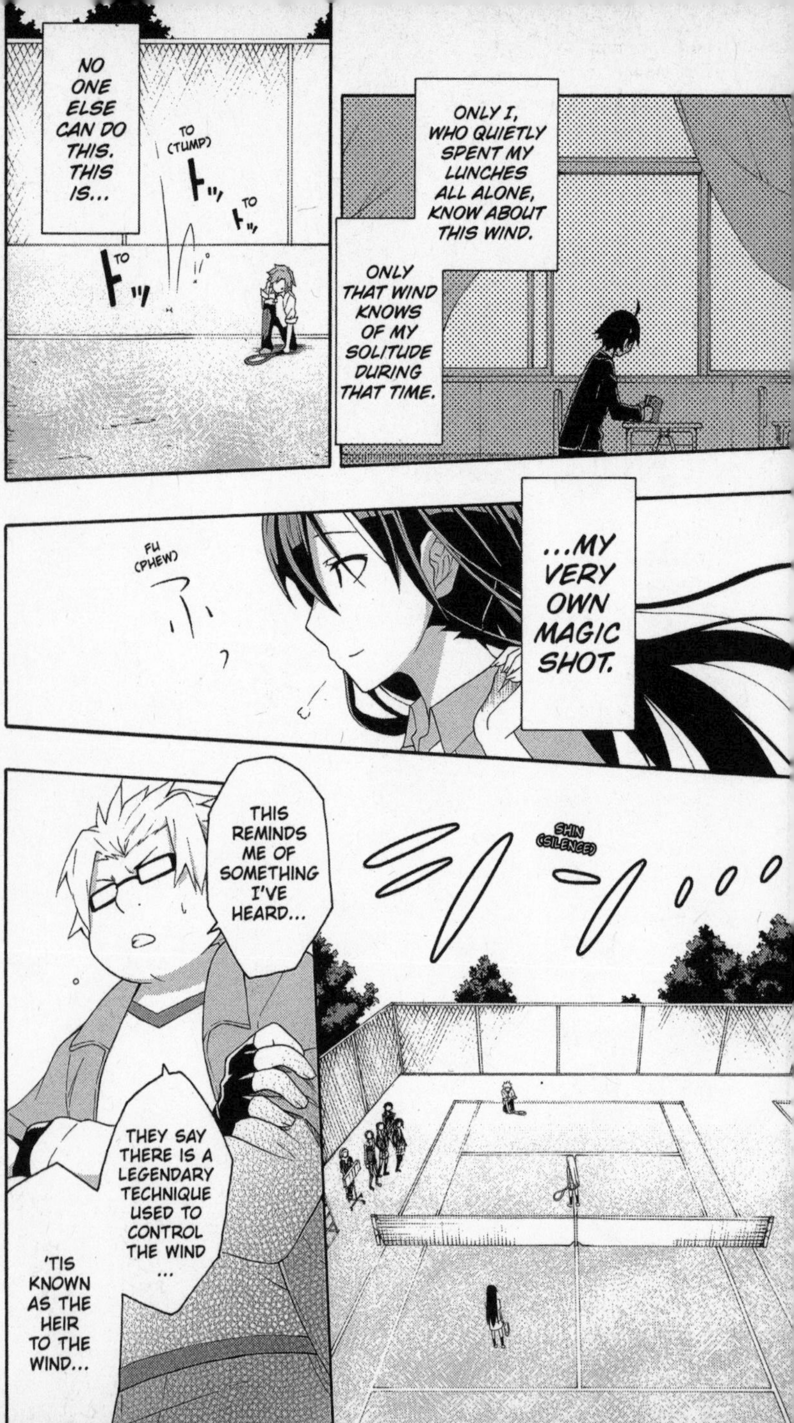
ONLY I, WHO QUIETLY SPENT MY LUNCHES ALL ALONE, KNOW ABOUT THIS WIND.
ONLY THAT WIND KNOWS OF MY SOLITUDE DURING THAT TIME.
NO ONE ELSE CAN DO THIS. THIS IS...
TO (TUMP)
トッ
TO
トッ
TO
トッ
...MY VERY OWN MAGIC SHOT.
FU (PHEW)
ふ
SHIN (SILENCE)
THIS REMINDS ME OF SOMETHING I'VE HEARD...
THEY SAY THERE IS A LEGENDARY TECHNIQUE USED TO CONTROL THE WIND...
'TIS KNOWN AS THE HEIR TO THE WIND...

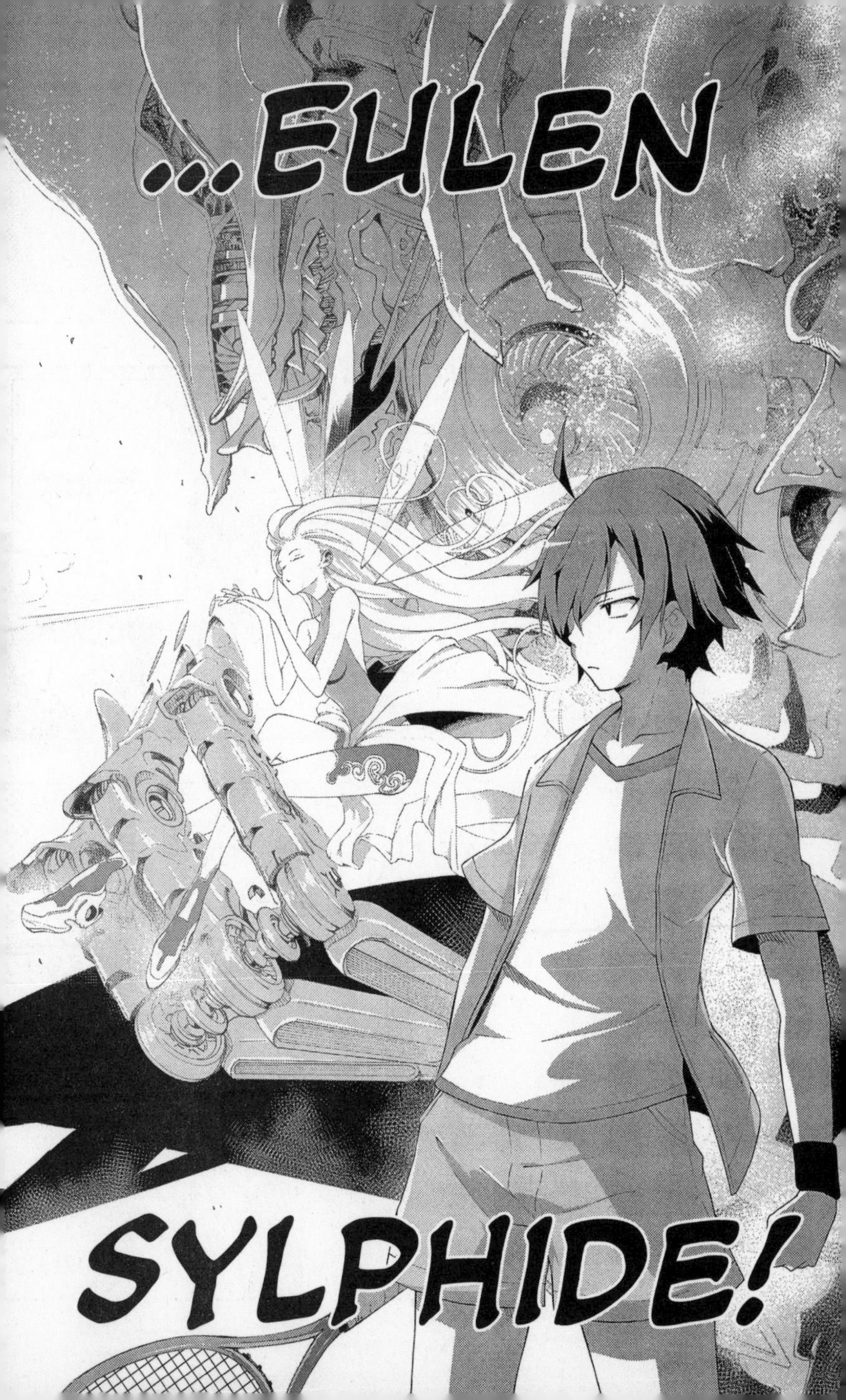
...EULEN
SYLPHIDE!

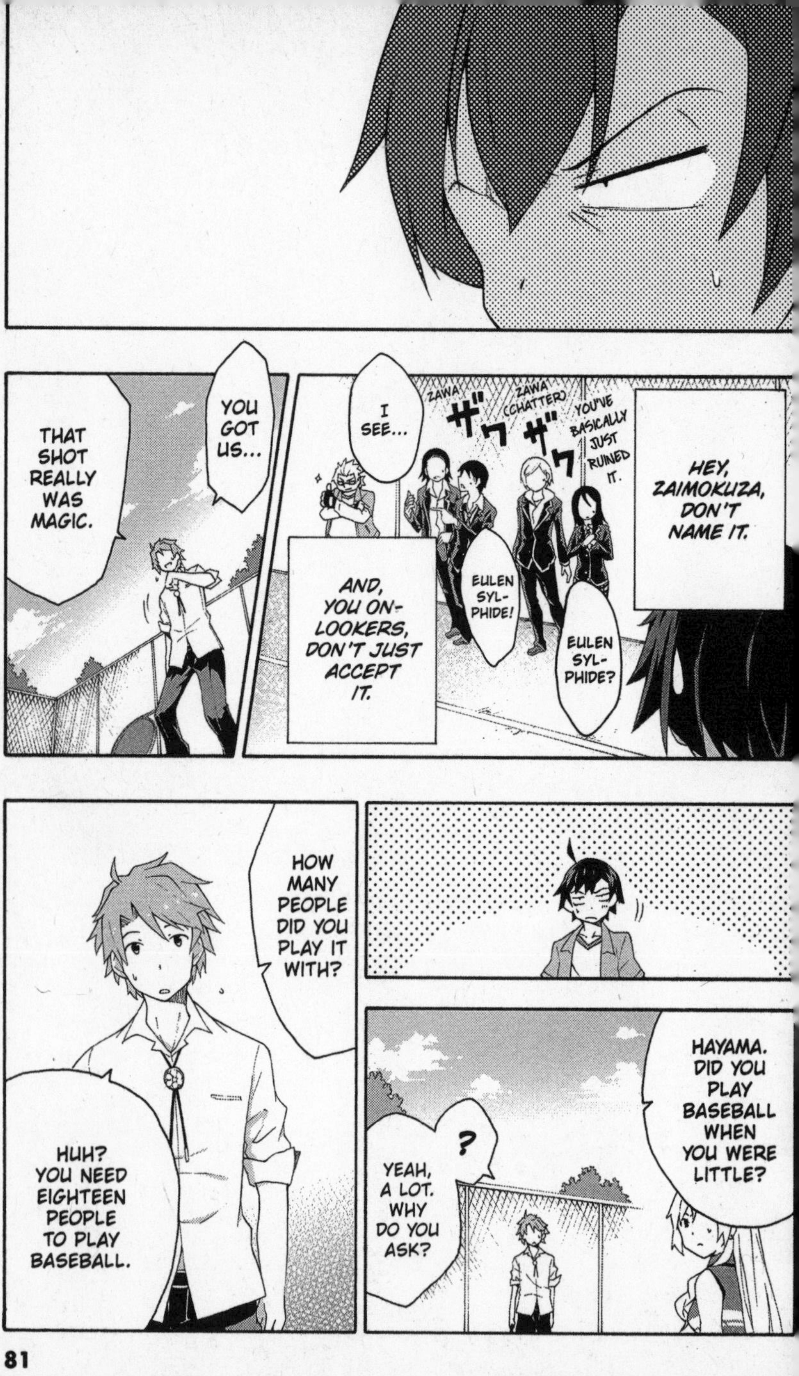
HEY, ZAIMOKUZA, DON'T NAME IT.
YOU'VE BASICALLY JUST RUINED IT.
ZAWA (CHATTER)
ZAWA
I SEE...
EULEN SYL-PHIDE?
EULEN SYL-PHIDE!
AND, YOU ON-LOOKERS, DON'T JUST ACCEPT IT.
YOU GOT US...
THAT SHOT REALLY WAS MAGIC.
HAYAMA. DID YOU PLAY BASEBALL WHEN YOU WERE LITTLE?
?
YEAH, A LOT. WHY DO YOU ASK?
HOW MANY PEOPLE DID YOU PLAY IT WITH?
HUH? YOU NEED EIGHTEEN PEOPLE TO PLAY BASEBALL.

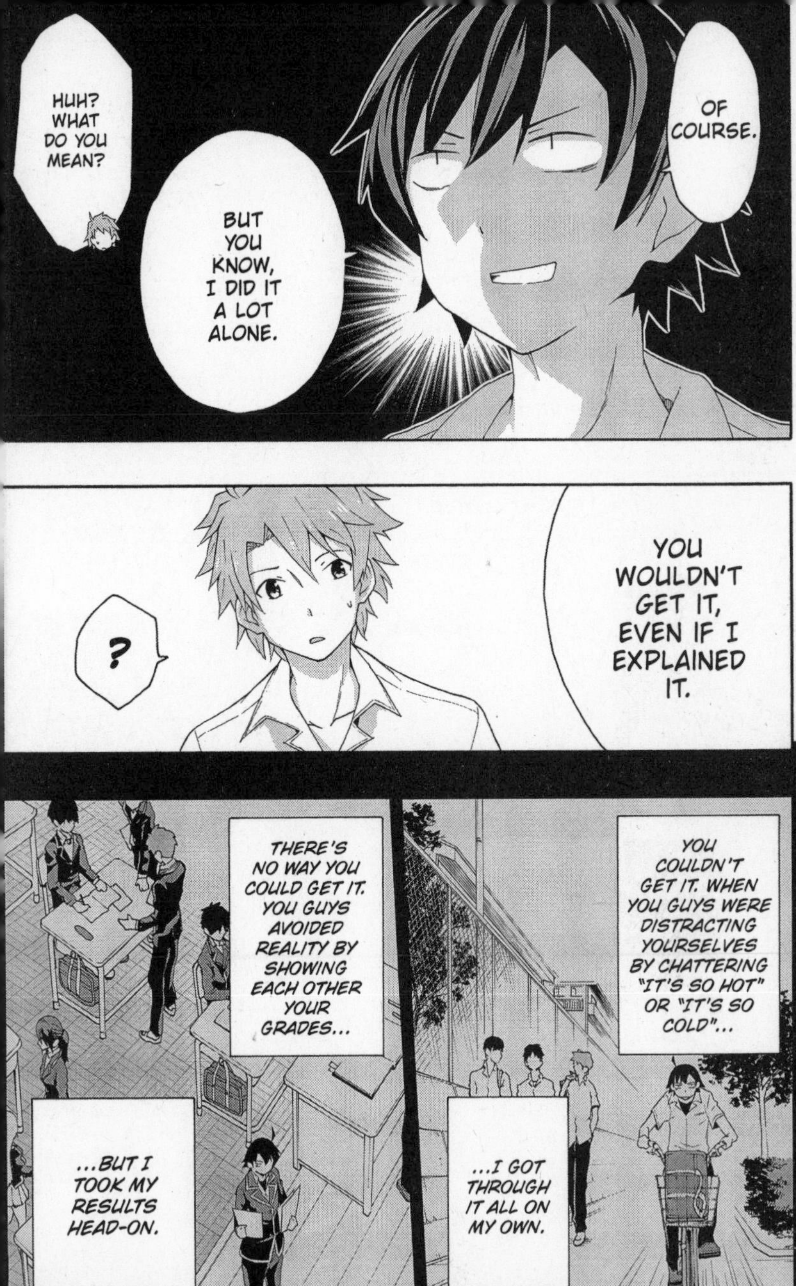
OF COURSE.
BUT YOU KNOW, I DID IT A LOT ALONE.
HUH? WHAT DO YOU MEAN?
YOU WOULDN'T GET IT, EVEN IF I EXPLAINED IT.
?
YOU COULDN'T GET IT. WHEN YOU GUYS WERE DISTRACTING YOURSELVES BY CHATTERING "IT'S SO HOT" OR "IT'S SO COLD"...
...I GOT THROUGH IT ALL ON MY OWN.
THERE'S NO WAY YOU COULD GET IT. YOU GUYS AVOIDED REALITY BY SHOWING EACH OTHER YOUR GRADES...
...BUT I TOOK MY RESULTS HEAD-ON.

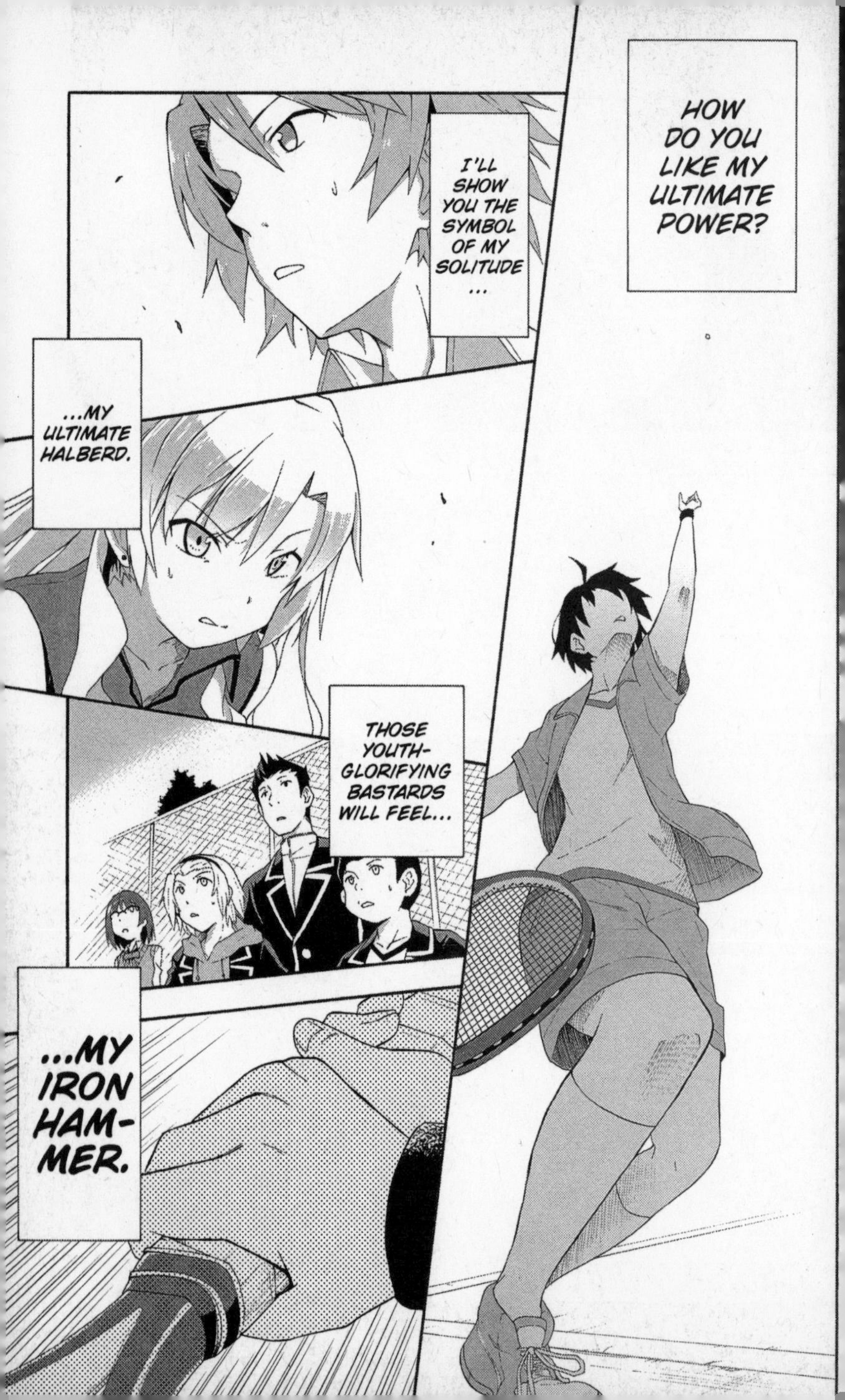
HOW DO YOU LIKE MY ULTIMATE POWER?
I'LL SHOW YOU THE SYMBOL OF MY SOLITUDE...
...MY ULTIMATE HALBERD.
THOSE YOUTH-GLORIFYING BASTARDS WILL FEEL...
...MY IRON HAM-MER.

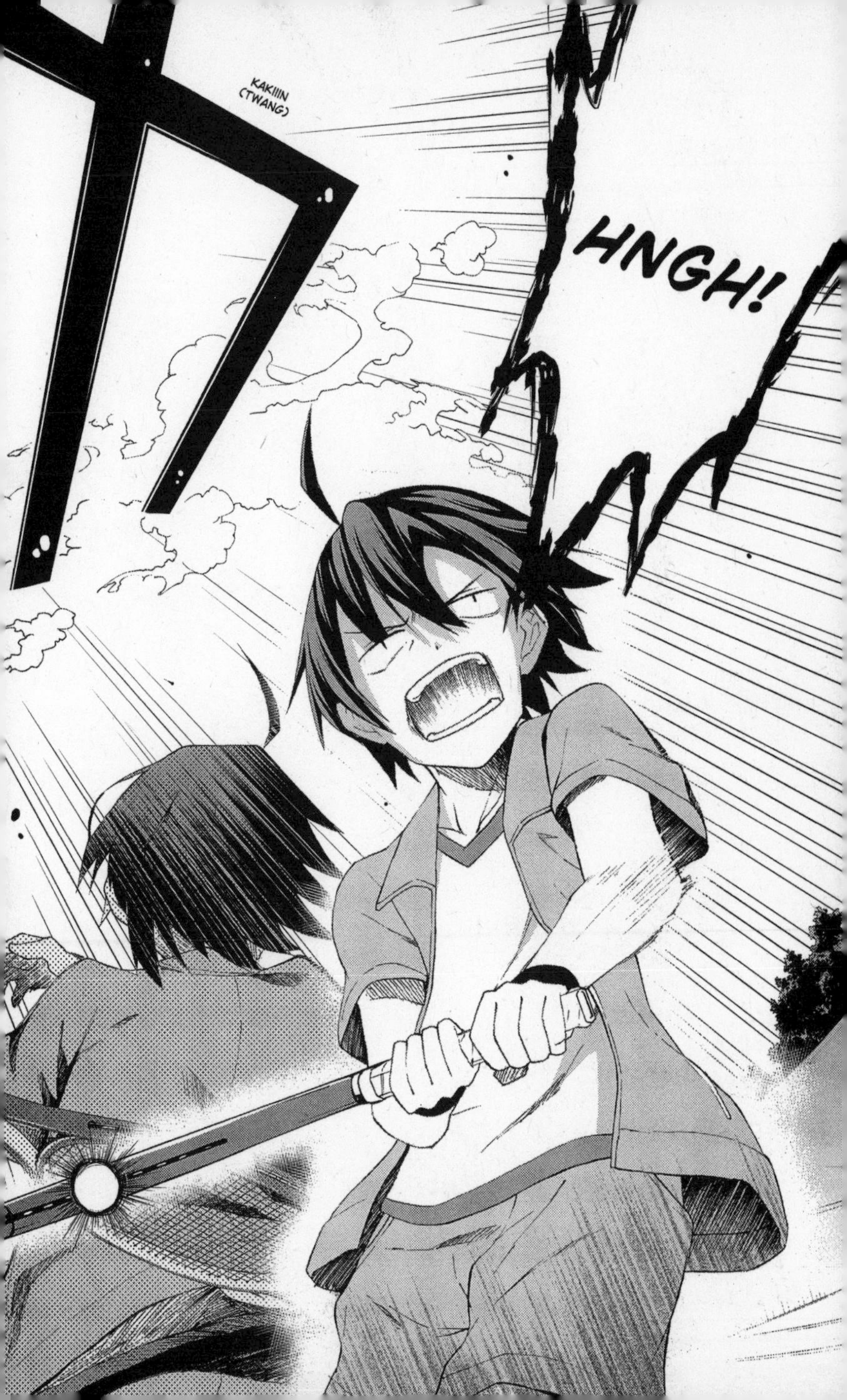
HNGH!
KAKIIN
(TWANG)

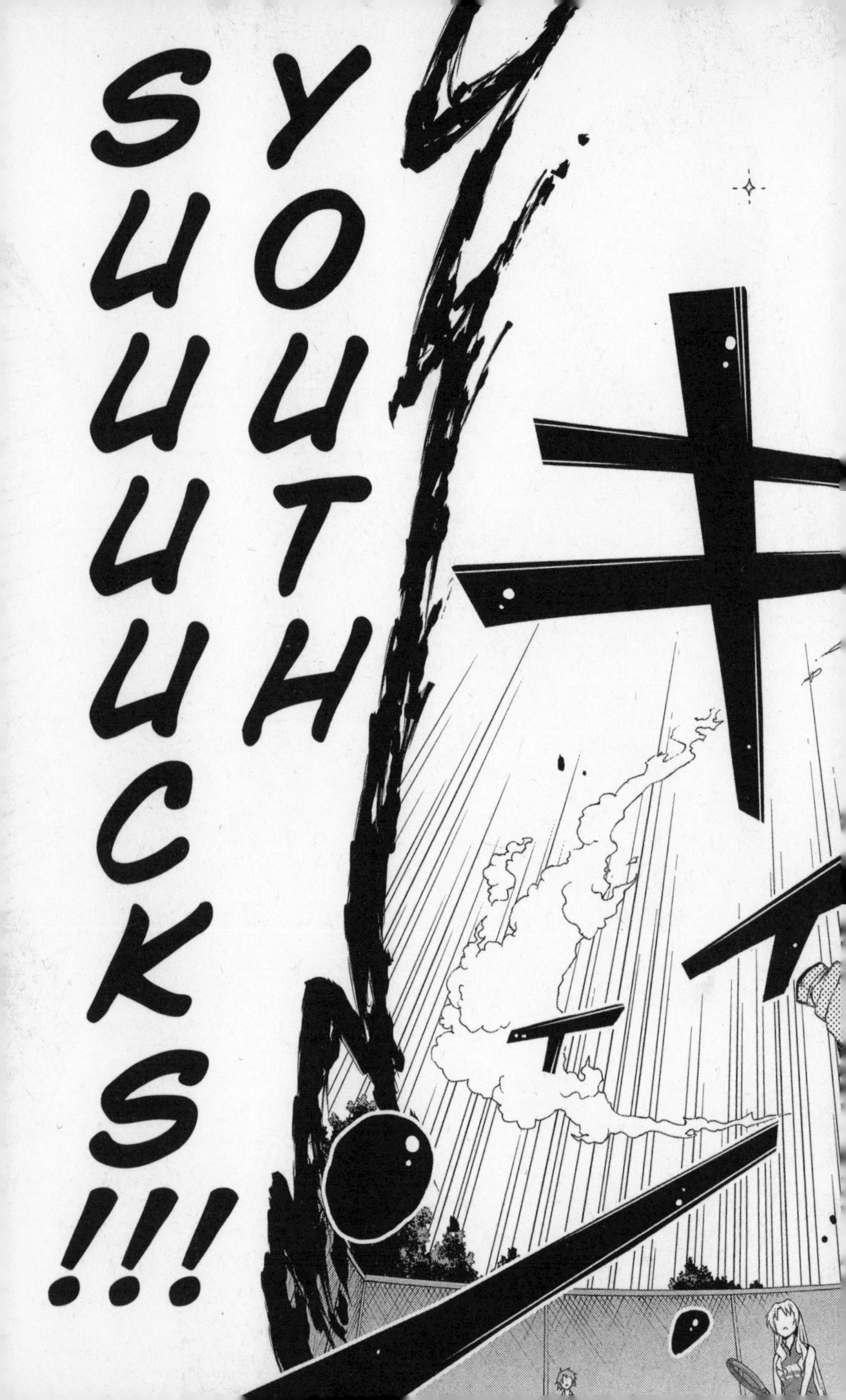
YOUTH SUUUUCKS!!!

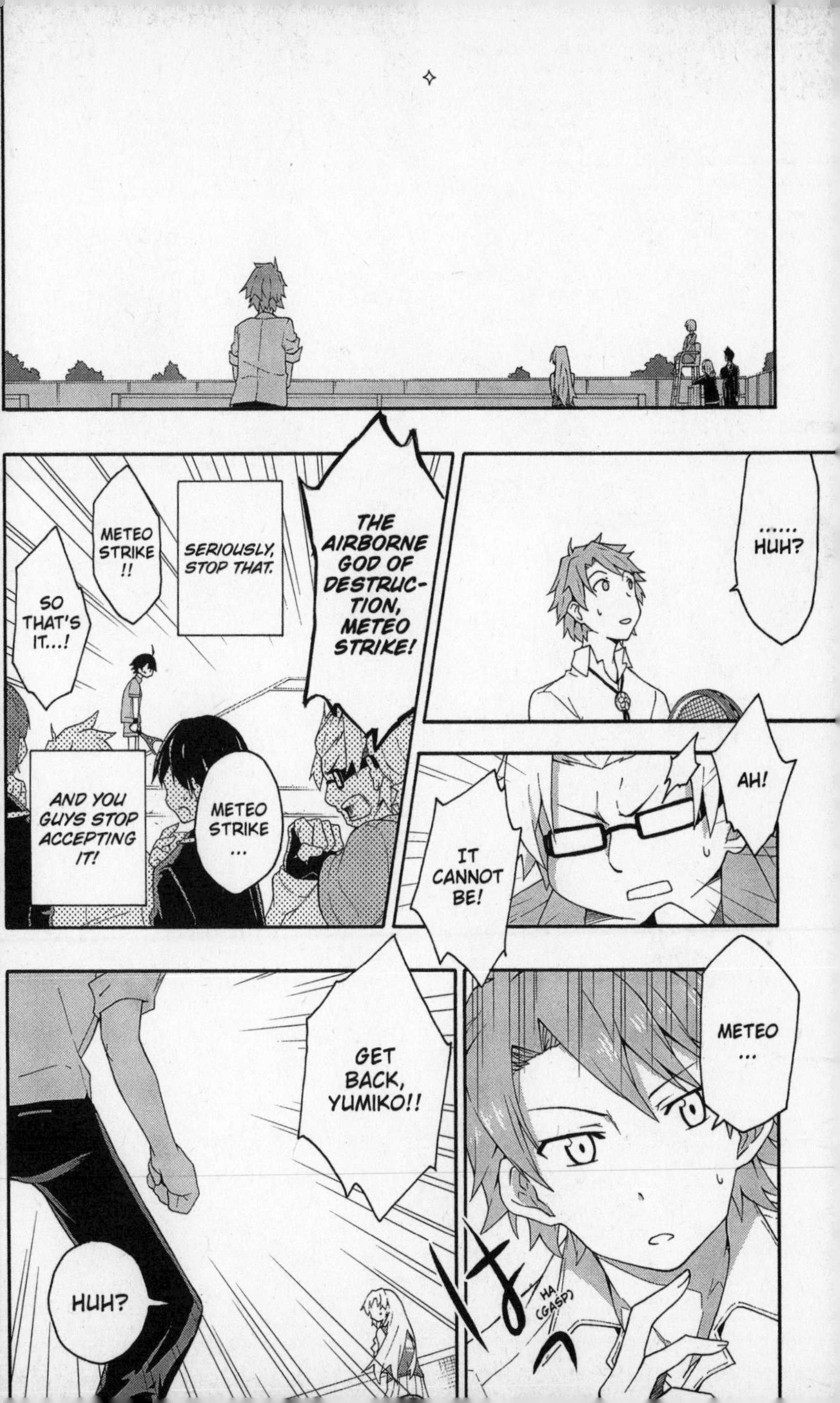

......HUH?
AH!
IT CANNOT BE!
THE AIRBORNE GOD OF DESTRUCTION, METEO STRIKE!
SERIOUSLY, STOP THAT.
METEO STRIKE!!
SO THAT'S IT...!
METEO STRIKE...
AND YOU GUYS STOP ACCEPTING IT!
METEO...
HA (GASP)
GET BACK, YUMIKO!!
HUH?

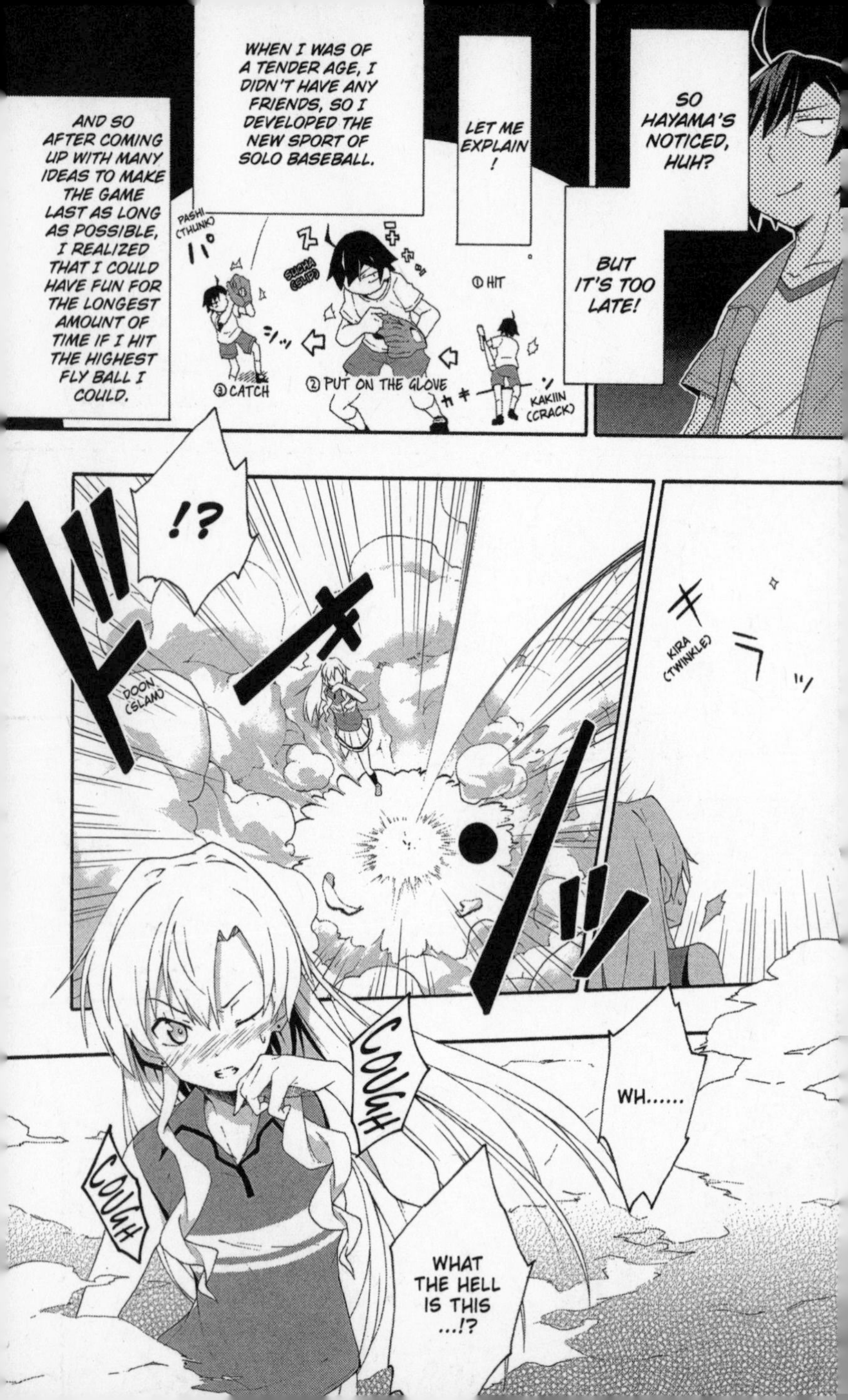
SO HAYAMA'S NOTICED, HUH?
BUT IT'S TOO LATE!
LET ME EXPLAIN!
WHEN I WAS OF A TENDER AGE, I DIDN'T HAVE ANY FRIENDS, SO I DEVELOPED THE NEW SPORT OF SOLO BASEBALL.
AND SO AFTER COMING UP WITH MANY IDEAS TO MAKE THE GAME LAST AS LONG AS POSSIBLE, I REALIZED THAT I COULD HAVE FUN FOR THE LONGEST AMOUNT OF TIME IF I HIT THE HIGHEST FLY BALL I COULD.
KAKIIN (CRACK)
① HIT
SUCHA (SLIP)
② PUT ON THE GLOVE
PASHI (THUNK)
③ CATCH
KIRA (TWINKLE)
!?
DOON (SLAM)
WH......
WHAT THE HELL IS THIS ...!?
COUGH
COUGH

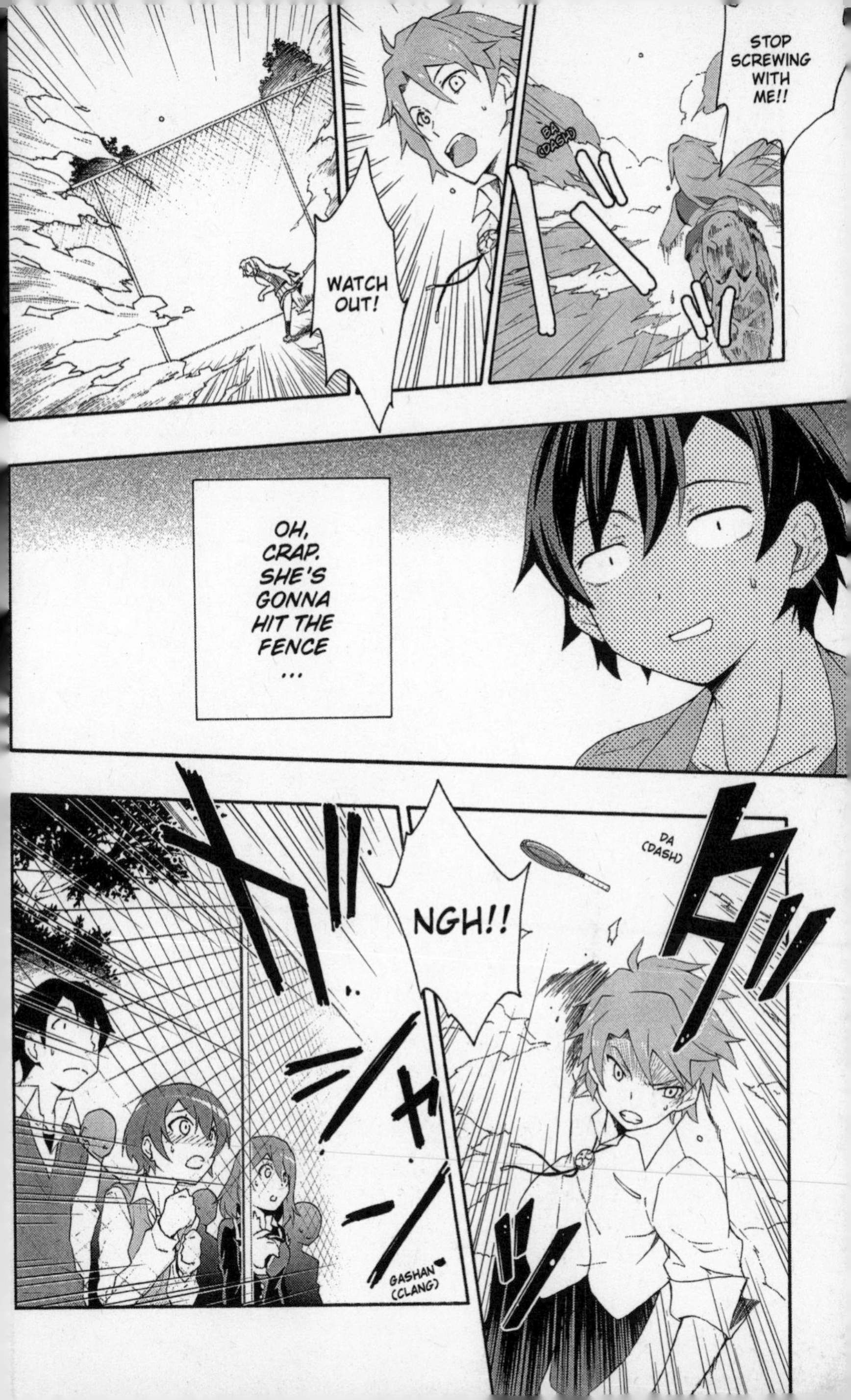
STOP SCREWING WITH ME!!
DA (DASH)
WATCH OUT!
OH, CRAP. SHE'S GONNA HIT THE FENCE...
DA (DASH)
NGH!!
GASHAN (CLANG)

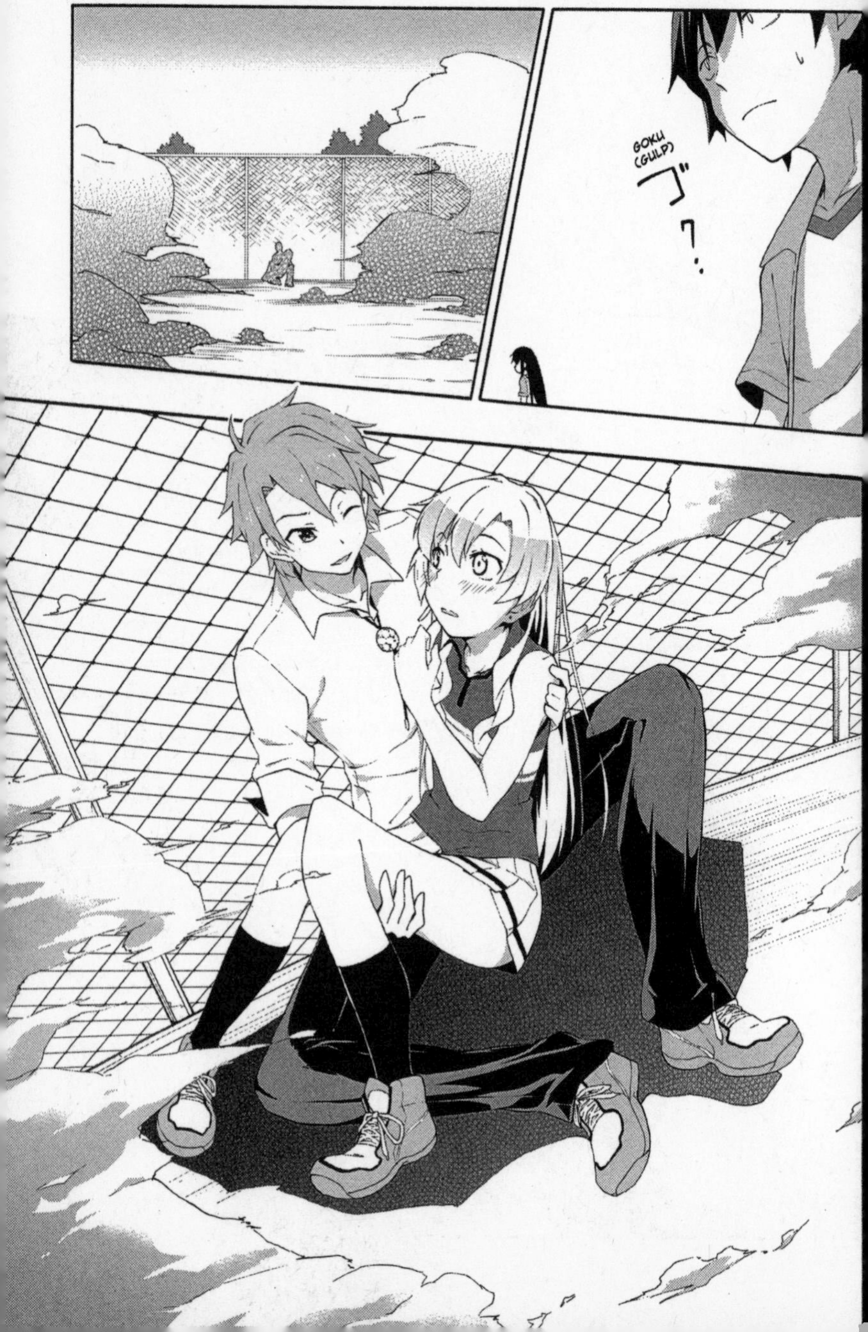
GOKU
(GULP)
ゴクッ

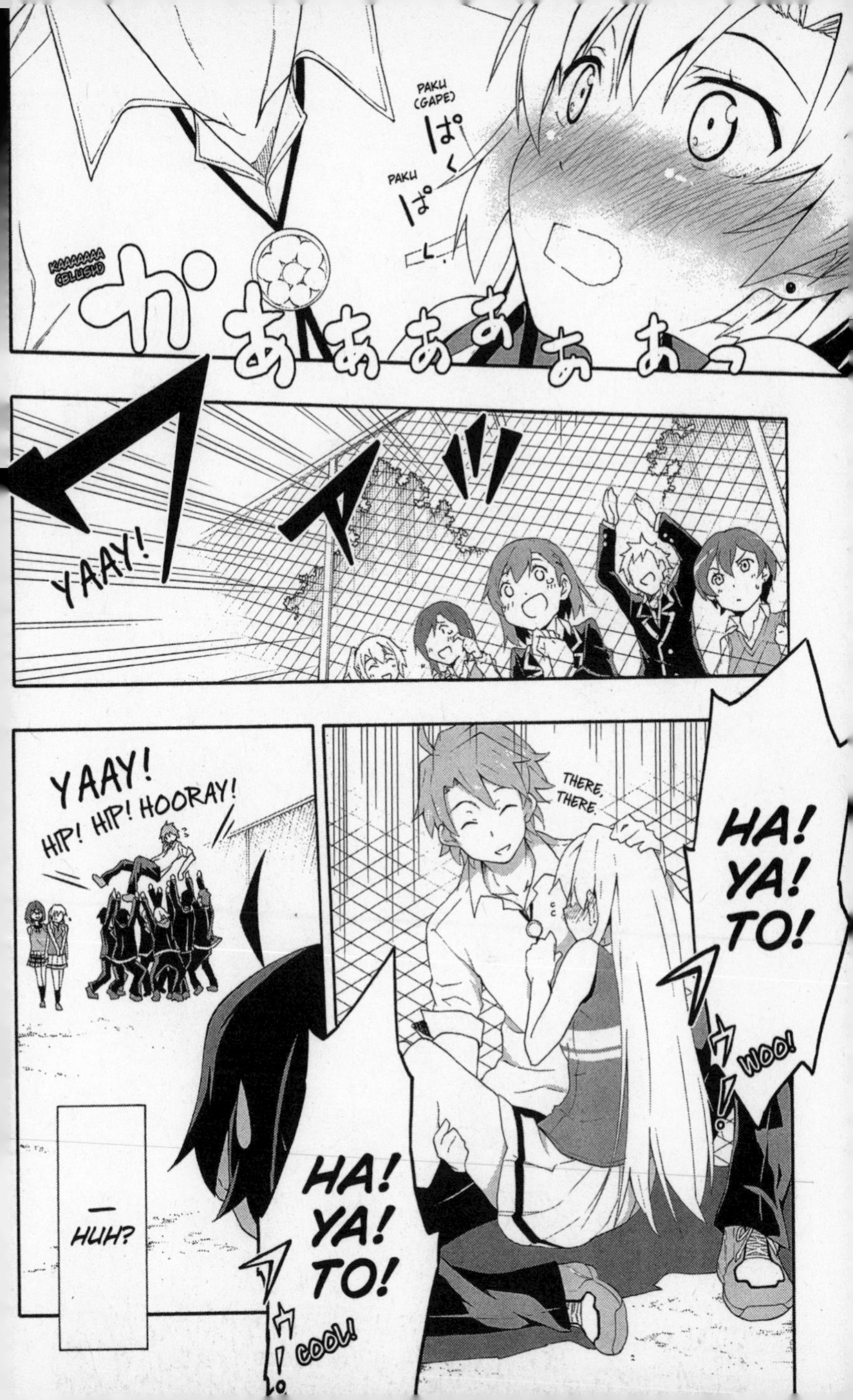
PAKU (GAPE)
ぱく
PAKU
ぱくっ
KAAAAAAA (BLUSH)
かぁぁぁぁぁぁっ
ワァッ
YAAY!
THERE, THERE.
HA! YA! TO!
ウ!
WOO!
HA! YA! TO!
ウ!
COOL!
YAAY!
HIP! HIP! HOORAY!
— HUH?

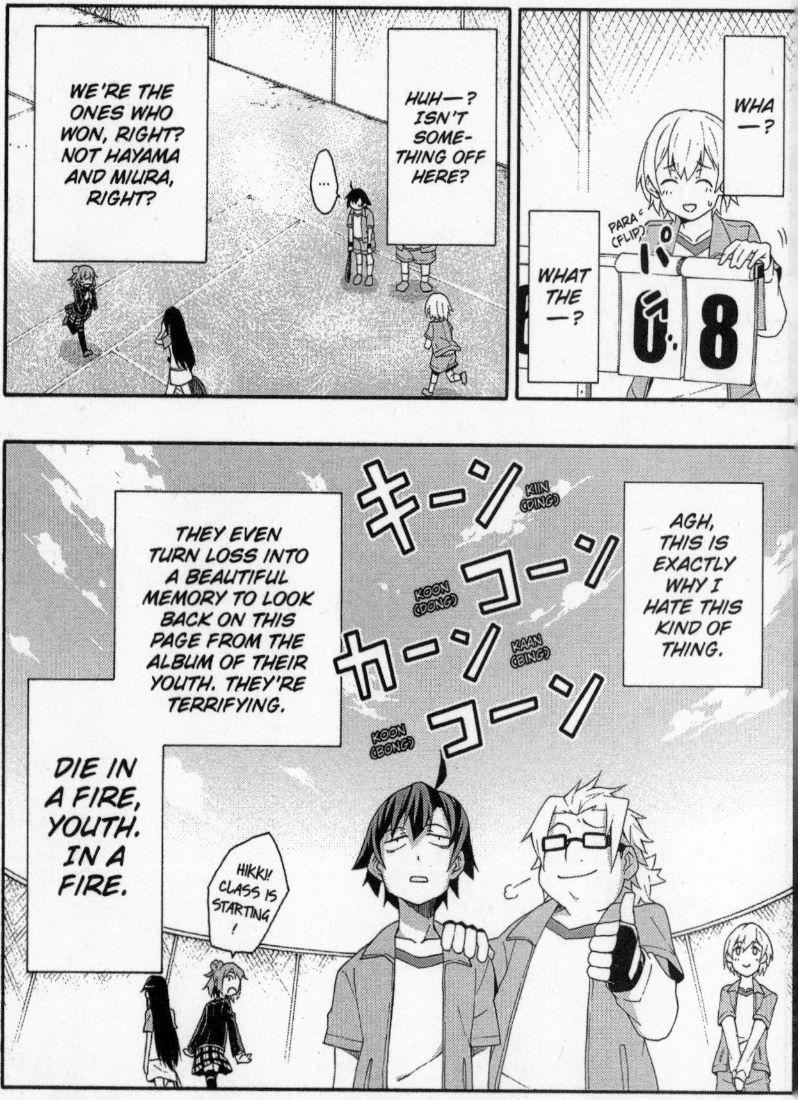
WHA—?
PARA (FLIP)
WHAT THE—?
HUH—? ISN'T SOMETHING OFF HERE?
...
WE'RE THE ONES WHO WON, RIGHT? NOT HAYAMA AND MIURA, RIGHT?
AGH, THIS IS EXACTLY WHY I HATE THIS KIND OF THING.
KIIN (DING)
KOON (DONG)
KAAN (BING)
KOON (BONG)
THEY EVEN TURN LOSS INTO A BEAUTIFUL MEMORY TO LOOK BACK ON THIS PAGE FROM THE ALBUM OF THEIR YOUTH. THEY'RE TERRIFYING.
DIE IN A FIRE, YOUTH. IN A FIRE.
HIKKI! CLASS IS STARTING!

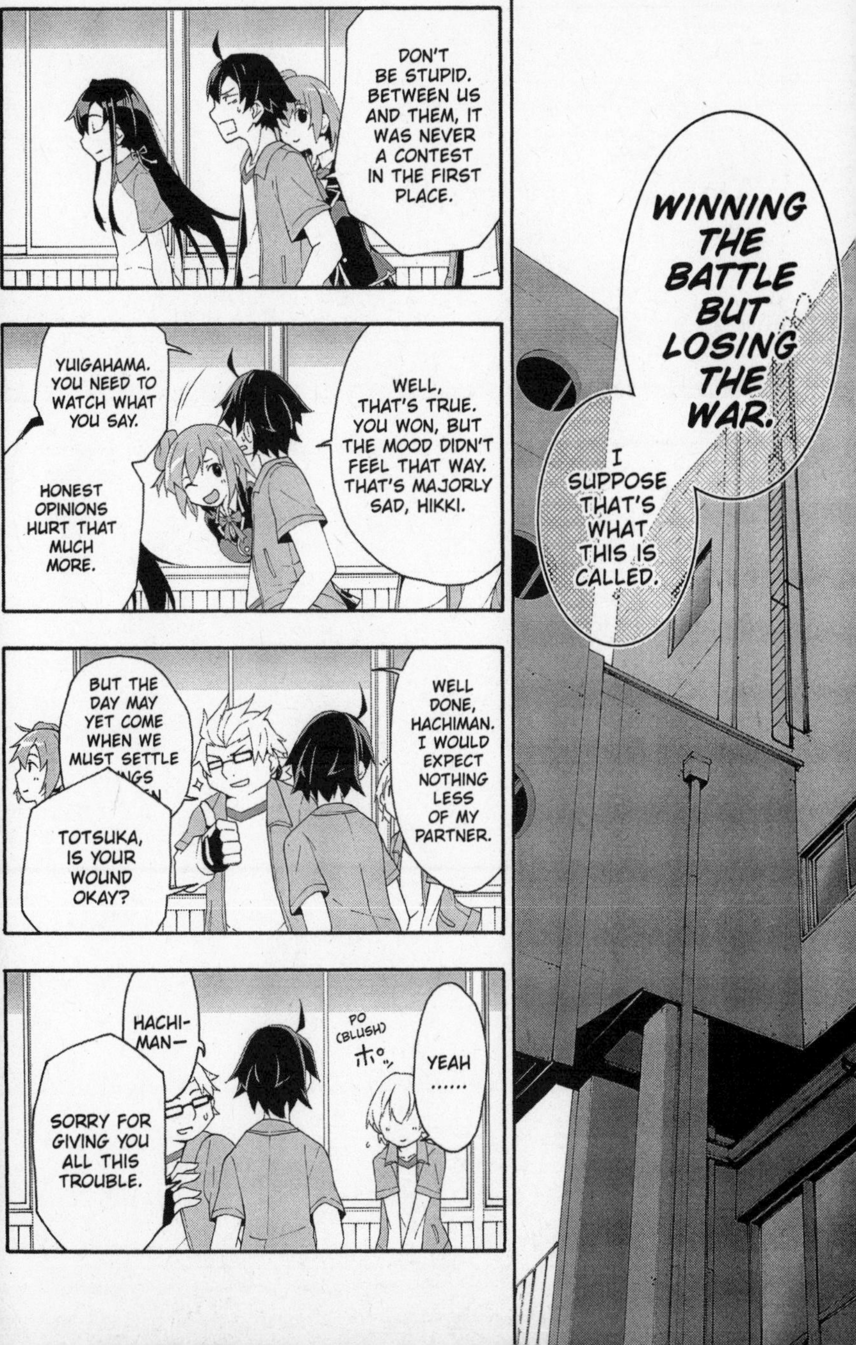
WINNING THE BATTLE BUT LOSING THE WAR.
I SUPPOSE THAT'S WHAT THIS IS CALLED.
DON'T BE STUPID. BETWEEN US AND THEM, IT WAS NEVER A CONTEST IN THE FIRST PLACE.
WELL, THAT'S TRUE. YOU WON, BUT THE MOOD DIDN'T FEEL THAT WAY. THAT'S MAJORLY SAD, HIKKI.
YUIGAHAMA. YOU NEED TO WATCH WHAT YOU SAY.
HONEST OPINIONS HURT THAT MUCH MORE.
WELL DONE, HACHIMAN. I WOULD EXPECT NOTHING LESS OF MY PARTNER.
BUT THE DAY MAY YET COME WHEN WE MUST SETTLE
TOTSUKA, IS YOUR WOUND OKAY?
YEAH ......
PO (BLUSH)
ホ。
HACHI-MAN—
SORRY FOR GIVING YOU ALL THIS TROUBLE.

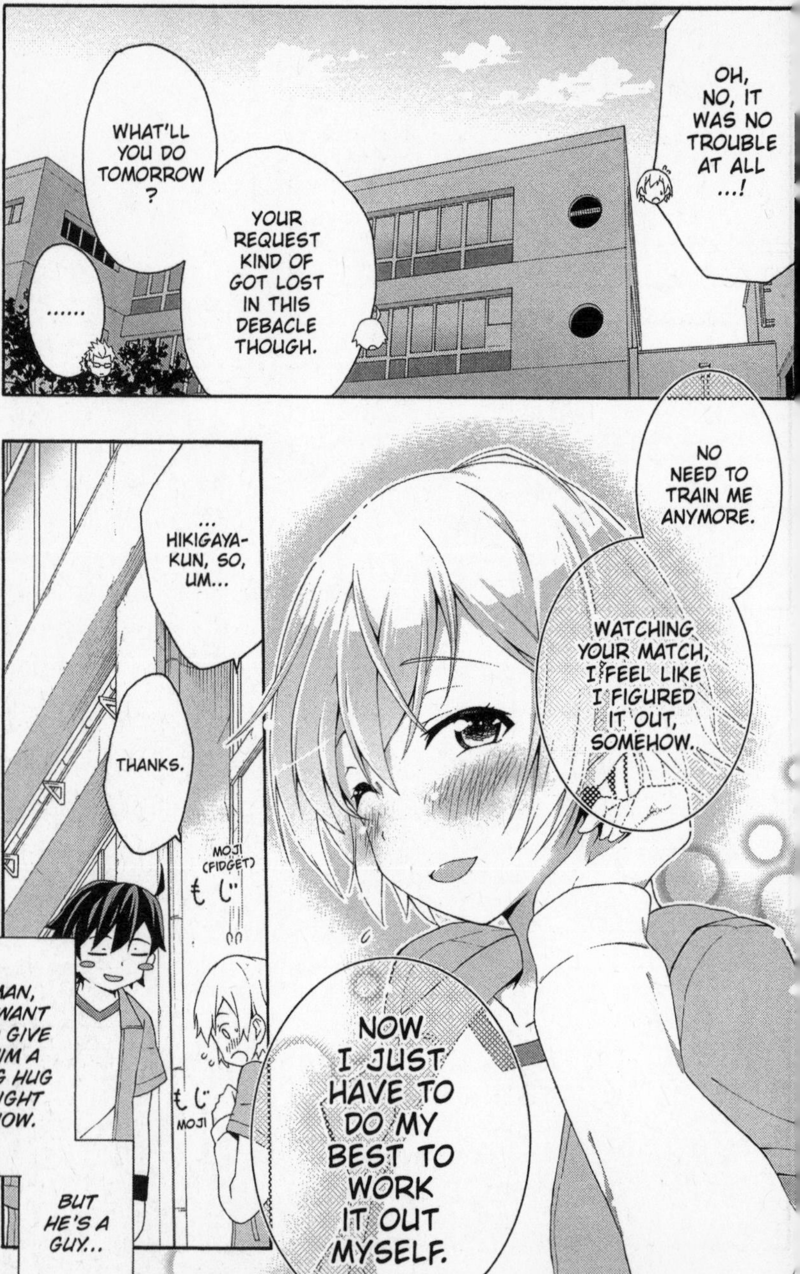
OH, NO, IT WAS NO TROUBLE AT ALL...!
YOUR REQUEST KIND OF GOT LOST IN THIS DEBACLE THOUGH.
WHAT'LL YOU DO TOMORROW?
......
...HIKIGAYA-KUN, SO, UM...
THANKS.
MOJI (FIDGET)
もじ
WATCHING YOUR MATCH, I FEEL LIKE I FIGURED IT OUT, SOMEHOW.
NO NEED TO TRAIN ME ANYMORE.
NOW I JUST HAVE TO DO MY BEST TO WORK IT OUT MYSELF.
もじ
MOJI
MAN, I WANT TO GIVE HIM A BIG HUG RIGHT NOW.
BUT HE'S A GUY...

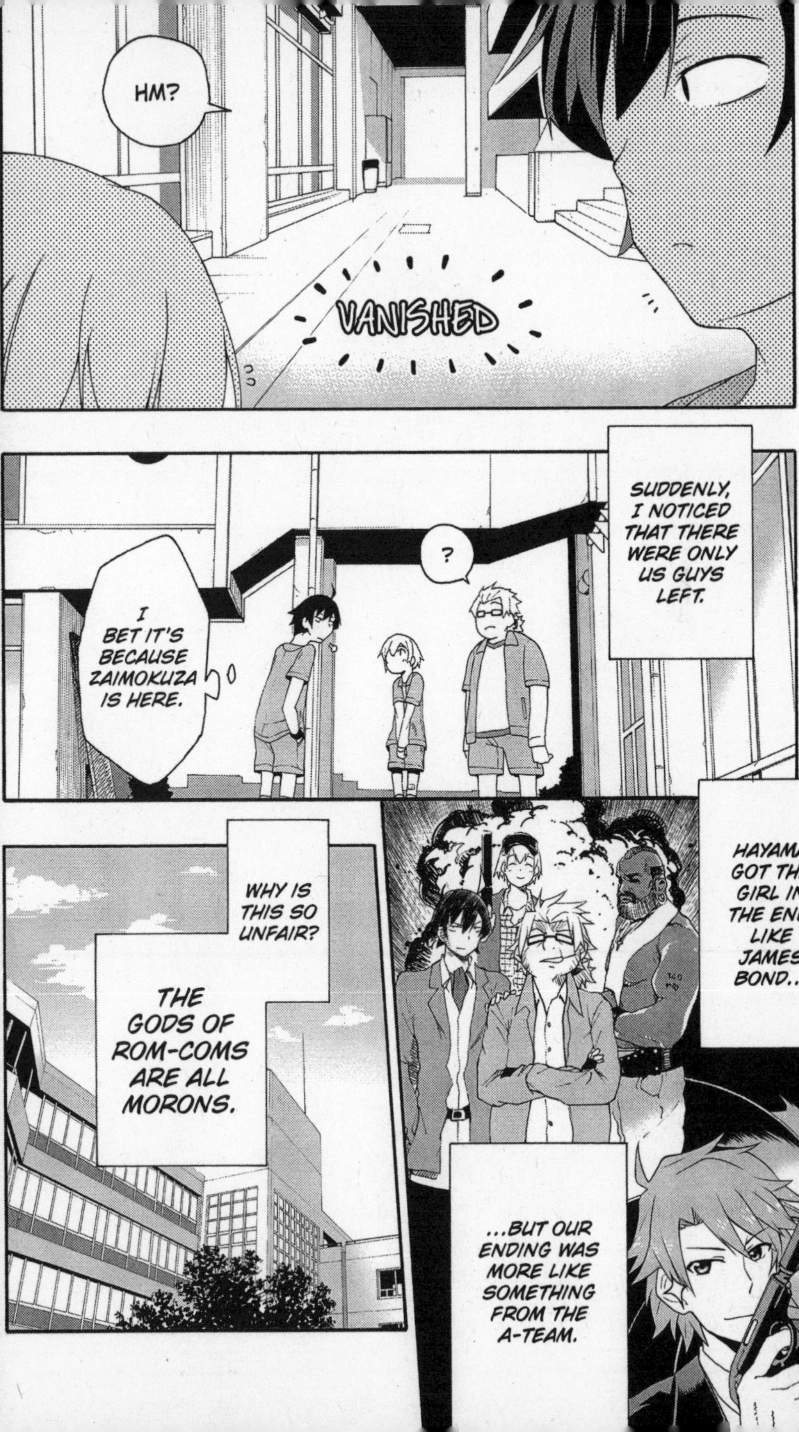
HM?
VANISHED
SUDDENLY, I NOTICED THAT THERE WERE ONLY US GUYS LEFT.
?
I BET IT'S BECAUSE ZAIMOKUZA IS HERE.
HAYAMA GOT THE GIRL IN THE END, LIKE JAMES BOND...
...BUT OUR ENDING WAS MORE LIKE SOMETHING FROM THE A-TEAM.
WHY IS THIS SO UNFAIR?
THE GODS OF ROM-COMS ARE ALL MORONS.

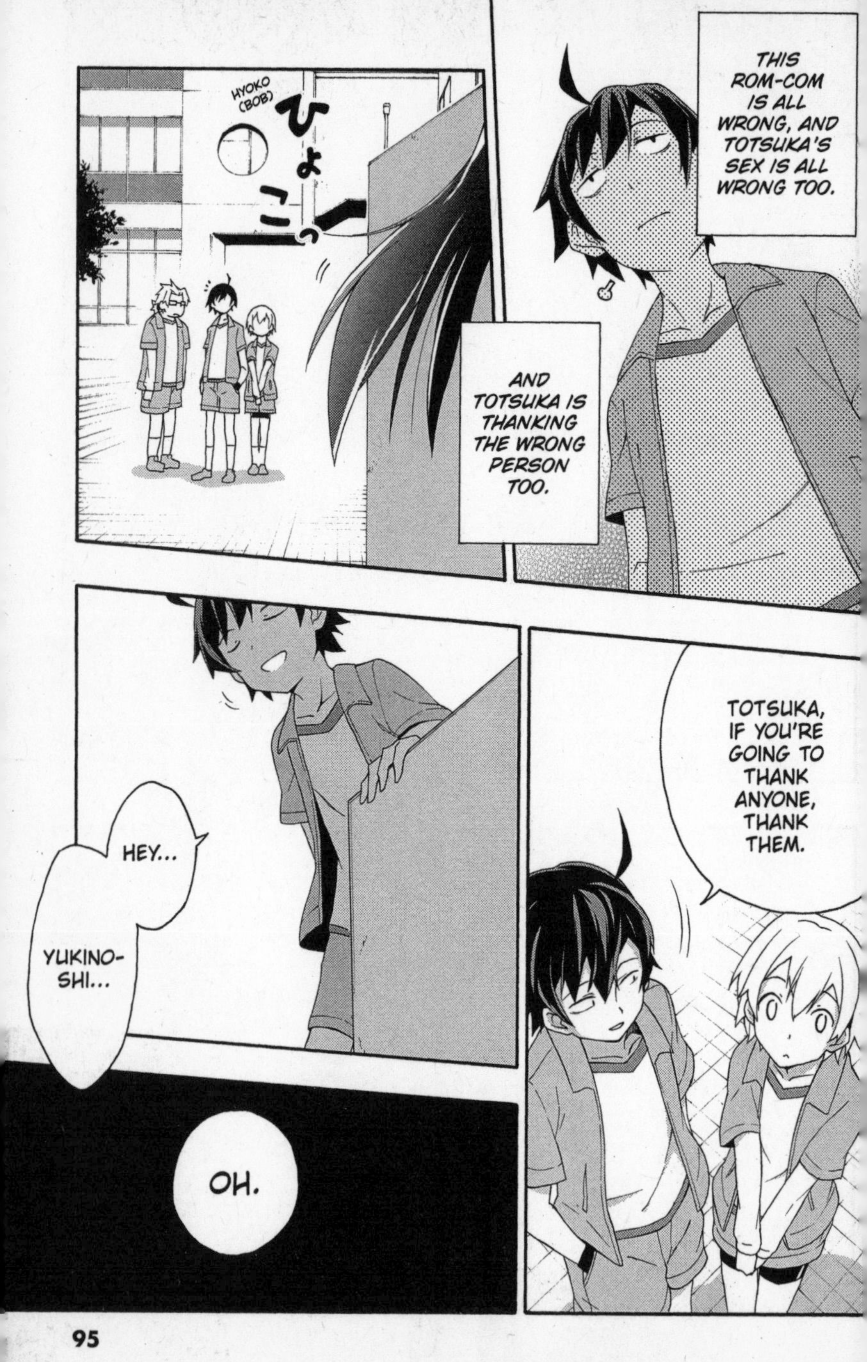
THIS ROM-COM IS ALL WRONG, AND TOTSUKA'S SEX IS ALL WRONG TOO.
AND TOTSUKA IS THANKING THE WRONG PERSON TOO.
ひょこっ
HYOKO (BOB)
TOTSUKA, IF YOU'RE GOING TO THANK ANYONE, THANK THEM.
HEY...
YUKINO-SHI...
OH.

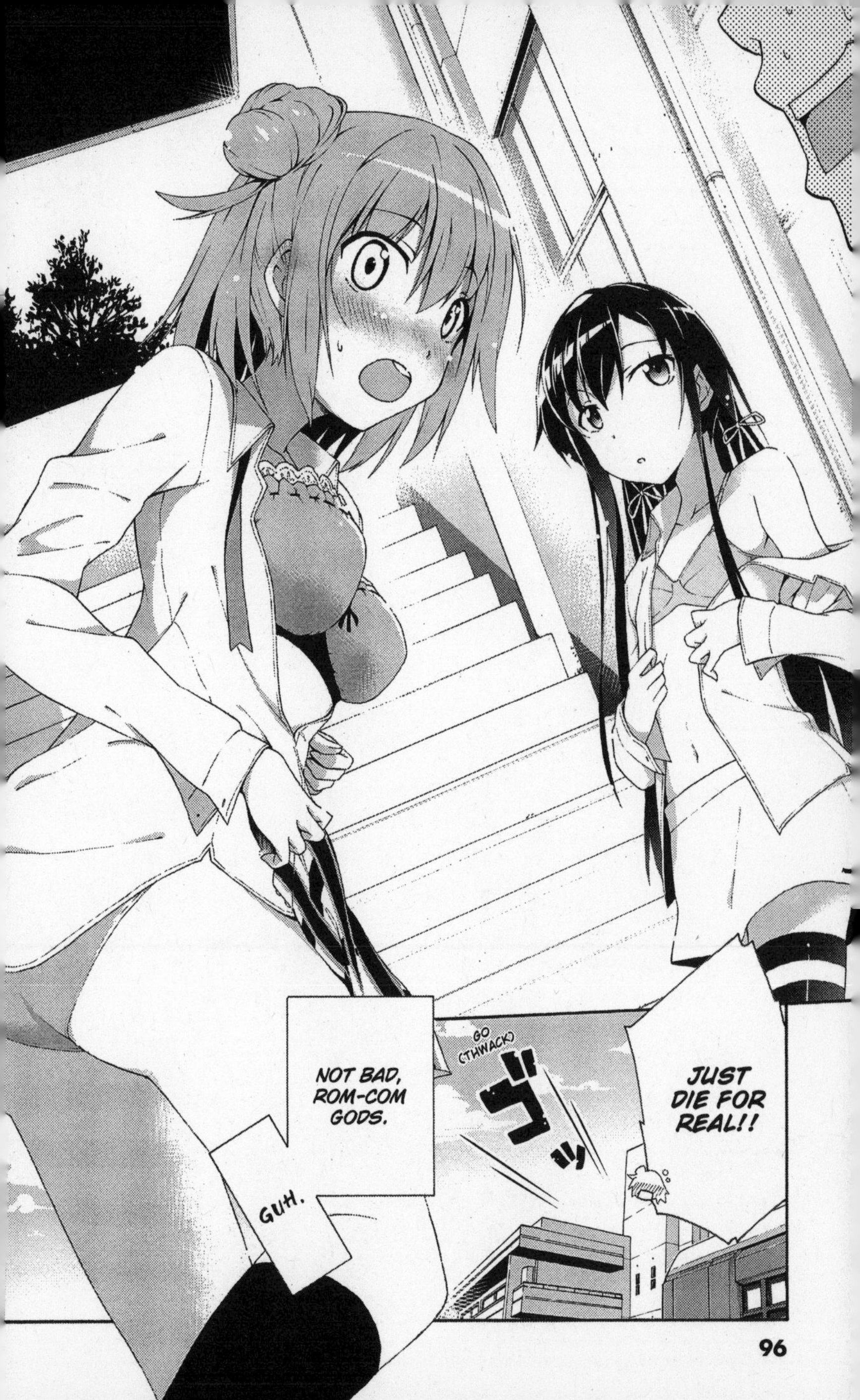
JUST DIE FOR REAL!!
GO (THWACK)
NOT BAD, ROM-COM GODS.
GUH.

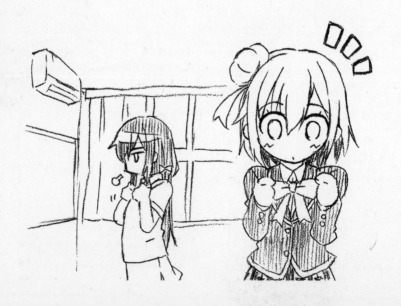

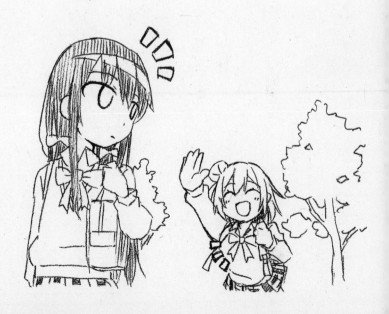

CHAPTER 9 ... AND THAT'S HOW YUI YUIGAHAMA DECIDED TO STUDY.

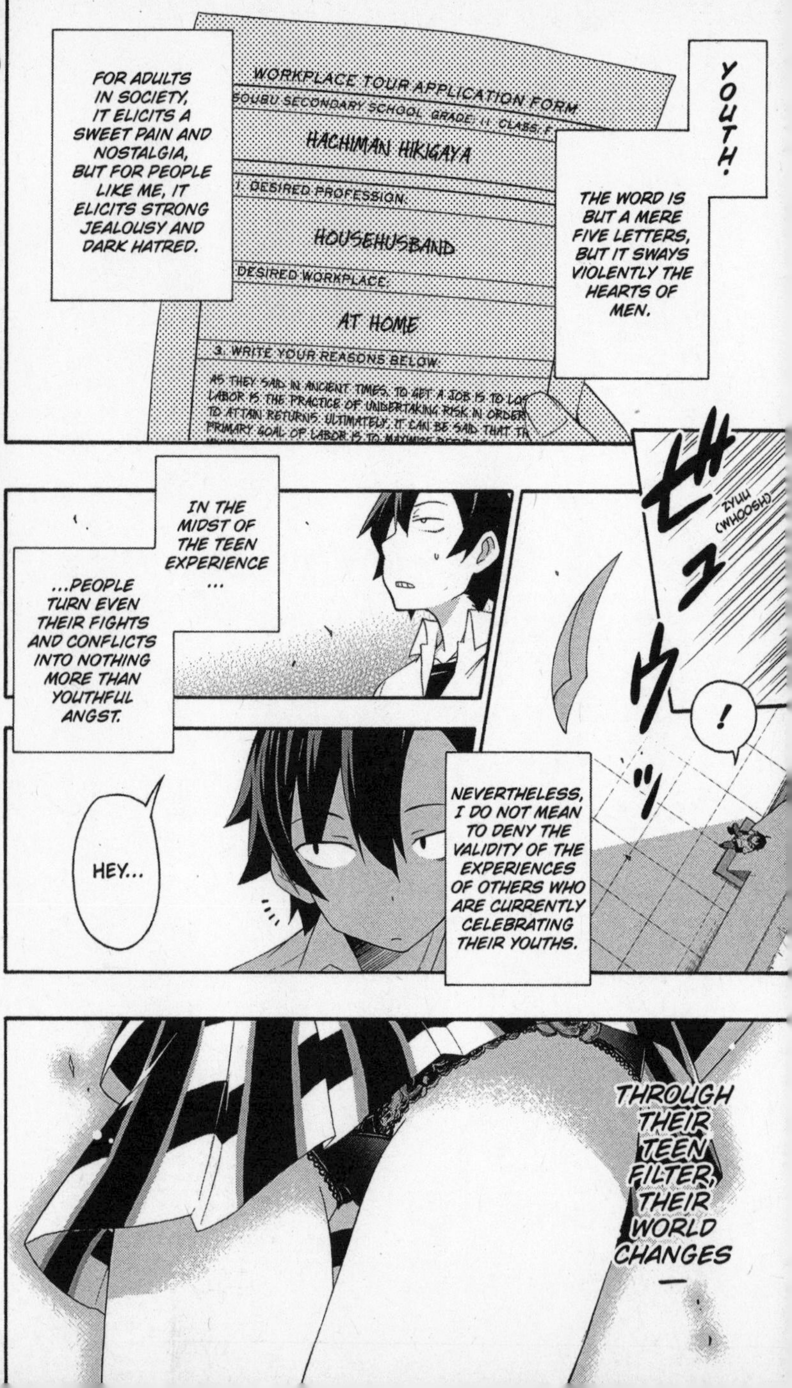

YOUTH!
THE WORD IS BUT A MERE FIVE LETTERS, BUT IT SWAYS VIOLENTLY THE HEARTS OF MEN.
WORKPLACE TOUR APPLICATION FORM
SOUBU SECONDARY SCHOOL GRADE: 11 CLASS: F
HACHIMAN HIKIGAYA
1. DESIRED PROFESSION:
HOUSEHUSBAND
DESIRED WORKPLACE:
AT HOME
3. WRITE YOUR REASONS BELOW.
AS THEY SAID IN ANCIENT TIMES, TO GET A JOB IS TO
LABOR IS THE PRACTICE OF UNDERTAKING RISK IN ORDER
TO ATTAIN RETURNS. ULTIMATELY, IT CAN BE SAID THAT
PRIMARY GOAL OF LABOR IS TO
FOR ADULTS IN SOCIETY, IT ELICITS A SWEET PAIN AND NOSTALGIA, BUT FOR PEOPLE LIKE ME, IT ELICITS STRONG JEALOUSY AND DARK HATRED.
ZYUU (WHOOSH)
!
IN THE MIDST OF THE TEEN EXPERIENCE...
...PEOPLE TURN EVEN THEIR FIGHTS AND CONFLICTS INTO NOTHING MORE THAN YOUTHFUL ANGST.
NEVERTHELESS, I DO NOT MEAN TO DENY THE VALIDITY OF THE EXPERIENCES OF OTHERS WHO ARE CURRENTLY CELEBRATING THEIR YOUTHS.
HEY...
THROUGH THEIR TEEN FILTER, THEIR WORLD CHANGES—

CHAPTER 9 ··· AND THAT'S HOW YUI YUIGAHAMA DECIDED TO STUDY.

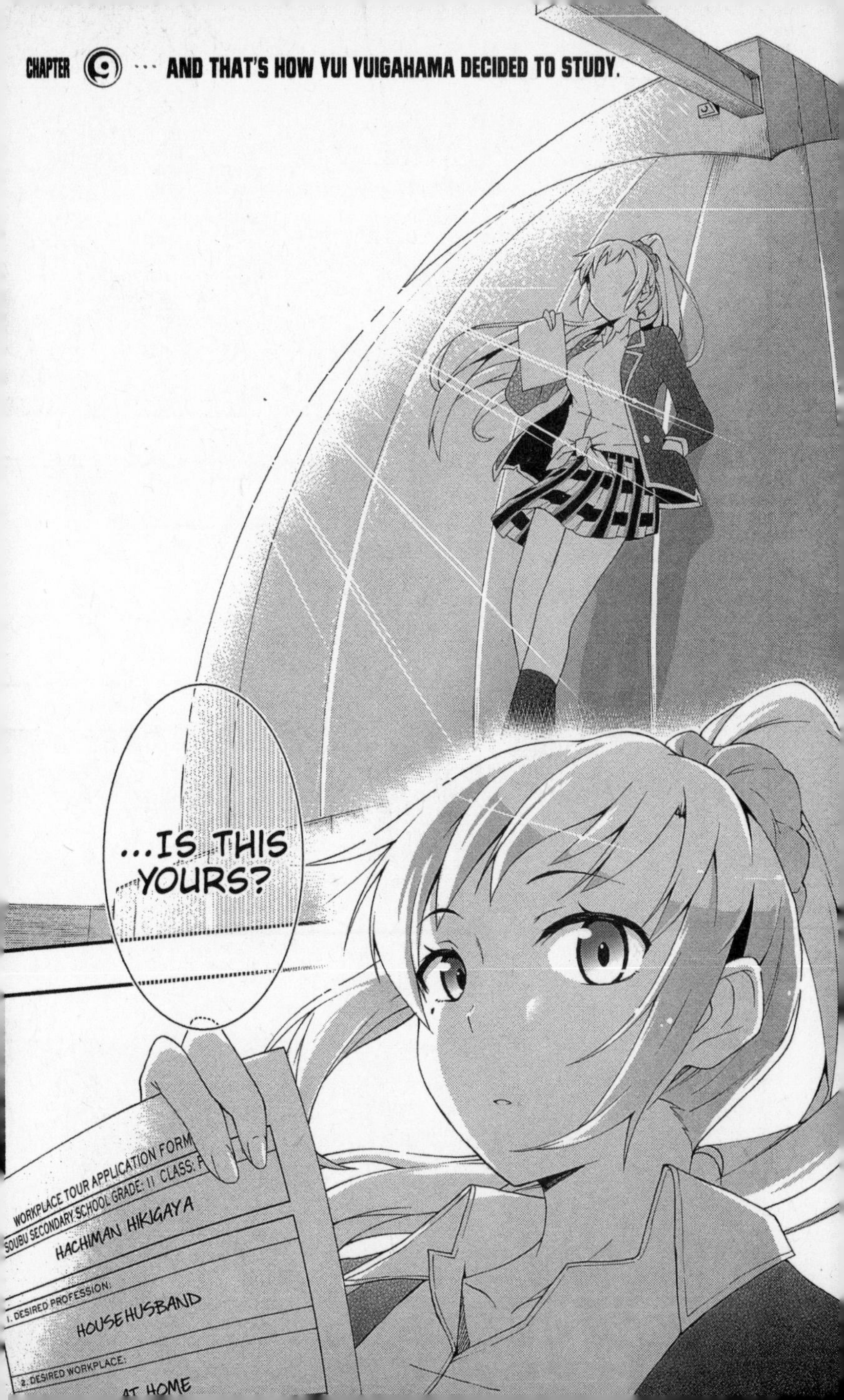
...IS THIS YOURS?
WORKPLACE TOUR APPLICATION FORM
SOUBU SECONDARY SCHOOL GRADE: 11 CLASS:
HACHIMAN HIKIGAYA
1. DESIRED PROFESSION:
HOUSEHUSBAND
2. DESIRED WORKPLACE:
AT HOME

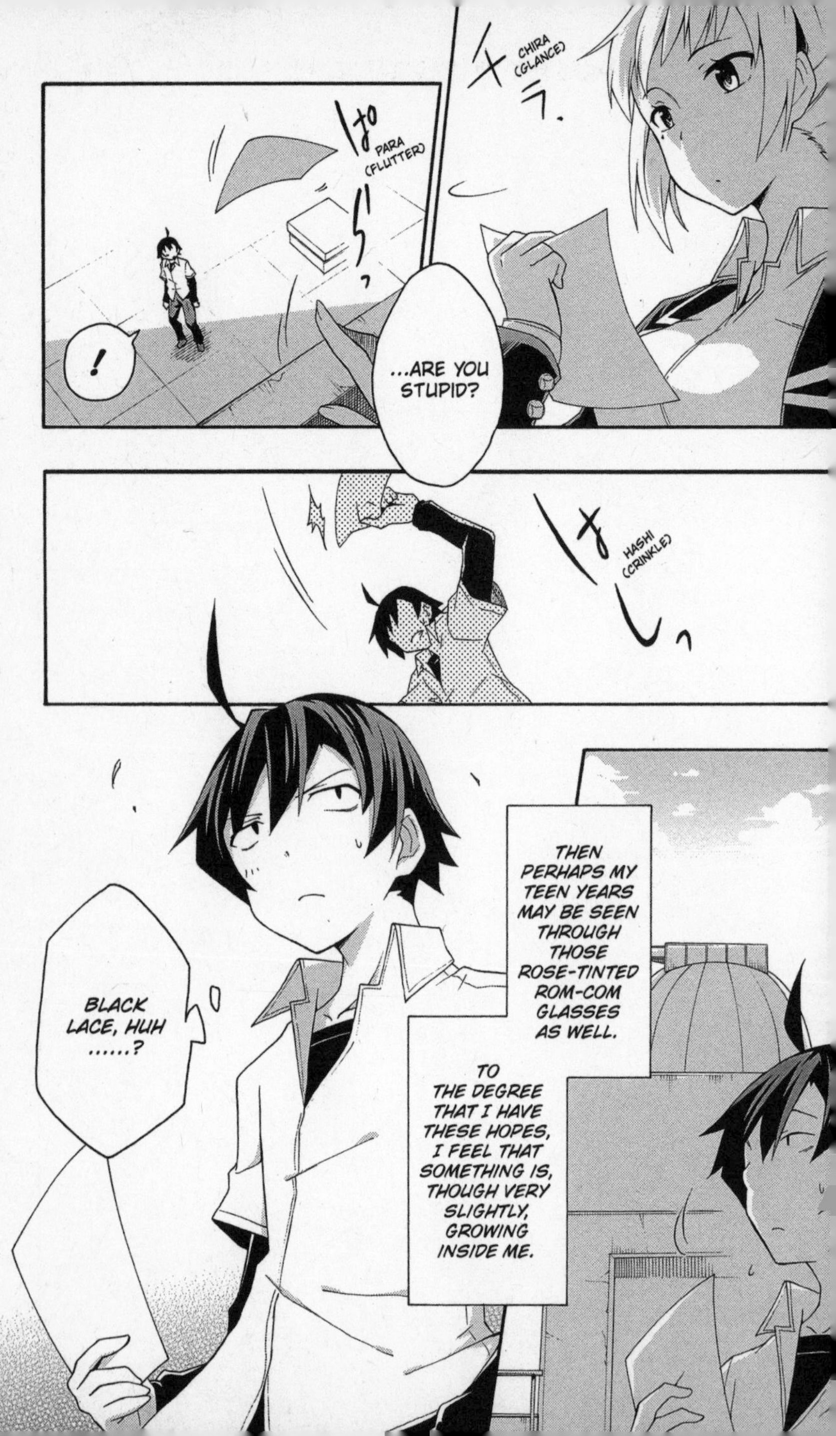

チラ
CHIRA (GLANCE)
ぱら
PARA (FLUTTER)
...ARE YOU STUPID?
!
はしっ
HASHI (CRINKLE)
THEN PERHAPS MY TEEN YEARS MAY BE SEEN THROUGH THOSE ROSE-TINTED ROM-COM GLASSES AS WELL.
TO THE DEGREE THAT I HAVE THESE HOPES, I FEEL THAT SOMETHING IS, THOUGH VERY SLIGHTLY, GROWING INSIDE ME.
BLACK LACE, HUH ......?

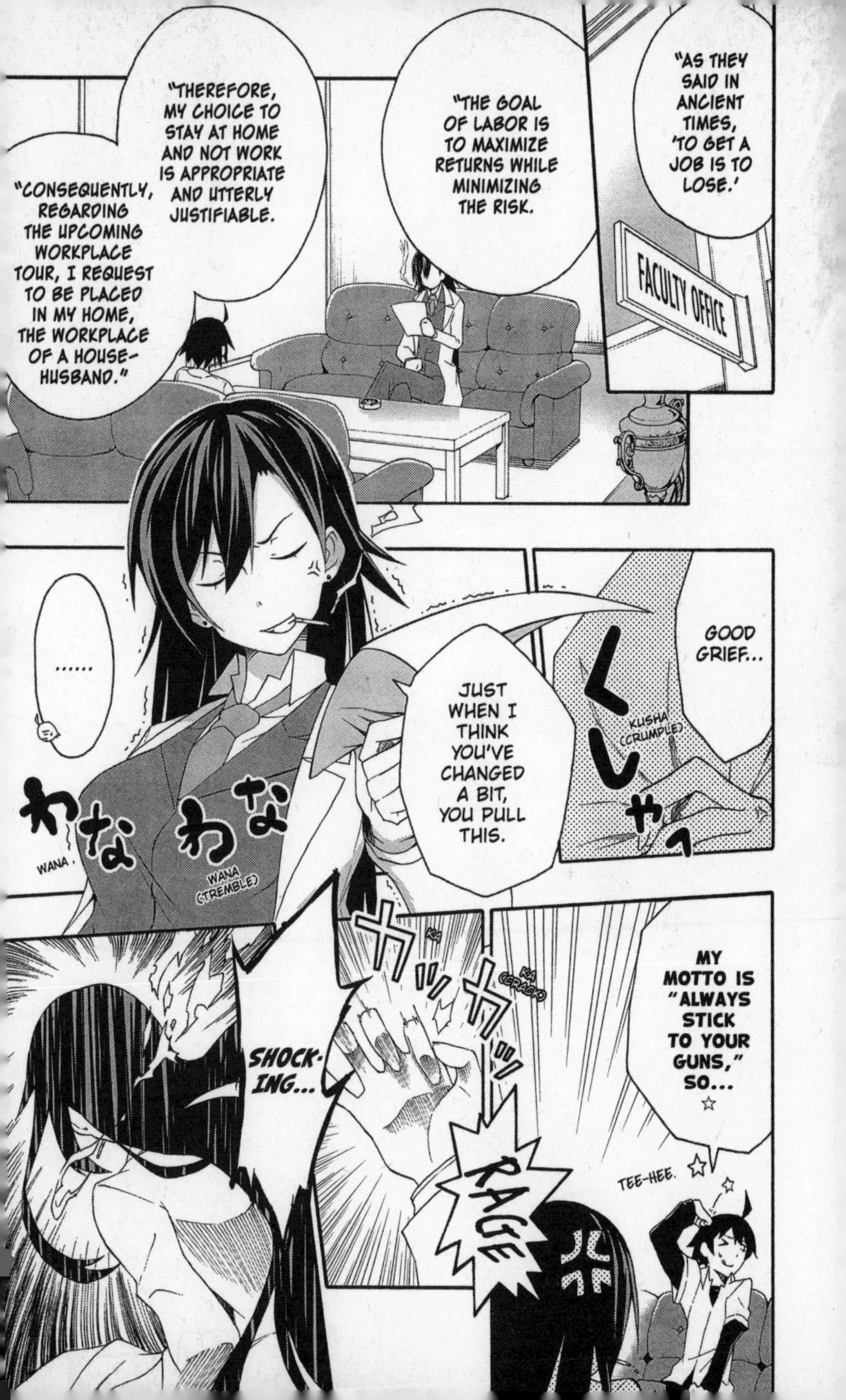

"AS THEY SAID IN ANCIENT TIMES, 'TO GET A JOB IS TO LOSE.'
FACULTY OFFICE
"THE GOAL OF LABOR IS TO MAXIMIZE RETURNS WHILE MINIMIZING THE RISK.
"THEREFORE, MY CHOICE TO STAY AT HOME AND NOT WORK IS APPROPRIATE AND UTTERLY JUSTIFIABLE.
"CONSEQUENTLY, REGARDING THE UPCOMING WORKPLACE TOUR, I REQUEST TO BE PLACED IN MY HOME, THE WORKPLACE OF A HOUSE-HUSBAND."
GOOD GRIEF...
KUSHA (CRUMPLE)
JUST WHEN I THINK YOU'VE CHANGED A BIT, YOU PULL THIS.
......
わなわな
WANA (TREMBLE)
WANA.
MY MOTTO IS "ALWAYS STICK TO YOUR GUNS," SO... ☆
TEE-HEE. ☆
KA
KA (CRACK)
RAGE
SHOCKING...

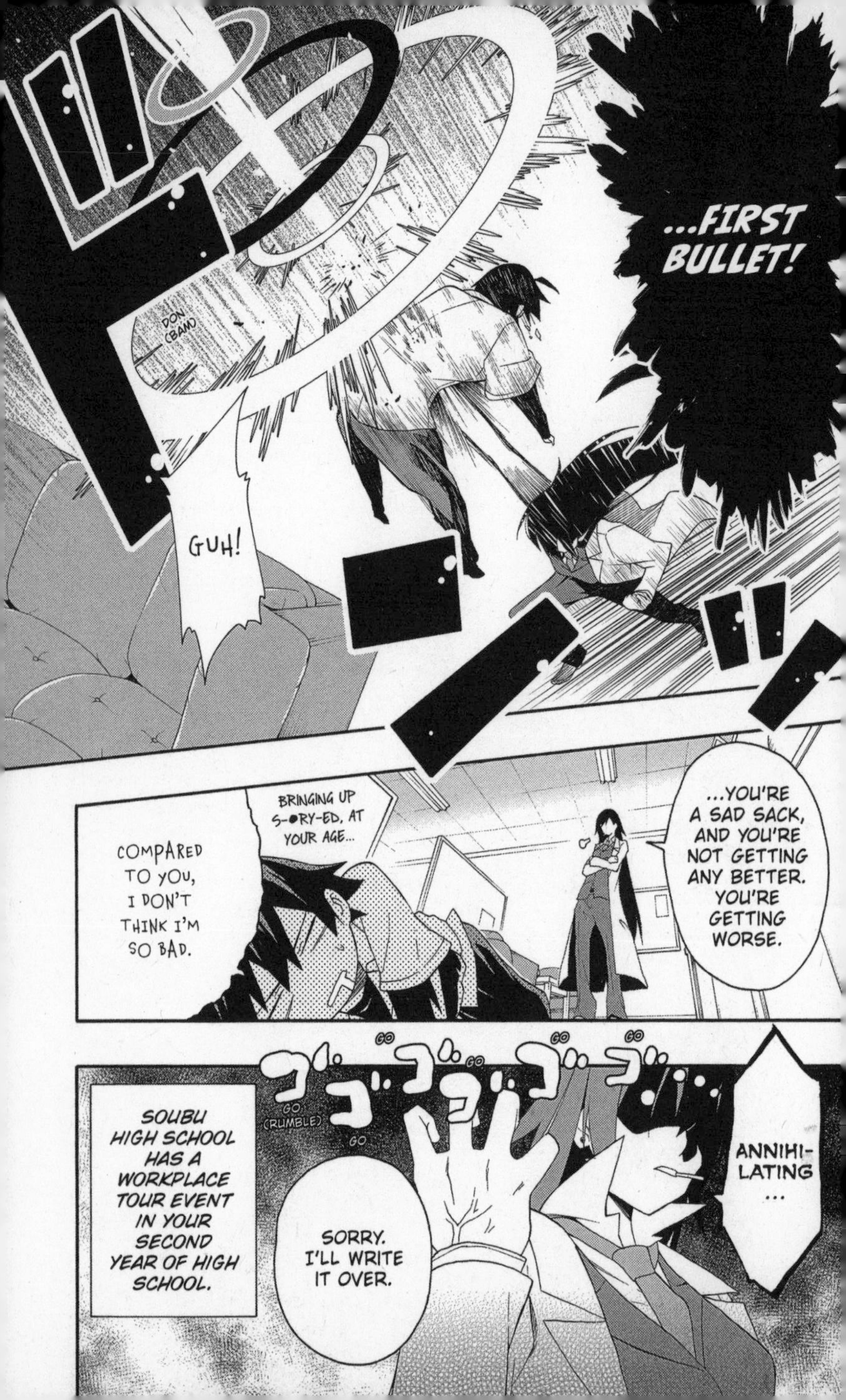
...FIRST BULLET!
DON (BAM)
GUH!
...YOU'RE A SAD SACK, AND YOU'RE NOT GETTING ANY BETTER. YOU'RE GETTING WORSE.
BRINGING UP S-●RY-ED, AT YOUR AGE...
COMPARED TO YOU, I DON'T THINK I'M SO BAD.
ANNIHI-LATING ...
GO GO GO GO GO GO (RUMBLE)
SOUBU HIGH SCHOOL HAS A WORKPLACE TOUR EVENT IN YOUR SECOND YEAR OF HIGH SCHOOL.
SORRY. I'LL WRITE IT OVER.

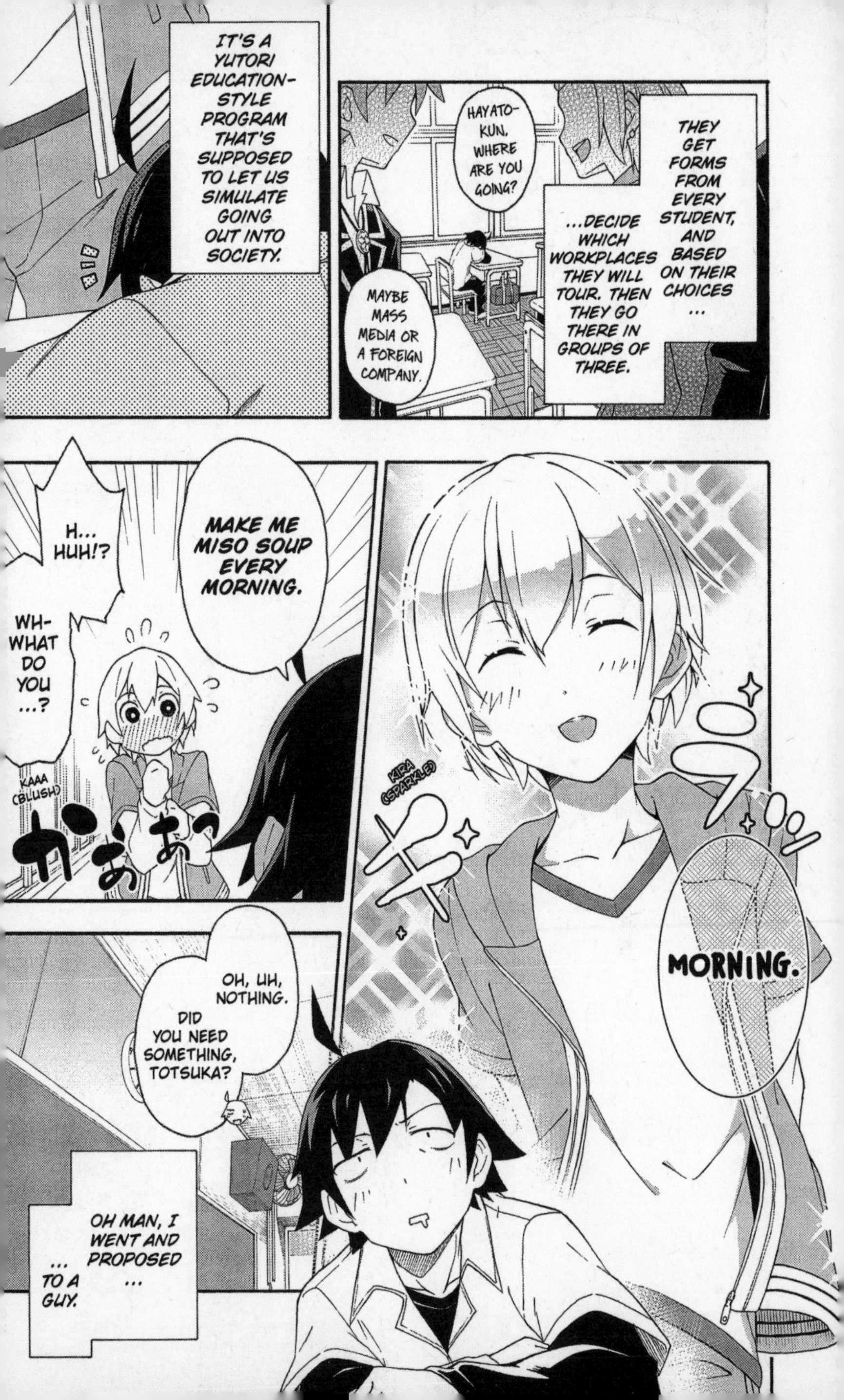
THEY GET FORMS FROM EVERY STUDENT, AND BASED ON THEIR CHOICES...
...DECIDE WHICH WORKPLACES THEY WILL TOUR. THEN THEY GO THERE IN GROUPS OF THREE.
HAYATO-KUN, WHERE ARE YOU GOING?
MAYBE MASS MEDIA OR A FOREIGN COMPANY.
IT'S A YUTORI EDUCATION-STYLE PROGRAM THAT'S SUPPOSED TO LET US SIMULATE GOING OUT INTO SOCIETY.
MORNING.
KIRA (SPARKLE)
MAKE ME MISO SOUP EVERY MORNING.
H... HUH!?
WH-WHAT DO YOU...?
KAAA (BLUSH)
OH, UH, NOTHING.
DID YOU NEED SOMETHING, TOTSUKA?
OH MAN, I WENT AND PROPOSED...
...TO A GUY.

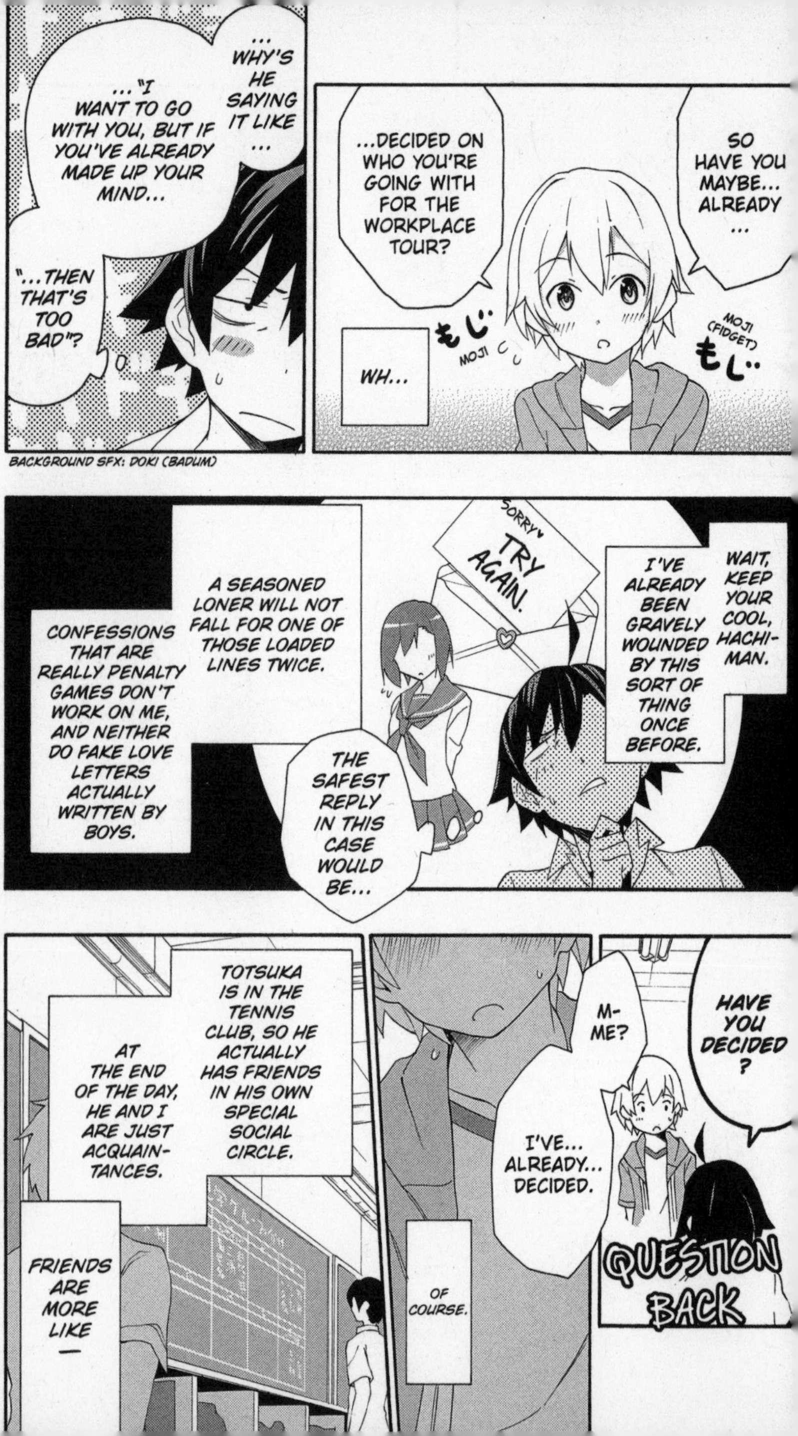
SO HAVE YOU MAYBE... ALREADY ...
...DECIDED ON WHO YOU'RE GOING WITH FOR THE WORKPLACE TOUR?
MOJI (FIDGET) もじ
もじ MOJI
WH...
... WHY'S HE SAYING IT LIKE ...
... "I WANT TO GO WITH YOU, BUT IF YOU'VE ALREADY MADE UP YOUR MIND...
"...THEN THAT'S TOO BAD"?
BACKGROUND SFX: DOKI (BADUM)
WAIT, KEEP YOUR COOL, HACHIMAN.
I'VE ALREADY BEEN GRAVELY WOUNDED BY THIS SORT OF THING ONCE BEFORE.
SORRY♥
TRY AGAIN.
A SEASONED LONER WILL NOT FALL FOR ONE OF THOSE LOADED LINES TWICE.
CONFESSIONS THAT ARE REALLY PENALTY GAMES DON'T WORK ON ME, AND NEITHER DO FAKE LOVE LETTERS ACTUALLY WRITTEN BY BOYS.
THE SAFEST REPLY IN THIS CASE WOULD BE...
HAVE YOU DECIDED?
M-ME?
QUESTION BACK
I'VE... ALREADY... DECIDED.
OF COURSE.
TOTSUKA IS IN THE TENNIS CLUB, SO HE ACTUALLY HAS FRIENDS IN HIS OWN SPECIAL SOCIAL CIRCLE.
AT THE END OF THE DAY, HE AND I ARE JUST ACQUAINTANCES.
FRIENDS ARE MORE LIKE —

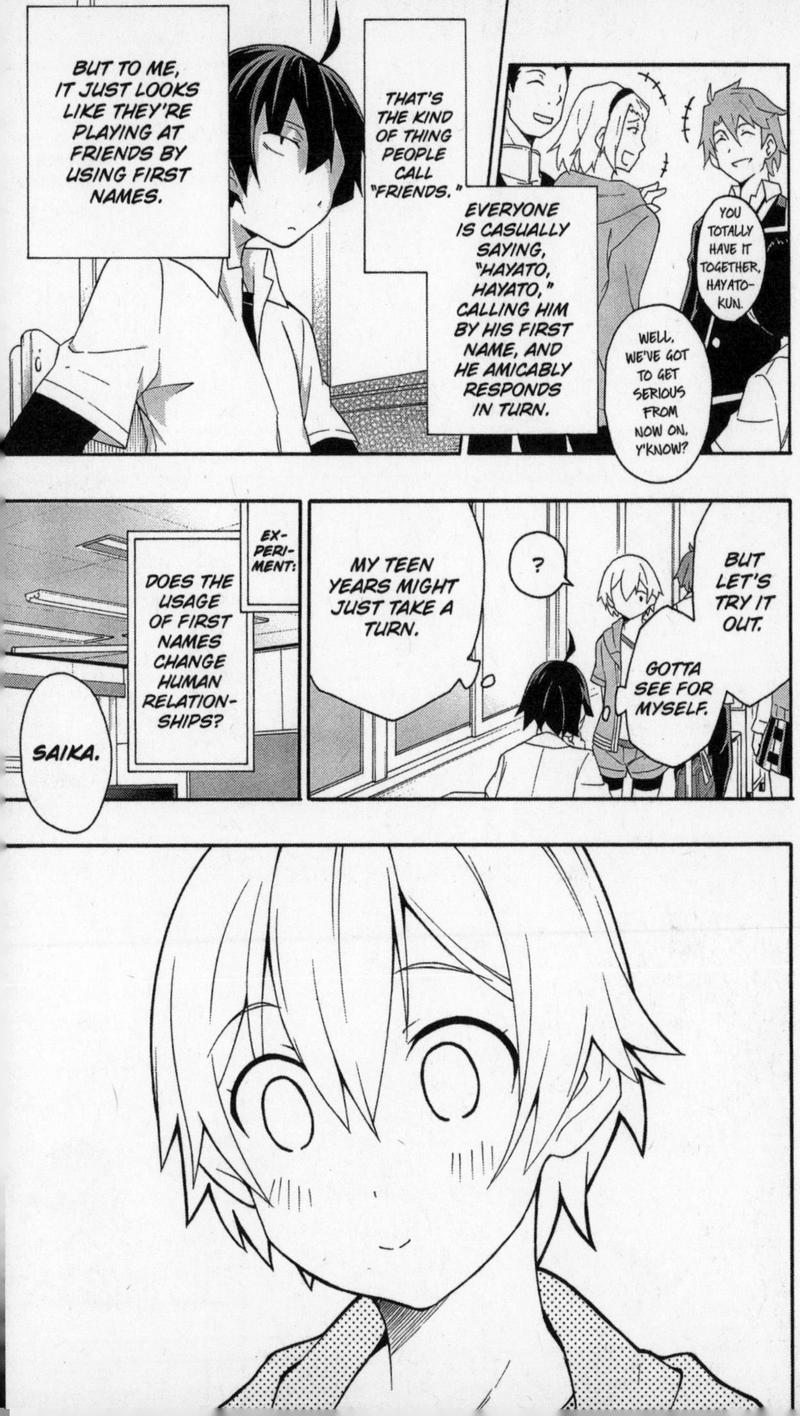
YOU TOTALLY HAVE IT TOGETHER, HAYATO-KUN.
WELL, WE'VE GOT TO GET SERIOUS FROM NOW ON, Y'KNOW?
EVERYONE IS CASUALLY SAYING, "HAYATO, HAYATO," CALLING HIM BY HIS FIRST NAME, AND HE AMICABLY RESPONDS IN TURN.
THAT'S THE KIND OF THING PEOPLE CALL "FRIENDS."
BUT TO ME, IT JUST LOOKS LIKE THEY'RE PLAYING AT FRIENDS BY USING FIRST NAMES.
BUT LET'S TRY IT OUT.
GOTTA SEE FOR MYSELF.
?
MY TEEN YEARS MIGHT JUST TAKE A TURN.
EXPERIMENT:
DOES THE USAGE OF FIRST NAMES CHANGE HUMAN RELATIONSHIPS?
SAIKA.

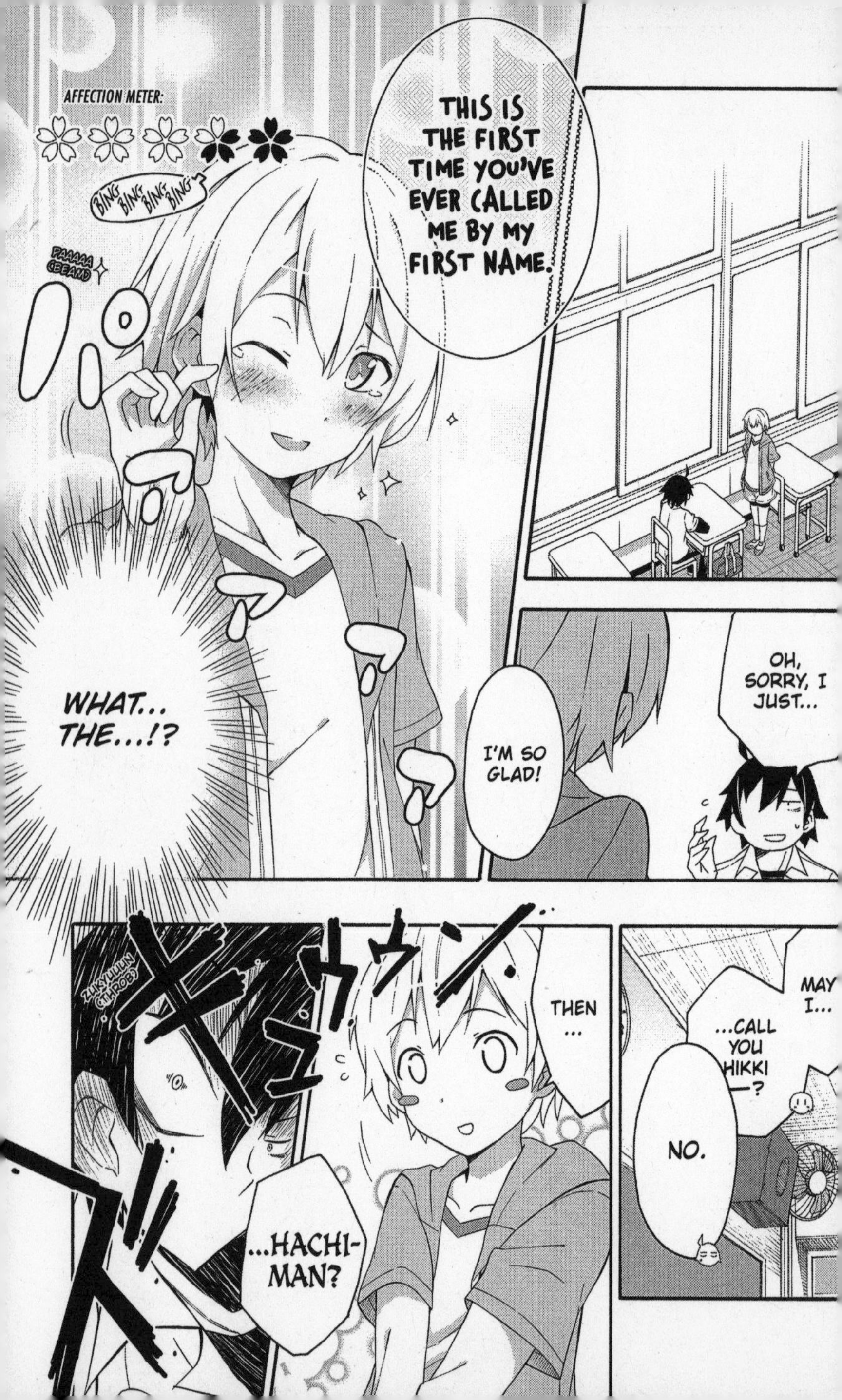
OH, SORRY, I JUST...
I'M SO GLAD!
THIS IS THE FIRST TIME YOU'VE EVER CALLED ME BY MY FIRST NAME.
AFFECTION METER:
BING BING BING BING
PAAAAA (BEAM)
WHAT... THE...!?
MAY I...
...CALL YOU HIKKI—?
NO.
THEN ...
...HACHI-MAN?
ZUKYUUUN (THROB)

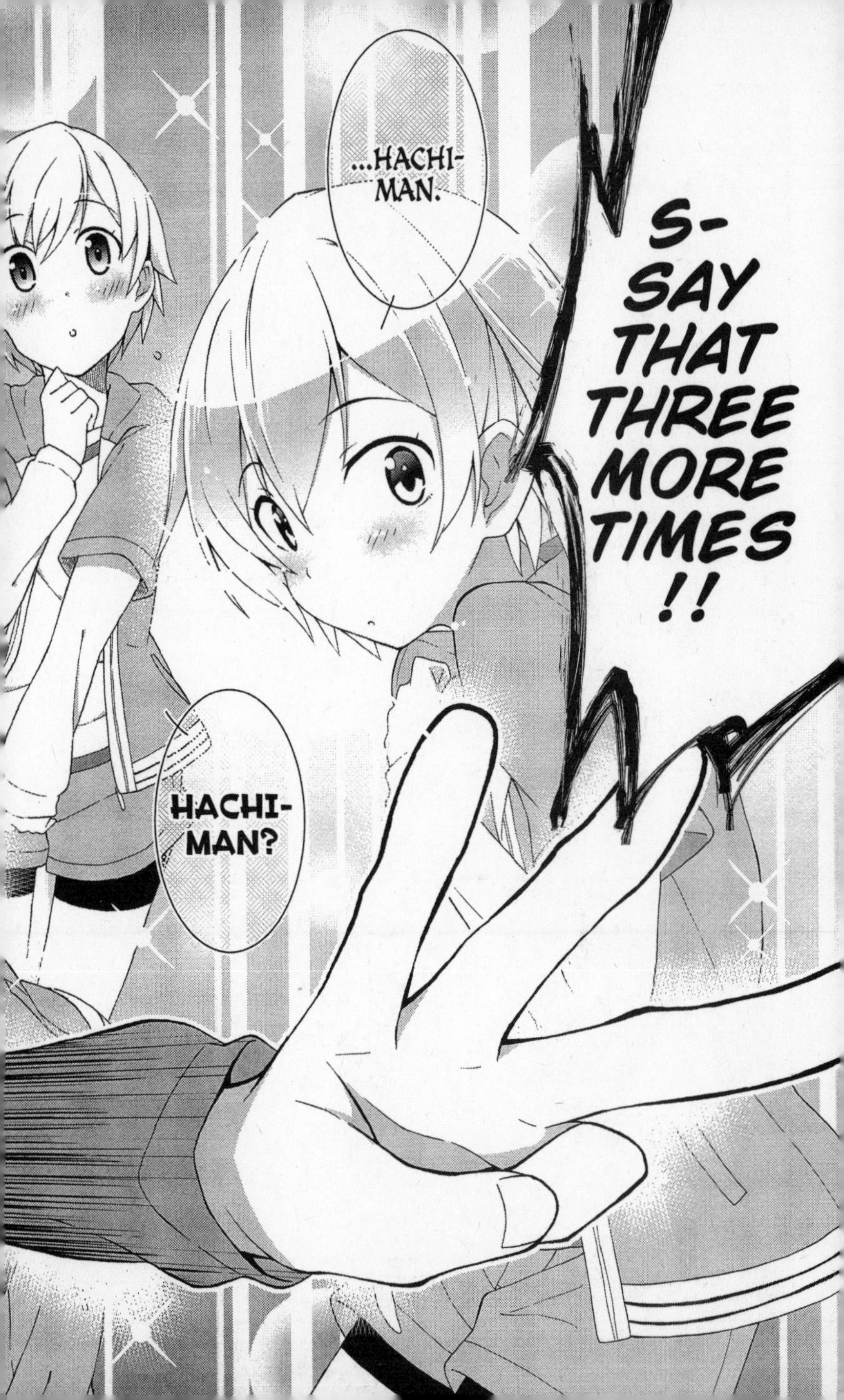
...HACHI-MAN.
S-SAY THAT THREE MORE TIMES!!
HACHI-MAN?

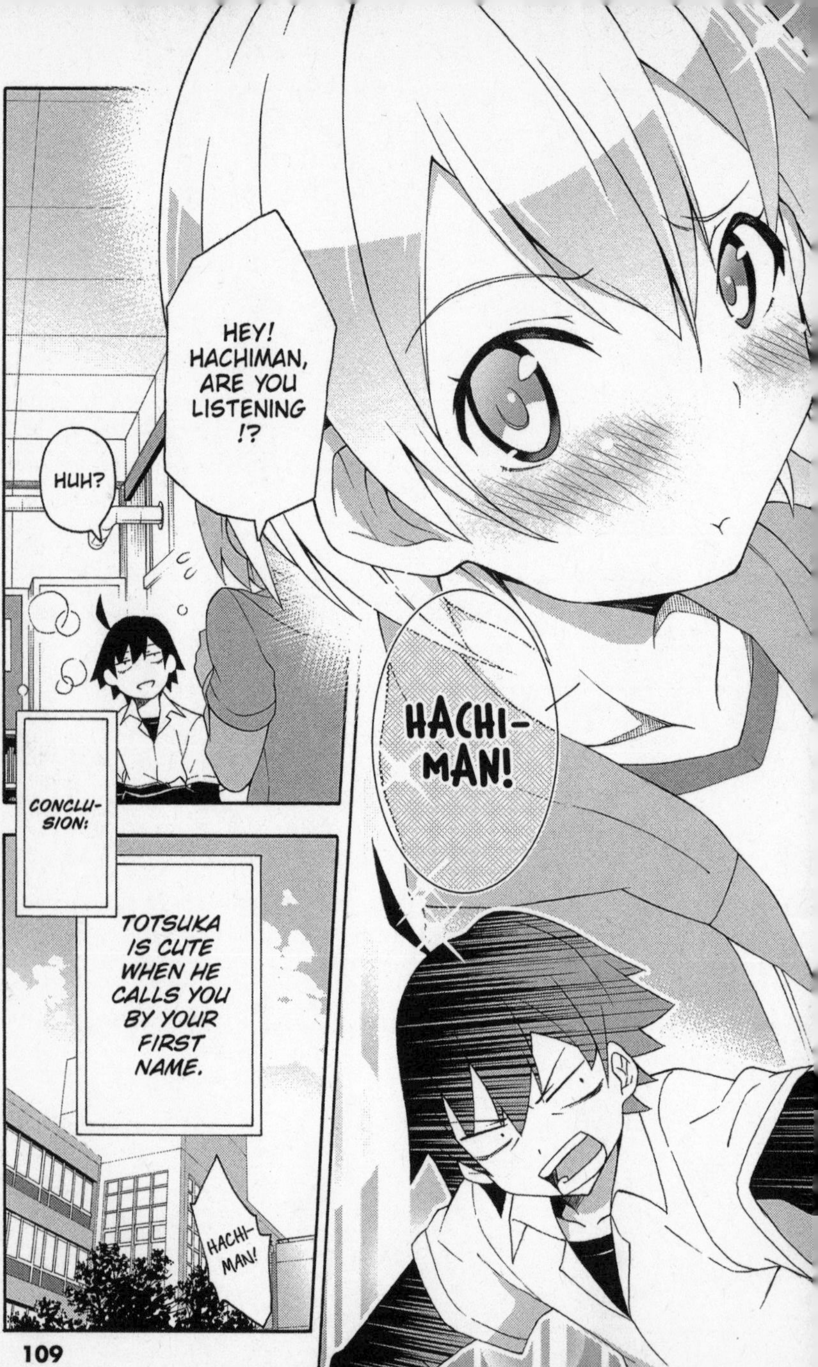
HACHI-MAN!
HEY! HACHIMAN, ARE YOU LISTENING!?
HUH?
CONCLUSION:
TOTSUKA IS CUTE WHEN HE CALLS YOU BY YOUR FIRST NAME.
HACHI-MAN!

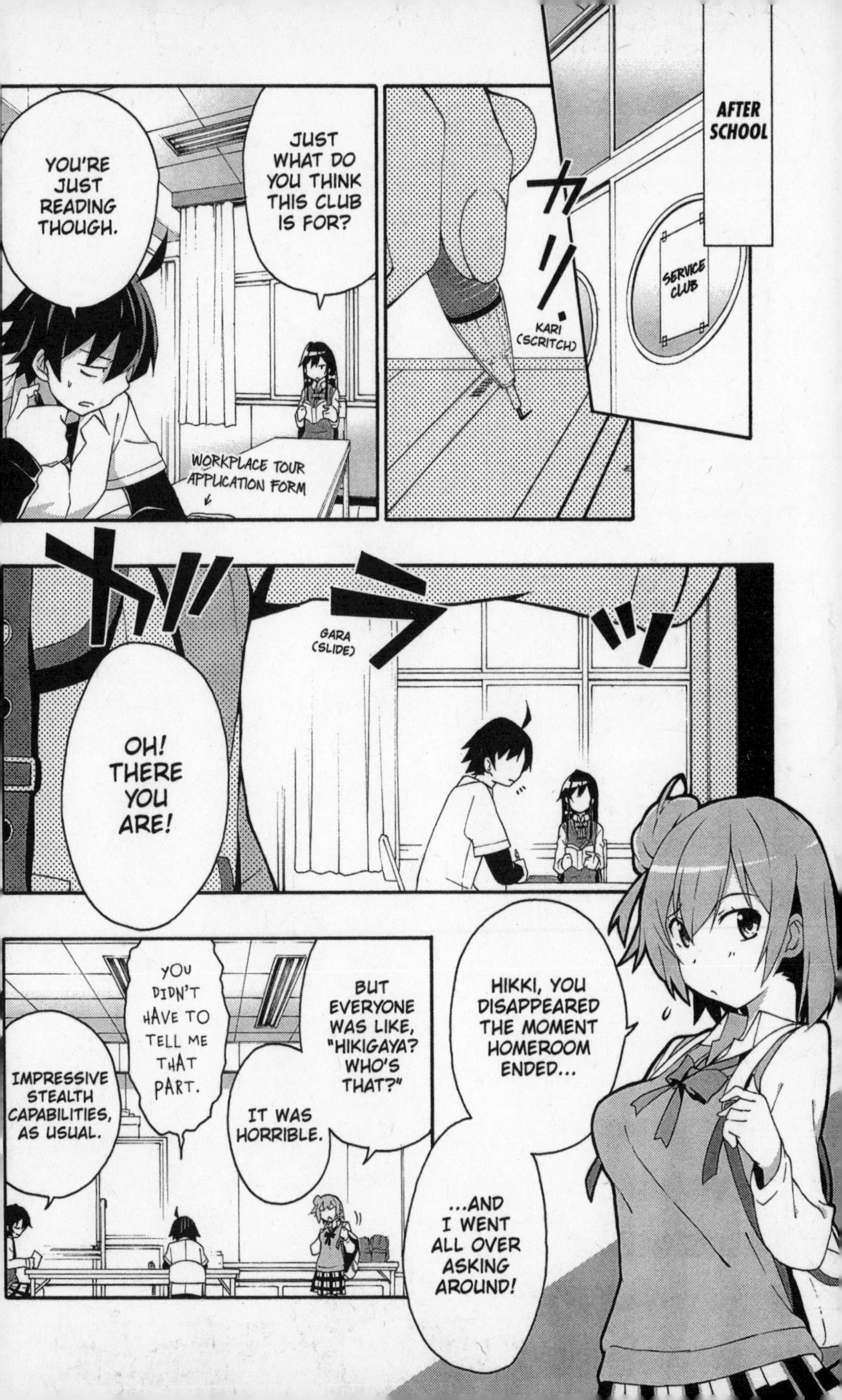
AFTER SCHOOL
SERVICE CLUB
KARI (SCRITCH)
JUST WHAT DO YOU THINK THIS CLUB IS FOR?
YOU'RE JUST READING THOUGH.
WORKPLACE TOUR APPLICATION FORM
GARA (SLIDE)
OH! THERE YOU ARE!
HIKKI, YOU DISAPPEARED THE MOMENT HOMEROOM ENDED...
...AND I WENT ALL OVER ASKING AROUND!
BUT EVERYONE WAS LIKE, "HIKIGAYA? WHO'S THAT?"
IT WAS HORRIBLE.
YOU DIDN'T HAVE TO TELL ME THAT PART.
IMPRESSIVE STEALTH CAPABILITIES, AS USUAL.

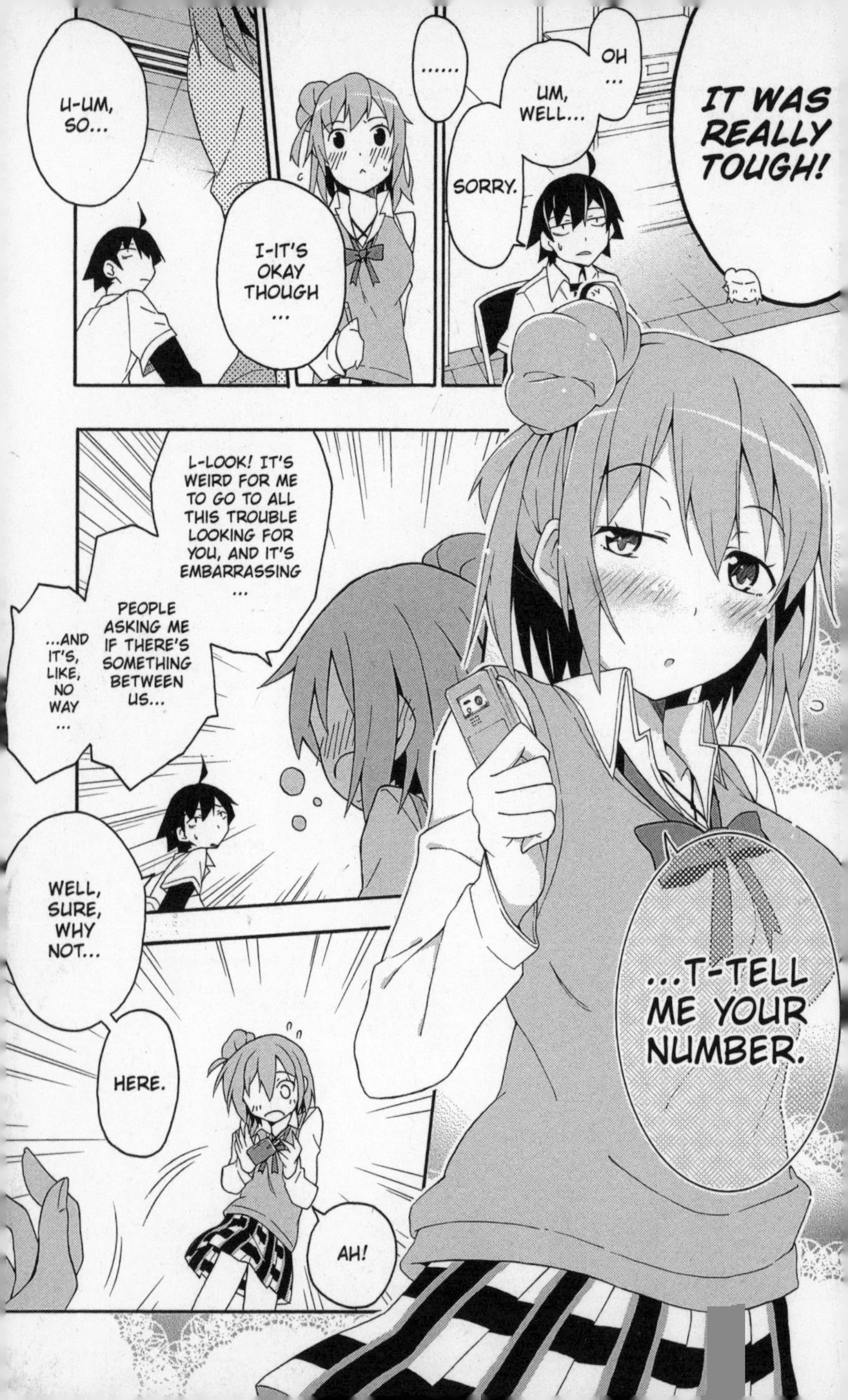
IT WAS REALLY TOUGH!
OH ...
UM, WELL...
SORRY.
......
I-IT'S OKAY THOUGH ...
U-UM, SO...
...T-TELL ME YOUR NUMBER.
L-LOOK! IT'S WEIRD FOR ME TO GO TO ALL THIS TROUBLE LOOKING FOR YOU, AND IT'S EMBARRASSING ...
PEOPLE ASKING ME IF THERE'S SOMETHING BETWEEN US...
...AND IT'S, LIKE, NO WAY ...
WELL, SURE, WHY NOT...
HERE.
AH!

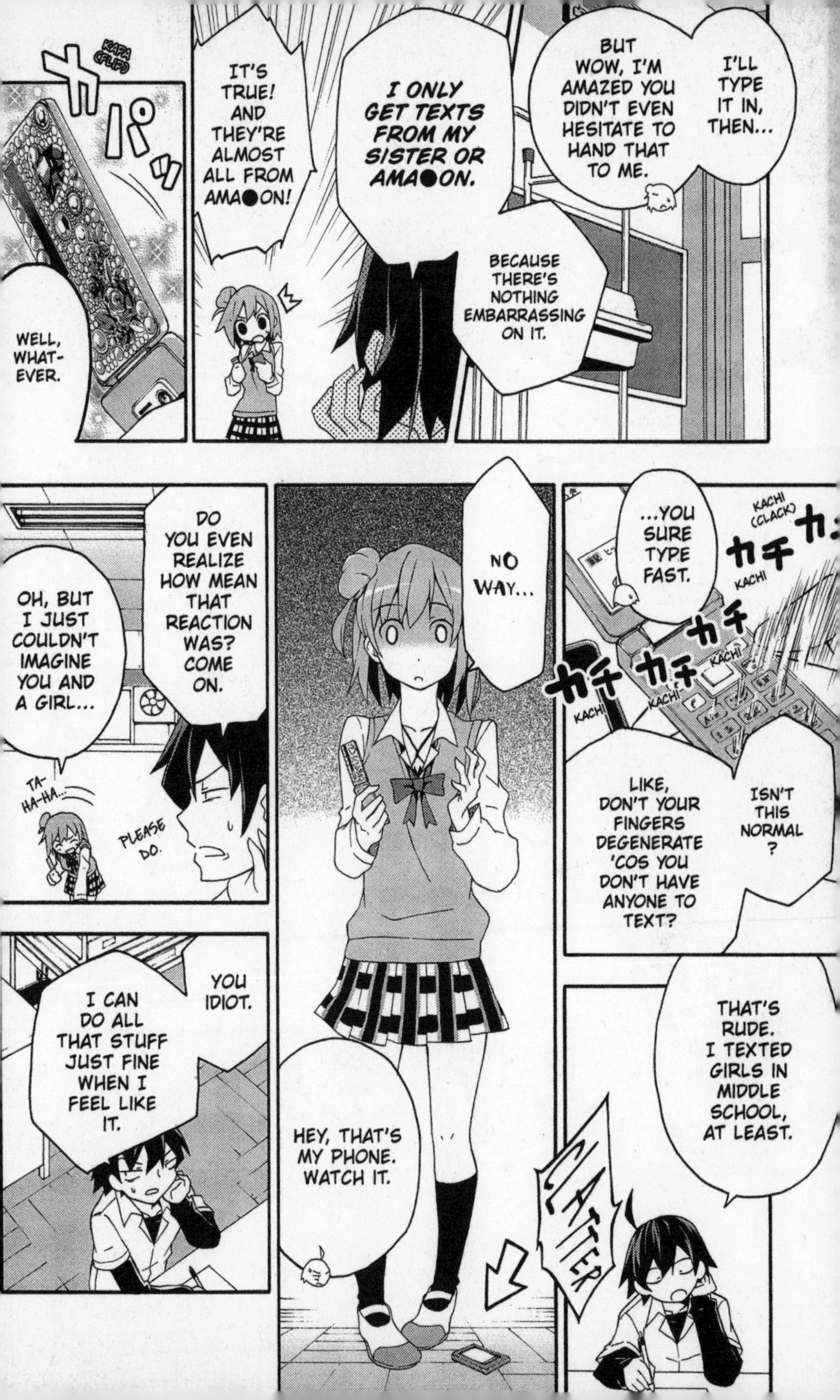
I'LL TYPE IT IN, THEN...
BUT WOW, I'M AMAZED YOU DIDN'T EVEN HESITATE TO HAND THAT TO ME.
BECAUSE THERE'S NOTHING EMBARRASSING ON IT.
I ONLY GET TEXTS FROM MY SISTER OR AMA●ON.
IT'S TRUE! AND THEY'RE ALMOST ALL FROM AMA●ON!
KAPA (FLIP)
WELL, WHAT-EVER.
KACHI (CLACK)
...YOU SURE TYPE FAST.
KACHI
KACHI
KACHI
KACHI
ISN'T THIS NORMAL?
LIKE, DON'T YOUR FINGERS DEGENERATE 'COS YOU DON'T HAVE ANYONE TO TEXT?
THAT'S RUDE. I TEXTED GIRLS IN MIDDLE SCHOOL, AT LEAST.
CLATTER
NO WAY...
HEY, THAT'S MY PHONE. WATCH IT.
DO YOU EVEN REALIZE HOW MEAN THAT REACTION WAS? COME ON.
OH, BUT I JUST COULDN'T IMAGINE YOU AND A GIRL...
TA-HA-HA...
PLEASE DO.
YOU IDIOT.
I CAN DO ALL THAT STUFF JUST FINE WHEN I FEEL LIKE IT.

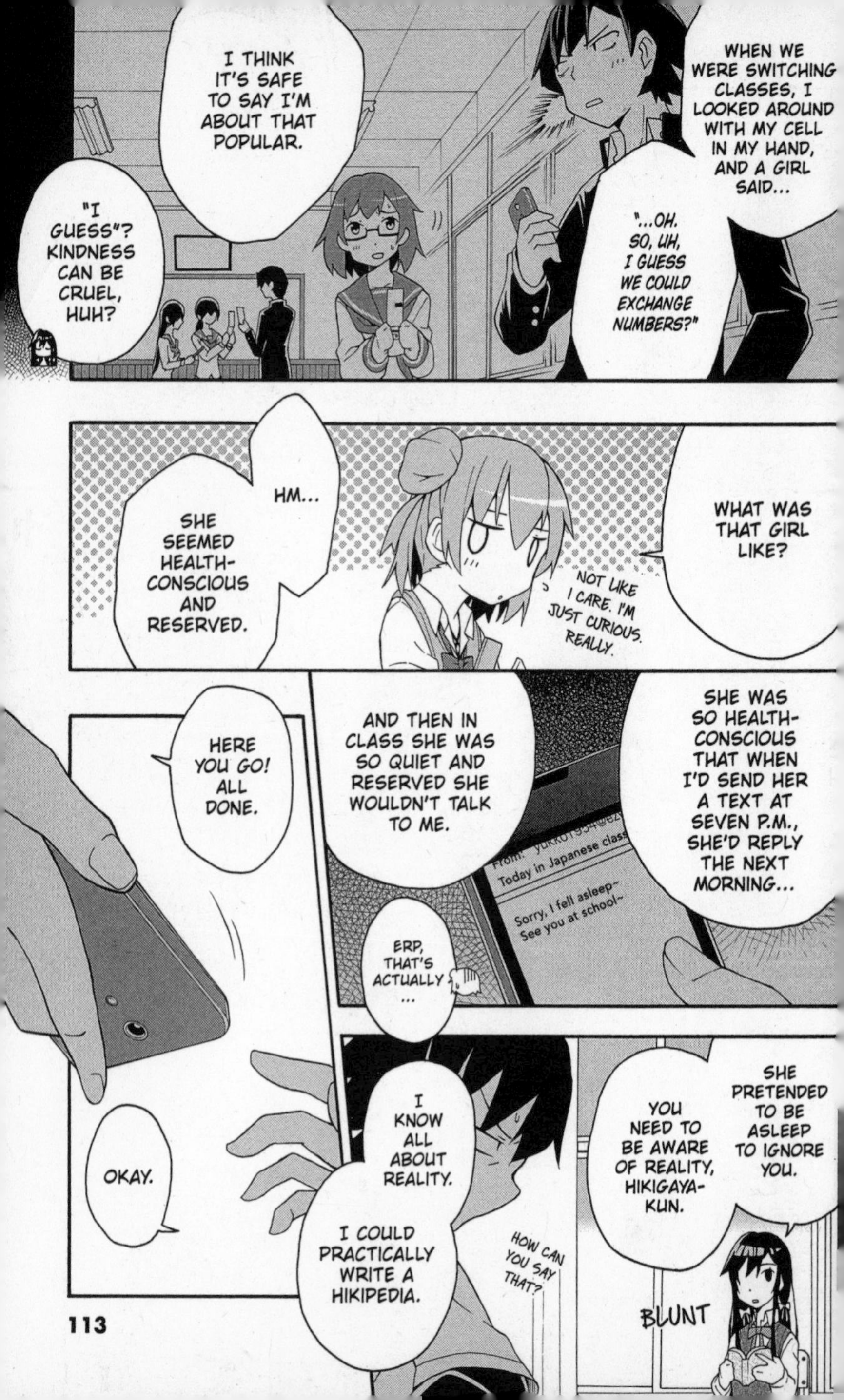
WHEN WE WERE SWITCHING CLASSES, I LOOKED AROUND WITH MY CELL IN MY HAND, AND A GIRL SAID...
"...OH. SO, UH, I GUESS WE COULD EXCHANGE NUMBERS?"
I THINK IT'S SAFE TO SAY I'M ABOUT THAT POPULAR.
"I GUESS"? KINDNESS CAN BE CRUEL, HUH?
WHAT WAS THAT GIRL LIKE?
NOT LIKE I CARE. I'M JUST CURIOUS. REALLY.
HM...
SHE SEEMED HEALTH-CONSCIOUS AND RESERVED.
SHE WAS SO HEALTH-CONSCIOUS THAT WHEN I'D SEND HER A TEXT AT SEVEN P.M., SHE'D REPLY THE NEXT MORNING...
AND THEN IN CLASS SHE WAS SO QUIET AND RESERVED SHE WOULDN'T TALK TO ME.
Today in Japanese class
Sorry, I fell asleep~ See you at school~
ERP, THAT'S ACTUALLY ...
SHE PRETENDED TO BE ASLEEP TO IGNORE YOU.
YOU NEED TO BE AWARE OF REALITY, HIKIGAYA-KUN.
BLUNT
I KNOW ALL ABOUT REALITY.
HOW CAN YOU SAY THAT?
I COULD PRACTICALLY WRITE A HIKIPEDIA.
HERE YOU GO! ALL DONE.
OKAY.

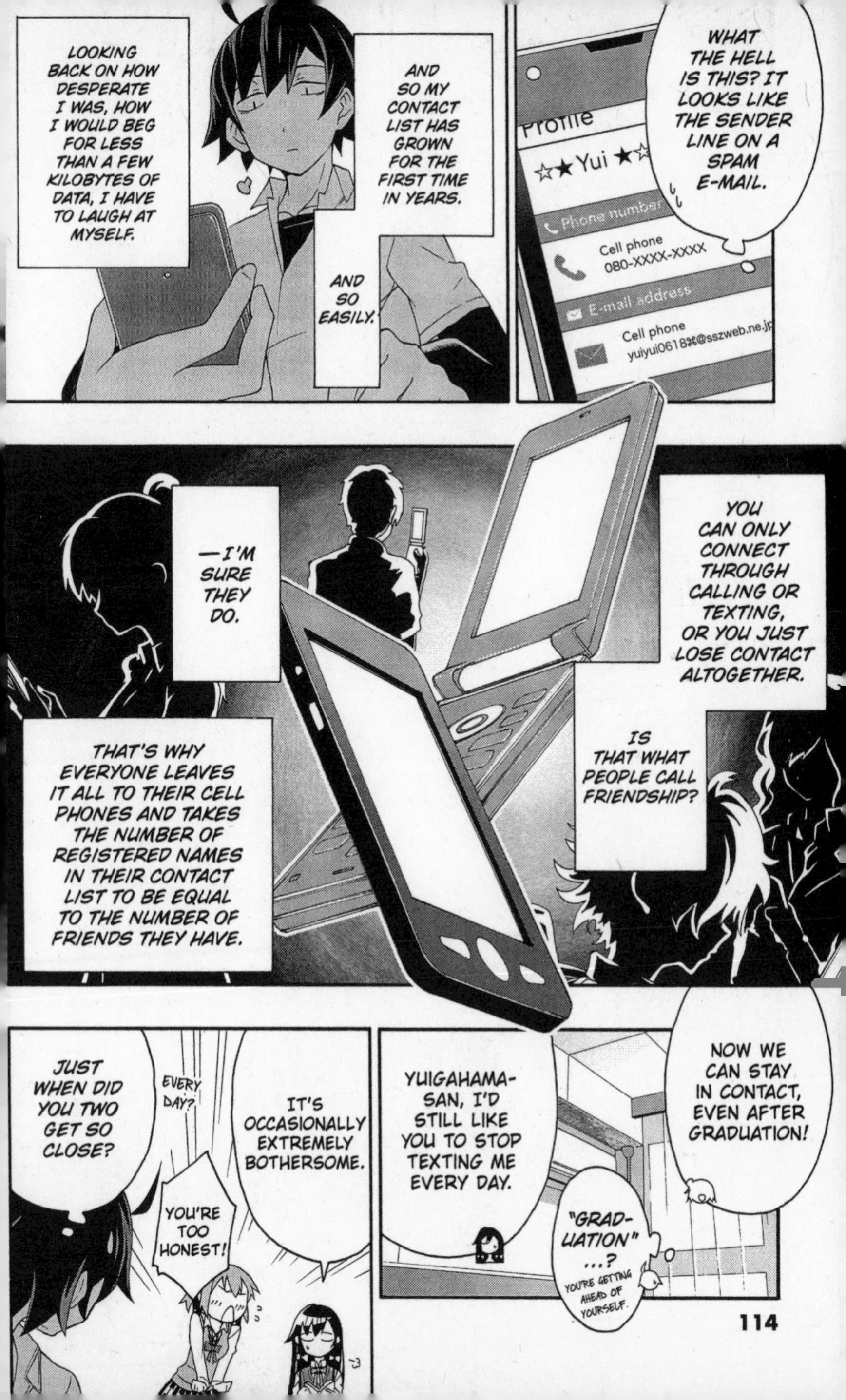
WHAT THE HELL IS THIS? IT LOOKS LIKE THE SENDER LINE ON A SPAM E-MAIL.
Profile
☆★Yui★☆
Phone number
Cell phone
080-XXXX-XXXX
E-mail address
Cell phone
yuiyui0618⌘@sszweb.ne.jp
AND SO MY CONTACT LIST HAS GROWN FOR THE FIRST TIME IN YEARS.
LOOKING BACK ON HOW DESPERATE I WAS, HOW I WOULD BEG FOR LESS THAN A FEW KILOBYTES OF DATA, I HAVE TO LAUGH AT MYSELF.
AND SO EASILY.
YOU CAN ONLY CONNECT THROUGH CALLING OR TEXTING, OR YOU JUST LOSE CONTACT ALTOGETHER.
IS THAT WHAT PEOPLE CALL FRIENDSHIP?
—I'M SURE THEY DO.
THAT'S WHY EVERYONE LEAVES IT ALL TO THEIR CELL PHONES AND TAKES THE NUMBER OF REGISTERED NAMES IN THEIR CONTACT LIST TO BE EQUAL TO THE NUMBER OF FRIENDS THEY HAVE.
NOW WE CAN STAY IN CONTACT, EVEN AFTER GRADUATION!
YUIGAHAMA-SAN, I'D STILL LIKE YOU TO STOP TEXTING ME EVERY DAY.
"GRAD-UATION" ...?
YOU'RE GETTING AHEAD OF YOURSELF.
IT'S OCCASIONALLY EXTREMELY BOTHERSOME.
EVERY DAY?
JUST WHEN DID YOU TWO GET SO CLOSE?
YOU'RE TOO HONEST!

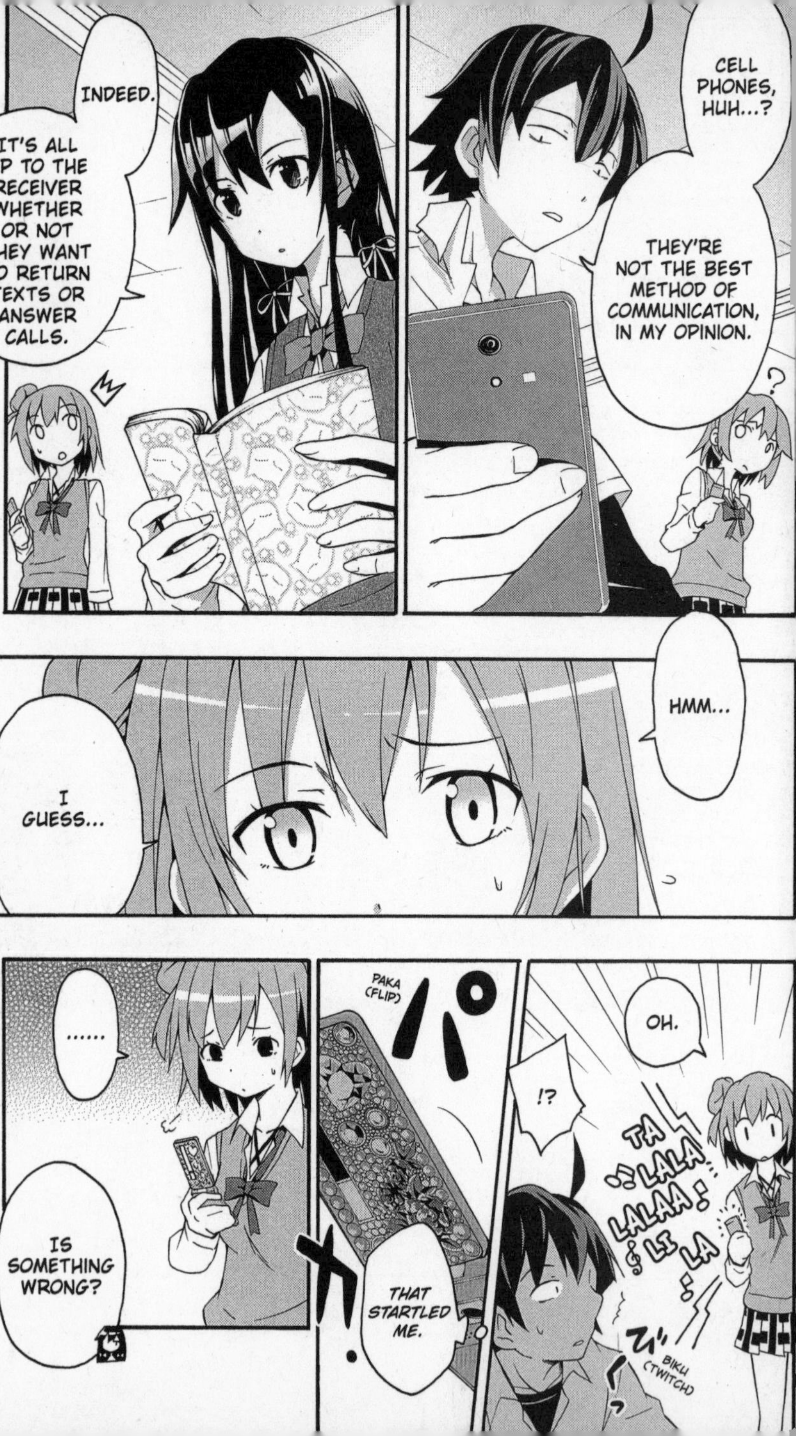
CELL PHONES, HUH...?
THEY'RE NOT THE BEST METHOD OF COMMUNICATION, IN MY OPINION.
INDEED.
IT'S ALL UP TO THE RECEIVER WHETHER OR NOT THEY WANT TO RETURN TEXTS OR ANSWER CALLS.
HMM...
I GUESS...
OH.
!?
TA LALA LALAA! LI LA
BIKU (TWITCH)
PAKA (FLIP)
THAT STARTLED ME.
......
IS SOMETHING WRONG?

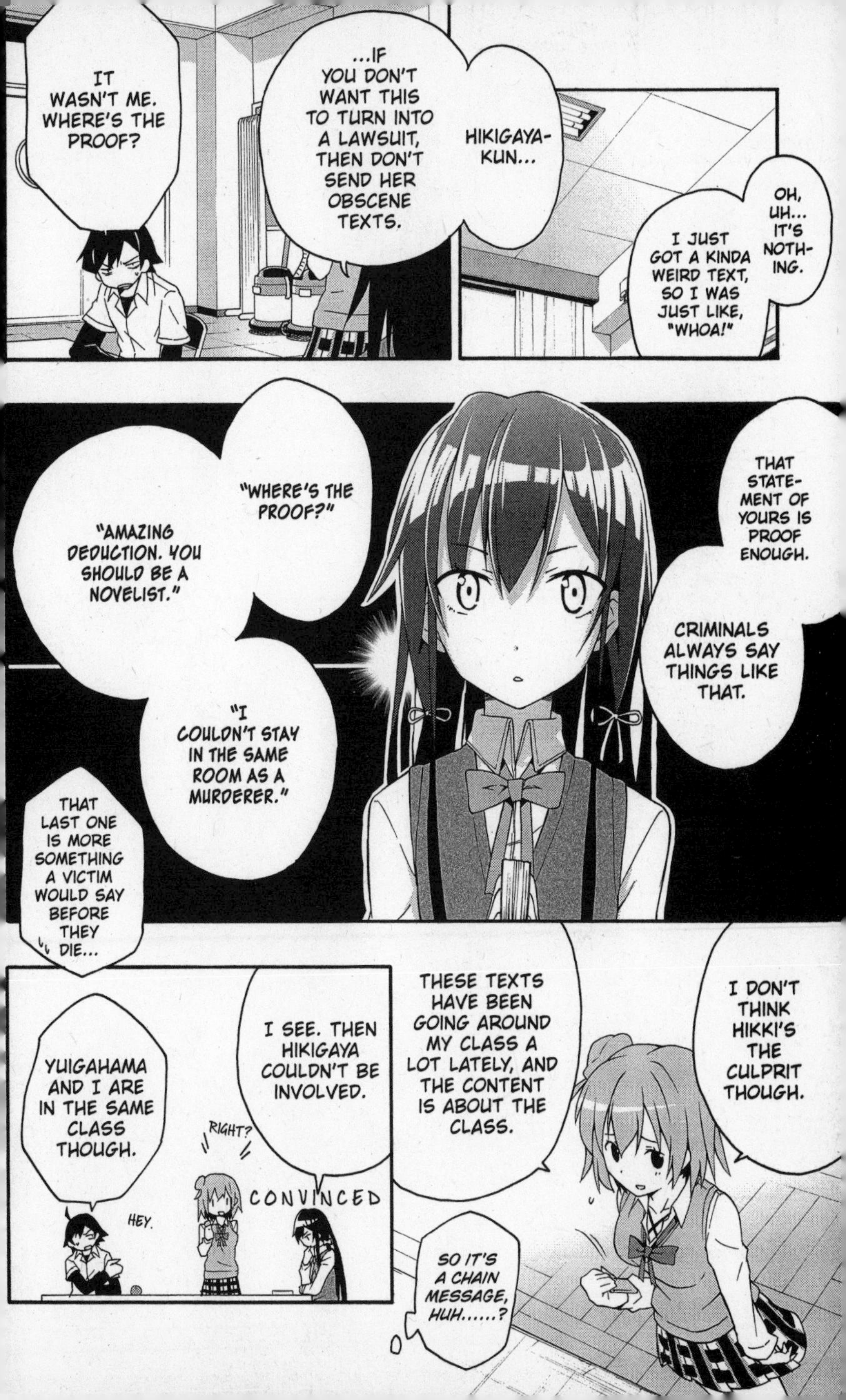
OH, UH... IT'S NOTHING.
I JUST GOT A KINDA WEIRD TEXT, SO I WAS JUST LIKE, "WHOA!"
HIKIGAYA-KUN...
...IF YOU DON'T WANT THIS TO TURN INTO A LAWSUIT, THEN DON'T SEND HER OBSCENE TEXTS.
IT WASN'T ME. WHERE'S THE PROOF?
THAT STATEMENT OF YOURS IS PROOF ENOUGH.
CRIMINALS ALWAYS SAY THINGS LIKE THAT.
"WHERE'S THE PROOF?"
"AMAZING DEDUCTION. YOU SHOULD BE A NOVELIST."
"I COULDN'T STAY IN THE SAME ROOM AS A MURDERER."
THAT LAST ONE IS MORE SOMETHING A VICTIM WOULD SAY BEFORE THEY DIE...
I DON'T THINK HIKKI'S THE CULPRIT THOUGH.
THESE TEXTS HAVE BEEN GOING AROUND MY CLASS A LOT LATELY, AND THE CONTENT IS ABOUT THE CLASS.
SO IT'S A CHAIN MESSAGE, HUH......?
I SEE. THEN HIKIGAYA COULDN'T BE INVOLVED.
RIGHT?
CONVINCED
YUIGAHAMA AND I ARE IN THE SAME CLASS THOUGH.
HEY.

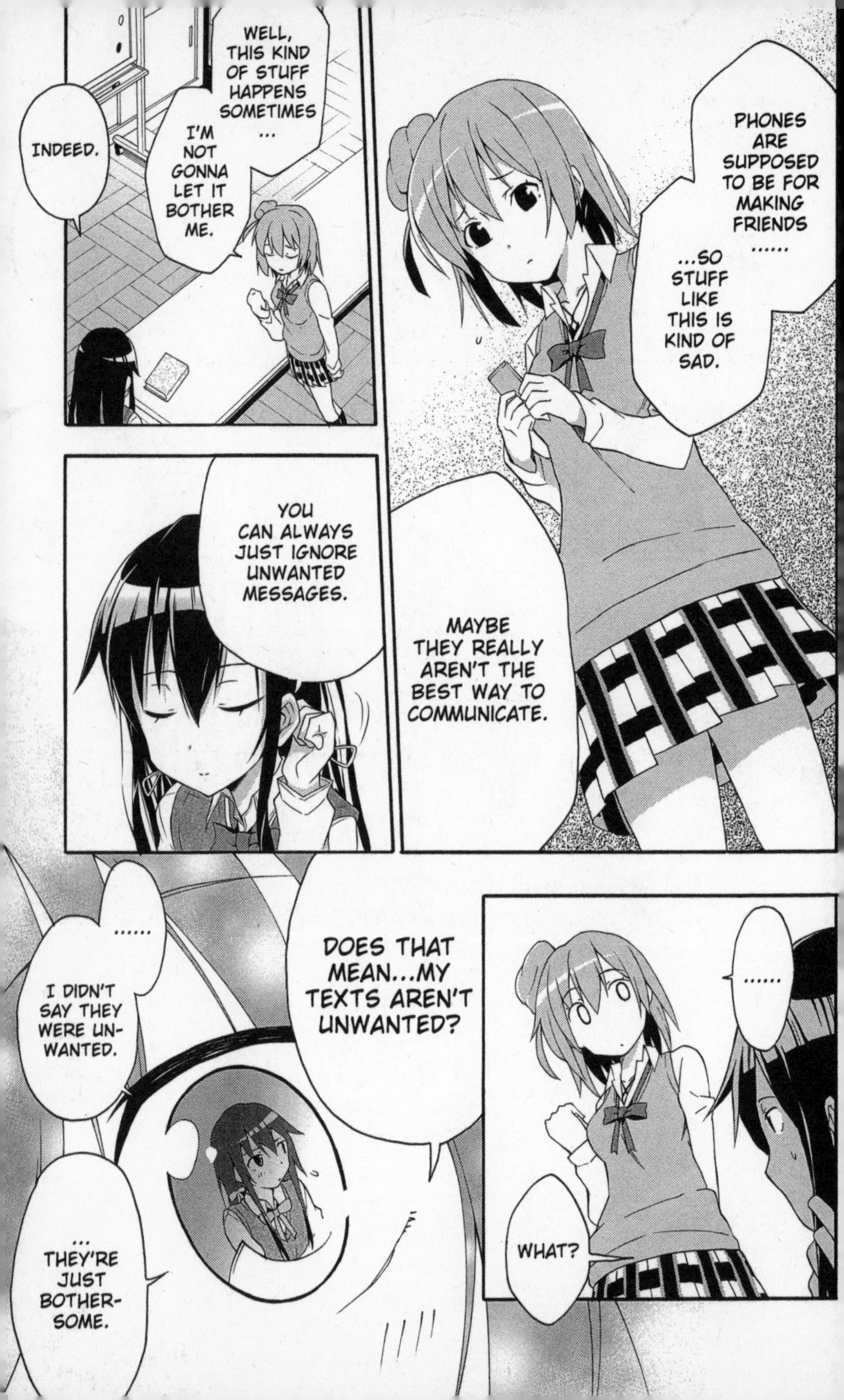
WELL, THIS KIND OF STUFF HAPPENS SOMETIMES...
I'M NOT GONNA LET IT BOTHER ME.
INDEED.
PHONES ARE SUPPOSED TO BE FOR MAKING FRIENDS......
...SO STUFF LIKE THIS IS KIND OF SAD.
MAYBE THEY REALLY AREN'T THE BEST WAY TO COMMUNICATE.
YOU CAN ALWAYS JUST IGNORE UNWANTED MESSAGES.
......
WHAT?
DOES THAT MEAN...MY TEXTS AREN'T UNWANTED?
......
I DIDN'T SAY THEY WERE UN-WANTED.
...THEY'RE JUST BOTHER-SOME.

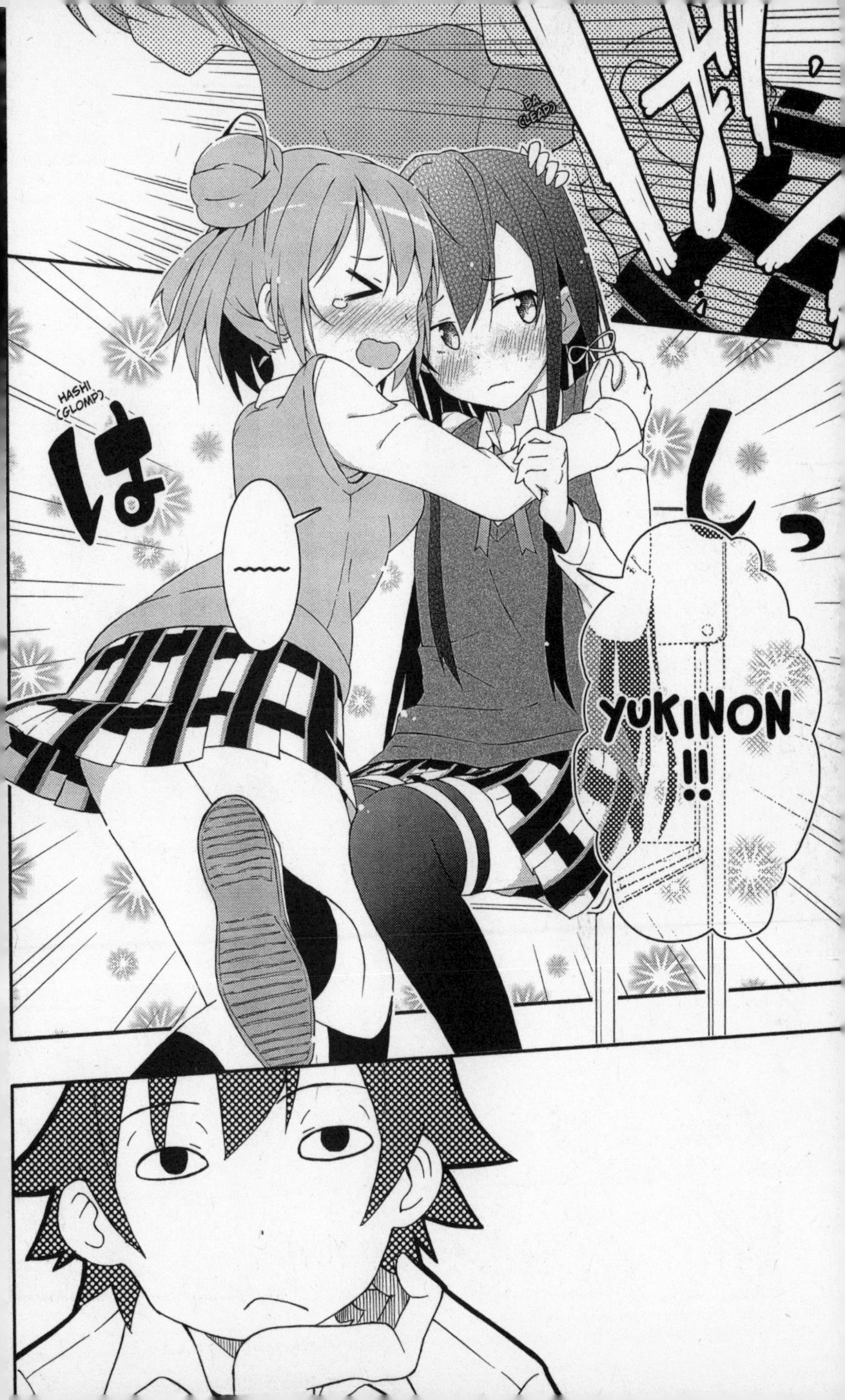

BA (LEAP)
HASHI (GLOMP)
はしっ
YUKINON!!
......

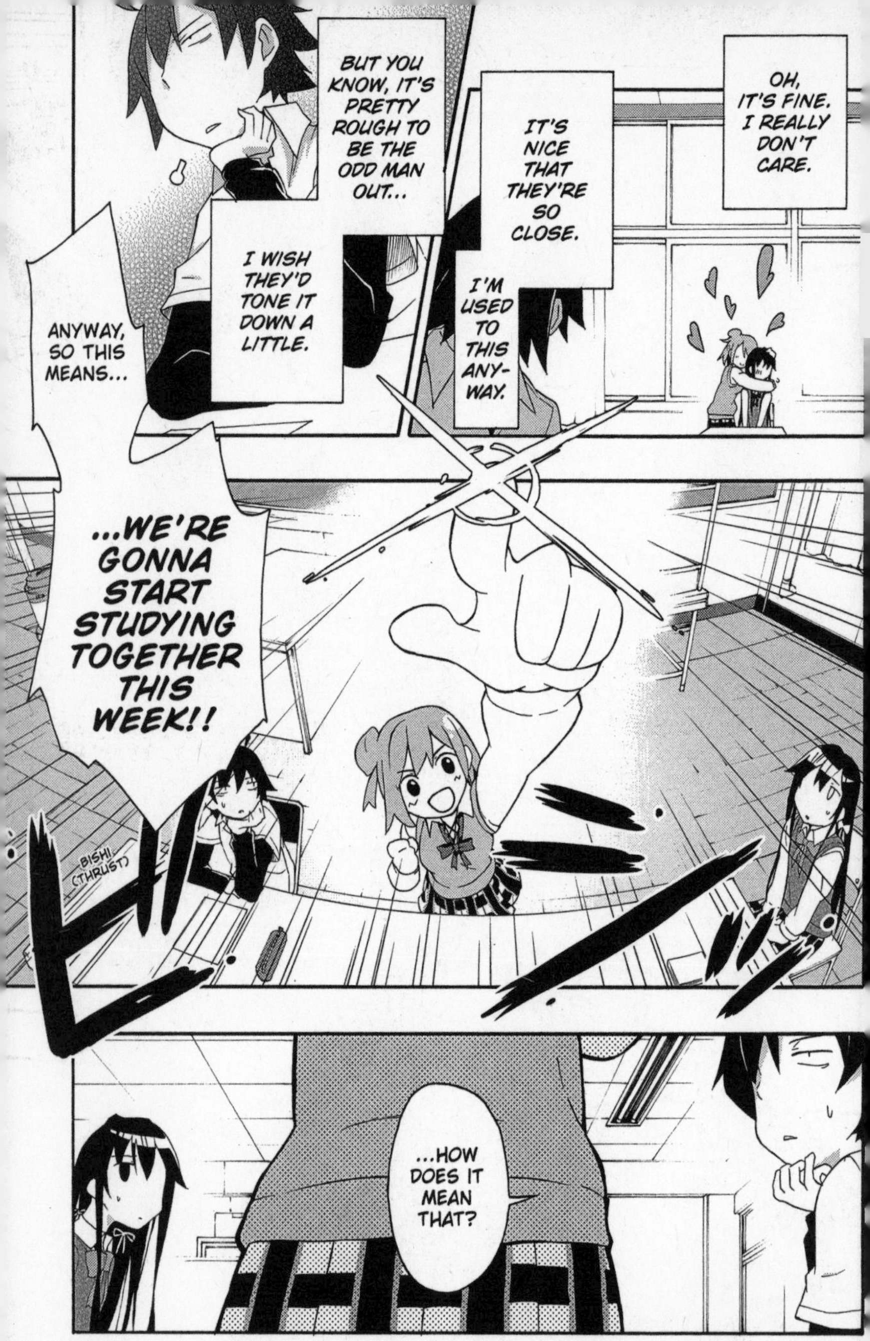
OH, IT'S FINE. I REALLY DON'T CARE.
IT'S NICE THAT THEY'RE SO CLOSE.
I'M USED TO THIS ANYWAY.
BUT YOU KNOW, IT'S PRETTY ROUGH TO BE THE ODD MAN OUT...
I WISH THEY'D TONE IT DOWN A LITTLE.
ANYWAY, SO THIS MEANS...
...WE'RE GONNA START STUDYING TOGETHER THIS WEEK!!
BISHI (THRUST)
...HOW DOES IT MEAN THAT?

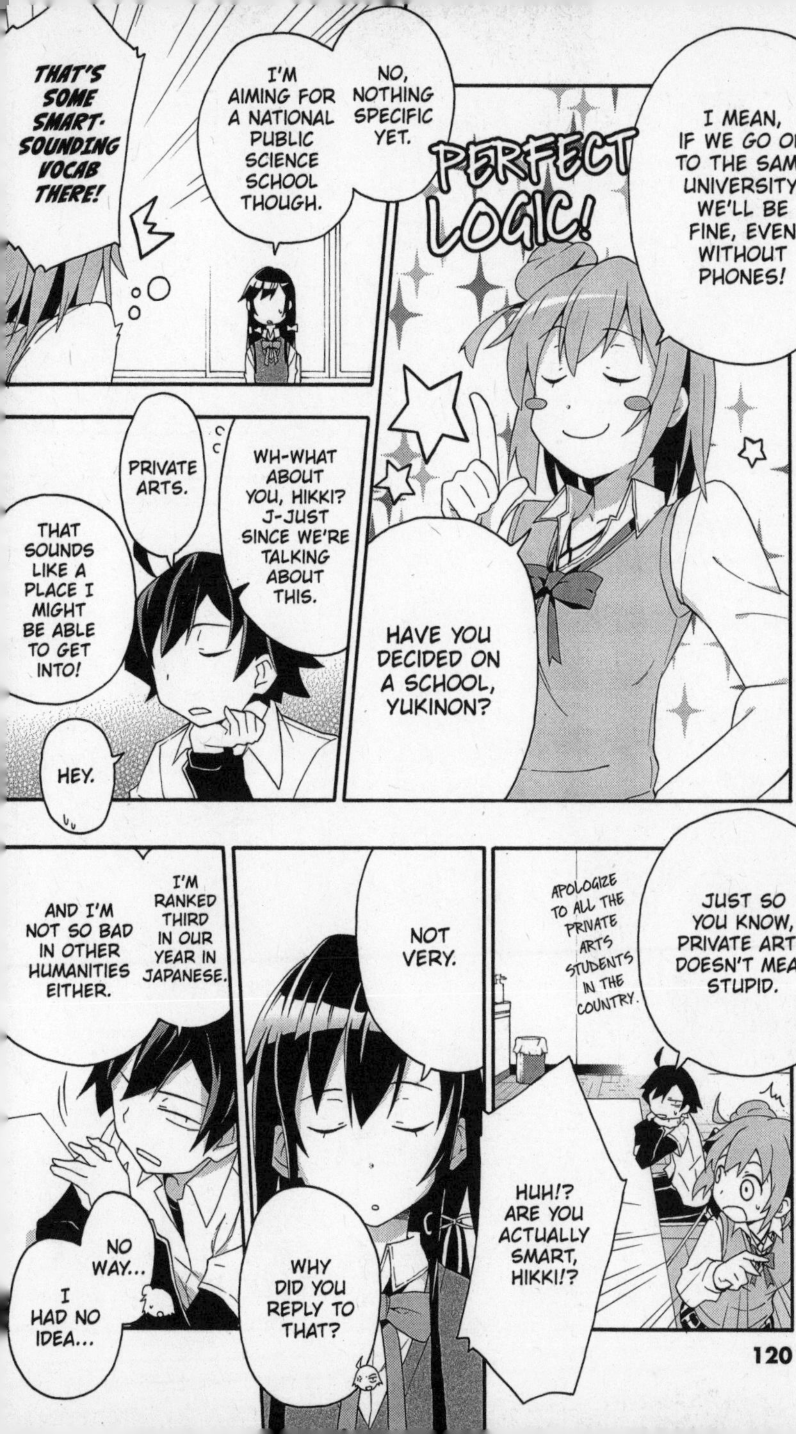
I MEAN, IF WE GO ON TO THE SAME UNIVERSITY, WE'LL BE FINE, EVEN WITHOUT PHONES!
PERFECT LOGIC!
HAVE YOU DECIDED ON A SCHOOL, YUKINON?
NO, NOTHING SPECIFIC YET.
I'M AIMING FOR A NATIONAL PUBLIC SCIENCE SCHOOL THOUGH.
THAT'S SOME SMART-SOUNDING VOCAB THERE!
WH-WHAT ABOUT YOU, HIKKI? J-JUST SINCE WE'RE TALKING ABOUT THIS.
PRIVATE ARTS.
THAT SOUNDS LIKE A PLACE I MIGHT BE ABLE TO GET INTO!
HEY.
JUST SO YOU KNOW, PRIVATE ARTS DOESN'T MEAN STUPID.
APOLOGIZE TO ALL THE PRIVATE ARTS STUDENTS IN THE COUNTRY.
HUH!? ARE YOU ACTUALLY SMART, HIKKI!?
NOT VERY.
WHY DID YOU REPLY TO THAT?
I'M RANKED THIRD IN OUR YEAR IN JAPANESE.
AND I'M NOT SO BAD IN OTHER HUMANITIES EITHER.
NO WAY... I HAD NO IDEA...

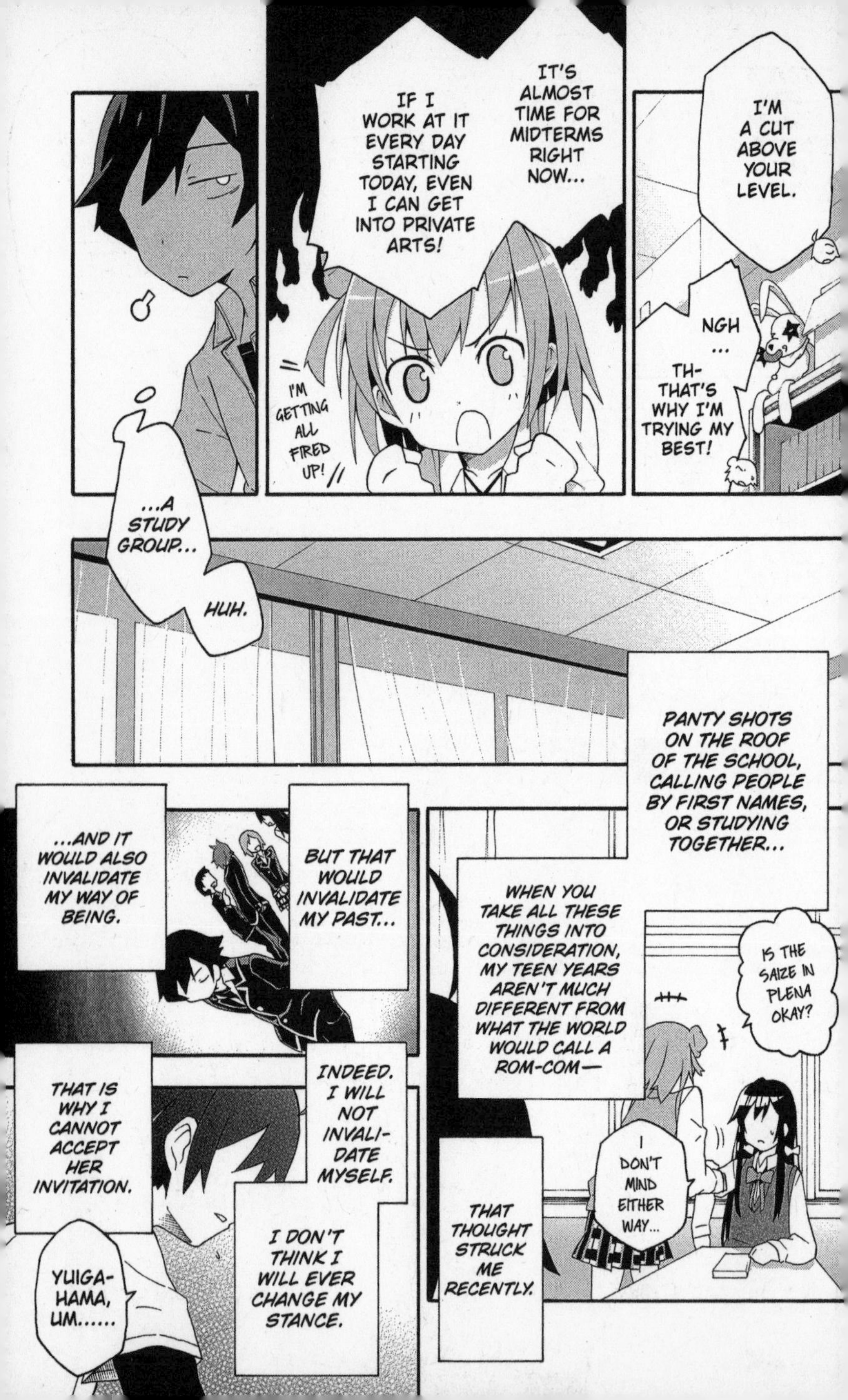
I'M A CUT ABOVE YOUR LEVEL.
NGH...
TH-THAT'S WHY I'M TRYING MY BEST!
IT'S ALMOST TIME FOR MIDTERMS RIGHT NOW...
IF I WORK AT IT EVERY DAY STARTING TODAY, EVEN I CAN GET INTO PRIVATE ARTS!
I'M GETTING ALL FIRED UP!
...A STUDY GROUP...
HUH.
PANTY SHOTS ON THE ROOF OF THE SCHOOL, CALLING PEOPLE BY FIRST NAMES, OR STUDYING TOGETHER...
WHEN YOU TAKE ALL THESE THINGS INTO CONSIDERATION, MY TEEN YEARS AREN'T MUCH DIFFERENT FROM WHAT THE WORLD WOULD CALL A ROM-COM—
IS THE SAIZE IN PLENA OKAY?
I DON'T MIND EITHER WAY...
THAT THOUGHT STRUCK ME RECENTLY.
BUT THAT WOULD INVALIDATE MY PAST...
...AND IT WOULD ALSO INVALIDATE MY WAY OF BEING.
INDEED. I WILL NOT INVALIDATE MYSELF.
THAT IS WHY I CANNOT ACCEPT HER INVITATION.
I DON'T THINK I WILL EVER CHANGE MY STANCE.
YUIGAHAMA, UM......

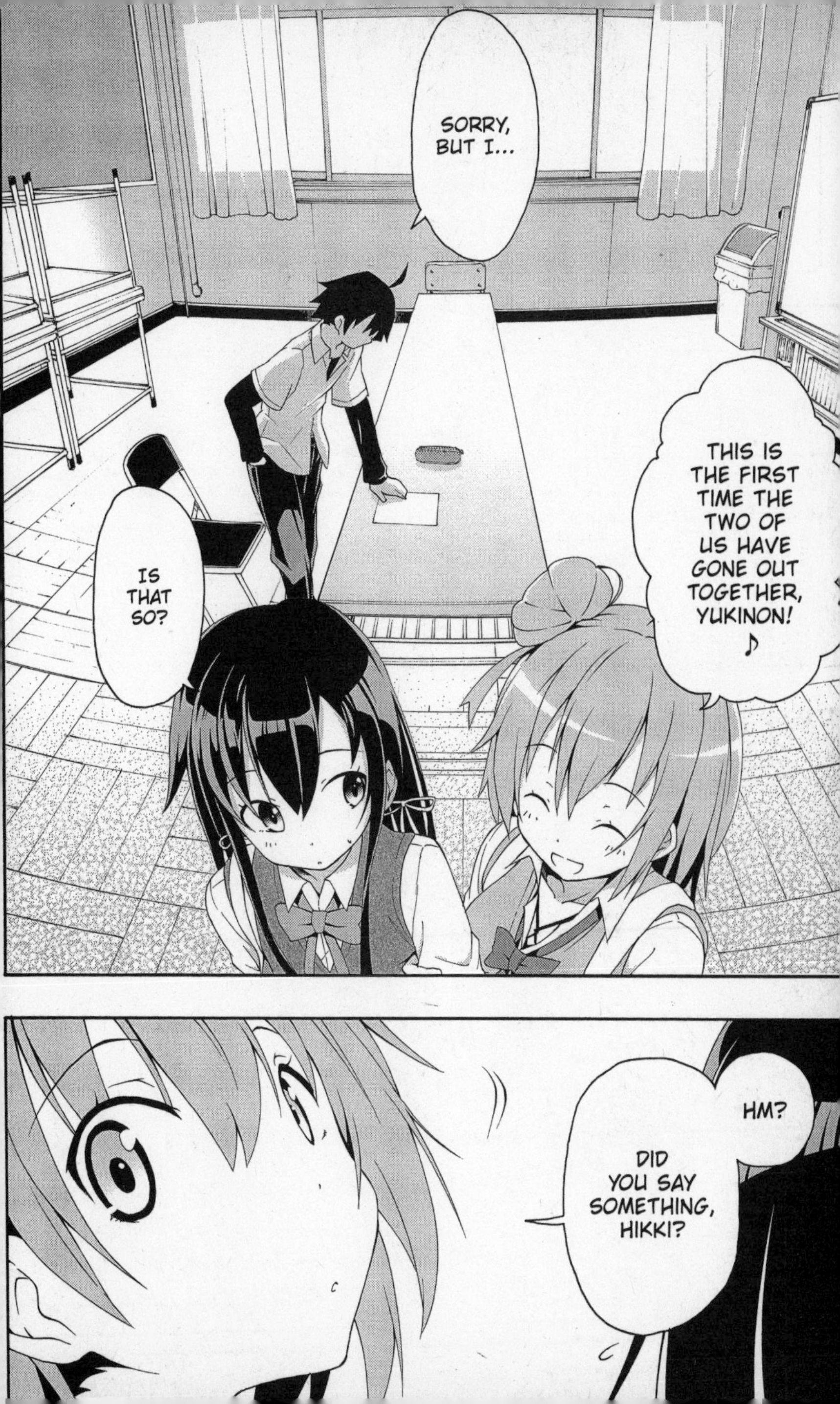
SORRY, BUT I...
THIS IS THE FIRST TIME THE TWO OF US HAVE GONE OUT TOGETHER, YUKINON! ♪
IS THAT SO?
HM?
DID YOU SAY SOMETHING, HIKKI?

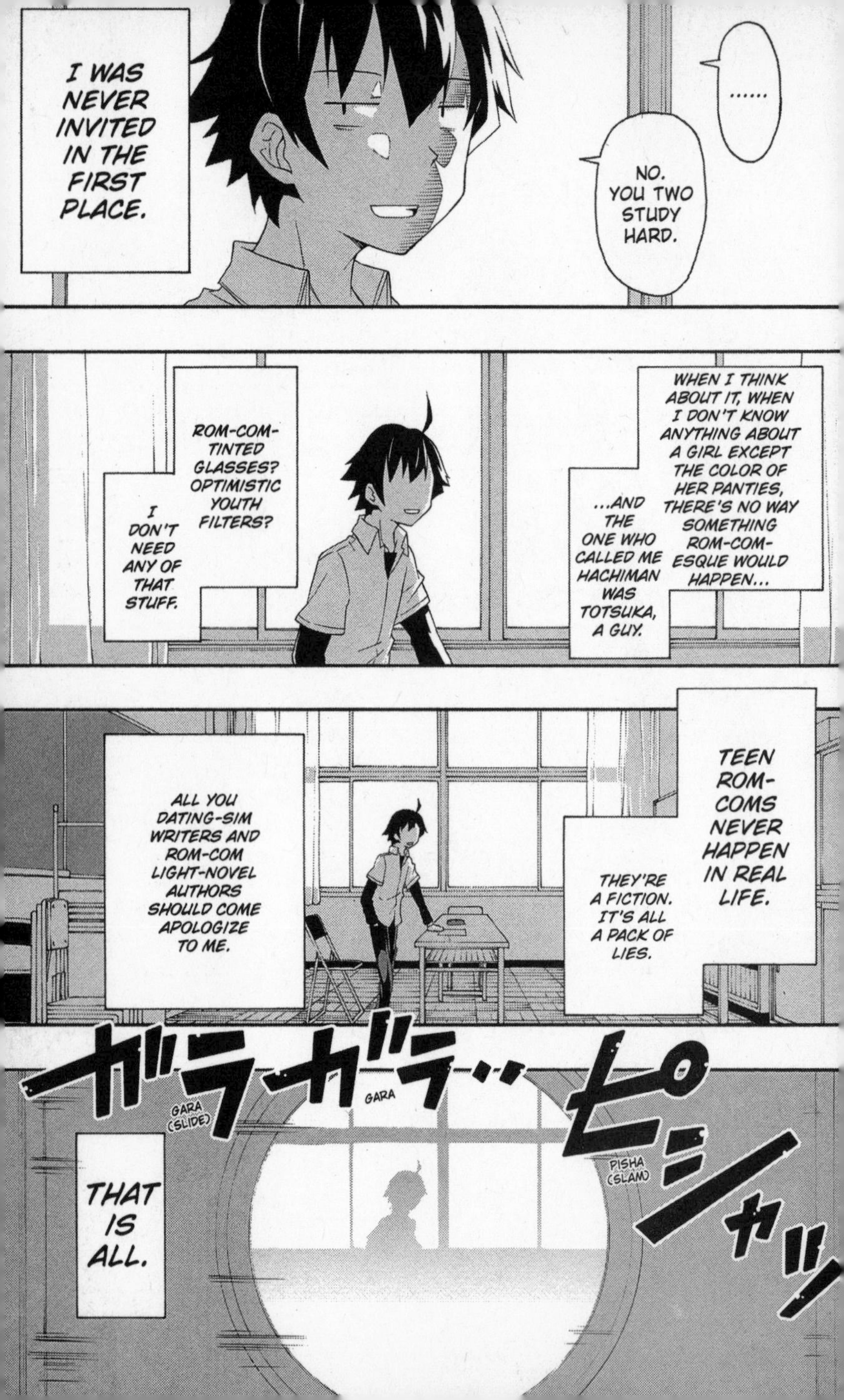

......
NO. YOU TWO STUDY HARD.
I WAS NEVER INVITED IN THE FIRST PLACE.
WHEN I THINK ABOUT IT, WHEN I DON'T KNOW ANYTHING ABOUT A GIRL EXCEPT THE COLOR OF HER PANTIES, THERE'S NO WAY SOMETHING ROM-COM-ESQUE WOULD HAPPEN...
...AND THE ONE WHO CALLED ME HACHIMAN WAS TOTSUKA, A GUY.
ROM-COM-TINTED GLASSES? OPTIMISTIC YOUTH FILTERS?
I DON'T NEED ANY OF THAT STUFF.
TEEN ROM-COMS NEVER HAPPEN IN REAL LIFE.
THEY'RE A FICTION. IT'S ALL A PACK OF LIES.
ALL YOU DATING-SIM WRITERS AND ROM-COM LIGHT-NOVEL AUTHORS SHOULD COME APOLOGIZE TO ME.
GARA (SLIDE)
GARA
PISHA (SLAM)
THAT IS ALL.

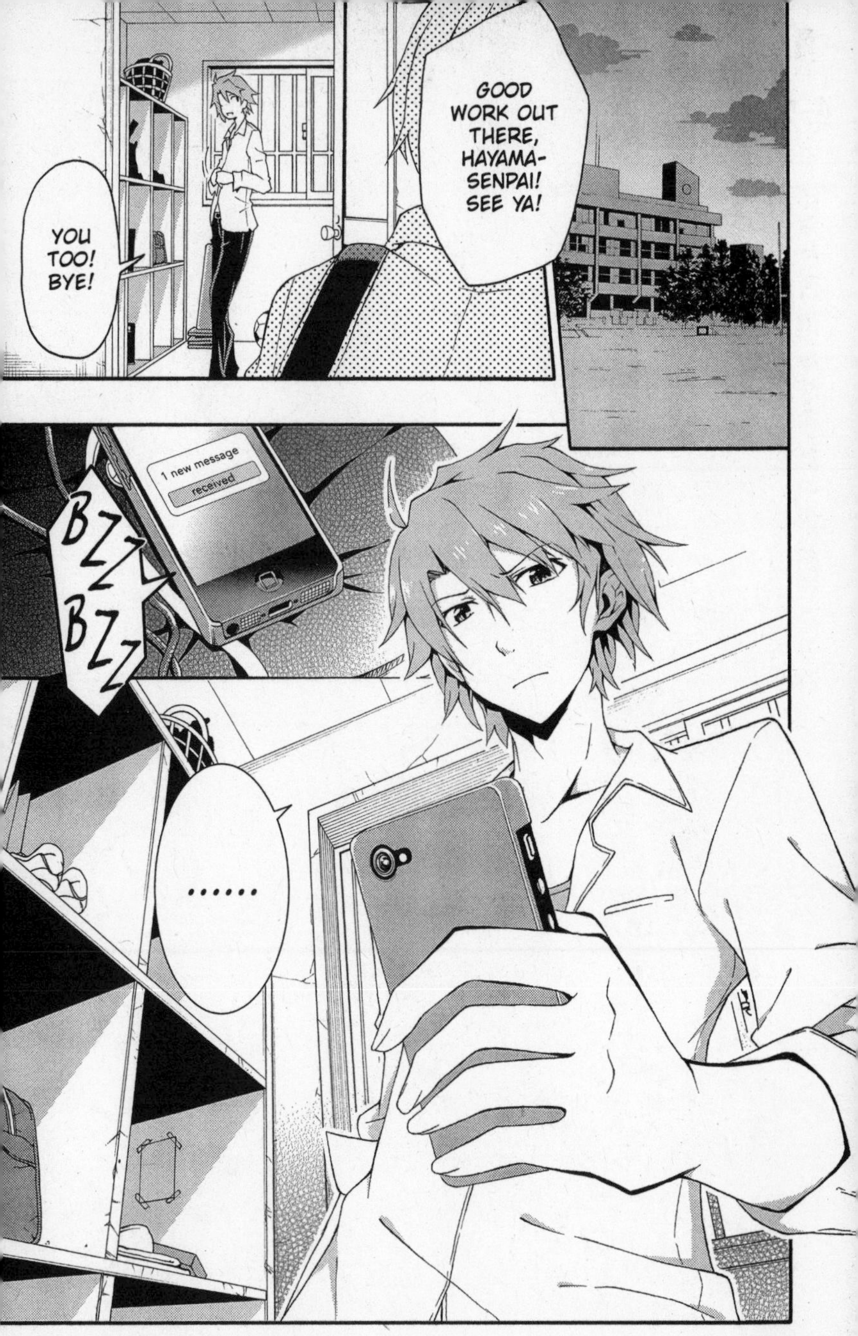
GOOD WORK OUT THERE, HAYAMA-SENPAI! SEE YA!
YOU TOO! BYE!
1 new message
received
BZZ BZZ
......

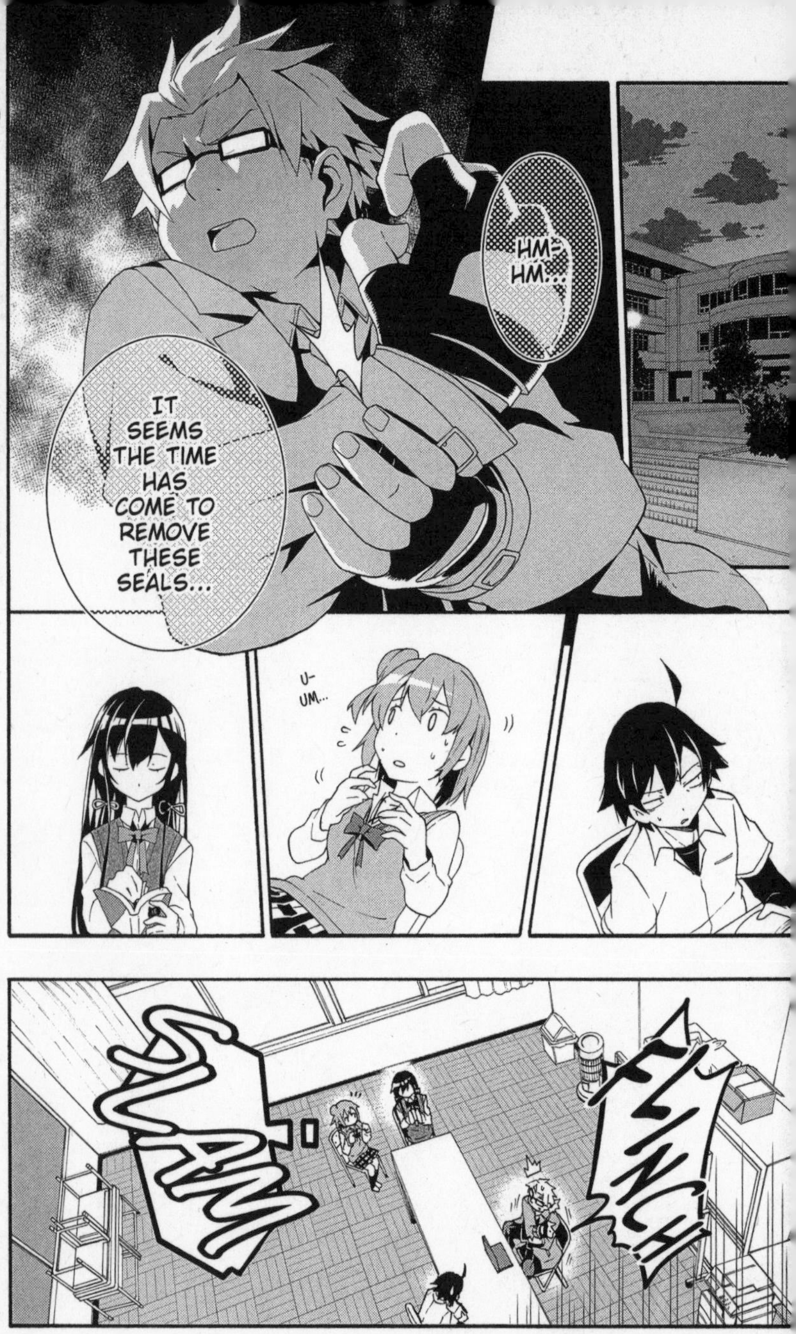
HM-HM...
IT SEEMS THE TIME HAS COME TO REMOVE THESE SEALS...
U-UM...
FLINCH!
SLAM!

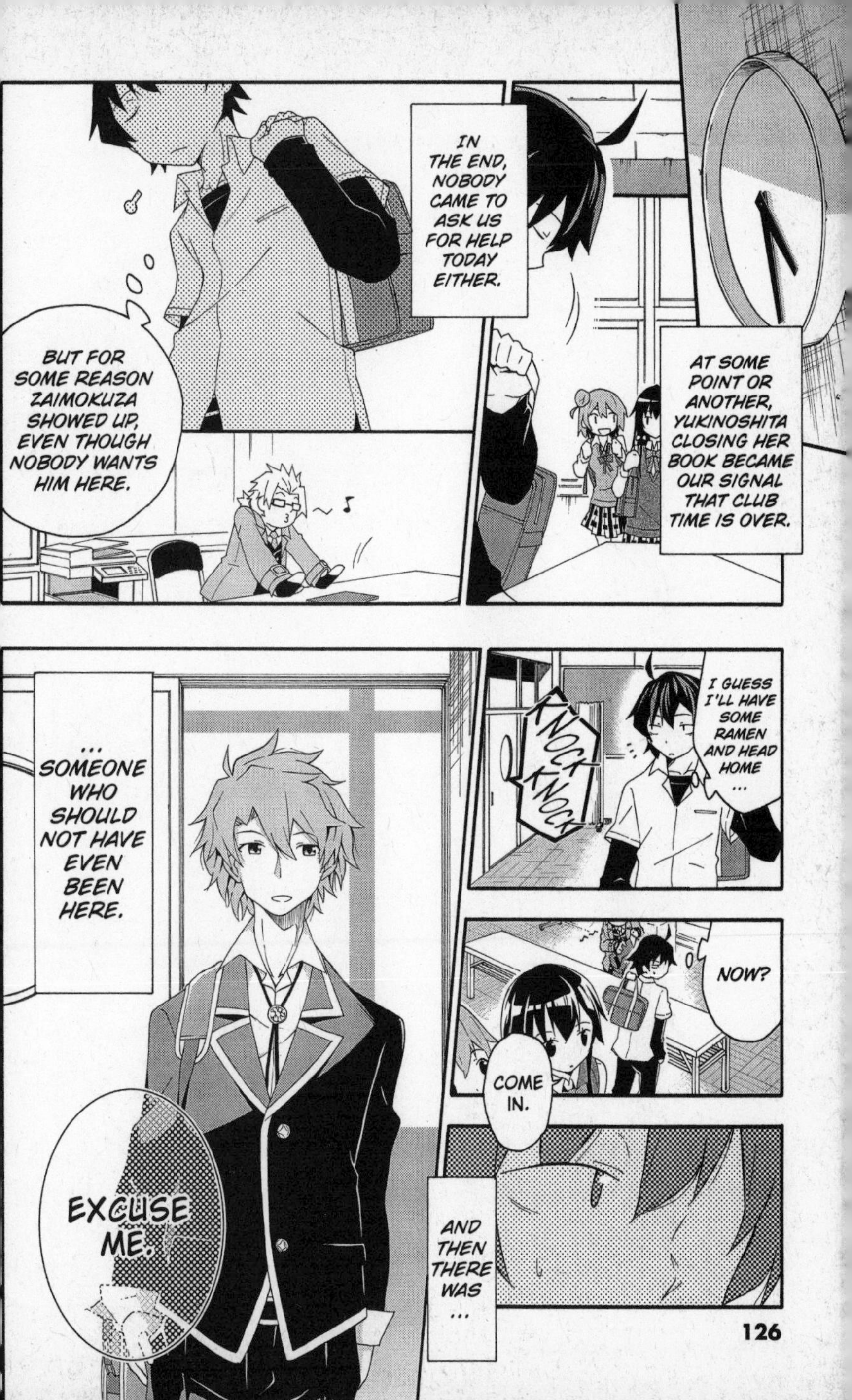
IN THE END, NOBODY CAME TO ASK US FOR HELP TODAY EITHER.
AT SOME POINT OR ANOTHER, YUKINOSHITA CLOSING HER BOOK BECAME OUR SIGNAL THAT CLUB TIME IS OVER.
BUT FOR SOME REASON ZAIMOKUZA SHOWED UP, EVEN THOUGH NOBODY WANTS HIM HERE.
I GUESS I'LL HAVE SOME RAMEN AND HEAD HOME ...
KNOCK KNOCK
NOW?
COME IN.
AND THEN THERE WAS ...
... SOMEONE WHO SHOULD NOT HAVE EVEN BEEN HERE.
EXCUSE ME.

CHAPTER 10 ··· HAYATO HAYAMA ALWAYS HAS IT TOGETHER.

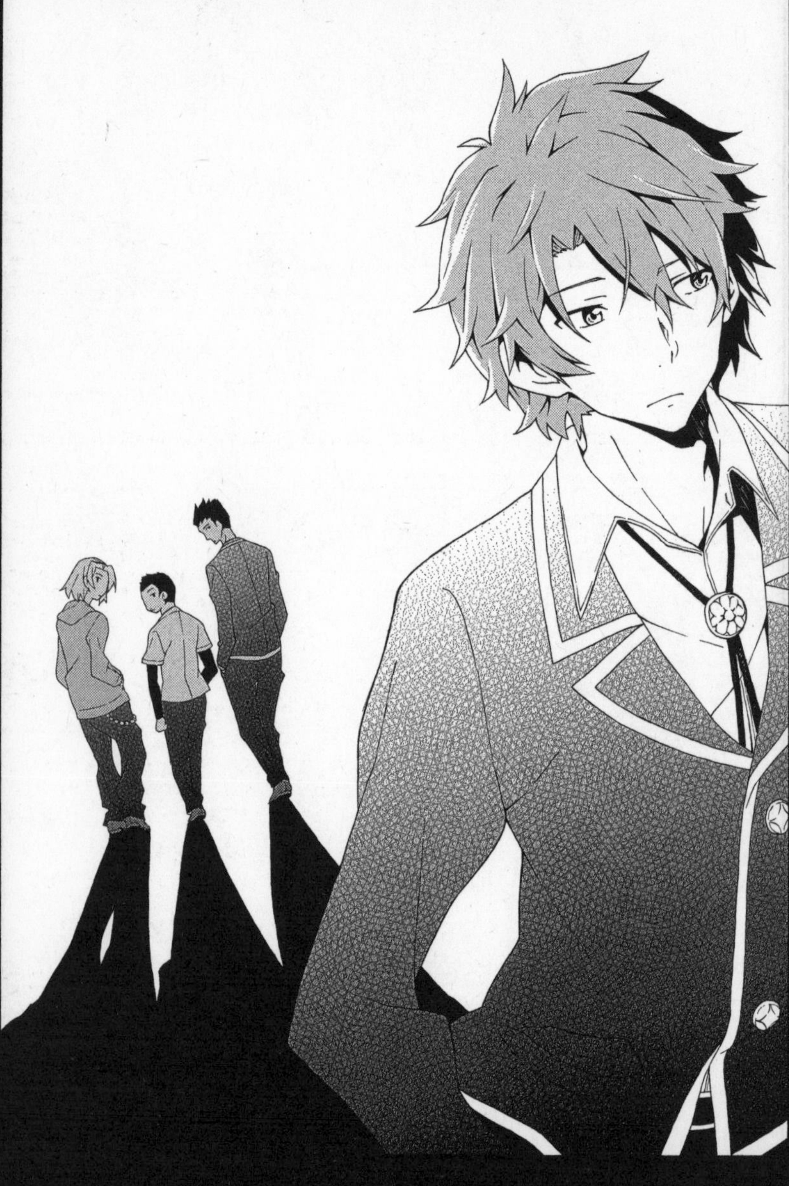

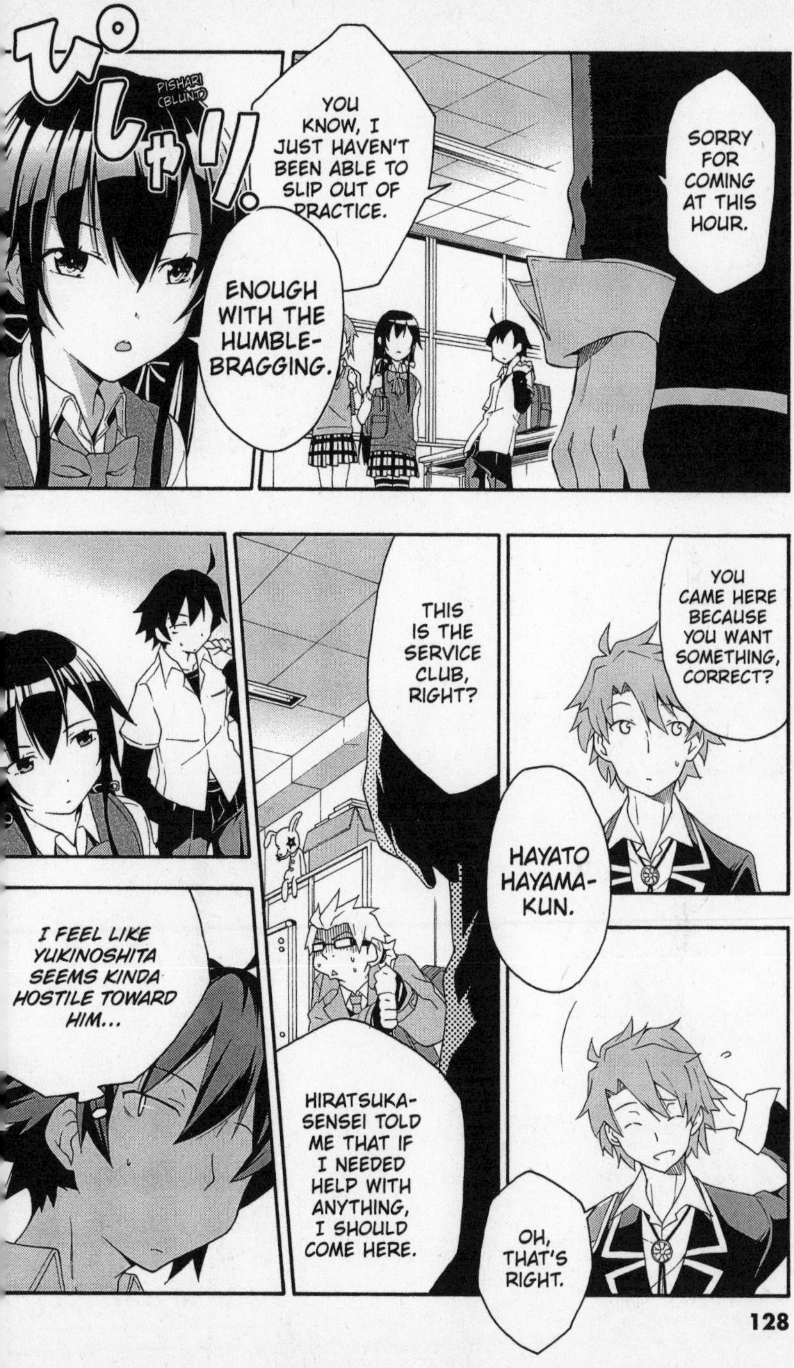
SORRY FOR COMING AT THIS HOUR.
YOU KNOW, I JUST HAVEN'T BEEN ABLE TO SLIP OUT OF PRACTICE.
ぴしゃり
PISHARI (BLUNT)
ENOUGH WITH THE HUMBLE-BRAGGING.
YOU CAME HERE BECAUSE YOU WANT SOMETHING, CORRECT?
HAYATO HAYAMA-KUN.
OH, THAT'S RIGHT.
THIS IS THE SERVICE CLUB, RIGHT?
HIRATSUKA-SENSEI TOLD ME THAT IF I NEEDED HELP WITH ANYTHING, I SHOULD COME HERE.
I FEEL LIKE YUKINOSHITA SEEMS KINDA HOSTILE TOWARD HIM...

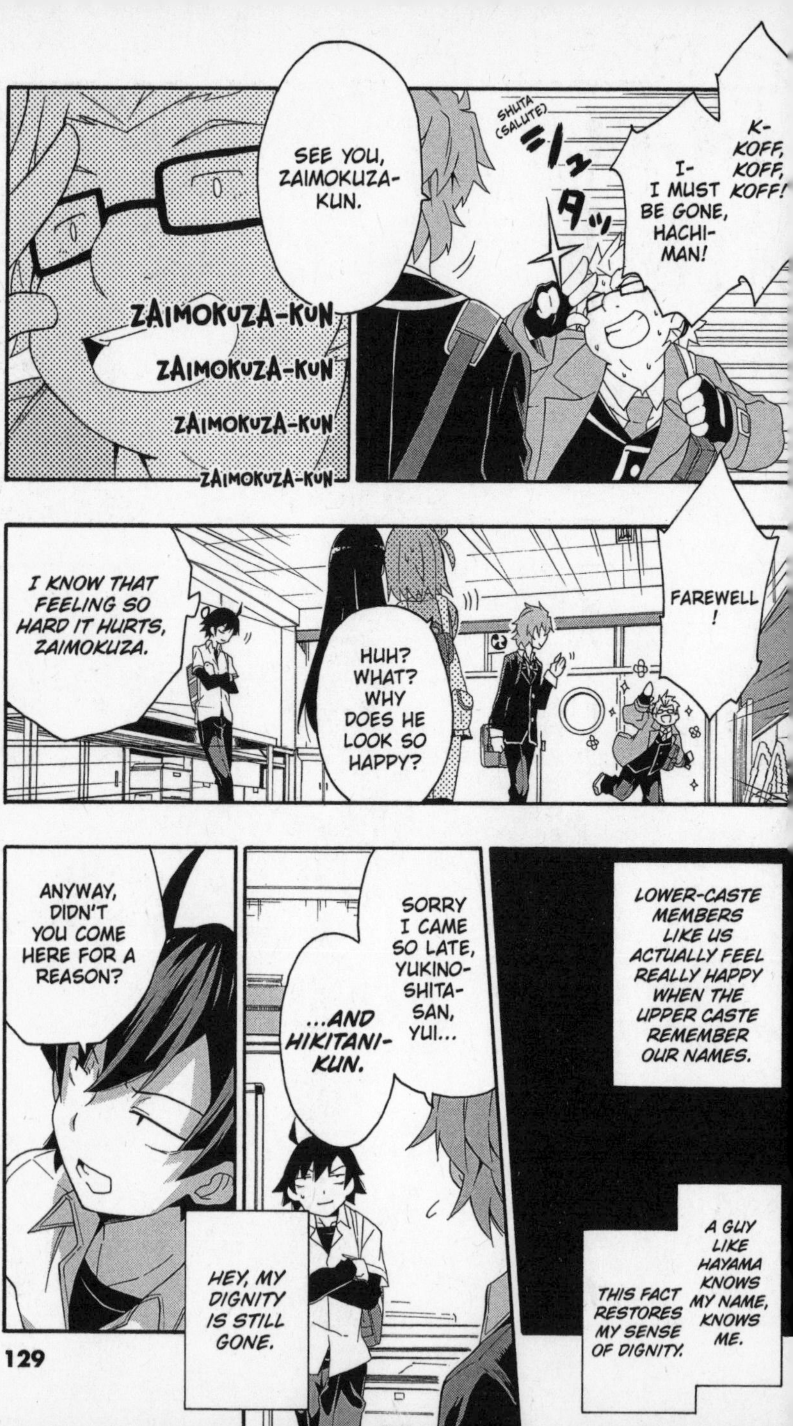
K-KOFF, KOFF, KOFF!
I- I MUST BE GONE, HACHIMAN!
SHUTA (SALUTE)
SEE YOU, ZAIMOKUZA-KUN.
ZAIMOKUZA-KUN
ZAIMOKUZA-KUN
ZAIMOKUZA-KUN
ZAIMOKUZA-KUN
FAREWELL!
HUH? WHAT? WHY DOES HE LOOK SO HAPPY?
I KNOW THAT FEELING SO HARD IT HURTS, ZAIMOKUZA.
LOWER-CASTE MEMBERS LIKE US ACTUALLY FEEL REALLY HAPPY WHEN THE UPPER CASTE REMEMBER OUR NAMES.
A GUY LIKE HAYAMA KNOWS MY NAME, KNOWS ME.
THIS FACT RESTORES MY SENSE OF DIGNITY.
SORRY I CAME SO LATE, YUKINO-SHITA-SAN, YUI...
...AND HIKITANI-KUN.
HEY, MY DIGNITY IS STILL GONE.
ANYWAY, DIDN'T YOU COME HERE FOR A REASON?

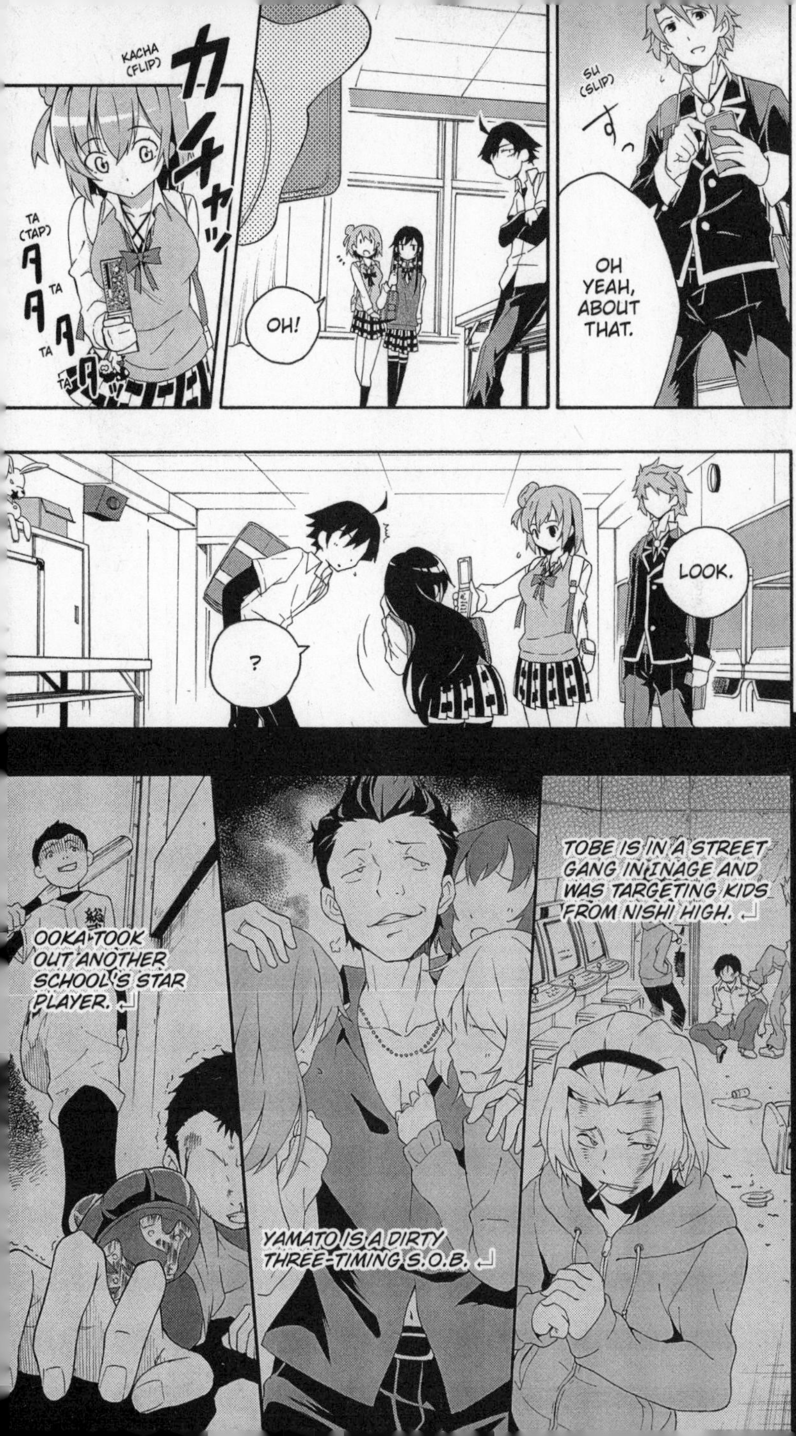
SU (SLIP)
すっ
OH YEAH, ABOUT THAT.
OH!
KACHA (FLIP)
カチャッ
TA (TAP)
タ
TA
タ
TA
タ
TA
タッ
LOOK.
?
TOBE IS IN A STREET GANG IN INAGE AND WAS TARGETING KIDS FROM NISHI HIGH. ↵
YAMATO IS A DIRTY THREE-TIMING S.O.B. ↵
OOKA TOOK OUT ANOTHER SCHOOL'S STAR PLAYER. ↵

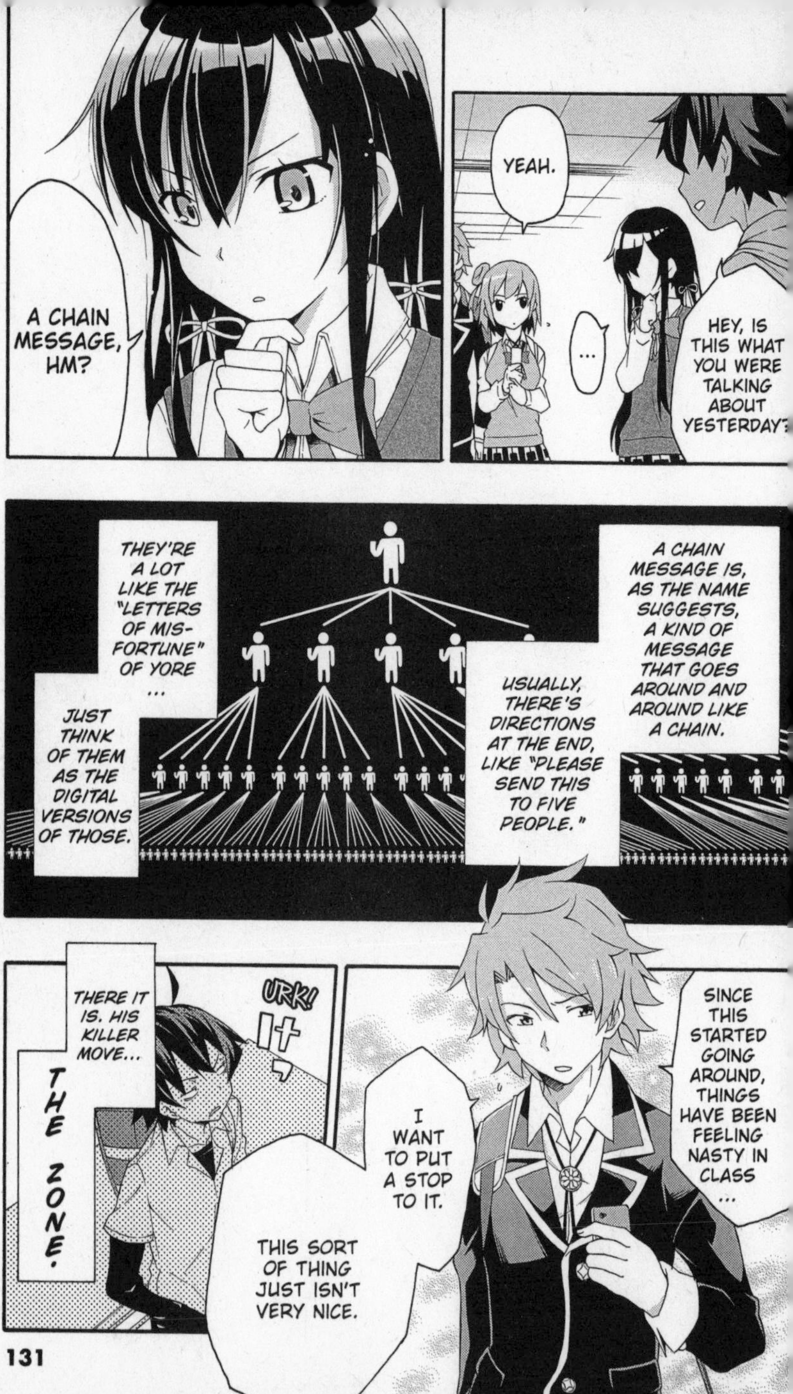
HEY, IS THIS WHAT YOU WERE TALKING ABOUT YESTERDAY?
...
YEAH.
A CHAIN MESSAGE, HM?
A CHAIN MESSAGE IS, AS THE NAME SUGGESTS, A KIND OF MESSAGE THAT GOES AROUND AND AROUND LIKE A CHAIN.
USUALLY, THERE'S DIRECTIONS AT THE END, LIKE "PLEASE SEND THIS TO FIVE PEOPLE."
THEY'RE A LOT LIKE THE "LETTERS OF MIS-FORTUNE" OF YORE ...
JUST THINK OF THEM AS THE DIGITAL VERSIONS OF THOSE.
SINCE THIS STARTED GOING AROUND, THINGS HAVE BEEN FEELING NASTY IN CLASS ...
I WANT TO PUT A STOP TO IT.
THIS SORT OF THING JUST ISN'T VERY NICE.
URK!
THERE IT IS. HIS KILLER MOVE...
THE ZONE.

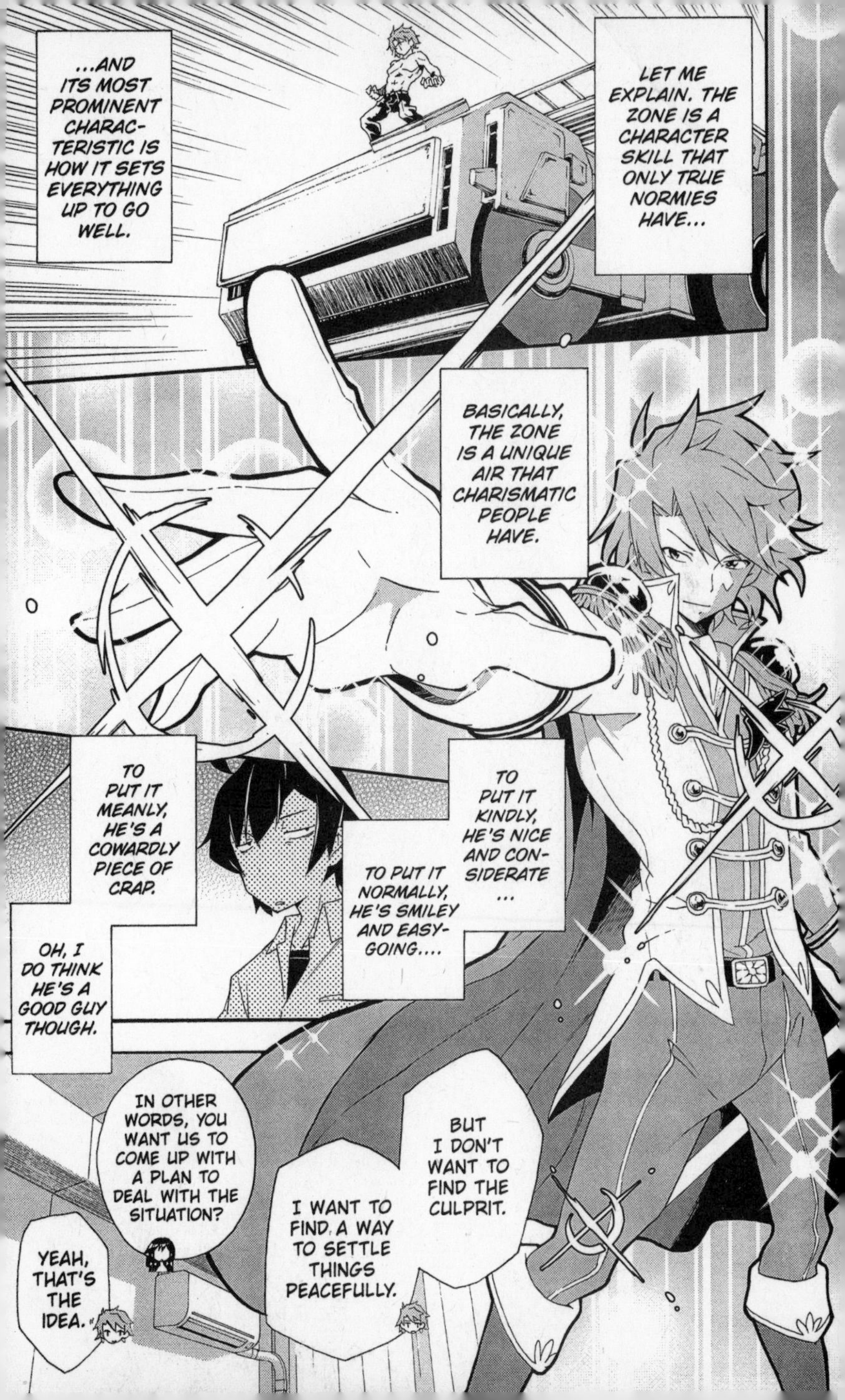
LET ME EXPLAIN. THE ZONE IS A CHARACTER SKILL THAT ONLY TRUE NORMIES HAVE...
...AND ITS MOST PROMINENT CHARAC-TERISTIC IS HOW IT SETS EVERYTHING UP TO GO WELL.
BASICALLY, THE ZONE IS A UNIQUE AIR THAT CHARISMATIC PEOPLE HAVE.
TO PUT IT KINDLY, HE'S NICE AND CON-SIDERATE...
TO PUT IT NORMALLY, HE'S SMILEY AND EASY-GOING....
TO PUT IT MEANLY, HE'S A COWARDLY PIECE OF CRAP.
OH, I DO THINK HE'S A GOOD GUY THOUGH.
BUT I DON'T WANT TO FIND THE CULPRIT.
I WANT TO FIND A WAY TO SETTLE THINGS PEACEFULLY.
IN OTHER WORDS, YOU WANT US TO COME UP WITH A PLAN TO DEAL WITH THE SITUATION?
YEAH, THAT'S THE IDEA.

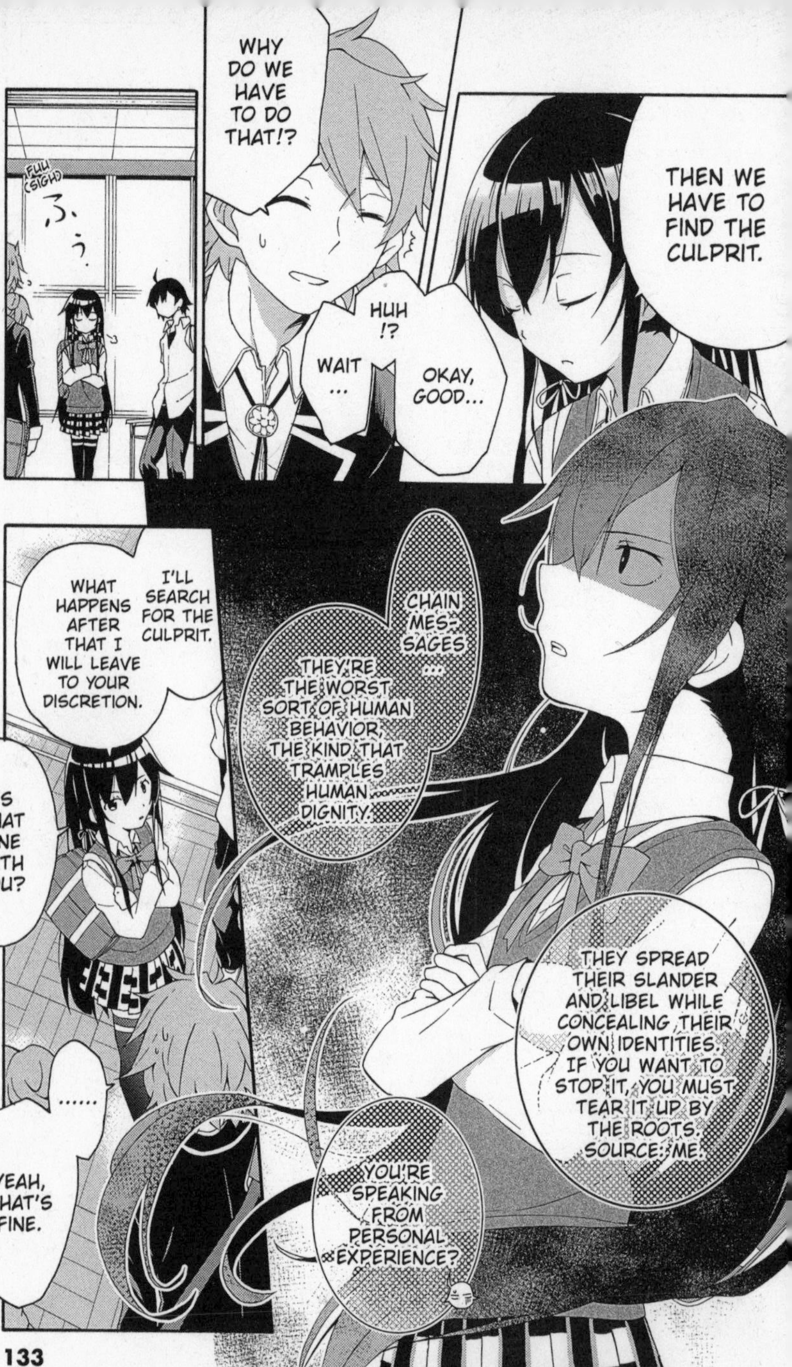
THEN WE HAVE TO FIND THE CULPRIT.
WHY DO WE HAVE TO DO THAT!?
HUH !?
OKAY, GOOD...
WAIT ...
FUU (SIGH)
ふう.
CHAIN MES-SAGES ...
THEY'RE THE WORST SORT OF HUMAN BEHAVIOR, THE KIND THAT TRAMPLES HUMAN DIGNITY.
THEY SPREAD THEIR SLANDER AND LIBEL WHILE CONCEALING THEIR OWN IDENTITIES. IF YOU WANT TO STOP IT, YOU MUST TEAR IT UP BY THE ROOTS. SOURCE: ME.
YOU'RE SPEAKING FROM PERSONAL EXPERIENCE?
I'LL SEARCH FOR THE CULPRIT.
WHAT HAPPENS AFTER THAT I WILL LEAVE TO YOUR DISCRETION.
IS THAT FINE WITH YOU?
......
YEAH, THAT'S FINE.

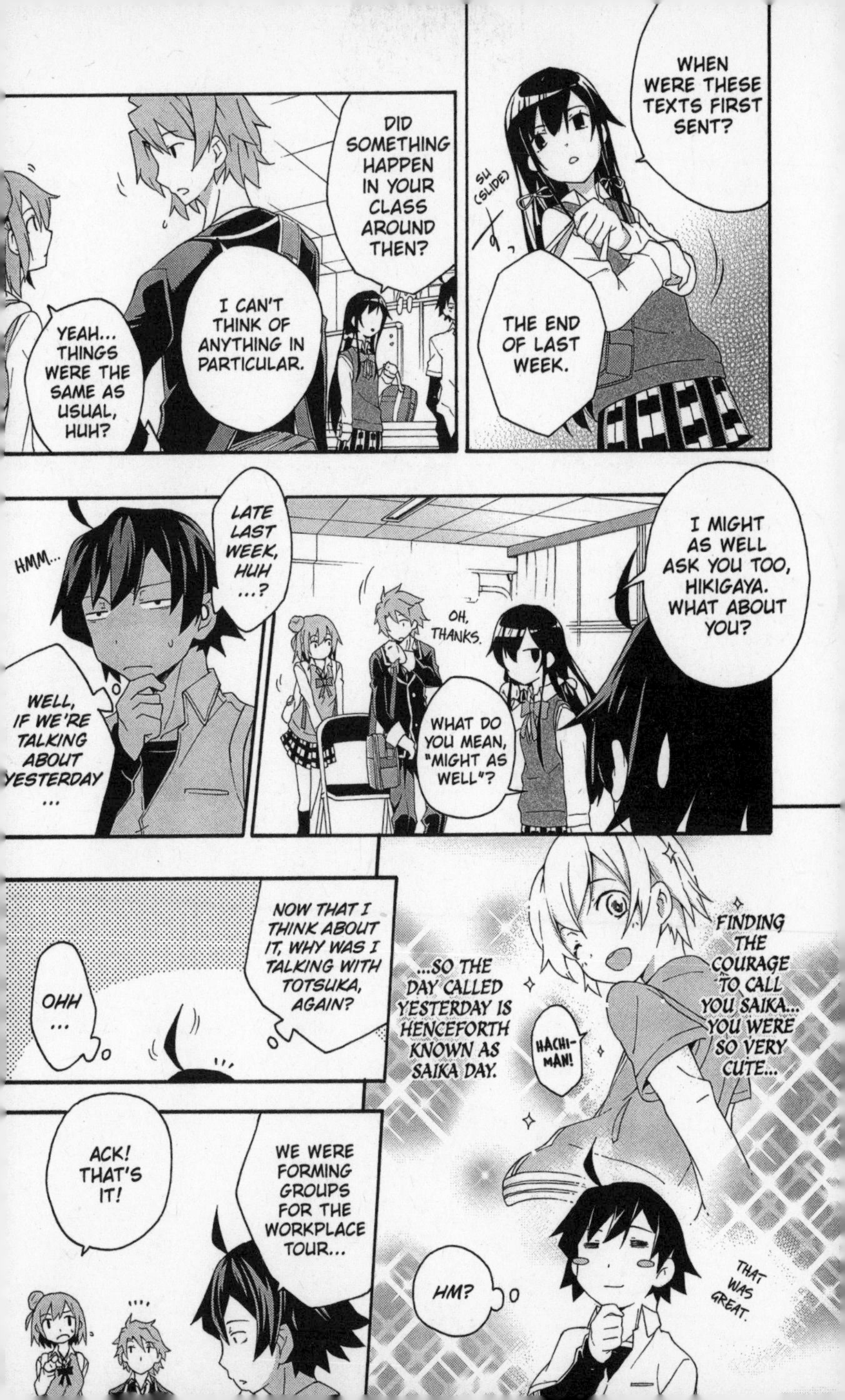
WHEN WERE THESE TEXTS FIRST SENT?
SU (SLIDE)
THE END OF LAST WEEK.
DID SOMETHING HAPPEN IN YOUR CLASS AROUND THEN?
I CAN'T THINK OF ANYTHING IN PARTICULAR.
YEAH... THINGS WERE THE SAME AS USUAL, HUH?
I MIGHT AS WELL ASK YOU TOO, HIKIGAYA. WHAT ABOUT YOU?
OH, THANKS.
WHAT DO YOU MEAN, "MIGHT AS WELL"?
LATE LAST WEEK, HUH ...?
HMM...
WELL, IF WE'RE TALKING ABOUT YESTERDAY ...
FINDING THE COURAGE TO CALL YOU SAIKA... YOU WERE SO VERY CUTE...
HACHI-MAN!
...SO THE DAY CALLED YESTERDAY IS HENCEFORTH KNOWN AS SAIKA DAY.
NOW THAT I THINK ABOUT IT, WHY WAS I TALKING WITH TOTSUKA, AGAIN?
OHH ...
THAT WAS GREAT.
HM?
WE WERE FORMING GROUPS FOR THE WORKPLACE TOUR...
ACK! THAT'S IT!

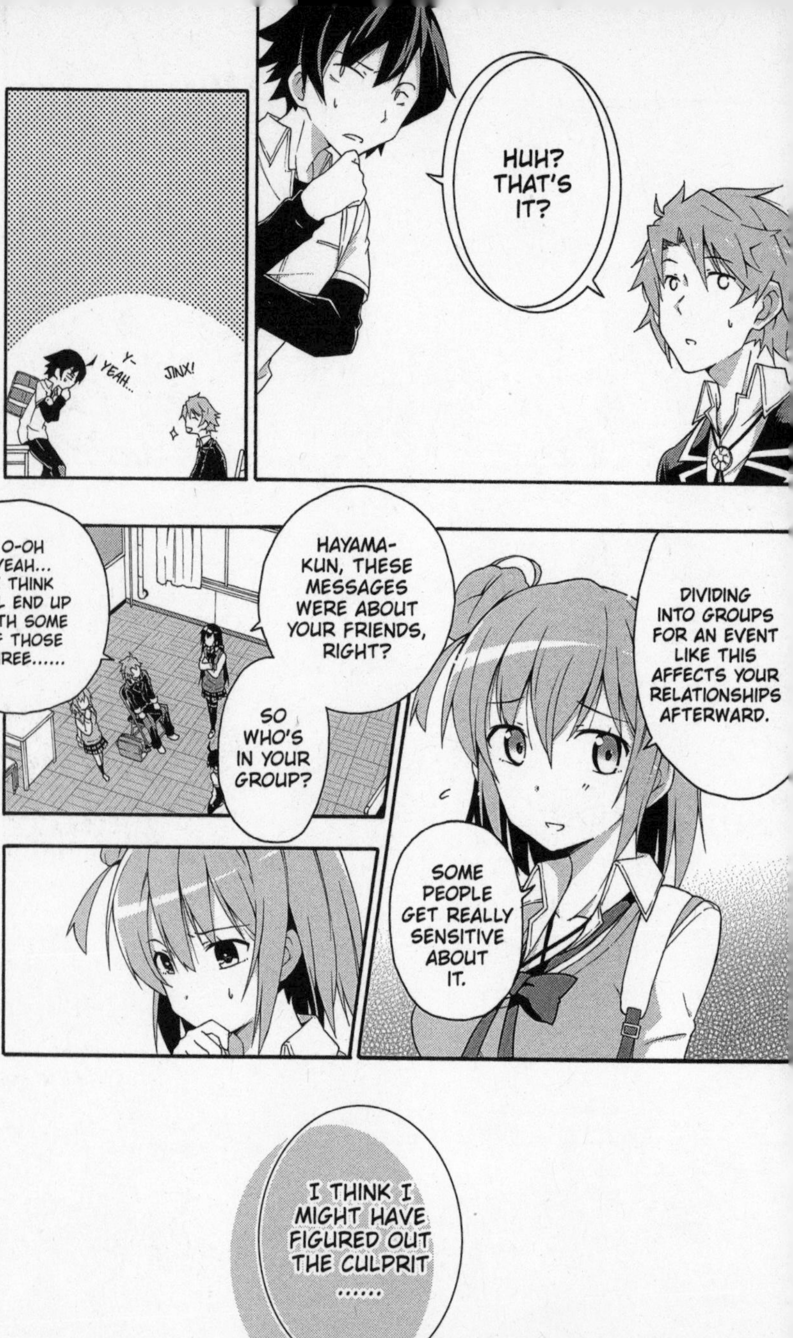
HUH? THAT'S IT?
Y-YEAH...
JINX!
DIVIDING INTO GROUPS FOR AN EVENT LIKE THIS AFFECTS YOUR RELATIONSHIPS AFTERWARD.
SOME PEOPLE GET REALLY SENSITIVE ABOUT IT.
HAYAMA-KUN, THESE MESSAGES WERE ABOUT YOUR FRIENDS, RIGHT?
SO WHO'S IN YOUR GROUP?
O-OH YEAH... I THINK I'LL END UP WITH SOME OF THOSE THREE......
I THINK I MIGHT HAVE FIGURED OUT THE CULPRIT ......

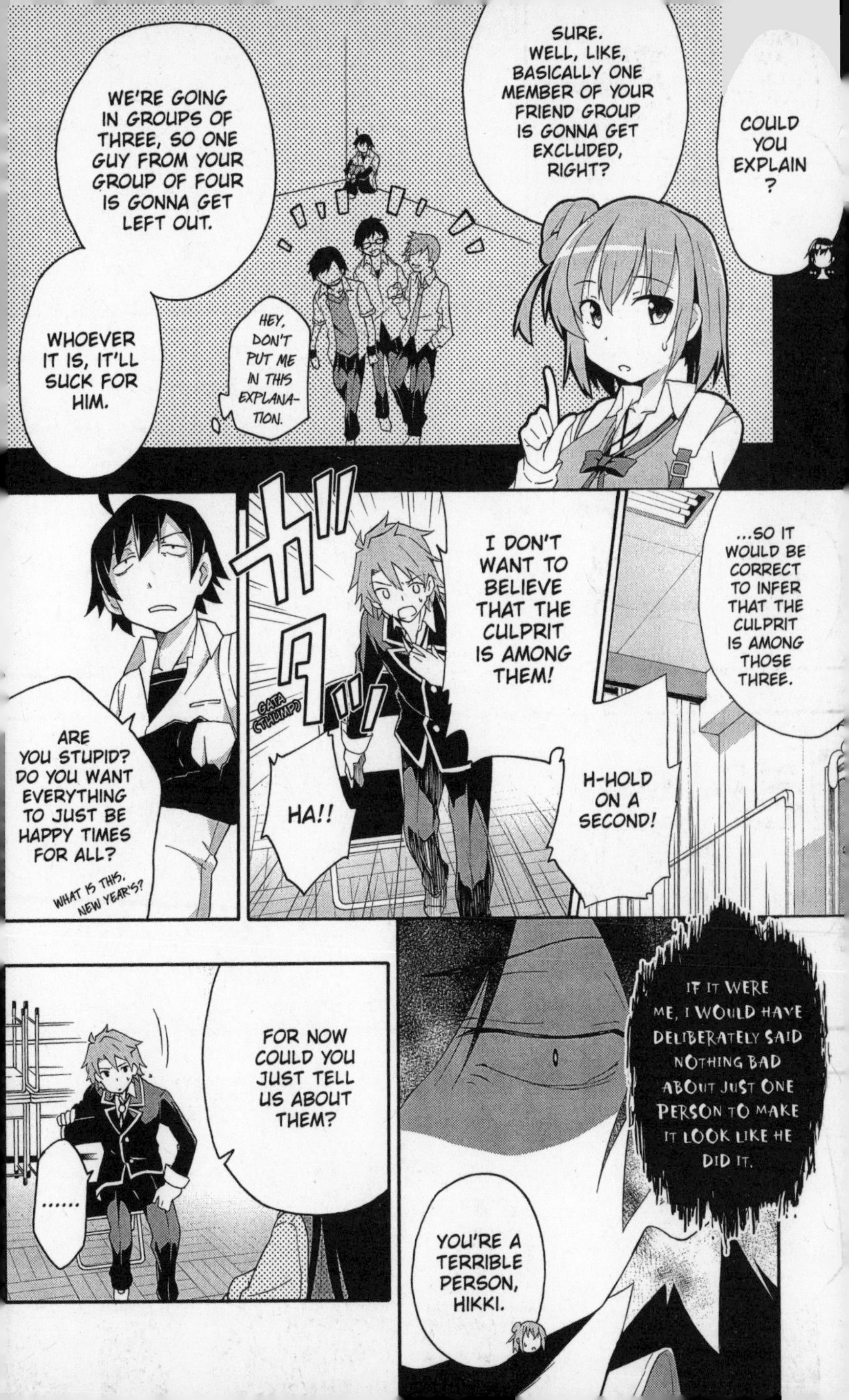
COULD YOU EXPLAIN?
SURE. WELL, LIKE, BASICALLY ONE MEMBER OF YOUR FRIEND GROUP IS GONNA GET EXCLUDED, RIGHT?
WE'RE GOING IN GROUPS OF THREE, SO ONE GUY FROM YOUR GROUP OF FOUR IS GONNA GET LEFT OUT.
HEY, DON'T PUT ME IN THIS EXPLANATION.
WHOEVER IT IS, IT'LL SUCK FOR HIM.
...SO IT WOULD BE CORRECT TO INFER THAT THE CULPRIT IS AMONG THOSE THREE.
I DON'T WANT TO BELIEVE THAT THE CULPRIT IS AMONG THEM!
H-HOLD ON A SECOND!
GATA (THUMP)
HA!!
ARE YOU STUPID? DO YOU WANT EVERYTHING TO JUST BE HAPPY TIMES FOR ALL?
WHAT IS THIS, NEW YEAR'S?
IF IT WERE ME, I WOULD HAVE DELIBERATELY SAID NOTHING BAD ABOUT JUST ONE PERSON TO MAKE IT LOOK LIKE HE DID IT.
YOU'RE A TERRIBLE PERSON, HIKKI.
FOR NOW COULD YOU JUST TELL US ABOUT THEM?
......

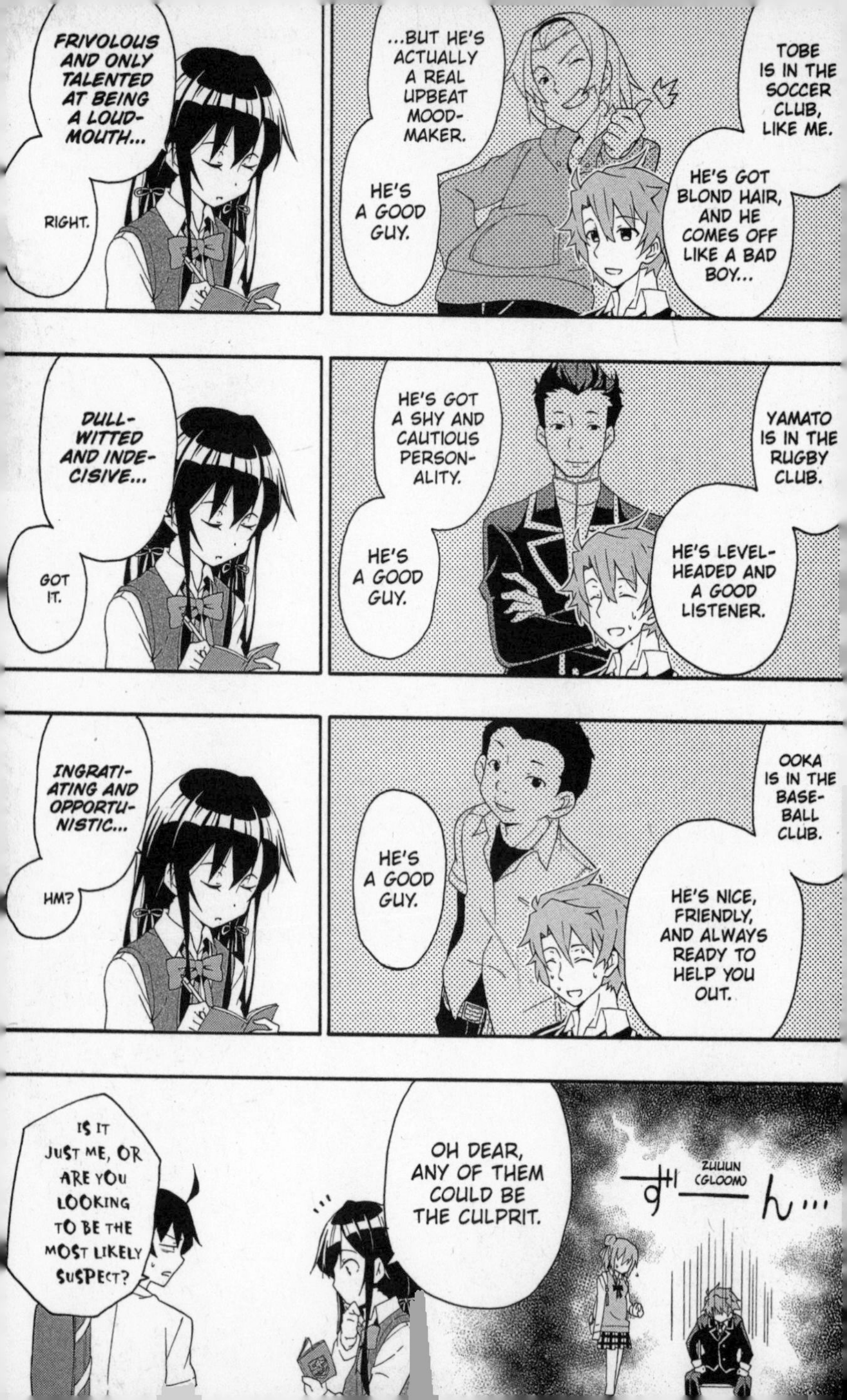
TOBE IS IN THE SOCCER CLUB, LIKE ME.
HE'S GOT BLOND HAIR, AND HE COMES OFF LIKE A BAD BOY...
...BUT HE'S ACTUALLY A REAL UPBEAT MOOD-MAKER.
HE'S A GOOD GUY.
FRIVOLOUS AND ONLY TALENTED AT BEING A LOUDMOUTH...
RIGHT.
YAMATO IS IN THE RUGBY CLUB.
HE'S LEVEL-HEADED AND A GOOD LISTENER.
HE'S GOT A SHY AND CAUTIOUS PERSONALITY.
HE'S A GOOD GUY.
DULL-WITTED AND INDECISIVE...
GOT IT.
OOKA IS IN THE BASEBALL CLUB.
HE'S NICE, FRIENDLY, AND ALWAYS READY TO HELP YOU OUT.
HE'S A GOOD GUY.
INGRATIATING AND OPPORTUNISTIC...
HM?
ZUUUN (GLOOM)
OH DEAR, ANY OF THEM COULD BE THE CULPRIT.
IS IT JUST ME, OR ARE YOU LOOKING TO BE THE MOST LIKELY SUSPECT?

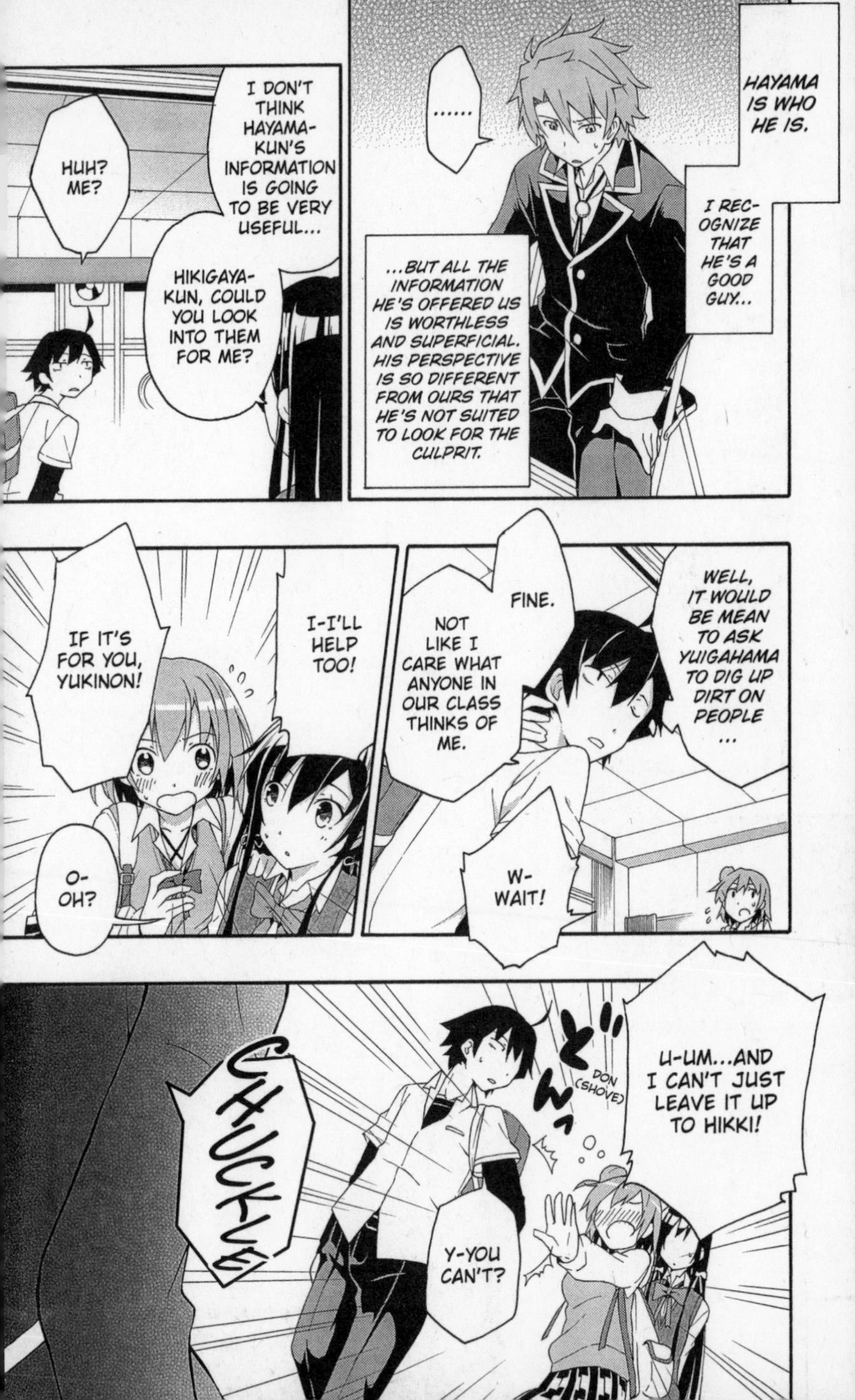
HAYAMA IS WHO HE IS.
I RECOGNIZE THAT HE'S A GOOD GUY...
......
...BUT ALL THE INFORMATION HE'S OFFERED US IS WORTHLESS AND SUPERFICIAL. HIS PERSPECTIVE IS SO DIFFERENT FROM OURS THAT HE'S NOT SUITED TO LOOK FOR THE CULPRIT.
I DON'T THINK HAYAMA-KUN'S INFORMATION IS GOING TO BE VERY USEFUL...
HIKIGAYA-KUN, COULD YOU LOOK INTO THEM FOR ME?
HUH? ME?
WELL, IT WOULD BE MEAN TO ASK YUIGAHAMA TO DIG UP DIRT ON PEOPLE ...
FINE.
NOT LIKE I CARE WHAT ANYONE IN OUR CLASS THINKS OF ME.
W-WAIT!
I-I'LL HELP TOO!
IF IT'S FOR YOU, YUKINON!
O-OH?
U-UM...AND I CAN'T JUST LEAVE IT UP TO HIKKI!
DON (SHOVE)
Y-YOU CAN'T?
CHUCKLE

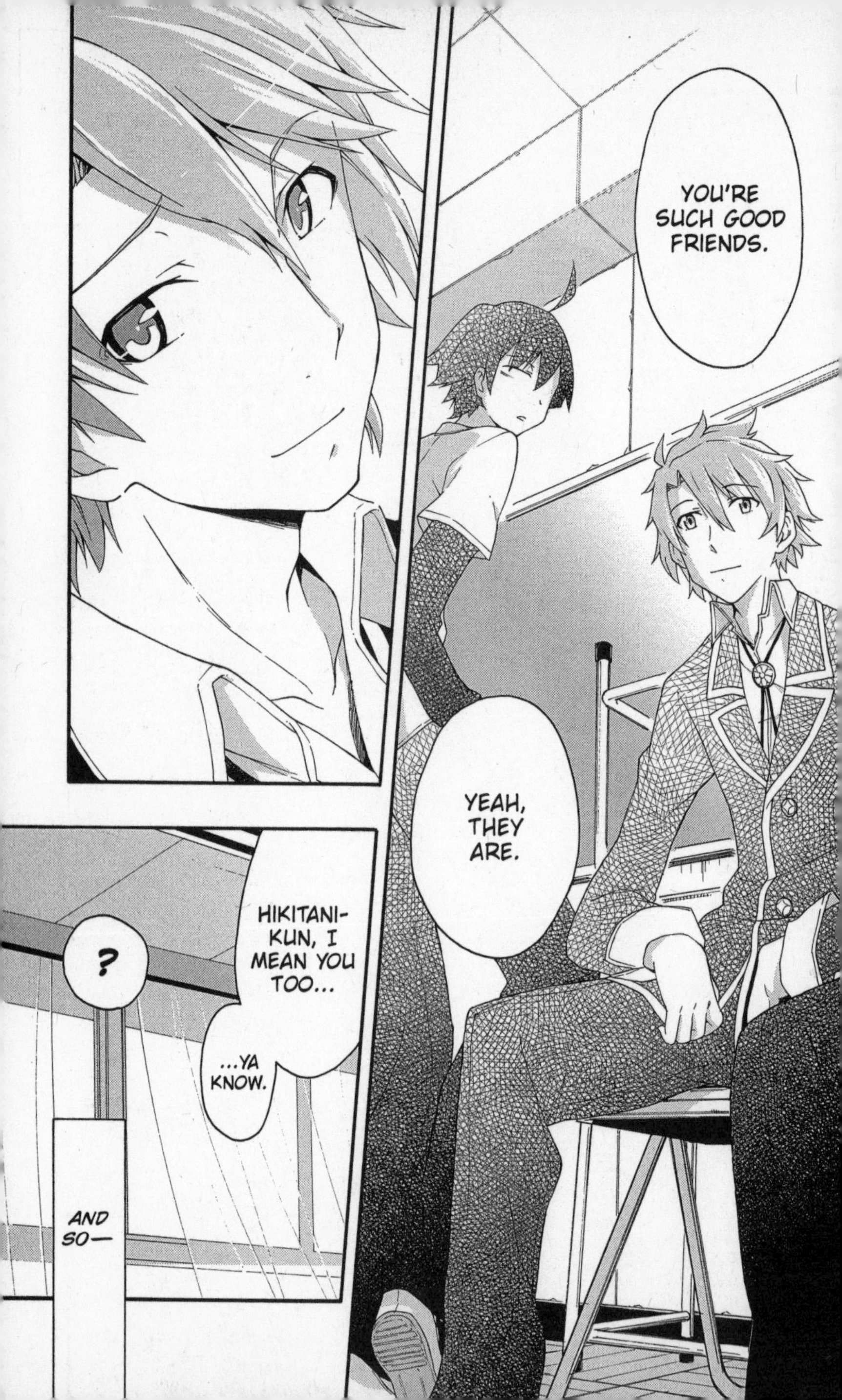
YOU'RE SUCH GOOD FRIENDS.
YEAH, THEY ARE.
HIKITANI-KUN, I MEAN YOU TOO...
?
...YA KNOW.
AND SO—

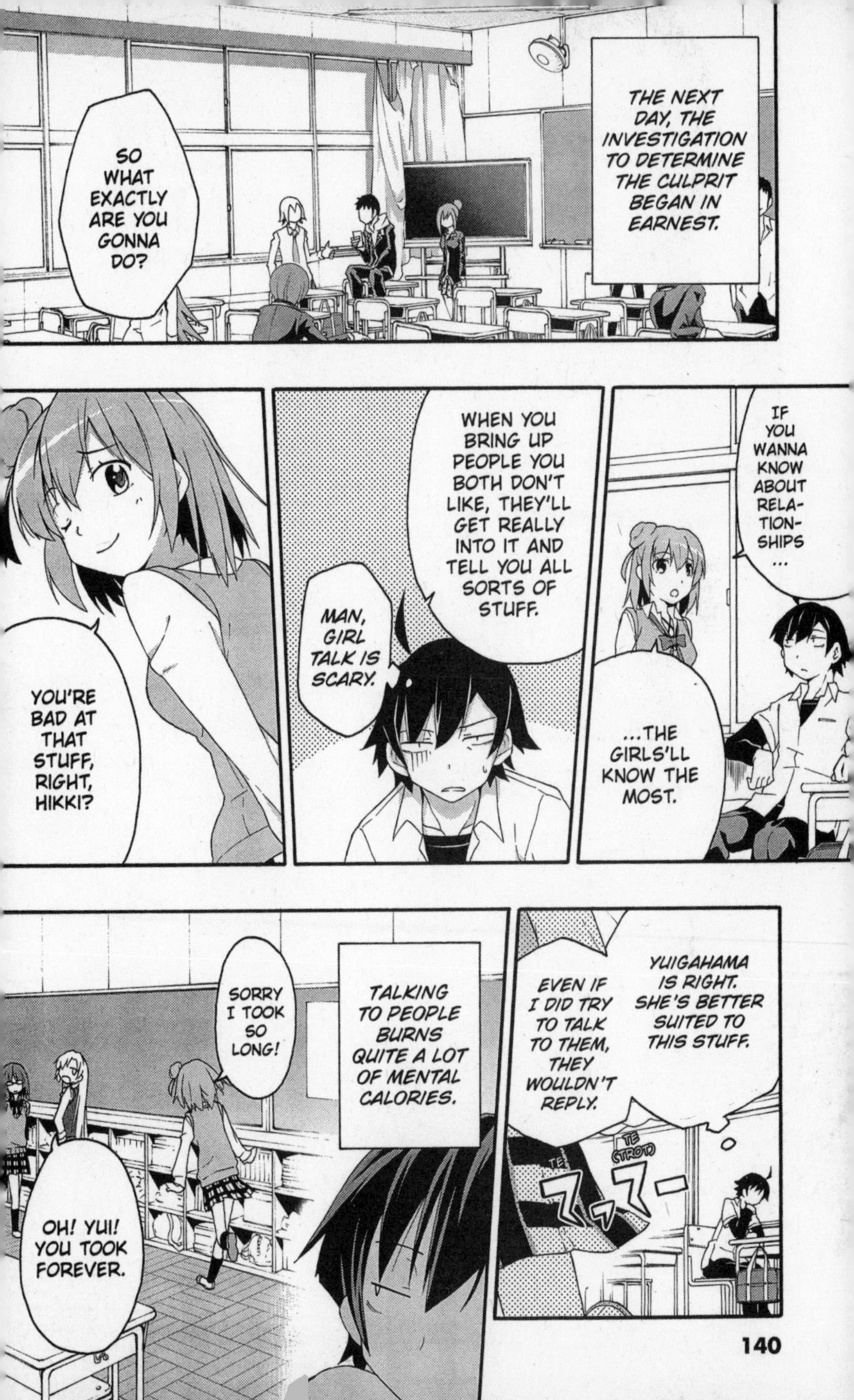
THE NEXT DAY, THE INVESTIGATION TO DETERMINE THE CULPRIT BEGAN IN EARNEST.
SO WHAT EXACTLY ARE YOU GONNA DO?
IF YOU WANNA KNOW ABOUT RELATIONSHIPS...
...THE GIRLS'LL KNOW THE MOST.
WHEN YOU BRING UP PEOPLE YOU BOTH DON'T LIKE, THEY'LL GET REALLY INTO IT AND TELL YOU ALL SORTS OF STUFF.
MAN, GIRL TALK IS SCARY.
YOU'RE BAD AT THAT STUFF, RIGHT, HIKKI?
YUIGAHAMA IS RIGHT. SHE'S BETTER SUITED TO THIS STUFF.
EVEN IF I DID TRY TO TALK TO THEM, THEY WOULDN'T REPLY.
TE TE (TROT)
TALKING TO PEOPLE BURNS QUITE A LOT OF MENTAL CALORIES.
SORRY I TOOK SO LONG!
OH! YUI! YOU TOOK FOREVER.

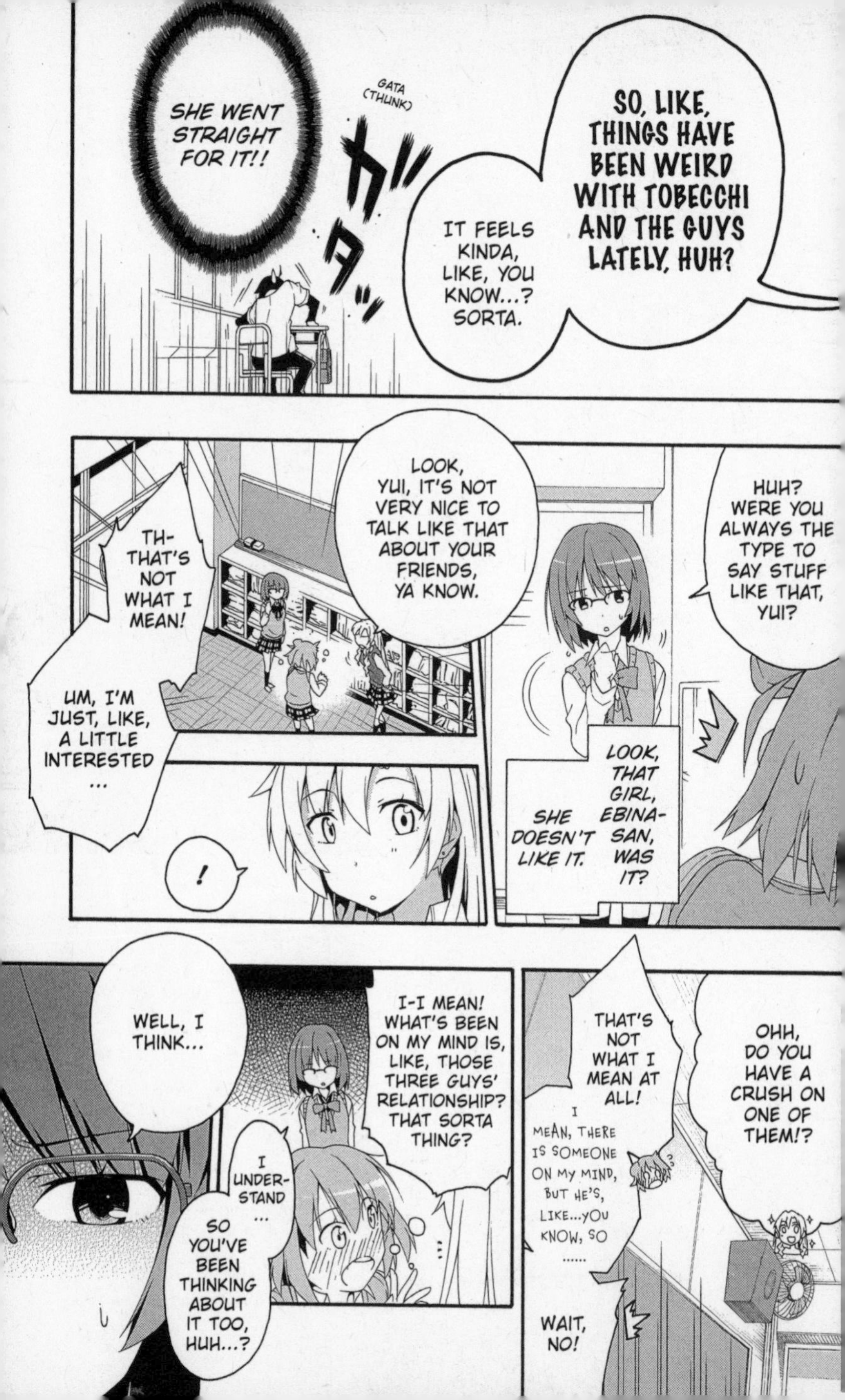
SO, LIKE, THINGS HAVE BEEN WEIRD WITH TOBECCHI AND THE GUYS LATELY, HUH?
IT FEELS KINDA, LIKE, YOU KNOW...? SORTA.
GATA (THUNK)
SHE WENT STRAIGHT FOR IT!!
HUH? WERE YOU ALWAYS THE TYPE TO SAY STUFF LIKE THAT, YUI?
LOOK, THAT GIRL, EBINA-SAN, WAS IT?
SHE DOESN'T LIKE IT.
LOOK, YUI, IT'S NOT VERY NICE TO TALK LIKE THAT ABOUT YOUR FRIENDS, YA KNOW.
TH- THAT'S NOT WHAT I MEAN!
UM, I'M JUST, LIKE, A LITTLE INTERESTED ...
!
OHH, DO YOU HAVE A CRUSH ON ONE OF THEM!?
THAT'S NOT WHAT I MEAN AT ALL!
I MEAN, THERE IS SOMEONE ON MY MIND, BUT HE'S, LIKE...YOU KNOW, SO ......
WAIT, NO!
I-I MEAN! WHAT'S BEEN ON MY MIND IS, LIKE, THOSE THREE GUYS' RELATIONSHIP? THAT SORTA THING?
I UNDERSTAND ...
SO YOU'VE BEEN THINKING ABOUT IT TOO, HUH...?
WELL, I THINK...

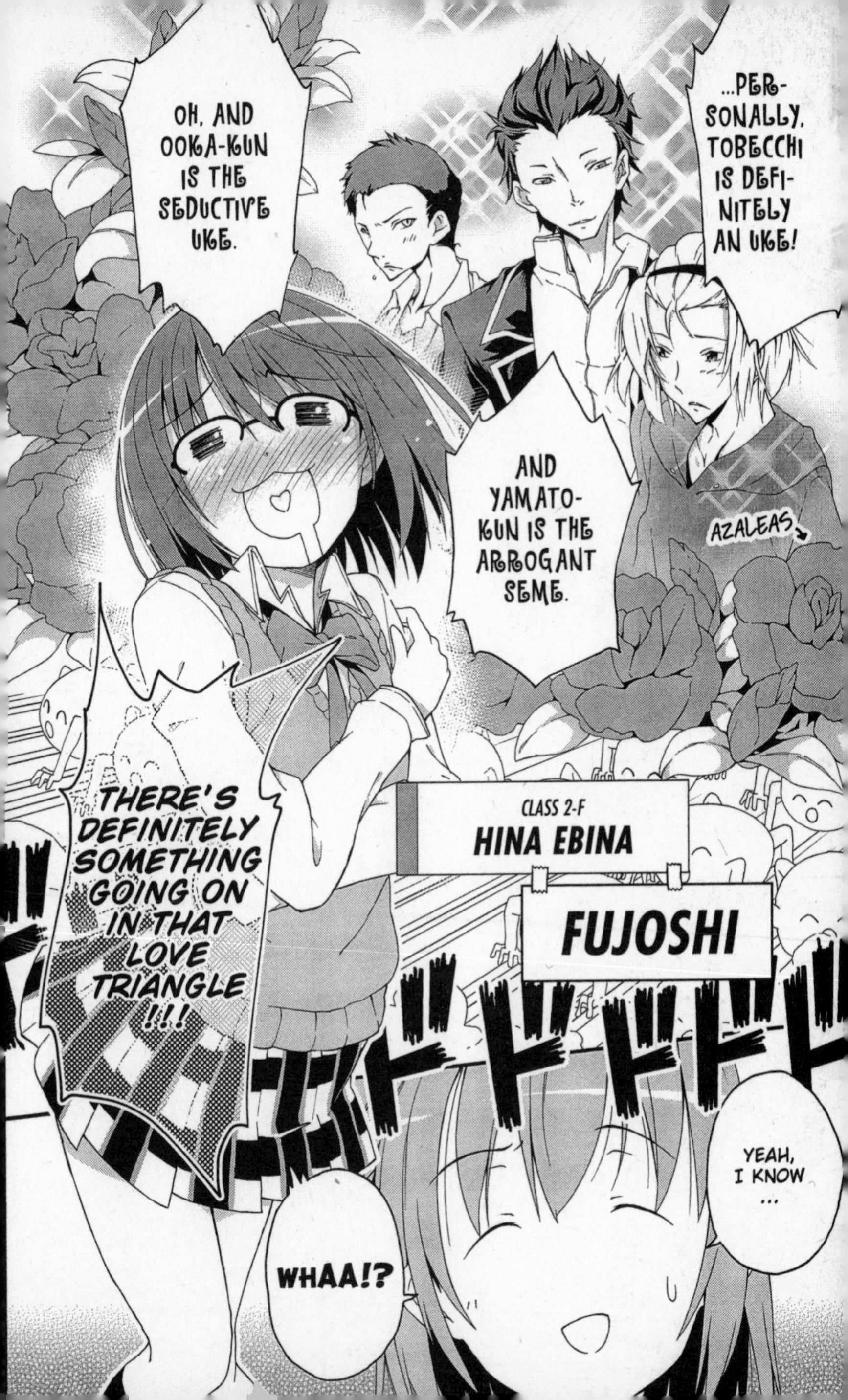
...PER-SONALLY, TOBECCHI IS DEFI-NITELY AN UKE!
OH, AND OOKA-KUN IS THE SEDUCTIVE UKE.
AND YAMATO-KUN IS THE ARROGANT SEME.
AZALEAS
CLASS 2-F
HINA EBINA
FUJOSHI
THERE'S DEFINITELY SOMETHING GOING ON IN THAT LOVE TRIANGLE !!!
YEAH, I KNOW ...
WHAA!?

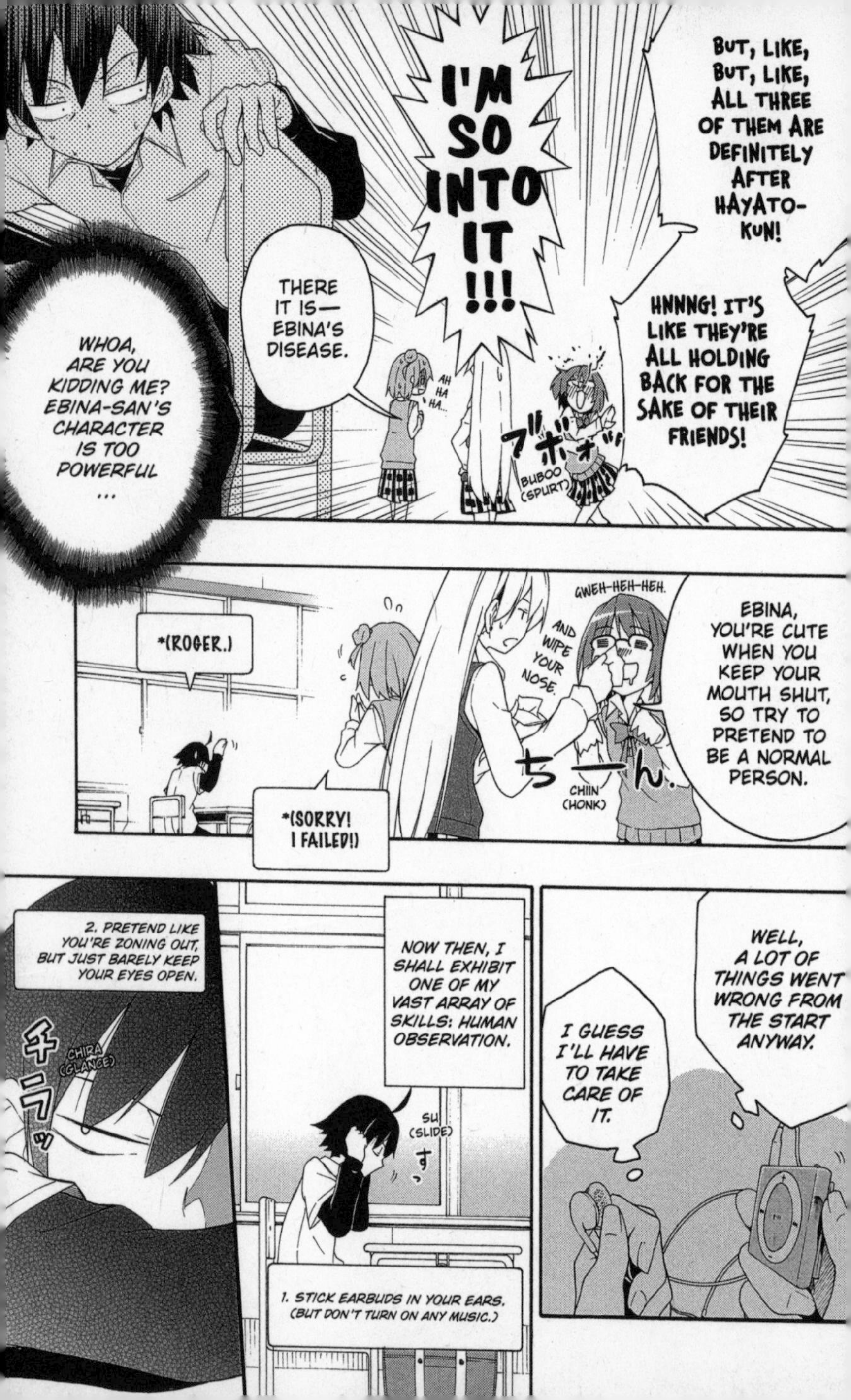
BUT, LIKE, BUT, LIKE, ALL THREE OF THEM ARE DEFINITELY AFTER HAYATO-KUN!
I'M SO INTO IT!!!
HNNNG! IT'S LIKE THEY'RE ALL HOLDING BACK FOR THE SAKE OF THEIR FRIENDS!
ブボォ
BUBOO (SPURT)
THERE IT IS— EBINA'S DISEASE.
AH HA HA...
WHOA, ARE YOU KIDDING ME? EBINA-SAN'S CHARACTER IS TOO POWERFUL...
EBINA, YOU'RE CUTE WHEN YOU KEEP YOUR MOUTH SHUT, SO TRY TO PRETEND TO BE A NORMAL PERSON.
GWEH-HEH-HEH.
AND WIPE YOUR NOSE.
ちーん.
CHIIN (HONK)
*(ROGER.)
*(SORRY! I FAILED!)
WELL, A LOT OF THINGS WENT WRONG FROM THE START ANYWAY.
I GUESS I'LL HAVE TO TAKE CARE OF IT.
NOW THEN, I SHALL EXHIBIT ONE OF MY VAST ARRAY OF SKILLS: HUMAN OBSERVATION.
SU (SLIDE)
す
1. STICK EARBUDS IN YOUR EARS. (BUT DON'T TURN ON ANY MUSIC.)
2. PRETEND LIKE YOU'RE ZONING OUT, BUT JUST BARELY KEEP YOUR EYES OPEN.
チラッ
CHIRA (GLANCE)

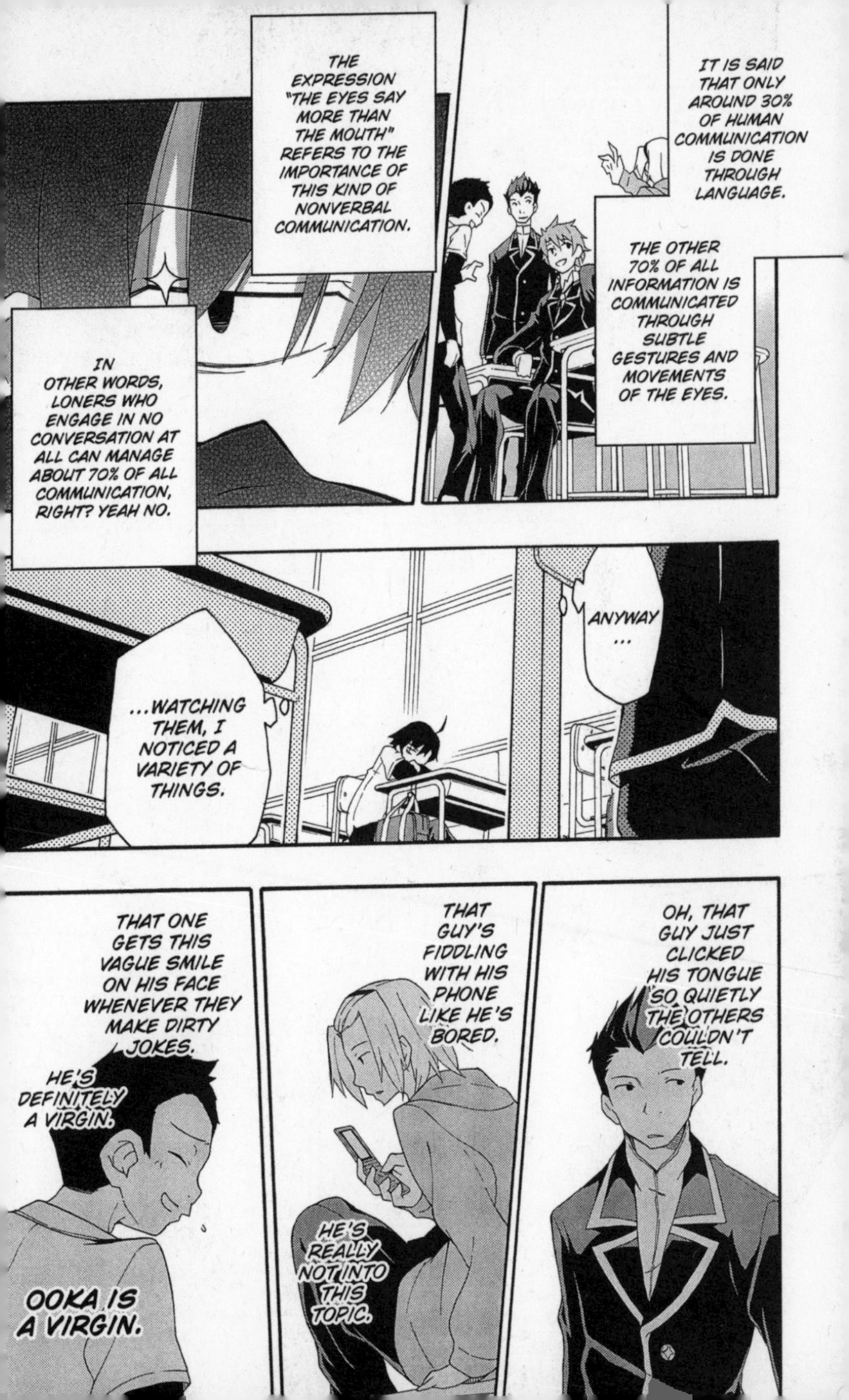
IT IS SAID THAT ONLY AROUND 30% OF HUMAN COMMUNICATION IS DONE THROUGH LANGUAGE.
THE OTHER 70% OF ALL INFORMATION IS COMMUNICATED THROUGH SUBTLE GESTURES AND MOVEMENTS OF THE EYES.
THE EXPRESSION "THE EYES SAY MORE THAN THE MOUTH" REFERS TO THE IMPORTANCE OF THIS KIND OF NONVERBAL COMMUNICATION.
IN OTHER WORDS, LONERS WHO ENGAGE IN NO CONVERSATION AT ALL CAN MANAGE ABOUT 70% OF ALL COMMUNICATION, RIGHT? YEAH NO.
ANYWAY...
...WATCHING THEM, I NOTICED A VARIETY OF THINGS.
OH, THAT GUY JUST CLICKED HIS TONGUE SO QUIETLY THE OTHERS COULDN'T TELL.
THAT GUY'S FIDDLING WITH HIS PHONE LIKE HE'S BORED.
HE'S REALLY NOT INTO THIS TOPIC.
THAT ONE GETS THIS VAGUE SMILE ON HIS FACE WHENEVER THEY MAKE DIRTY JOKES.
HE'S DEFINITELY A VIRGIN.
OOKA IS A VIRGIN.

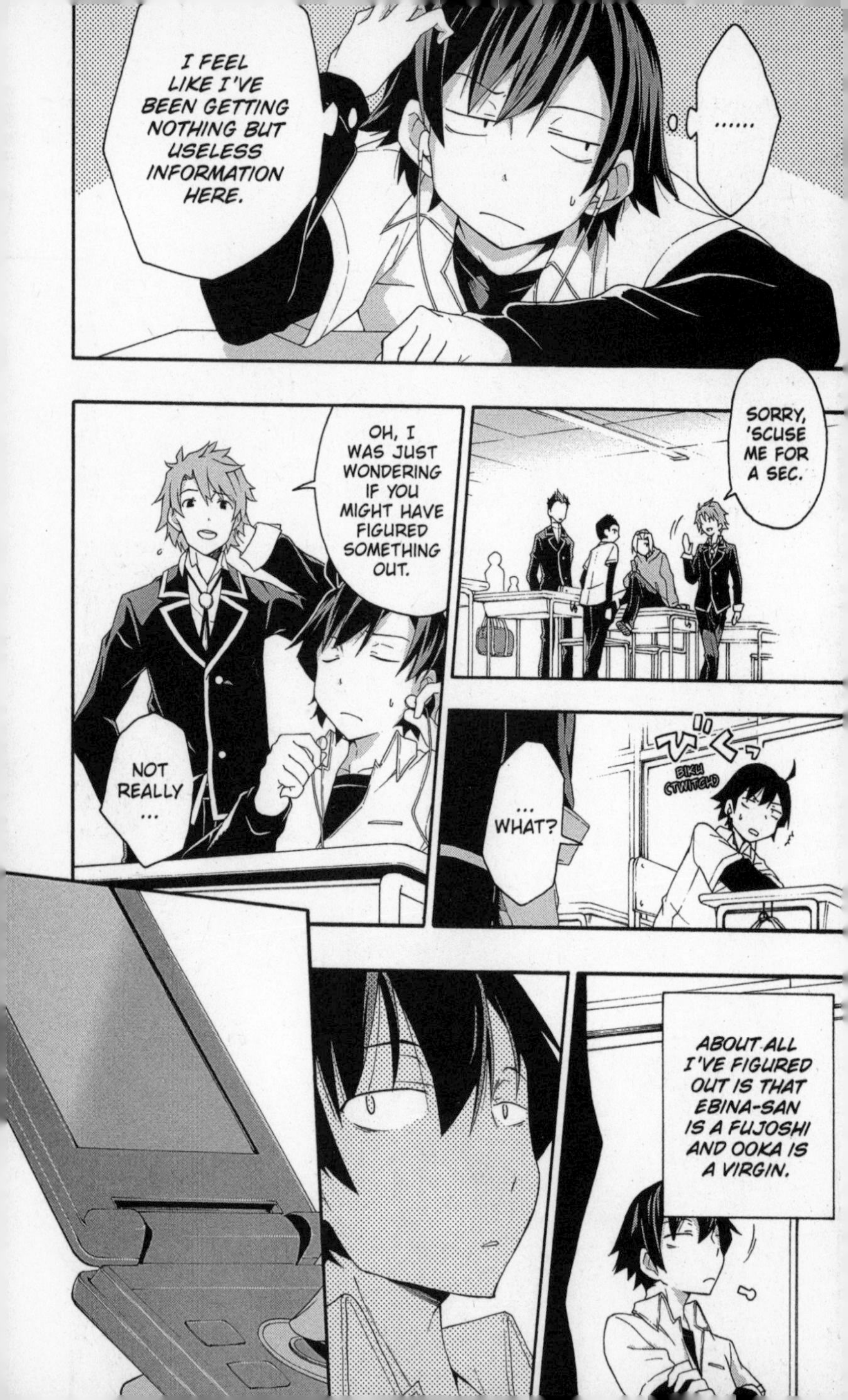
......
I FEEL LIKE I'VE BEEN GETTING NOTHING BUT USELESS INFORMATION HERE.
SORRY, 'SCUSE ME FOR A SEC.
BIKU (TWITCH)
...WHAT?
OH, I WAS JUST WONDERING IF YOU MIGHT HAVE FIGURED SOMETHING OUT.
NOT REALLY...
ABOUT ALL I'VE FIGURED OUT IS THAT EBINA-SAN IS A FUJOSHI AND OOKA IS A VIRGIN.

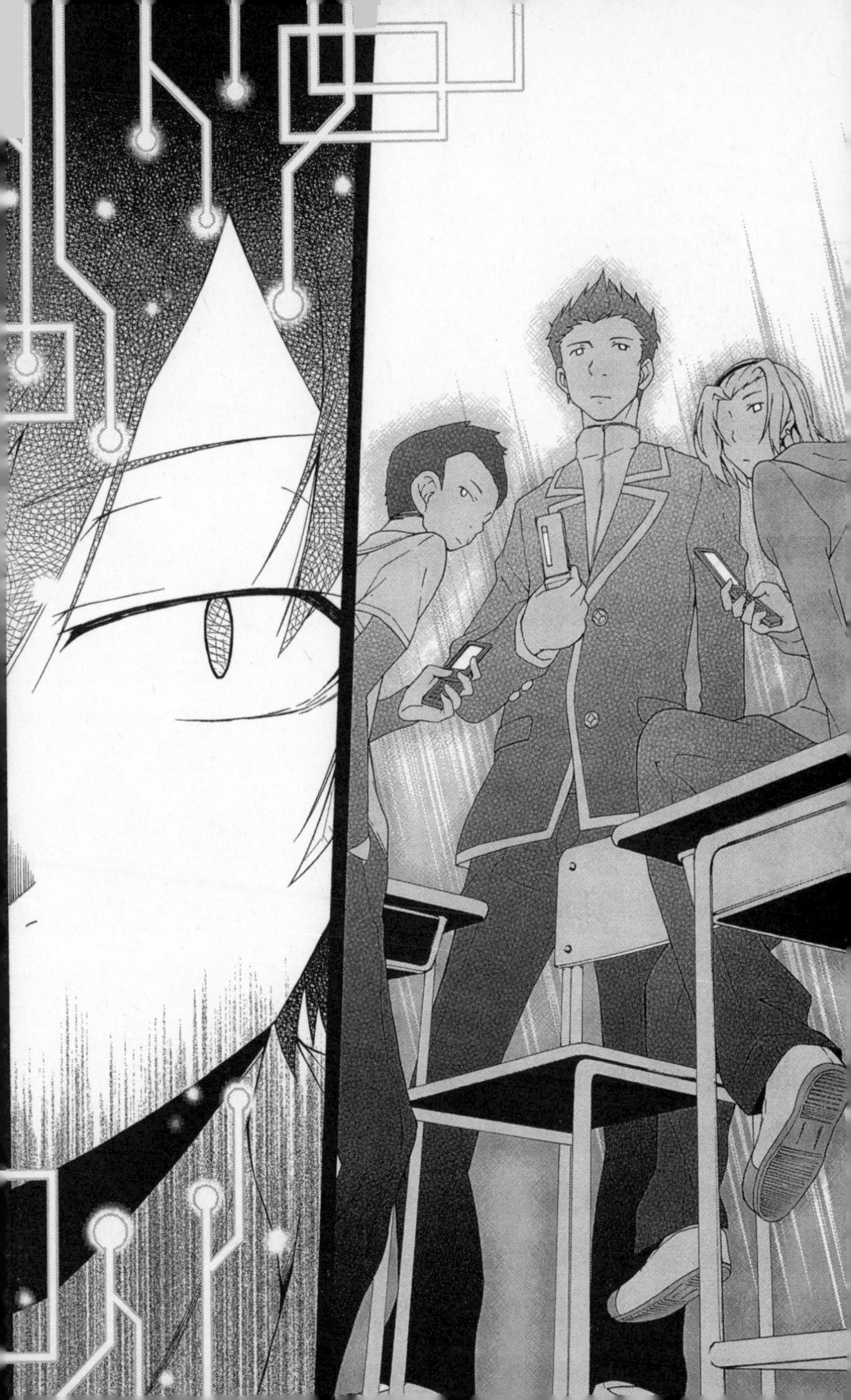

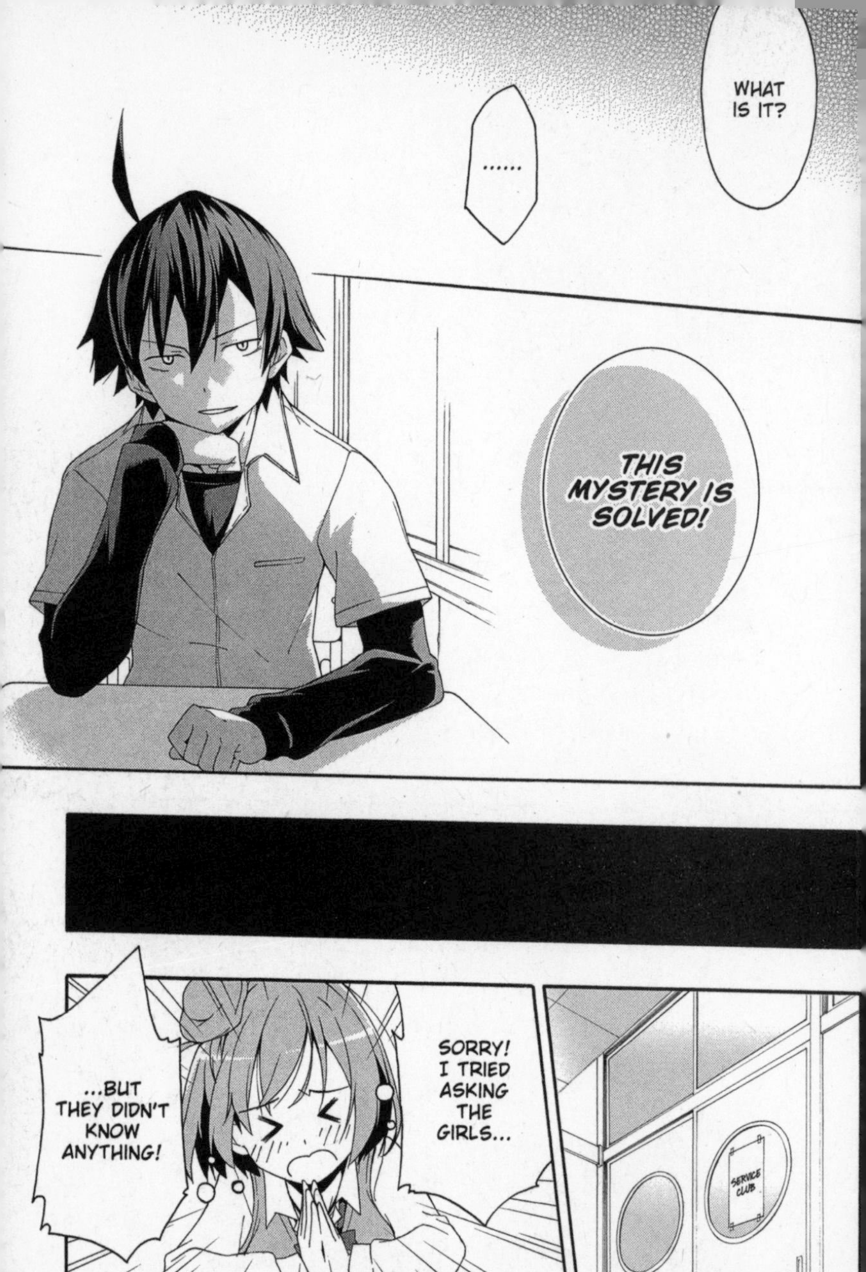
WHAT IS IT?
......
THIS MYSTERY IS SOLVED!
SERVICE CLUB
SORRY! I TRIED ASKING THE GIRLS...
...BUT THEY DIDN'T KNOW ANYTHING!

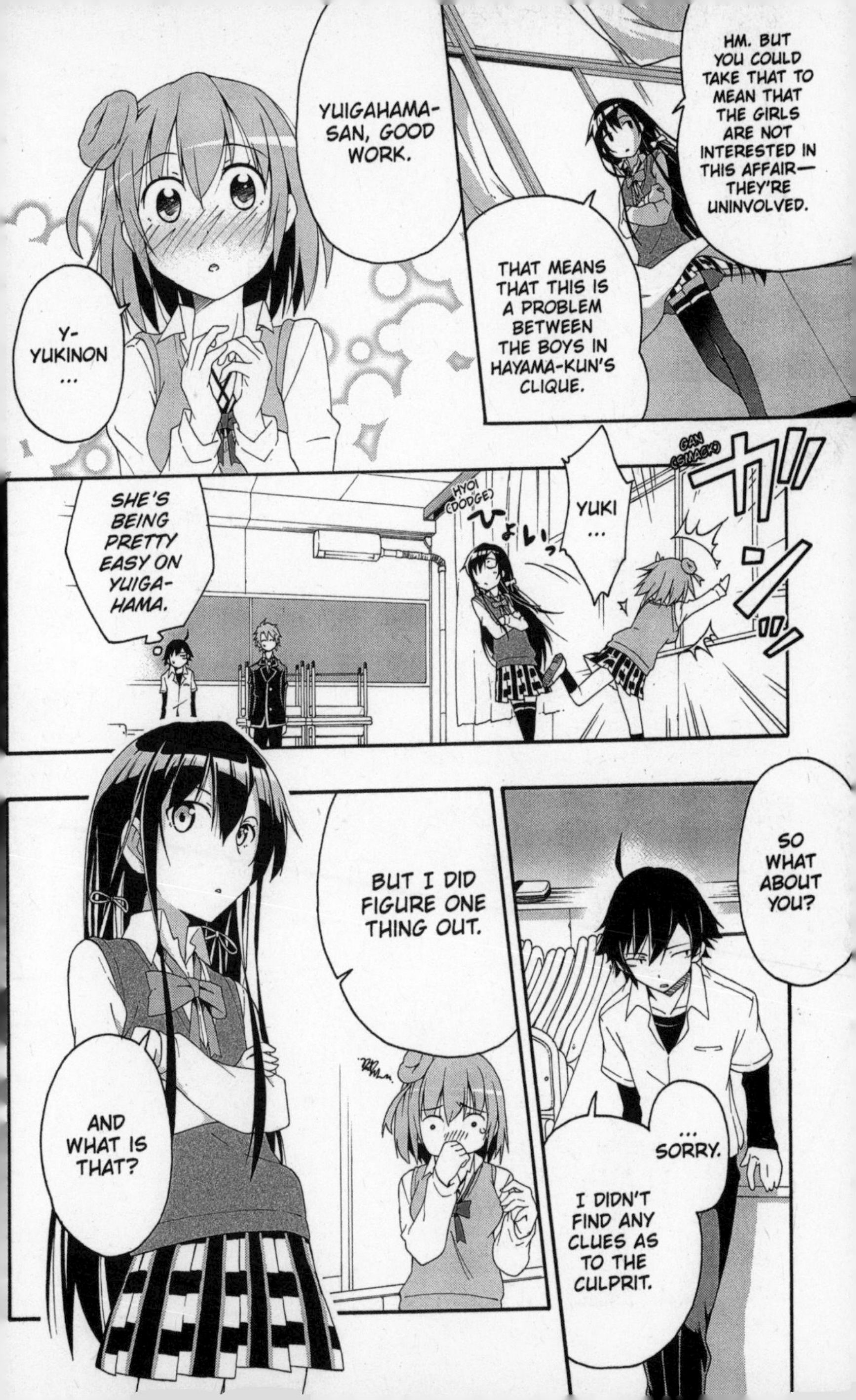
HM. BUT YOU COULD TAKE THAT TO MEAN THAT THE GIRLS ARE NOT INTERESTED IN THIS AFFAIR—THEY'RE UNINVOLVED.
THAT MEANS THAT THIS IS A PROBLEM BETWEEN THE BOYS IN HAYAMA-KUN'S CLIQUE.
YUIGAHAMA-SAN, GOOD WORK.
Y-YUKINON ...
GAN (SMACK)
YUKI ...
HYOI (DODGE)
SHE'S BEING PRETTY EASY ON YUIGA-HAMA.
SO WHAT ABOUT YOU?
... SORRY.
I DIDN'T FIND ANY CLUES AS TO THE CULPRIT.
BUT I DID FIGURE ONE THING OUT.
AND WHAT IS THAT?

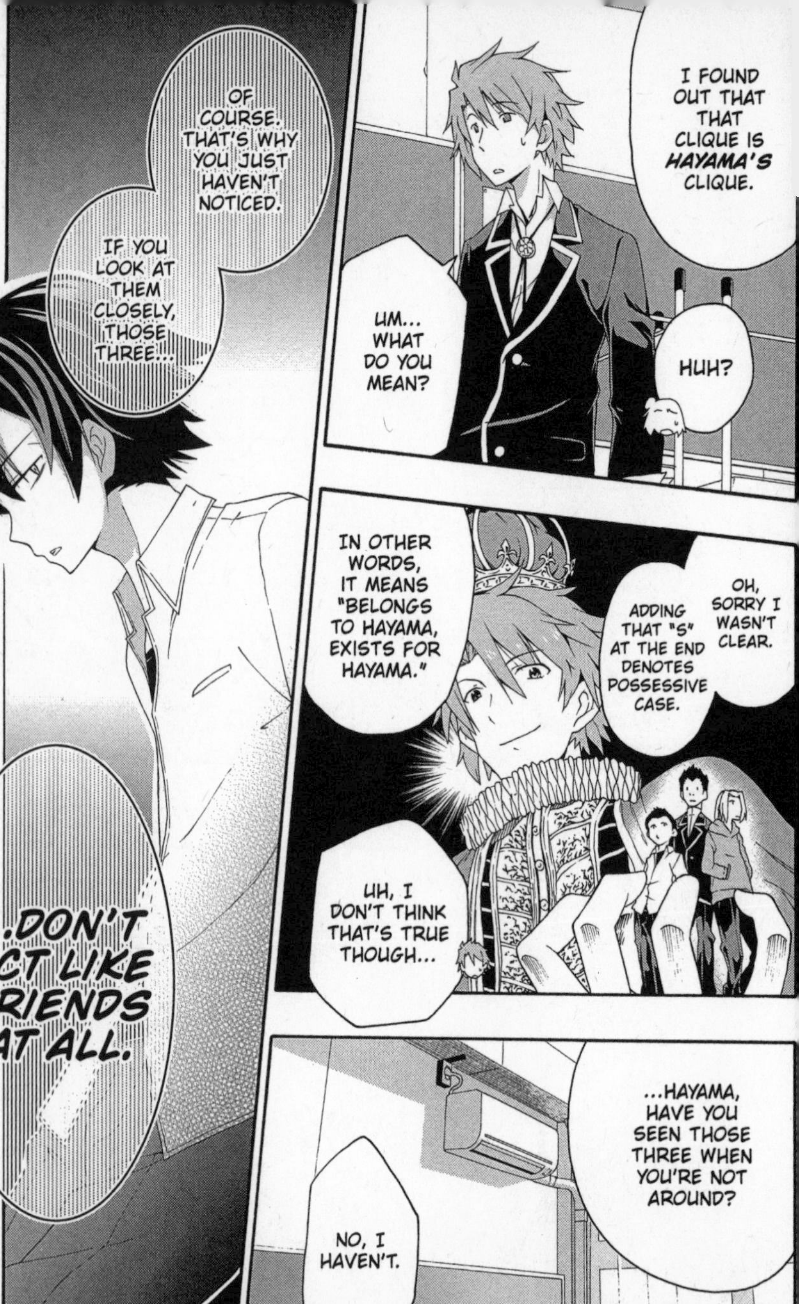

I FOUND OUT THAT THAT CLIQUE IS ***HAYAMA'S*** CLIQUE.
HUH?
UM... WHAT DO YOU MEAN?
OH, SORRY I WASN'T CLEAR.
ADDING THAT "S" AT THE END DENOTES POSSESSIVE CASE.
IN OTHER WORDS, IT MEANS "BELONGS TO HAYAMA, EXISTS FOR HAYAMA."
UH, I DON'T THINK THAT'S TRUE THOUGH...
...HAYAMA, HAVE YOU SEEN THOSE THREE WHEN YOU'RE NOT AROUND?
NO, I HAVEN'T.
OF COURSE. THAT'S WHY YOU JUST HAVEN'T NOTICED.
IF YOU LOOK AT THEM CLOSELY, THOSE THREE...
...DON'T ACT LIKE FRIENDS AT ALL.

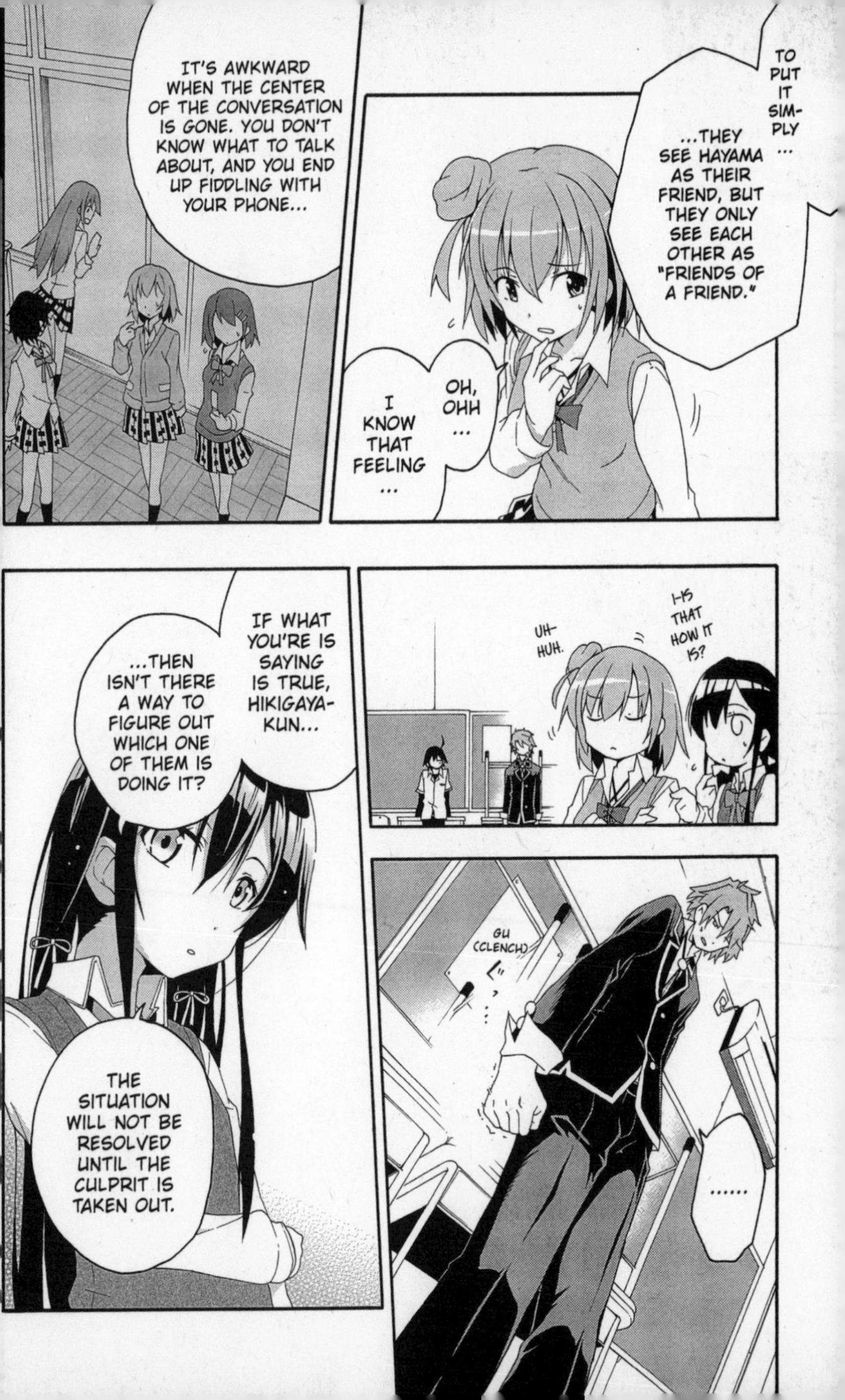
TO PUT IT SIMPLY...
...THEY SEE HAYAMA AS THEIR FRIEND, BUT THEY ONLY SEE EACH OTHER AS "FRIENDS OF A FRIEND."
OH, OHH...
I KNOW THAT FEELING...
IT'S AWKWARD WHEN THE CENTER OF THE CONVERSATION IS GONE. YOU DON'T KNOW WHAT TO TALK ABOUT, AND YOU END UP FIDDLING WITH YOUR PHONE...
I-IS THAT HOW IT IS?
UH-HUH.
GU (CLENCH)
......
IF WHAT YOU'RE IS SAYING IS TRUE, HIKIGAYA-KUN...
...THEN ISN'T THERE A WAY TO FIGURE OUT WHICH ONE OF THEM IS DOING IT?
THE SITUATION WILL NOT BE RESOLVED UNTIL THE CULPRIT IS TAKEN OUT.

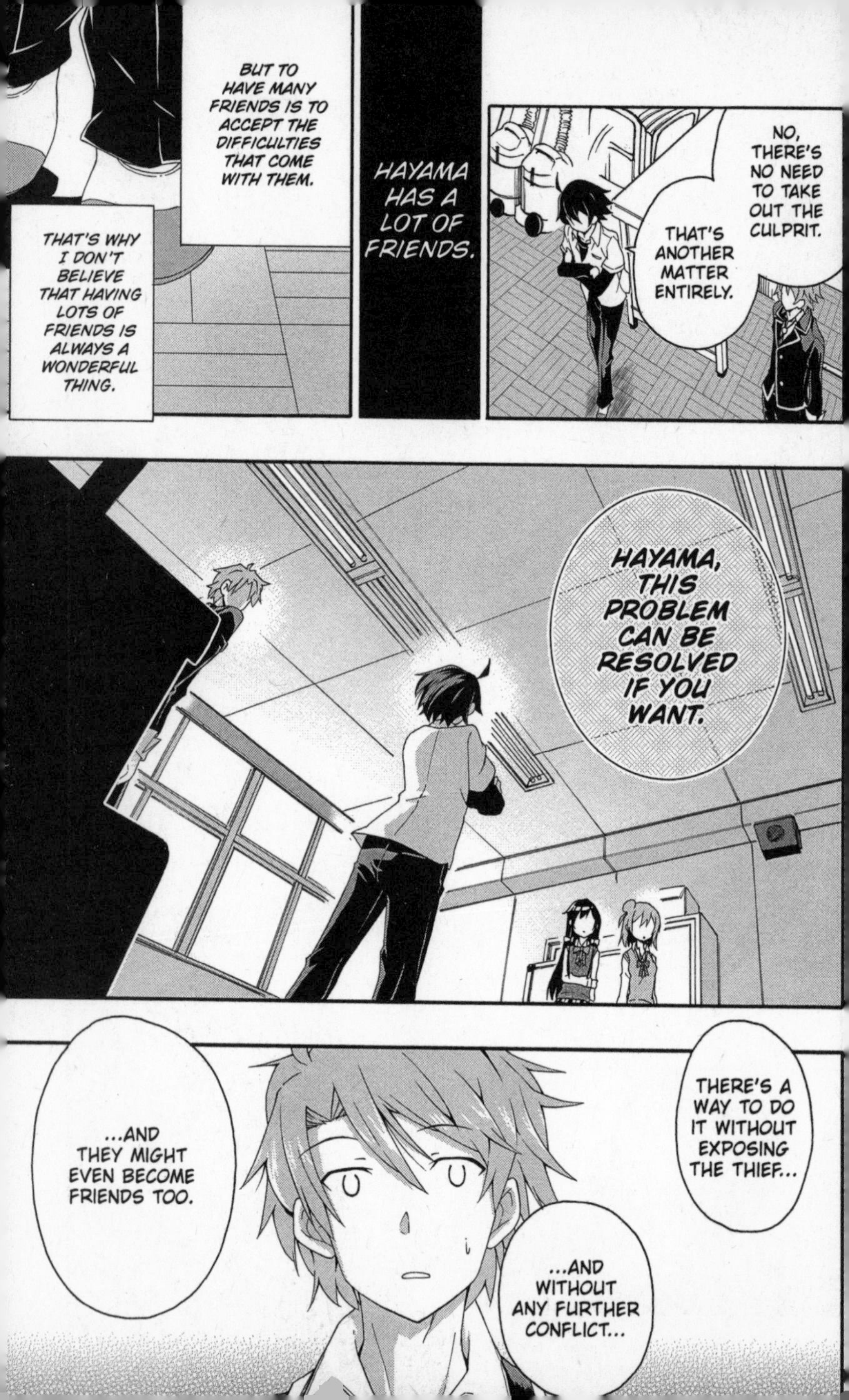
NO, THERE'S NO NEED TO TAKE OUT THE CULPRIT.
THAT'S ANOTHER MATTER ENTIRELY.
HAYAMA HAS A LOT OF FRIENDS.
BUT TO HAVE MANY FRIENDS IS TO ACCEPT THE DIFFICULTIES THAT COME WITH THEM.
THAT'S WHY I DON'T BELIEVE THAT HAVING LOTS OF FRIENDS IS ALWAYS A WONDERFUL THING.
HAYAMA, THIS PROBLEM CAN BE RESOLVED IF YOU WANT.
THERE'S A WAY TO DO IT WITHOUT EXPOSING THE THIEF...
...AND WITHOUT ANY FURTHER CONFLICT...
...AND THEY MIGHT EVEN BECOME FRIENDS TOO.

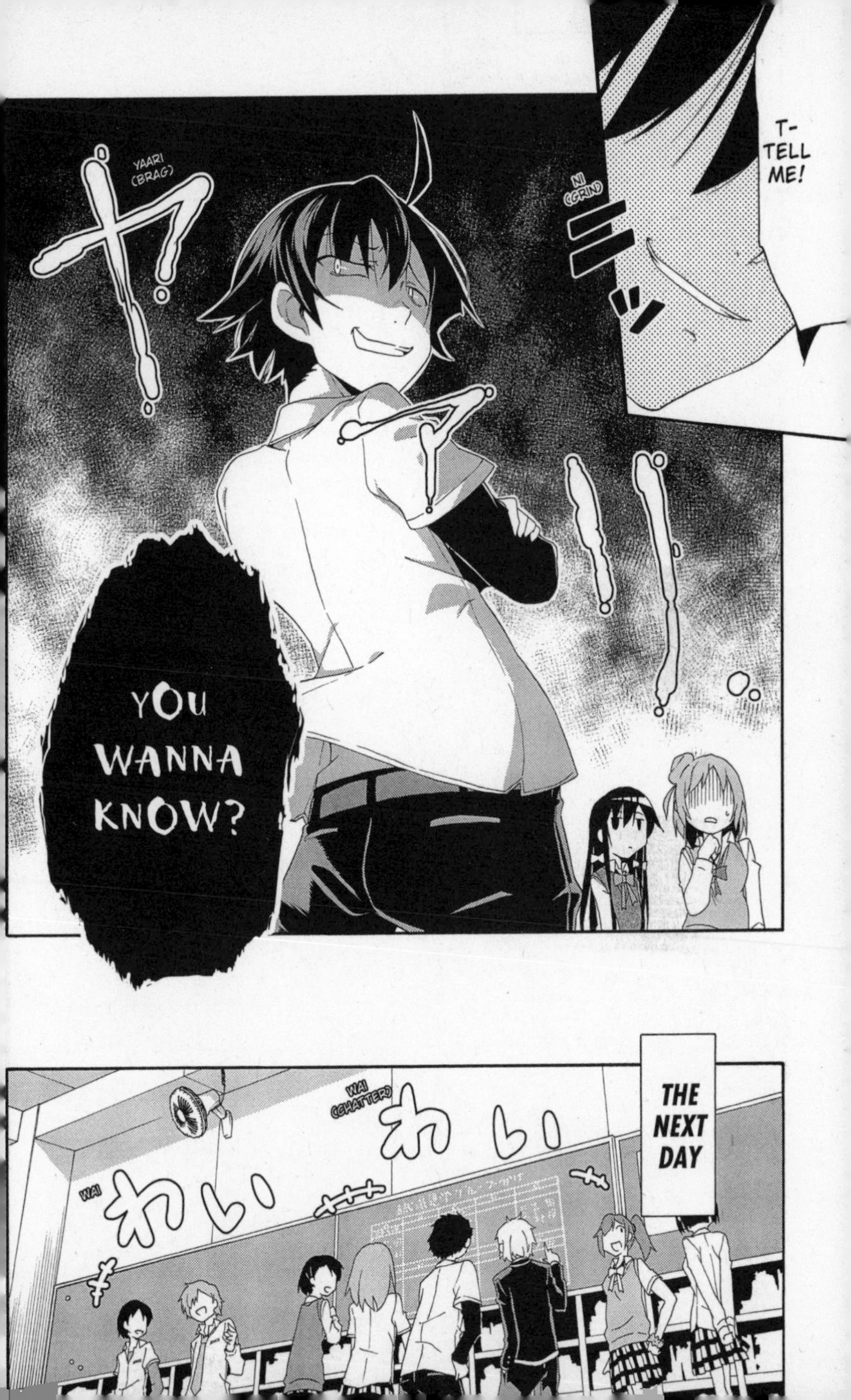
T-TELL ME!
NI (GRIN)
YAARI (BRAG)
YOU WANNA KNOW?
THE NEXT DAY
WAI (CHATTER)
WAI

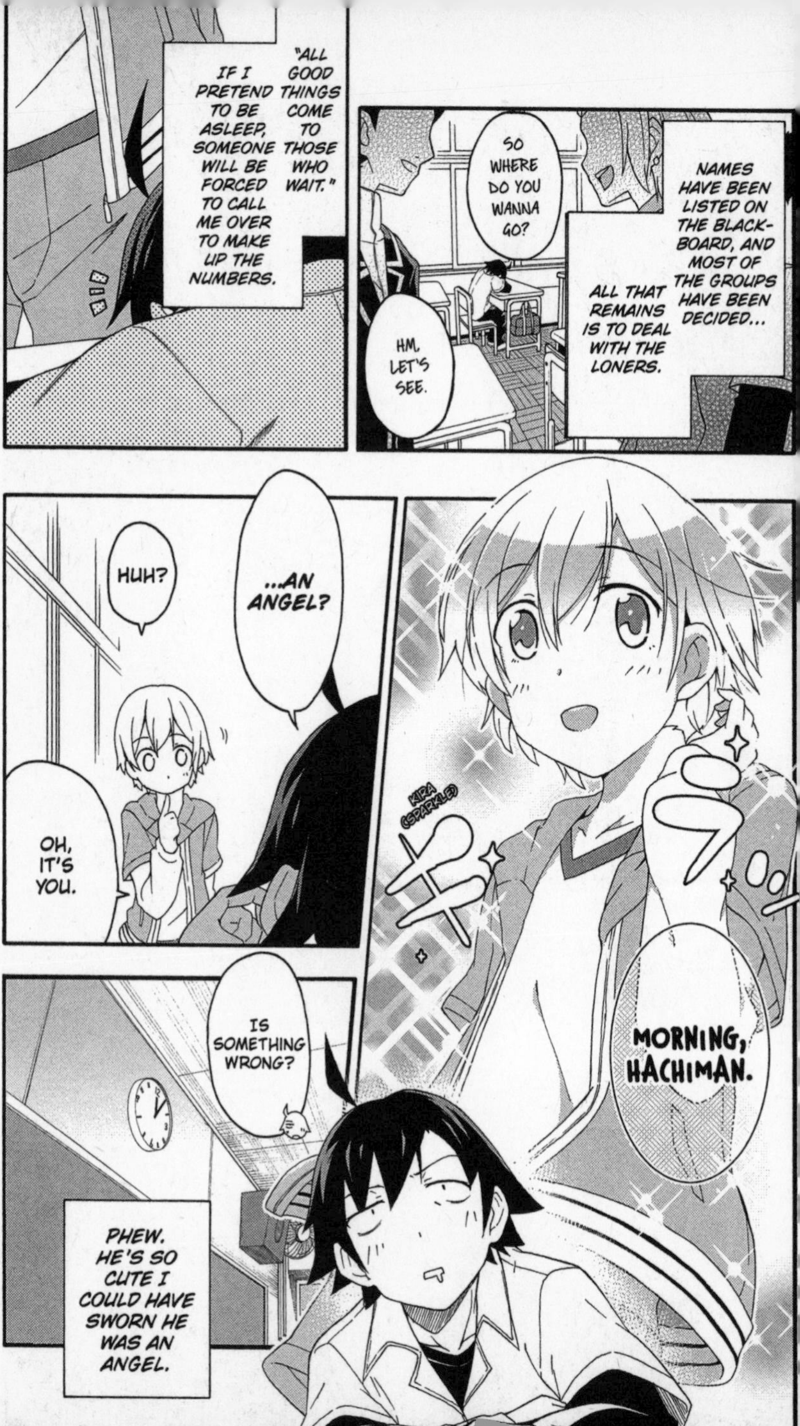
NAMES HAVE BEEN LISTED ON THE BLACKBOARD, AND MOST OF THE GROUPS HAVE BEEN DECIDED...
ALL THAT REMAINS IS TO DEAL WITH THE LONERS.
SO WHERE DO YOU WANNA GO?
HM, LET'S SEE.
"ALL GOOD THINGS COME TO THOSE WHO WAIT."
IF I PRETEND TO BE ASLEEP, SOMEONE WILL BE FORCED TO CALL ME OVER TO MAKE UP THE NUMBERS.
KIRA (SPARKLE)
MORNING, HACHIMAN.
...AN ANGEL?
HUH?
OH, IT'S YOU.
IS SOMETHING WRONG?
PHEW. HE'S SO CUTE I COULD HAVE SWORN HE WAS AN ANGEL.

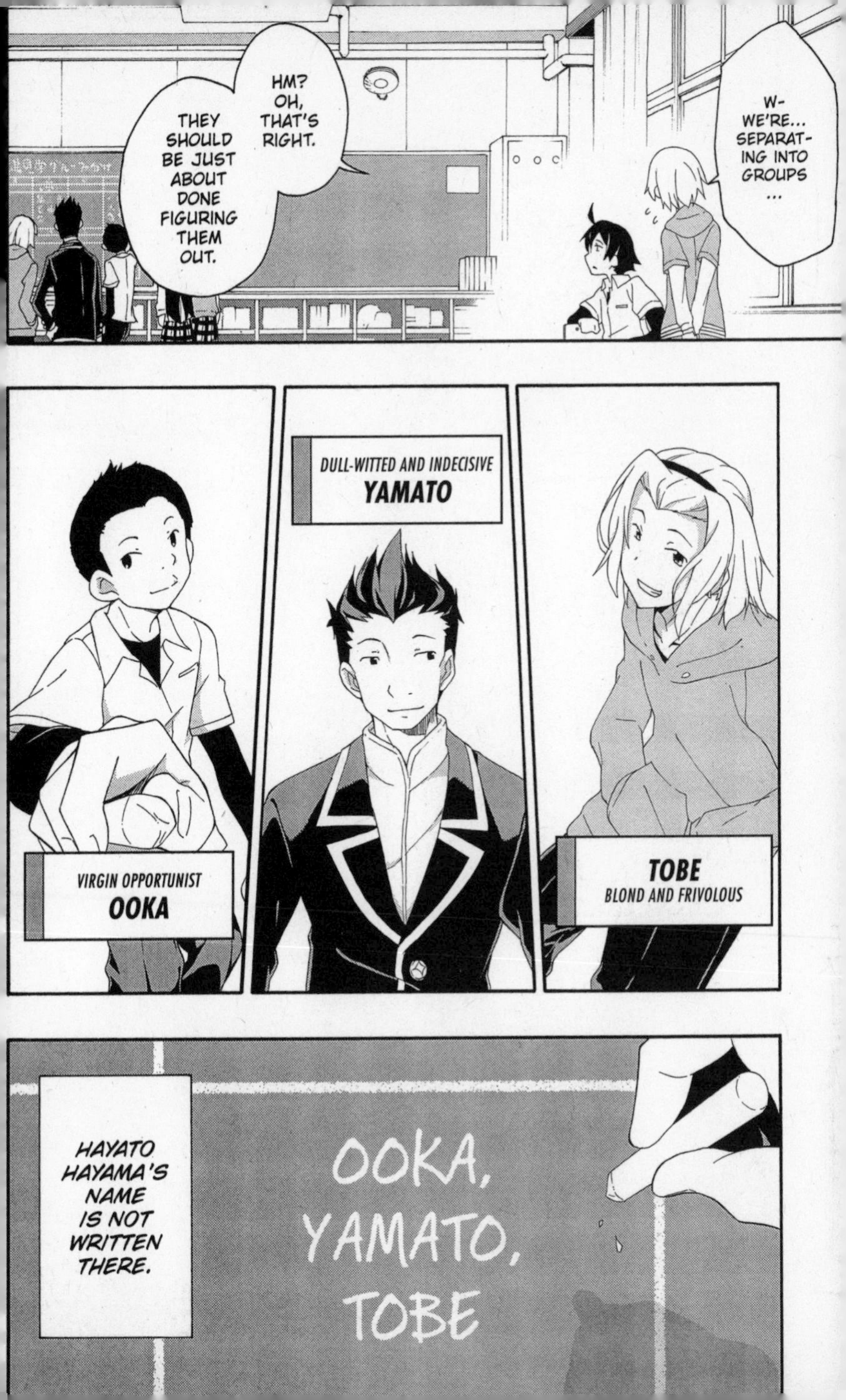

W-WE'RE... SEPARAT-ING INTO GROUPS...
HM? OH, THAT'S RIGHT.
THEY SHOULD BE JUST ABOUT DONE FIGURING THEM OUT.
TOBE
BLOND AND FRIVOLOUS
DULL-WITTED AND INDECISIVE
YAMATO
VIRGIN OPPORTUNIST
OOKA
OOKA, YAMATO, TOBE
HAYATO HAYAMA'S NAME IS NOT WRITTEN THERE.

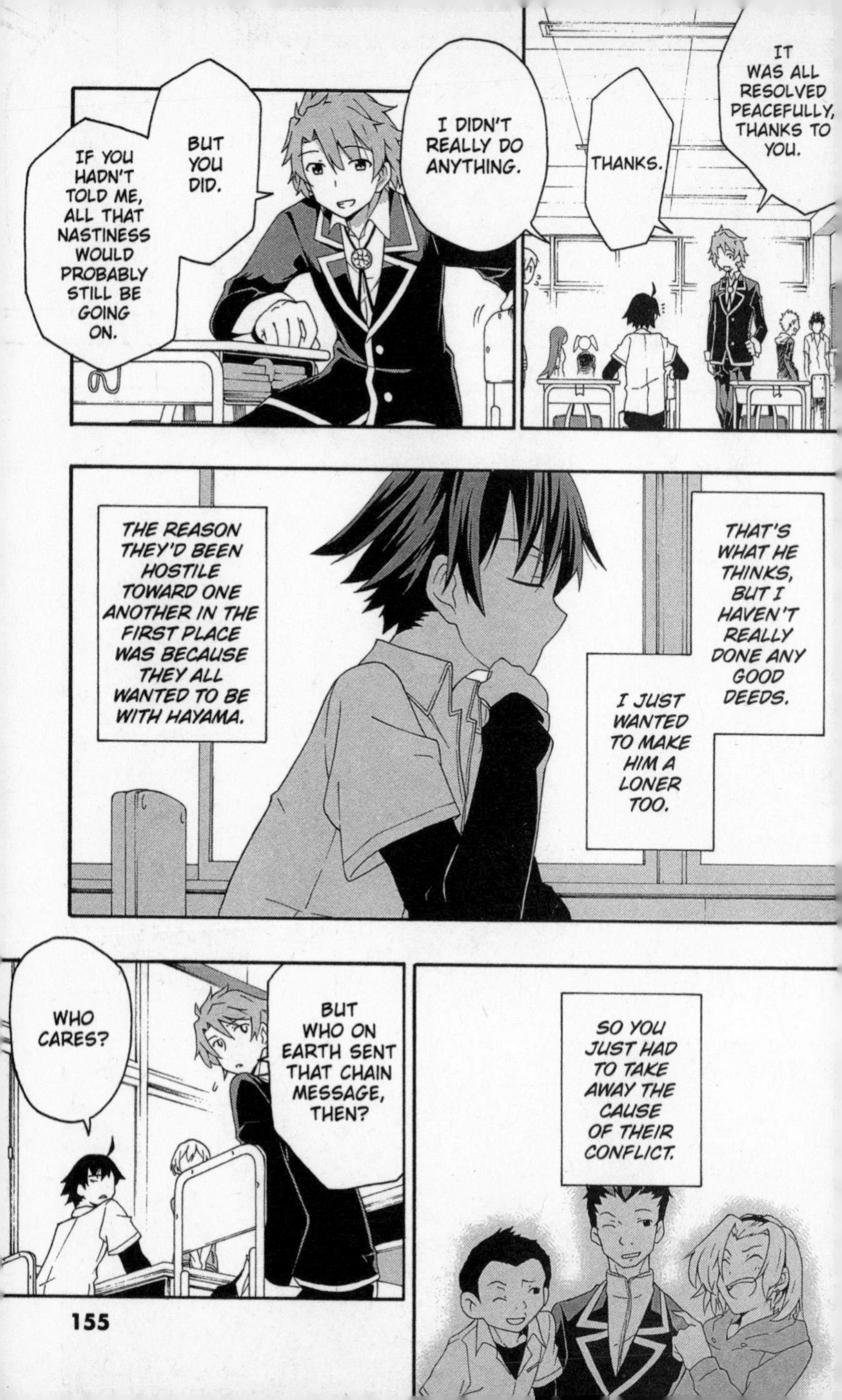
IT WAS ALL RESOLVED PEACEFULLY, THANKS TO YOU.
THANKS.
I DIDN'T REALLY DO ANYTHING.
BUT YOU DID.
IF YOU HADN'T TOLD ME, ALL THAT NASTINESS WOULD PROBABLY STILL BE GOING ON.
THAT'S WHAT HE THINKS, BUT I HAVEN'T REALLY DONE ANY GOOD DEEDS.
I JUST WANTED TO MAKE HIM A LONER TOO.
THE REASON THEY'D BEEN HOSTILE TOWARD ONE ANOTHER IN THE FIRST PLACE WAS BECAUSE THEY ALL WANTED TO BE WITH HAYAMA.
SO YOU JUST HAD TO TAKE AWAY THE CAUSE OF THEIR CONFLICT.
BUT WHO ON EARTH SENT THAT CHAIN MESSAGE, THEN?
WHO CARES?

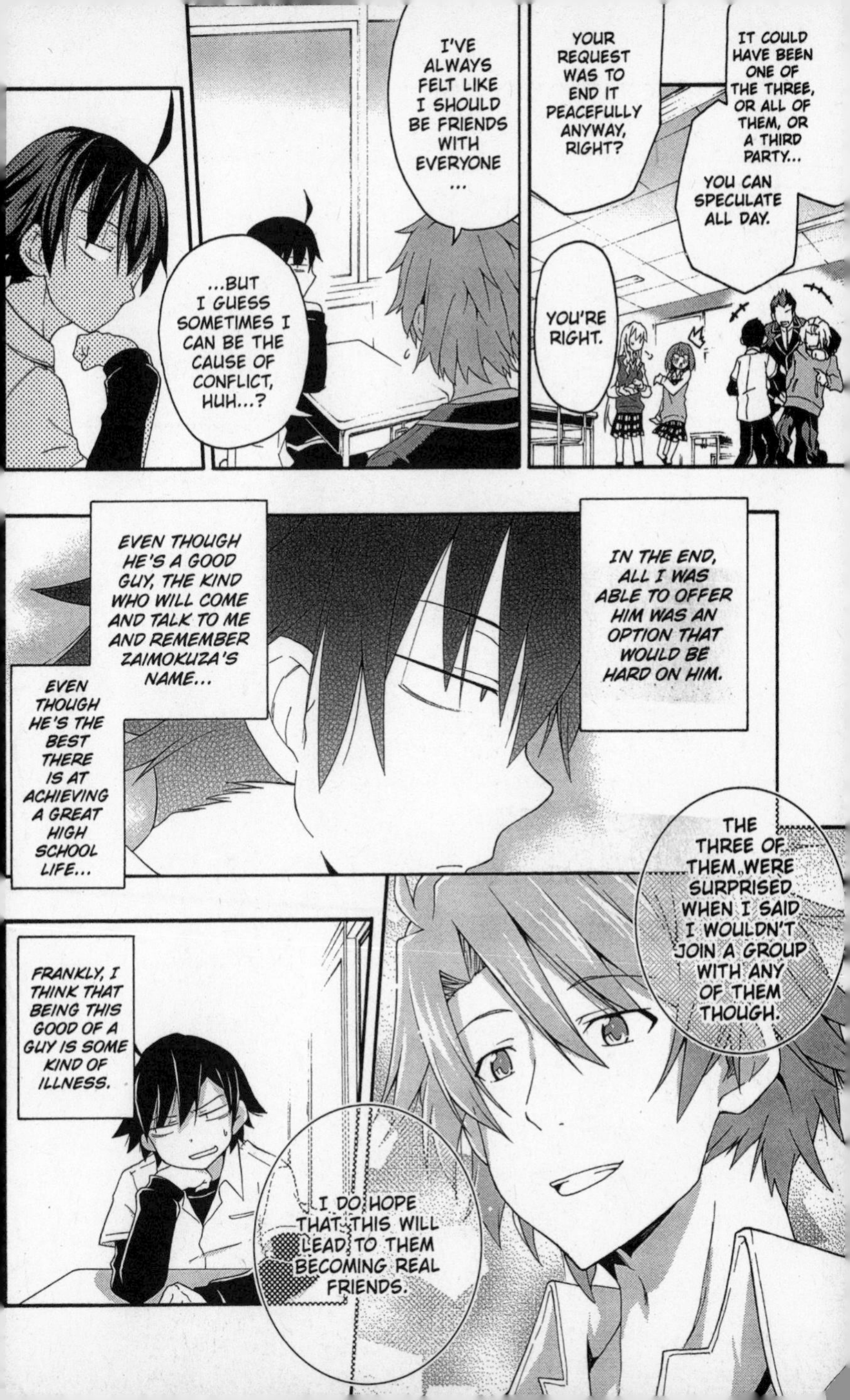
IT COULD HAVE BEEN ONE OF THE THREE, OR ALL OF THEM, OR A THIRD PARTY...
YOU CAN SPECULATE ALL DAY.
YOUR REQUEST WAS TO END IT PEACEFULLY ANYWAY, RIGHT?
YOU'RE RIGHT.
I'VE ALWAYS FELT LIKE I SHOULD BE FRIENDS WITH EVERYONE...
...BUT I GUESS SOMETIMES I CAN BE THE CAUSE OF CONFLICT, HUH...?
IN THE END, ALL I WAS ABLE TO OFFER HIM WAS AN OPTION THAT WOULD BE HARD ON HIM.
EVEN THOUGH HE'S A GOOD GUY, THE KIND WHO WILL COME AND TALK TO ME AND REMEMBER ZAIMOKUZA'S NAME...
EVEN THOUGH HE'S THE BEST THERE IS AT ACHIEVING A GREAT HIGH SCHOOL LIFE...
THE THREE OF THEM WERE SURPRISED WHEN I SAID I WOULDN'T JOIN A GROUP WITH ANY OF THEM THOUGH.
I DO HOPE THAT THIS WILL LEAD TO THEM BECOMING REAL FRIENDS.
FRANKLY, I THINK THAT BEING THIS GOOD OF A GUY IS SOME KIND OF ILLNESS.

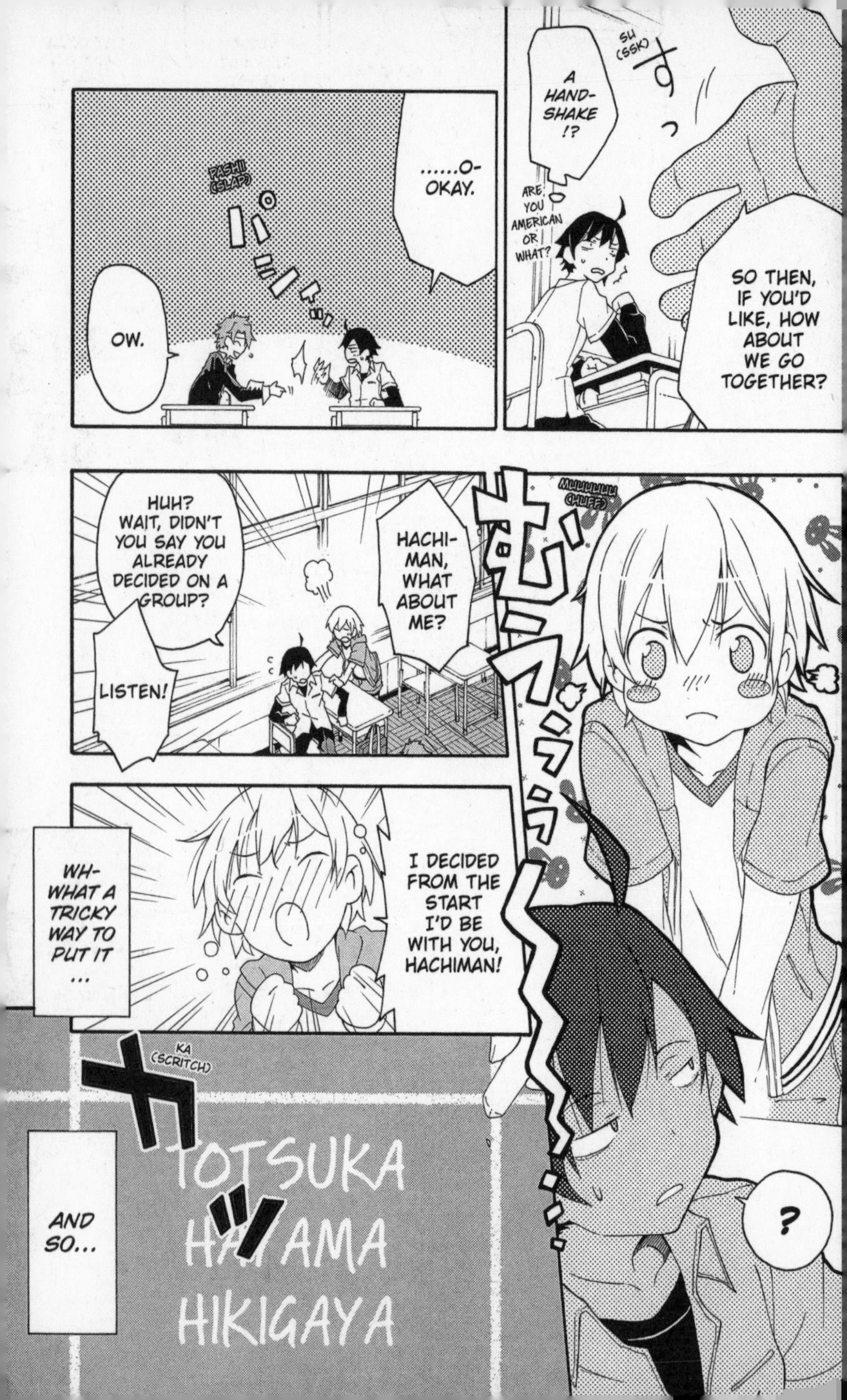
SU (SSK)
A HAND-SHAKE!?
ARE YOU AMERICAN OR WHAT?
SO THEN, IF YOU'D LIKE, HOW ABOUT WE GO TOGETHER?
......O-OKAY.
PASHI (SLAP)
OW.
MUUUUUU (HUFF)
?
HACHI-MAN, WHAT ABOUT ME?
HUH? WAIT, DIDN'T YOU SAY YOU ALREADY DECIDED ON A GROUP?
LISTEN!
I DECIDED FROM THE START I'D BE WITH YOU, HACHIMAN!
WH-WHAT A TRICKY WAY TO PUT IT ...
KA (SCRITCH)
TOTSUKA
HA AMA
HIKIGAYA
AND SO...

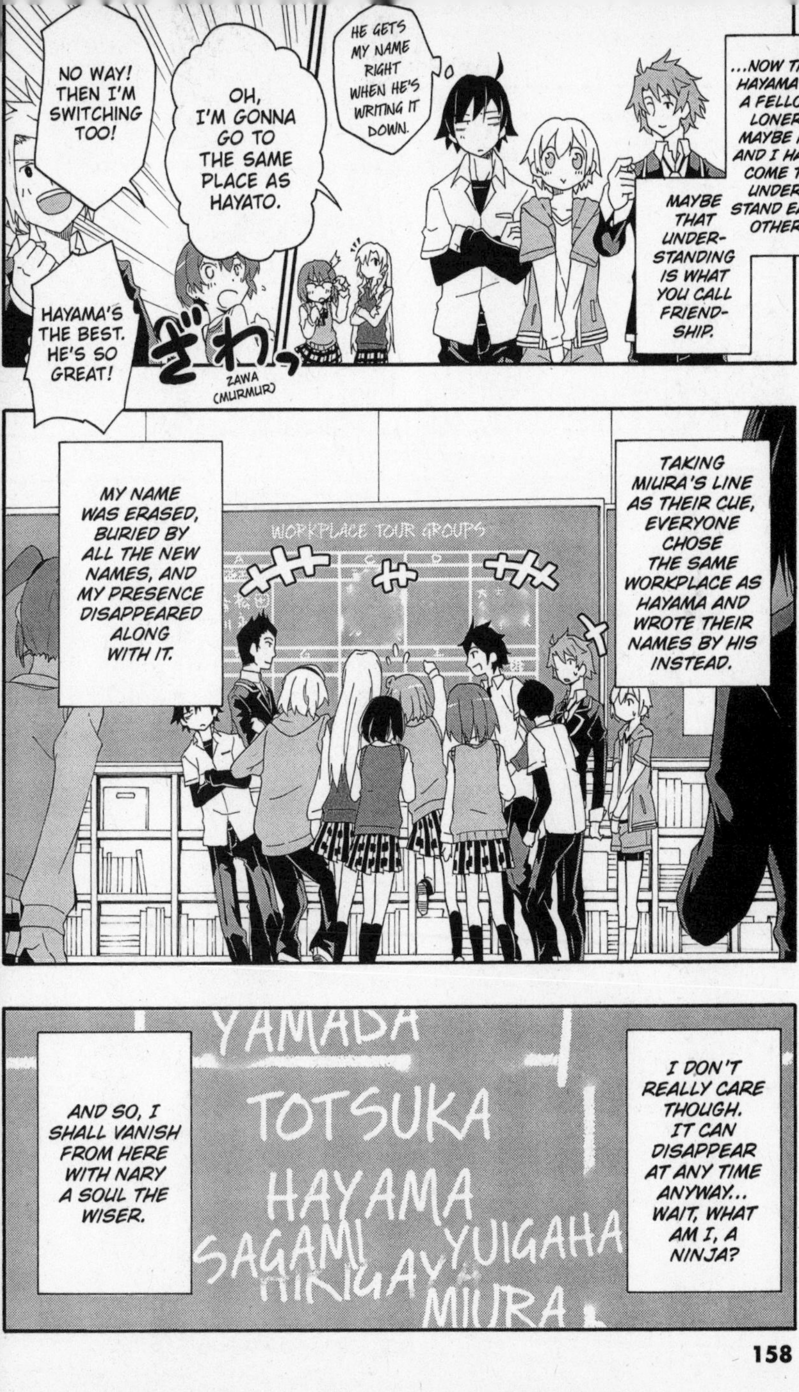
...NOW THAT HAYAMA IS A FELLOW LONER, MAYBE HE AND I HAVE COME TO UNDERSTAND EACH OTHER.
MAYBE THAT UNDERSTANDING IS WHAT YOU CALL FRIENDSHIP.
HE GETS MY NAME RIGHT WHEN HE'S WRITING IT DOWN.
OH, I'M GONNA GO TO THE SAME PLACE AS HAYATO.
NO WAY! THEN I'M SWITCHING TOO!
ざわっ
ZAWA (MURMUR)
HAYAMA'S THE BEST. HE'S SO GREAT!
TAKING MIURA'S LINE AS THEIR CUE, EVERYONE CHOSE THE SAME WORKPLACE AS HAYAMA AND WROTE THEIR NAMES BY HIS INSTEAD.
WORKPLACE TOUR GROUPS
MY NAME WAS ERASED, BURIED BY ALL THE NEW NAMES, AND MY PRESENCE DISAPPEARED ALONG WITH IT.
I DON'T REALLY CARE THOUGH. IT CAN DISAPPEAR AT ANY TIME ANYWAY... WAIT, WHAT AM I, A NINJA?
YAMADA
TOTSUKA
HAYAMA
SAGAMI
YUIGAHA
MIURA
AND SO, I SHALL VANISH FROM HERE WITH NARY A SOUL THE WISER.

CHAPTER 1 ... SAKI KAWASAKI HAS SOME STUFF GOING ON, SO SHE'S SULKING. (PART ONE)

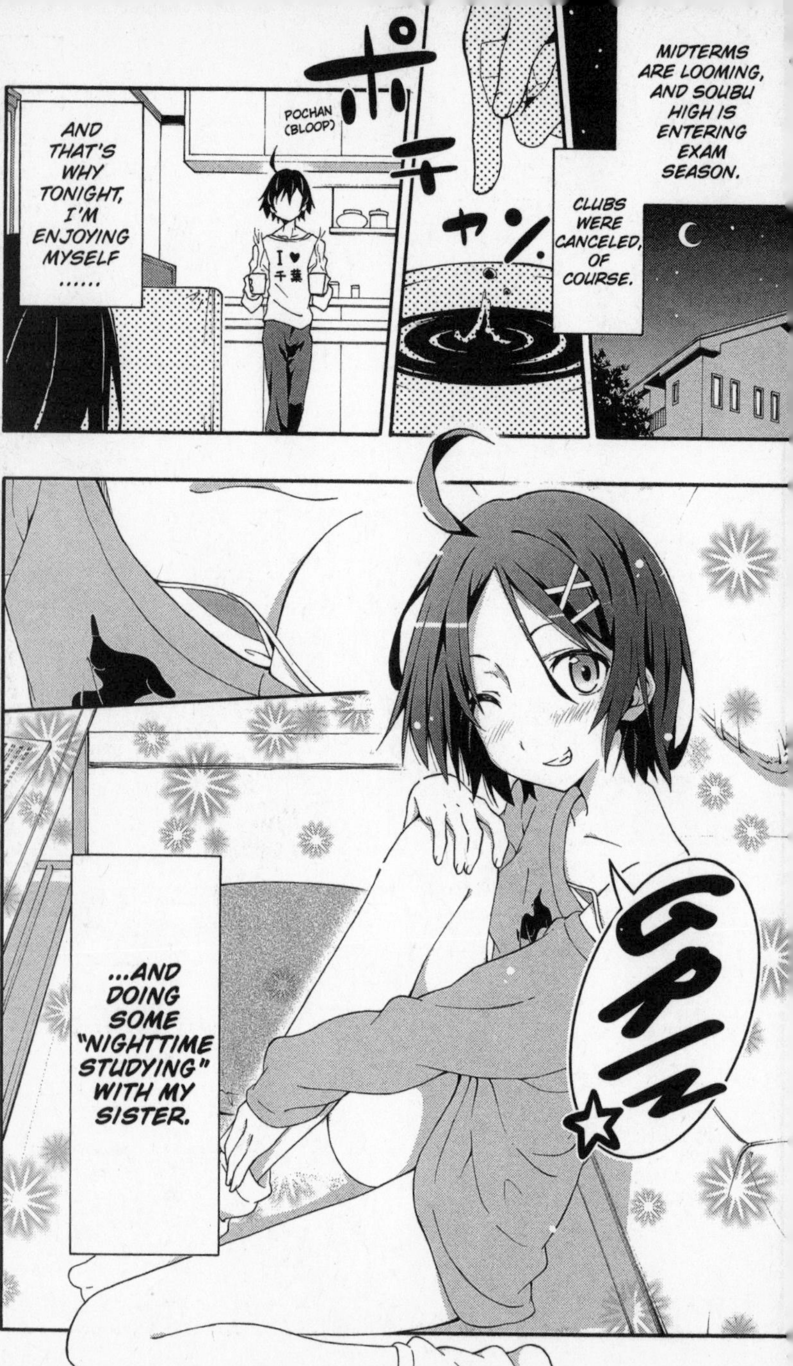
MIDTERMS ARE LOOMING, AND SOUBU HIGH IS ENTERING EXAM SEASON.
CLUBS WERE CANCELED, OF COURSE.
ポチャン
POCHAN (BLOOP)
AND THAT'S WHY TONIGHT, I'M ENJOYING MYSELF ......
I ♥ 千葉
GRIN
...AND DOING SOME "NIGHTTIME STUDYING" WITH MY SISTER.

CHAPTER 11 ... SAKI KAWASAKI HAS SOME STUFF GOING ON, SO SHE'S SULKING. (PART ONE)

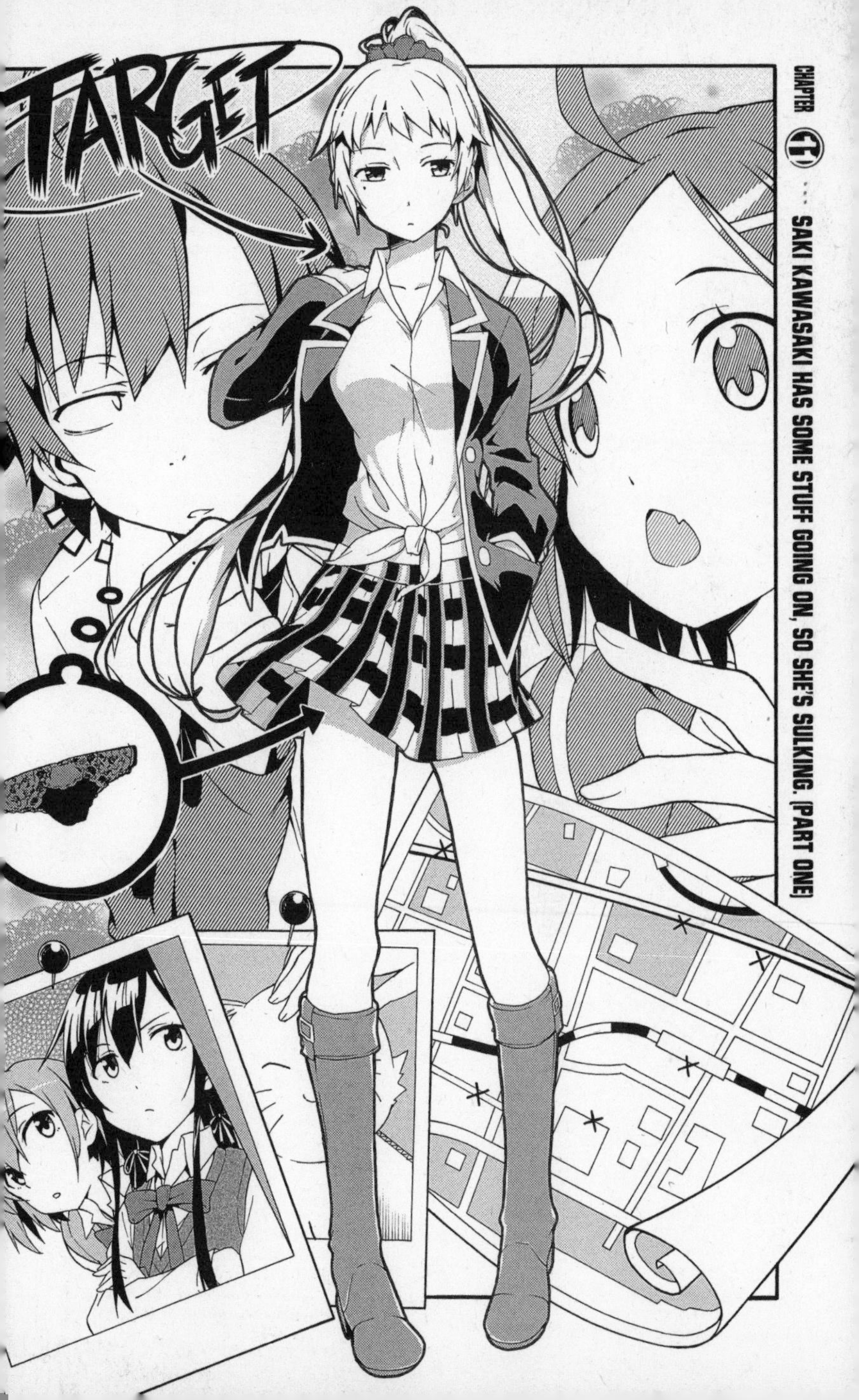
TARGET

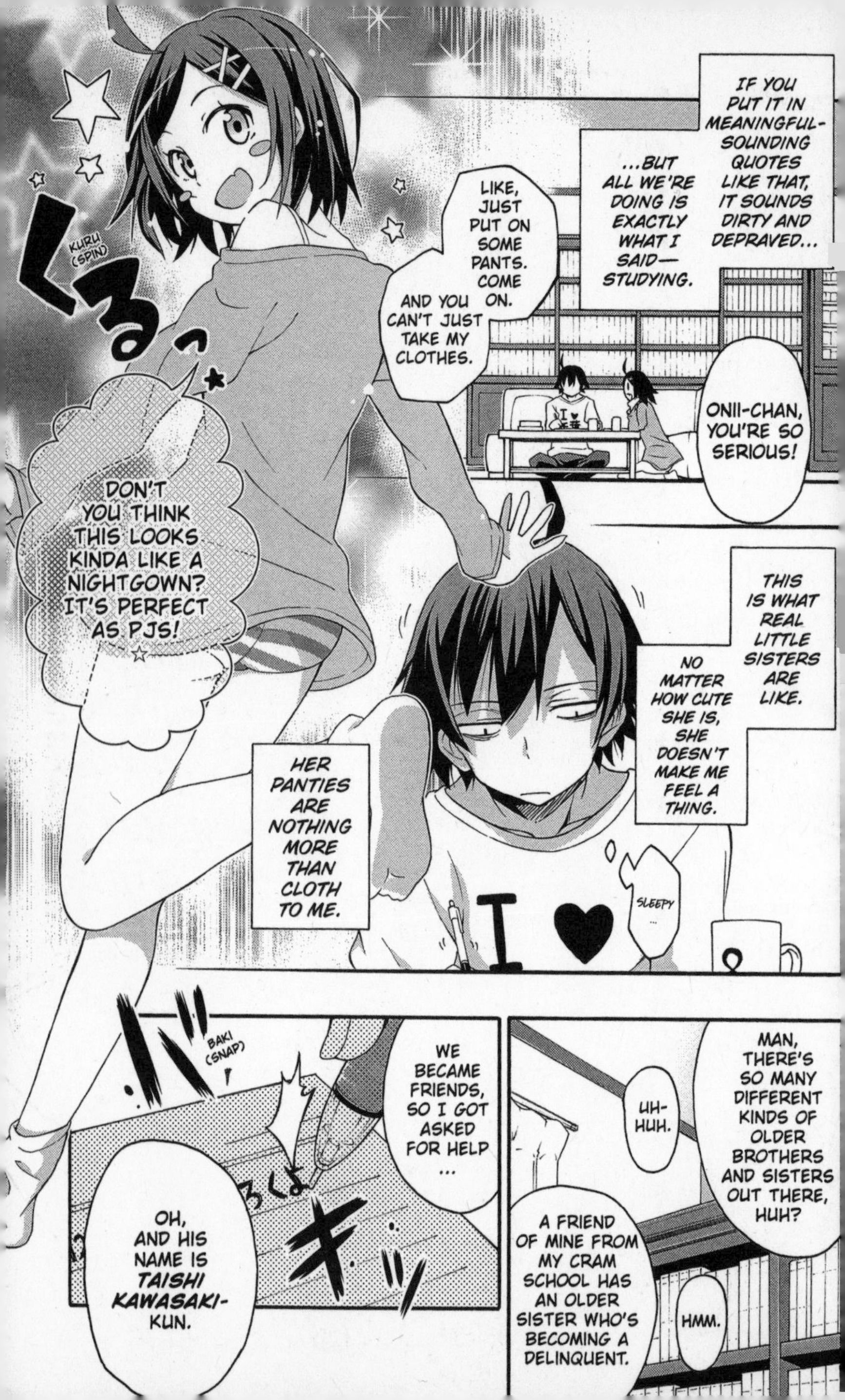
IF YOU PUT IT IN MEANINGFUL-SOUNDING QUOTES LIKE THAT, IT SOUNDS DIRTY AND DEPRAVED...
...BUT ALL WE'RE DOING IS EXACTLY WHAT I SAID—STUDYING.
LIKE, JUST PUT ON SOME PANTS. COME ON.
AND YOU CAN'T JUST TAKE MY CLOTHES.
ONII-CHAN, YOU'RE SO SERIOUS!
KURU (SPIN)
DON'T YOU THINK THIS LOOKS KINDA LIKE A NIGHTGOWN? IT'S PERFECT AS PJS!
THIS IS WHAT REAL LITTLE SISTERS ARE LIKE.
NO MATTER HOW CUTE SHE IS, SHE DOESN'T MAKE ME FEEL A THING.
HER PANTIES ARE NOTHING MORE THAN CLOTH TO ME.
SLEEPY...
MAN, THERE'S SO MANY DIFFERENT KINDS OF OLDER BROTHERS AND SISTERS OUT THERE, HUH?
UH-HUH.
A FRIEND OF MINE FROM MY CRAM SCHOOL HAS AN OLDER SISTER WHO'S BECOMING A DELINQUENT.
HMM.
WE BECAME FRIENDS, SO I GOT ASKED FOR HELP...
BAKI (SNAP)
OH, AND HIS NAME IS TAISHI KAWASAKI-KUN.

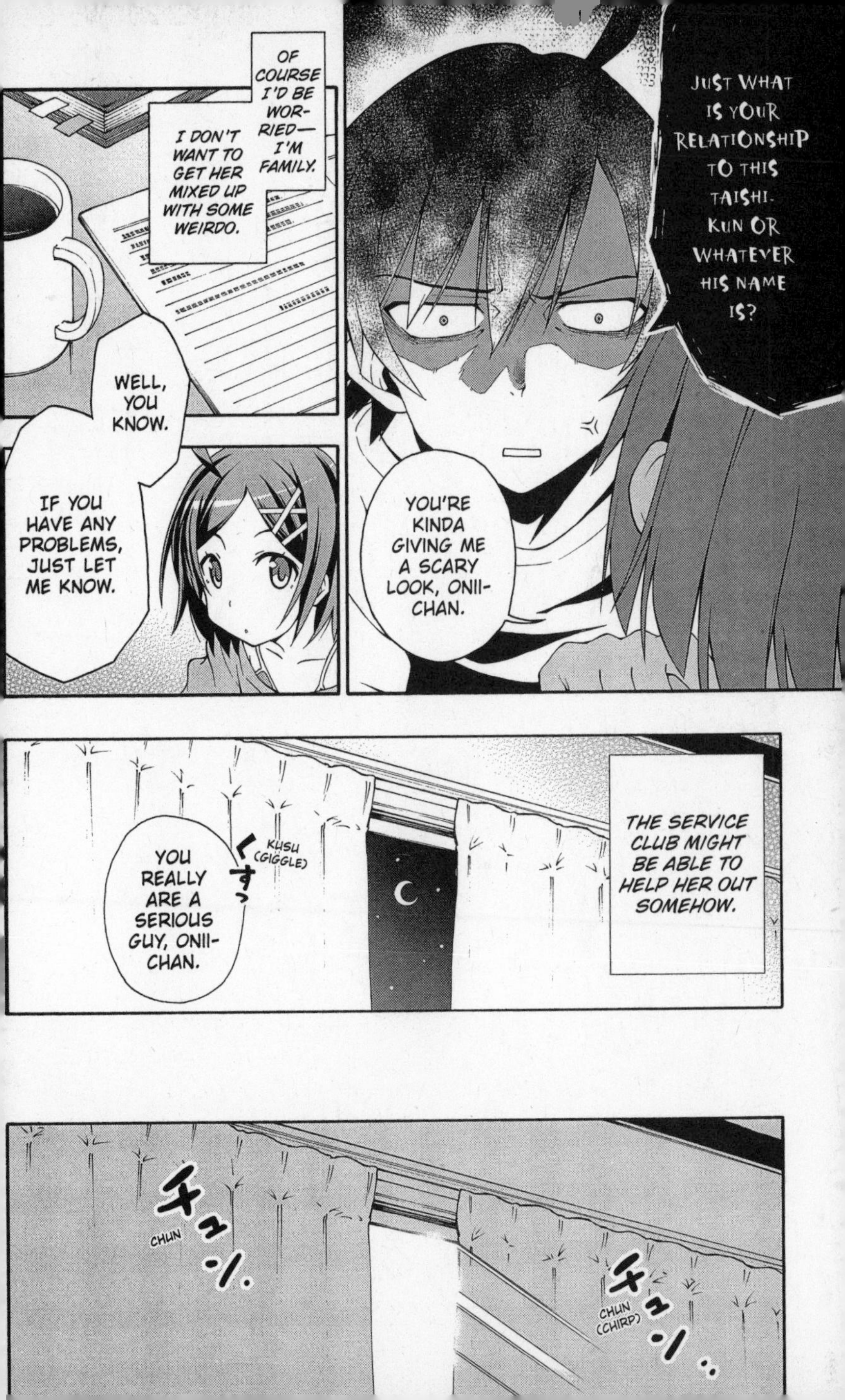
JUST WHAT IS YOUR RELATIONSHIP TO THIS TAISHI-KUN OR WHATEVER HIS NAME IS?
YOU'RE KINDA GIVING ME A SCARY LOOK, ONII-CHAN.
OF COURSE I'D BE WORRIED—I'M FAMILY.
I DON'T WANT TO GET HER MIXED UP WITH SOME WEIRDO.
WELL, YOU KNOW.
IF YOU HAVE ANY PROBLEMS, JUST LET ME KNOW.
THE SERVICE CLUB MIGHT BE ABLE TO HELP HER OUT SOMEHOW.
くすっ
KUSU (GIGGLE)
YOU REALLY ARE A SERIOUS GUY, ONII-CHAN.
チュン
CHUN (CHIRP)
チュン
CHUN

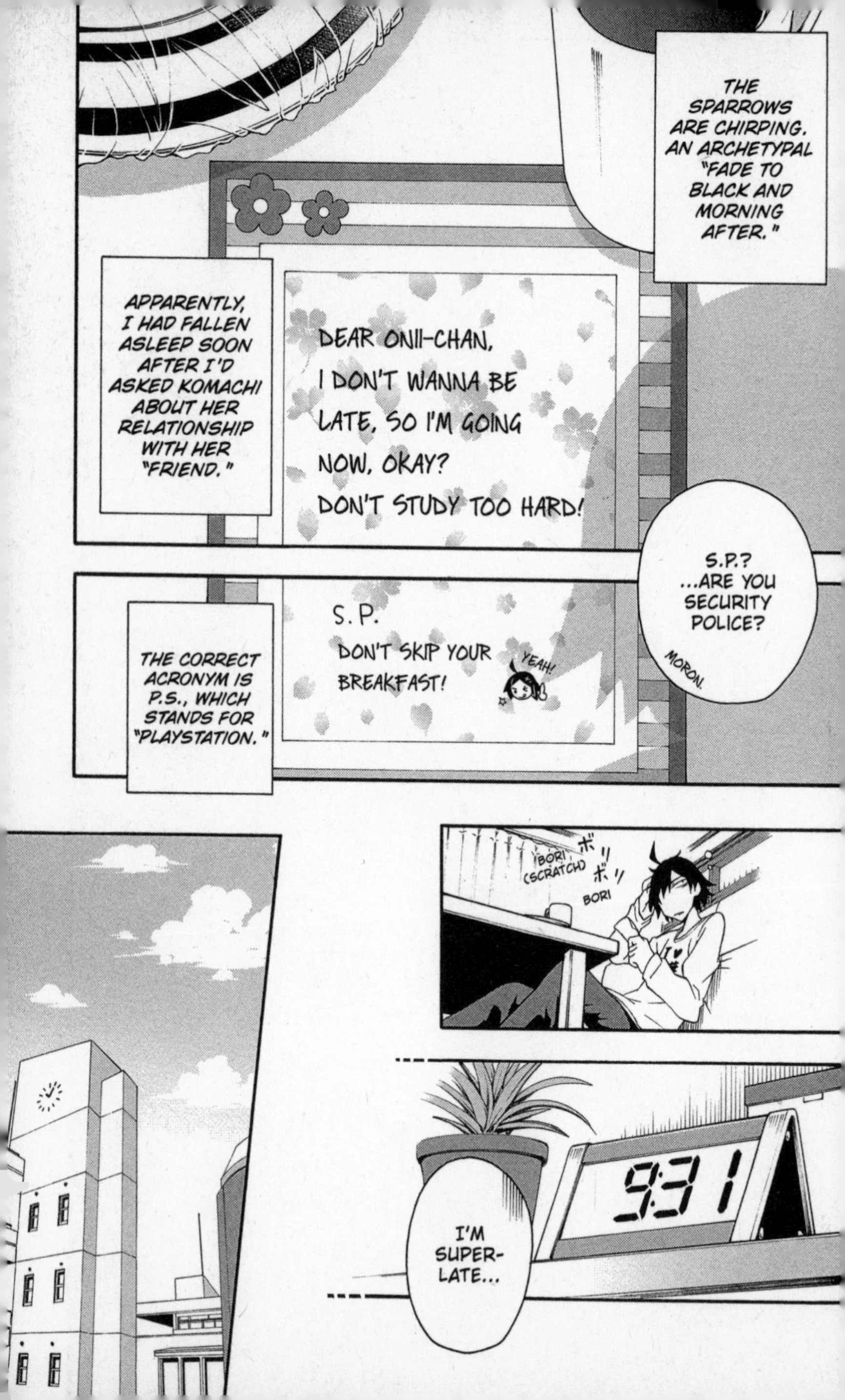
THE SPARROWS ARE CHIRPING. AN ARCHETYPAL "FADE TO BLACK AND MORNING AFTER."
DEAR ONII-CHAN,
I DON'T WANNA BE LATE, SO I'M GOING NOW, OKAY?
DON'T STUDY TOO HARD!
APPARENTLY, I HAD FALLEN ASLEEP SOON AFTER I'D ASKED KOMACHI ABOUT HER RELATIONSHIP WITH HER "FRIEND."
S.P.? ...ARE YOU SECURITY POLICE?
MORON.
S. P.
DON'T SKIP YOUR BREAKFAST!
YEAH!
THE CORRECT ACRONYM IS P.S., WHICH STANDS FOR "PLAYSTATION."
ボリ BORI (SCRATCH)
ボリ BORI
9:31
I'M SUPER-LATE...

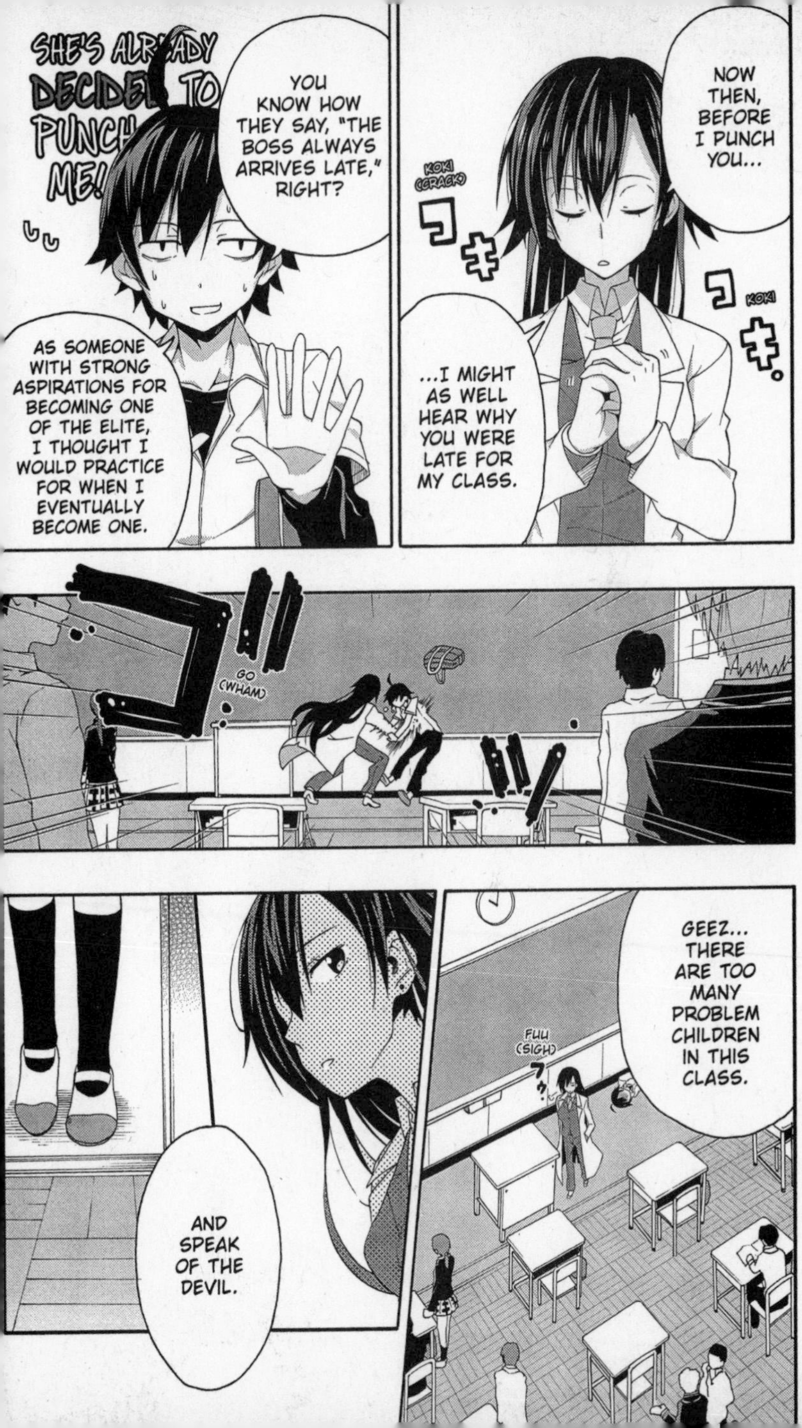
NOW THEN, BEFORE I PUNCH YOU...
KOKI (CRACK)
KOKI
...I MIGHT AS WELL HEAR WHY YOU WERE LATE FOR MY CLASS.
YOU KNOW HOW THEY SAY, "THE BOSS ALWAYS ARRIVES LATE," RIGHT?
SHE'S ALREADY DECIDED TO PUNCH ME!
AS SOMEONE WITH STRONG ASPIRATIONS FOR BECOMING ONE OF THE ELITE, I THOUGHT I WOULD PRACTICE FOR WHEN I EVENTUALLY BECOME ONE.
GO (WHAM)
GEEZ... THERE ARE TOO MANY PROBLEM CHILDREN IN THIS CLASS.
FUU (SIGH)
AND SPEAK OF THE DEVIL.

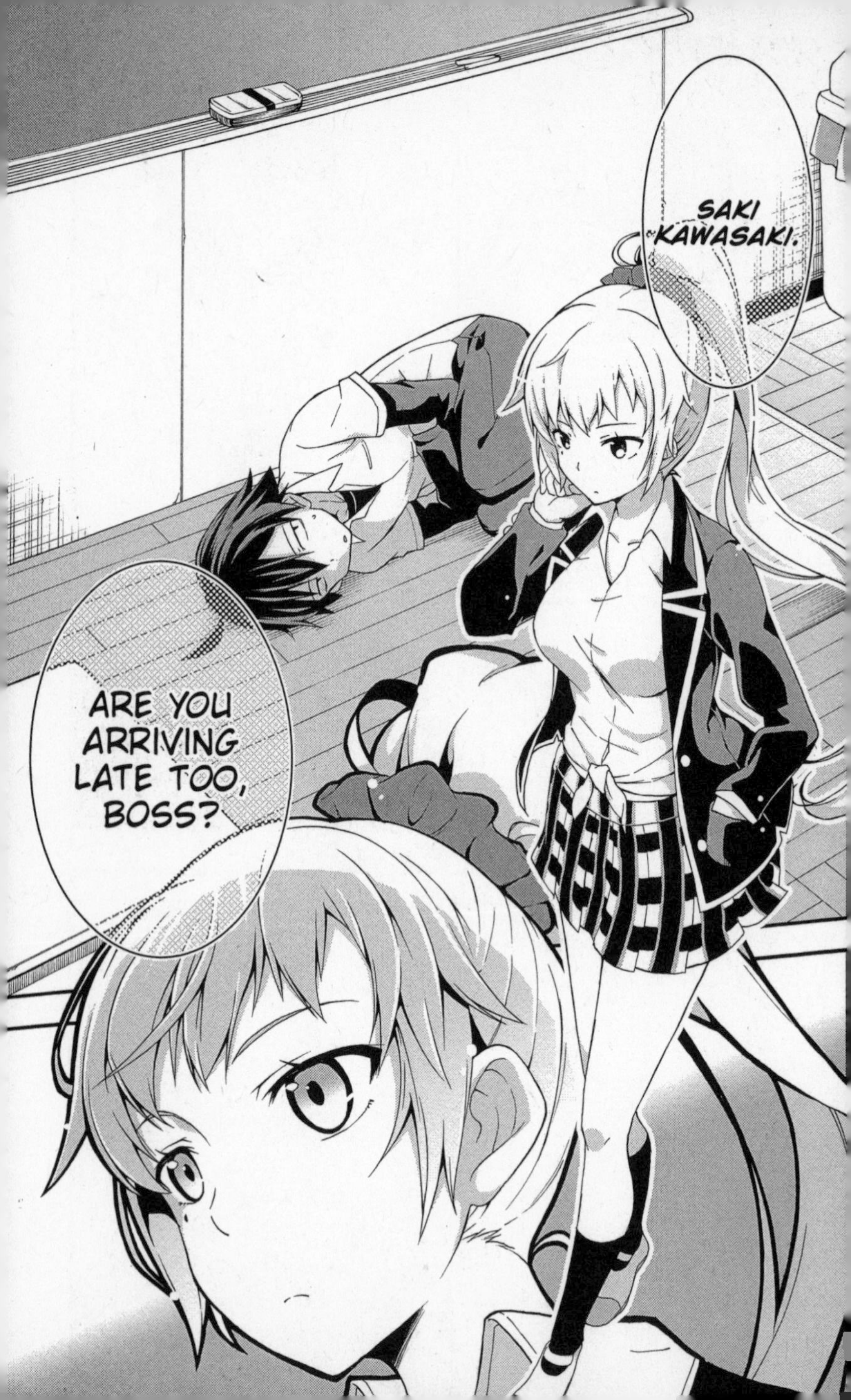
SAKI KAWASAKI.
ARE YOU ARRIVING LATE TOO, BOSS?

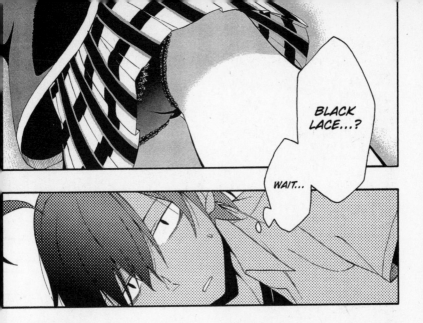

BLACK LACE...?

WAIT...

SAKI KAWA-SAKI...

HUH...

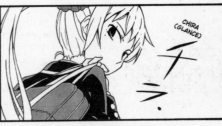

CHIRA (GLANCE)

HIKIGAYA, DON'T MUTTER THE NAME OF A GIRL WHOSE SKIRT YOU'VE PEEKED UP IN THAT DEEP AND EMOTIONAL TONE.

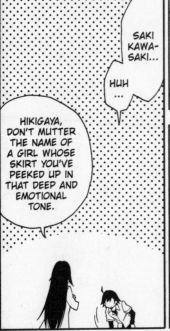

...ARE YOU STUPID?

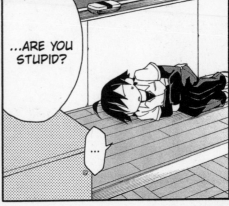

...

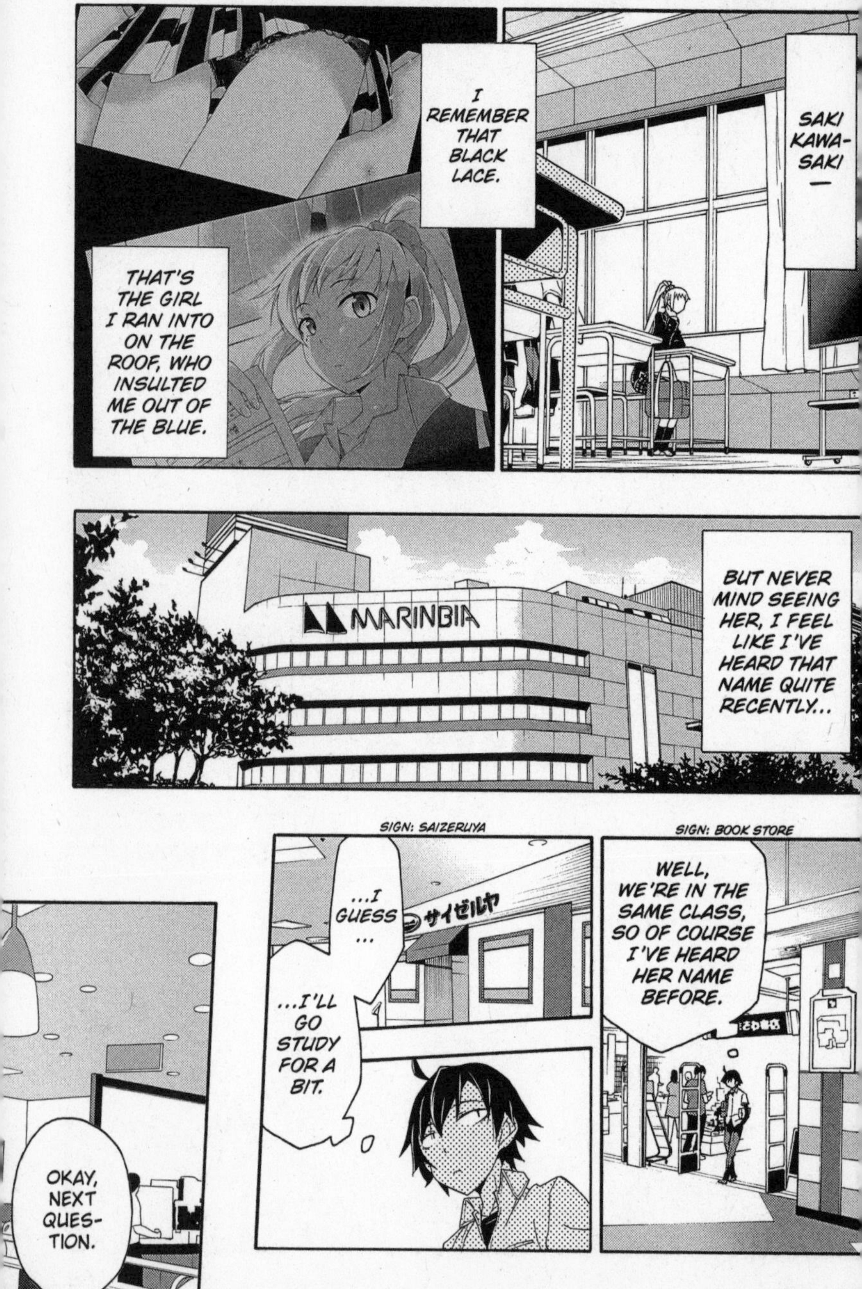
SAKI KAWA-SAKI —
I REMEMBER THAT BLACK LACE.
THAT'S THE GIRL I RAN INTO ON THE ROOF, WHO INSULTED ME OUT OF THE BLUE.
MARINBIA
BUT NEVER MIND SEEING HER, I FEEL LIKE I'VE HEARD THAT NAME QUITE RECENTLY...
SIGN: BOOK STORE
WELL, WE'RE IN THE SAME CLASS, SO OF COURSE I'VE HEARD HER NAME BEFORE.
SIGN: SAIZERUYA
サイゼルヤ
...I GUESS ...
...I'LL GO STUDY FOR A BIT.
OKAY, NEXT QUES-TION.

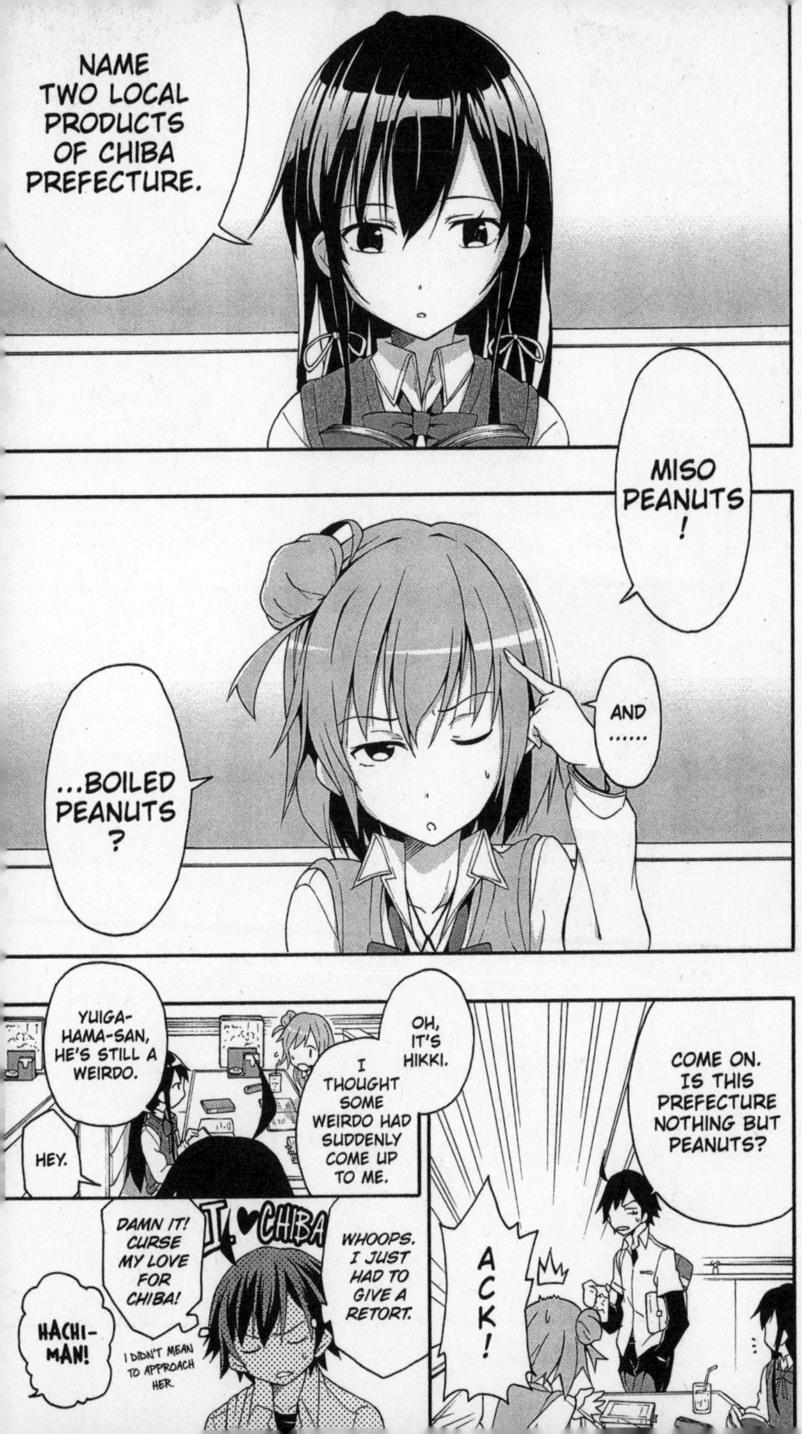
NAME TWO LOCAL PRODUCTS OF CHIBA PREFECTURE.
MISO PEANUTS!
AND ......
...BOILED PEANUTS?
COME ON. IS THIS PREFECTURE NOTHING BUT PEANUTS?
ACK!
OH, IT'S HIKKI.
I THOUGHT SOME WEIRDO HAD SUDDENLY COME UP TO ME.
YUIGA-HAMA-SAN, HE'S STILL A WEIRDO.
HEY.
WHOOPS. I JUST HAD TO GIVE A RETORT.
I ♥ CHIBA
DAMN IT! CURSE MY LOVE FOR CHIBA!
HACHI-MAN!
I DIDN'T MEAN TO APPROACH HER.

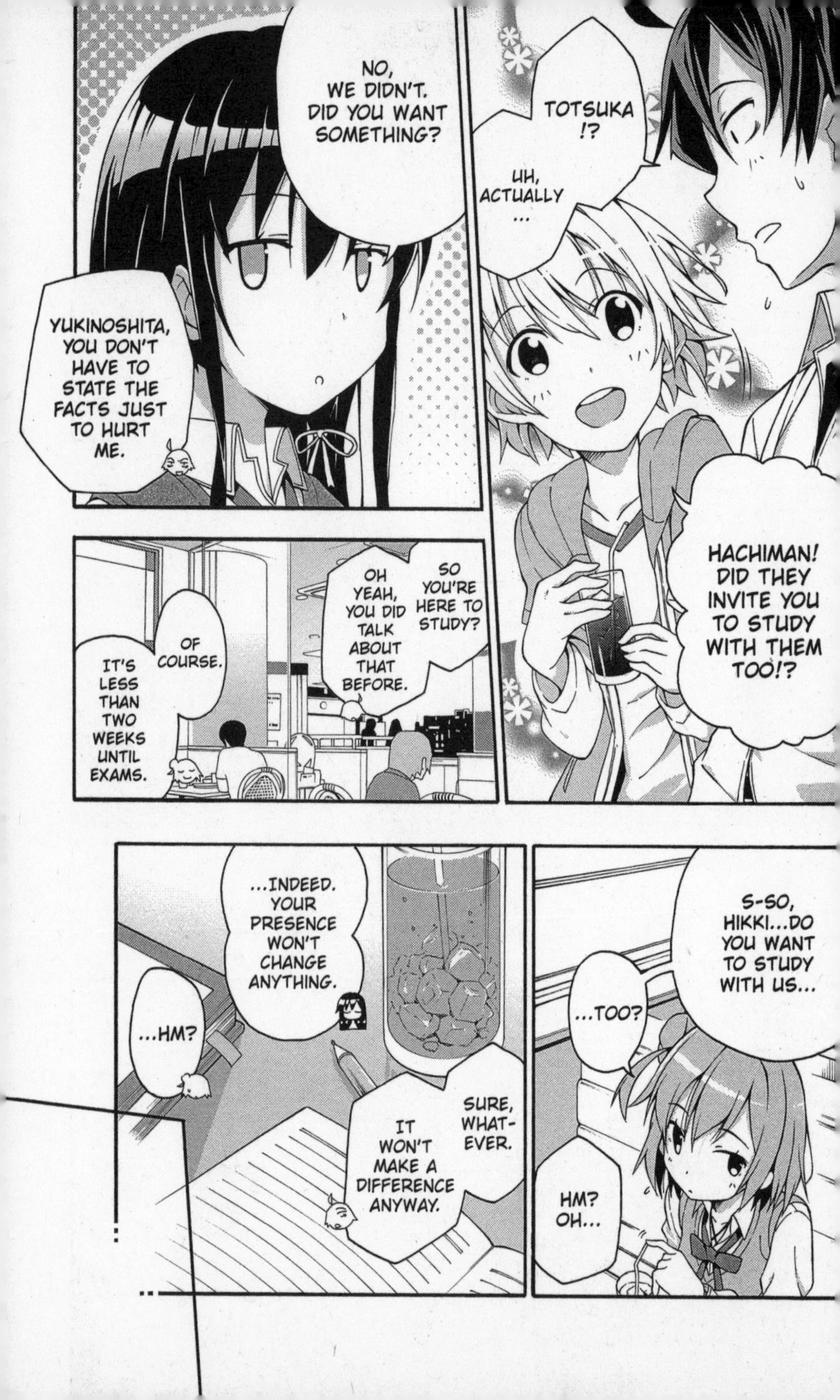
TOTSUKA !?
UH, ACTUALLY ...
HACHIMAN! DID THEY INVITE YOU TO STUDY WITH THEM TOO!?
NO, WE DIDN'T. DID YOU WANT SOMETHING?
YUKINOSHITA, YOU DON'T HAVE TO STATE THE FACTS JUST TO HURT ME.
SO YOU'RE HERE TO STUDY?
OH YEAH, YOU DID TALK ABOUT THAT BEFORE.
OF COURSE.
IT'S LESS THAN TWO WEEKS UNTIL EXAMS.
S-SO, HIKKI...DO YOU WANT TO STUDY WITH US...
...TOO?
HM? OH...
...INDEED. YOUR PRESENCE WON'T CHANGE ANYTHING.
...HM?
SURE, WHAT-EVER.
IT WON'T MAKE A DIFFERENCE ANYWAY.

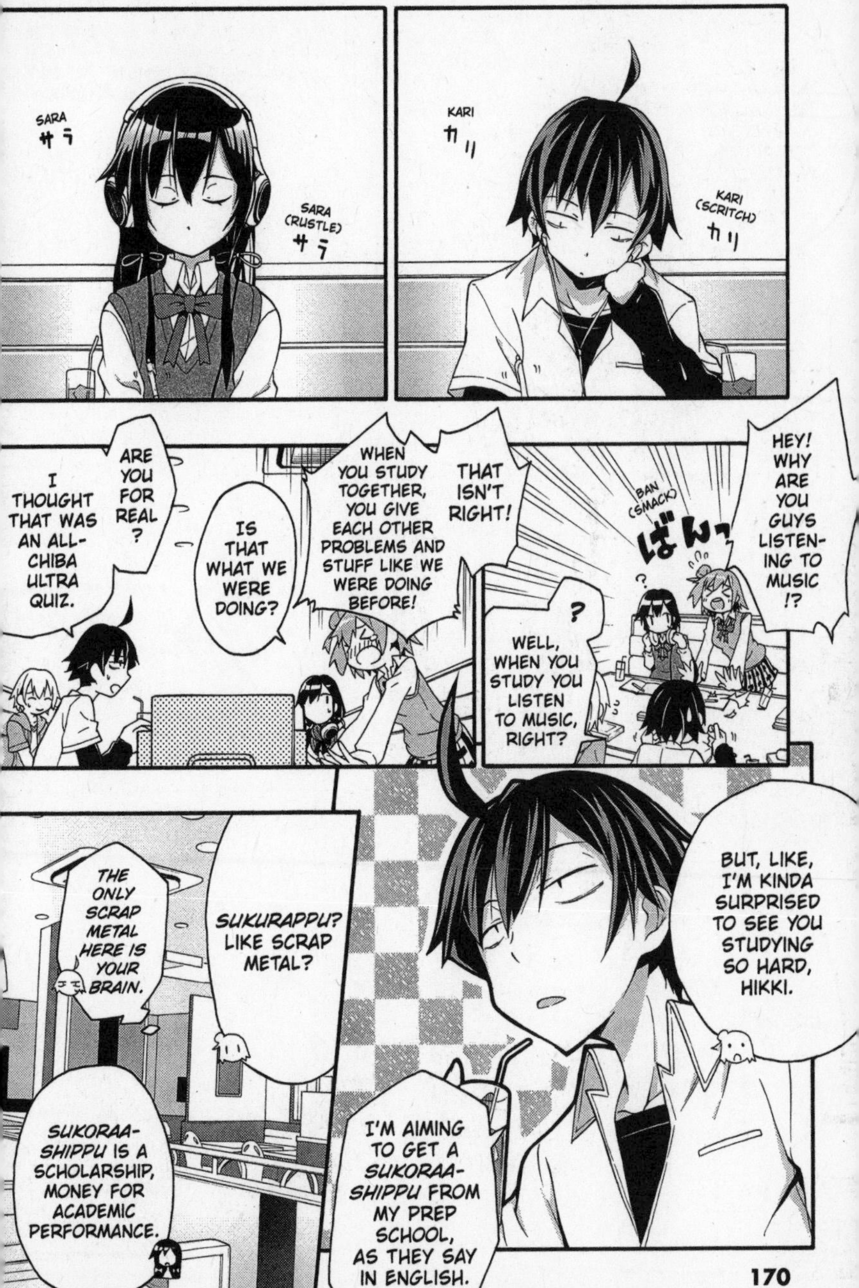
KARI
カリ
KARI (SCRITCH)
カリ
SARA
サラ
SARA (RUSTLE)
サラ
HEY! WHY ARE YOU GUYS LISTENING TO MUSIC!?
BAN (SMACK)
ばんっ
?
WELL, WHEN YOU STUDY YOU LISTEN TO MUSIC, RIGHT?
THAT ISN'T RIGHT!
WHEN YOU STUDY TOGETHER, YOU GIVE EACH OTHER PROBLEMS AND STUFF LIKE WE WERE DOING BEFORE!
IS THAT WHAT WE WERE DOING?
ARE YOU FOR REAL?
I THOUGHT THAT WAS AN ALL-CHIBA ULTRA QUIZ.
BUT, LIKE, I'M KINDA SURPRISED TO SEE YOU STUDYING SO HARD, HIKKI.
I'M AIMING TO GET A SUKORAA-SHIPPU FROM MY PREP SCHOOL, AS THEY SAY IN ENGLISH.
SUKURAPPU? LIKE SCRAP METAL?
THE ONLY SCRAP METAL HERE IS YOUR BRAIN.
SUKORAA-SHIPPU IS A SCHOLARSHIP, MONEY FOR ACADEMIC PERFORMANCE.

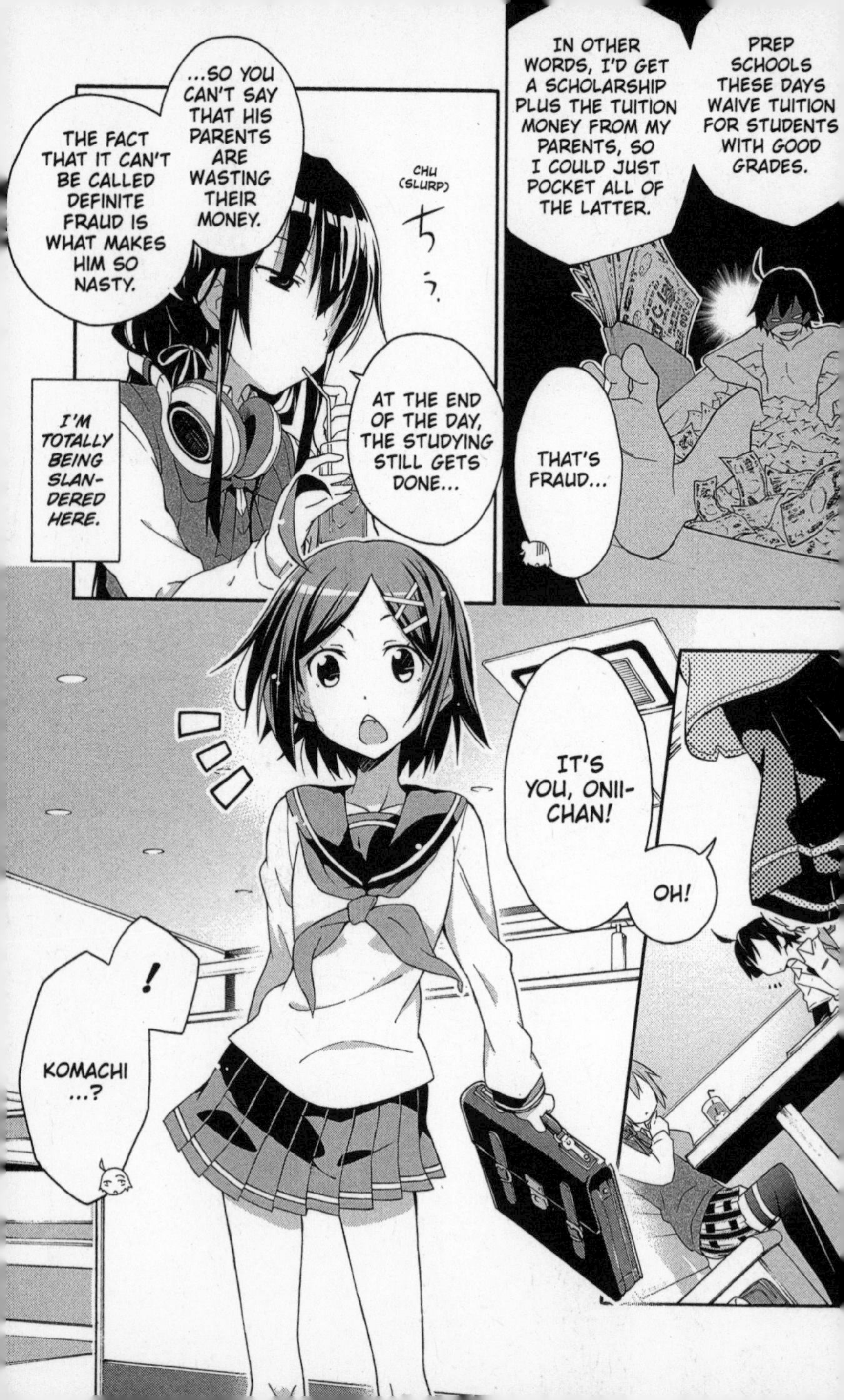
PREP SCHOOLS THESE DAYS WAIVE TUITION FOR STUDENTS WITH GOOD GRADES.
IN OTHER WORDS, I'D GET A SCHOLARSHIP PLUS THE TUITION MONEY FROM MY PARENTS, SO I COULD JUST POCKET ALL OF THE LATTER.
THAT'S FRAUD...
CHU (SLURP)
AT THE END OF THE DAY, THE STUDYING STILL GETS DONE...
...SO YOU CAN'T SAY THAT HIS PARENTS ARE WASTING THEIR MONEY.
THE FACT THAT IT CAN'T BE CALLED DEFINITE FRAUD IS WHAT MAKES HIM SO NASTY.
I'M TOTALLY BEING SLANDERED HERE.
OH!
IT'S YOU, ONII-CHAN!
!
KOMACHI ...?

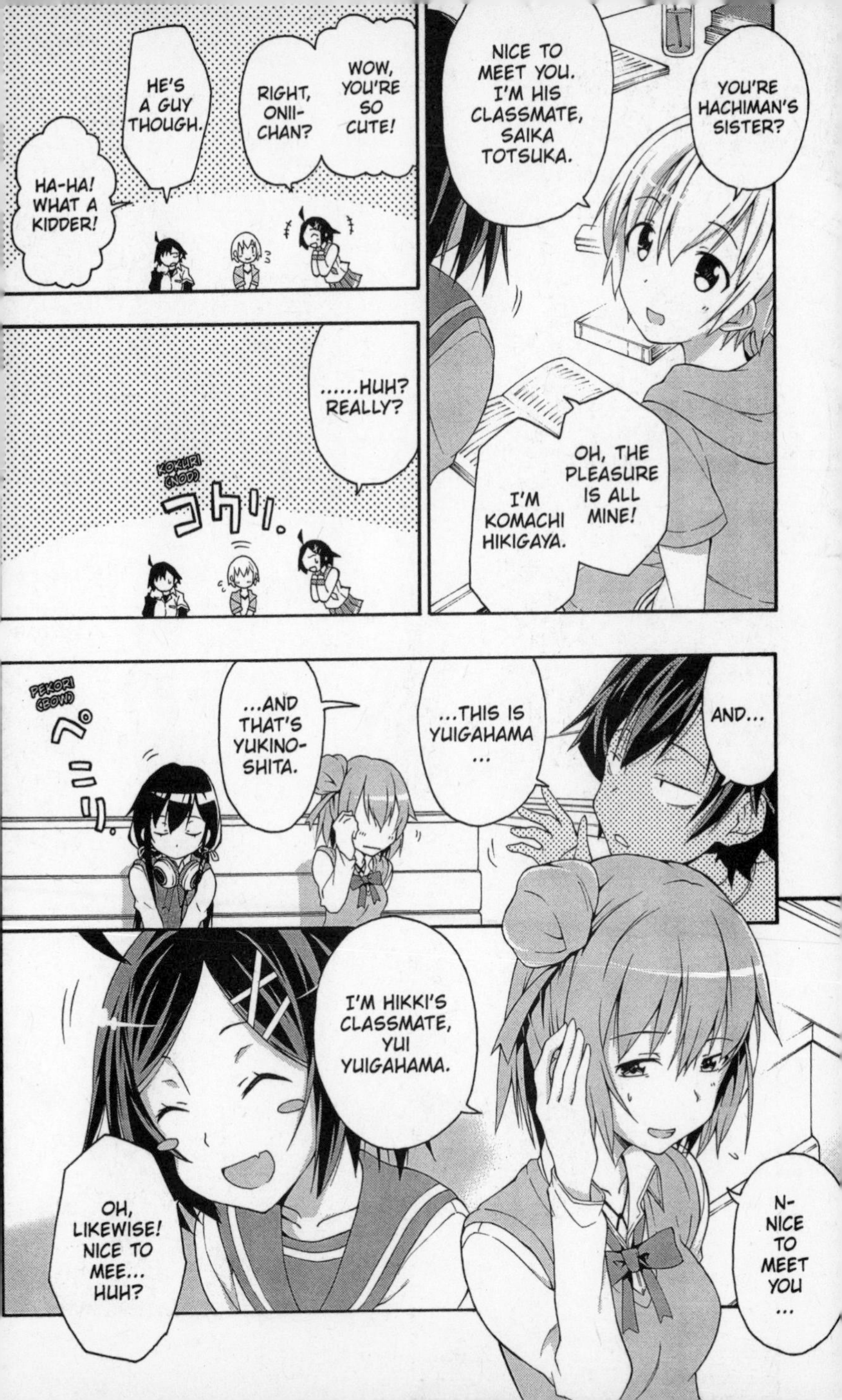
YOU'RE HACHIMAN'S SISTER?
NICE TO MEET YOU. I'M HIS CLASSMATE, SAIKA TOTSUKA.
OH, THE PLEASURE IS ALL MINE!
I'M KOMACHI HIKIGAYA.
WOW, YOU'RE SO CUTE!
RIGHT, ONII-CHAN?
HE'S A GUY THOUGH.
HA-HA! WHAT A KIDDER!
......HUH? REALLY?
KOKURI (NOD)
AND...
...THIS IS YUIGAHAMA ...
...AND THAT'S YUKINO-SHITA.
PEKORI (BOW)
N-NICE TO MEET YOU ...
I'M HIKKI'S CLASSMATE, YUI YUIGAHAMA.
OH, LIKEWISE! NICE TO MEE... HUH?

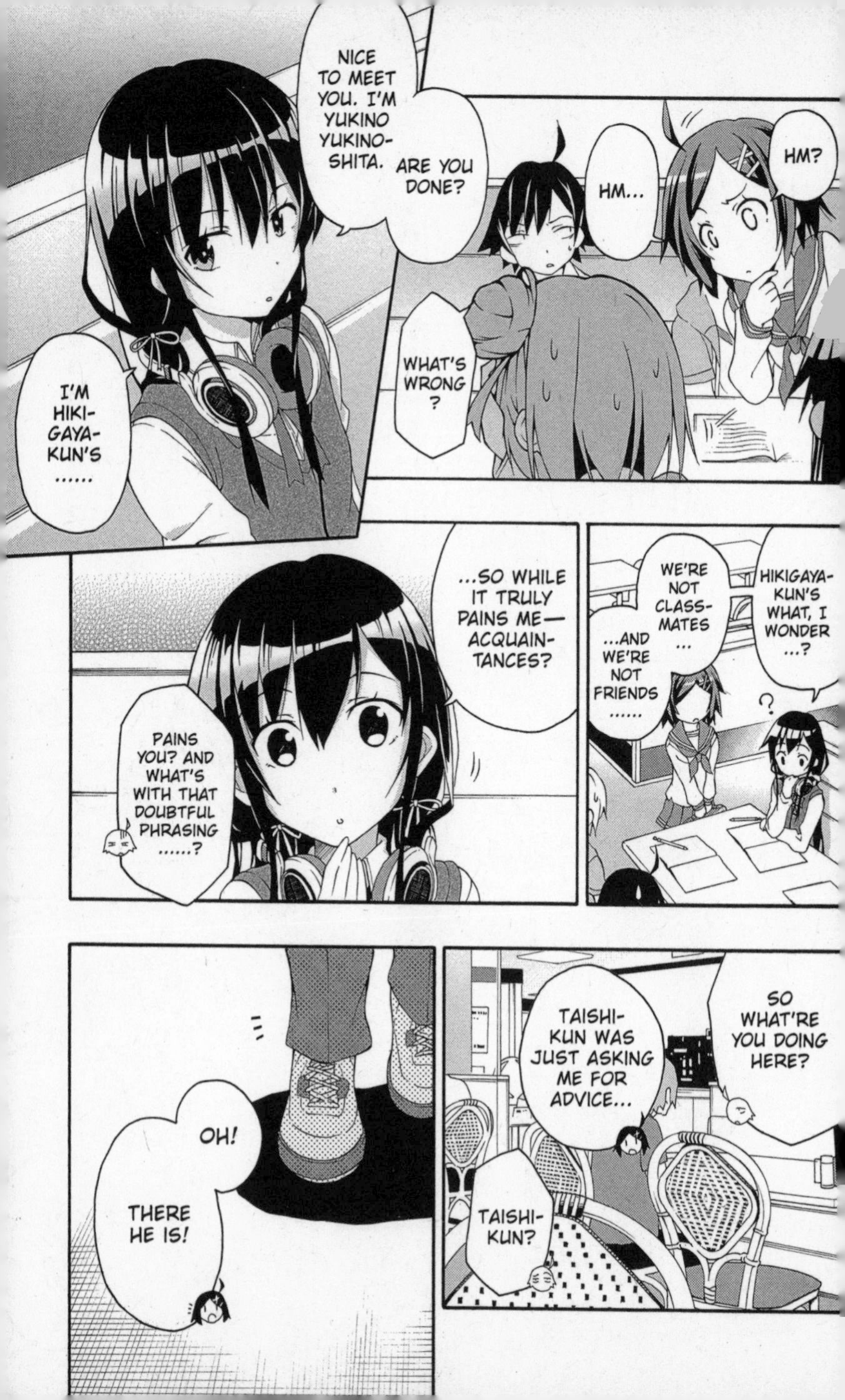
HM?
HM...
ARE YOU DONE?
WHAT'S WRONG?
NICE TO MEET YOU. I'M YUKINO YUKINOSHITA.
I'M HIKIGAYA-KUN'S ......
HIKIGAYA-KUN'S WHAT, I WONDER ...?
WE'RE NOT CLASSMATES ...
...AND WE'RE NOT FRIENDS ......
...SO WHILE IT TRULY PAINS ME— ACQUAINTANCES?
PAINS YOU? AND WHAT'S WITH THAT DOUBTFUL PHRASING ......?
SO WHAT'RE YOU DOING HERE?
TAISHI-KUN WAS JUST ASKING ME FOR ADVICE...
TAISHI-KUN?
OH!
THERE HE IS!

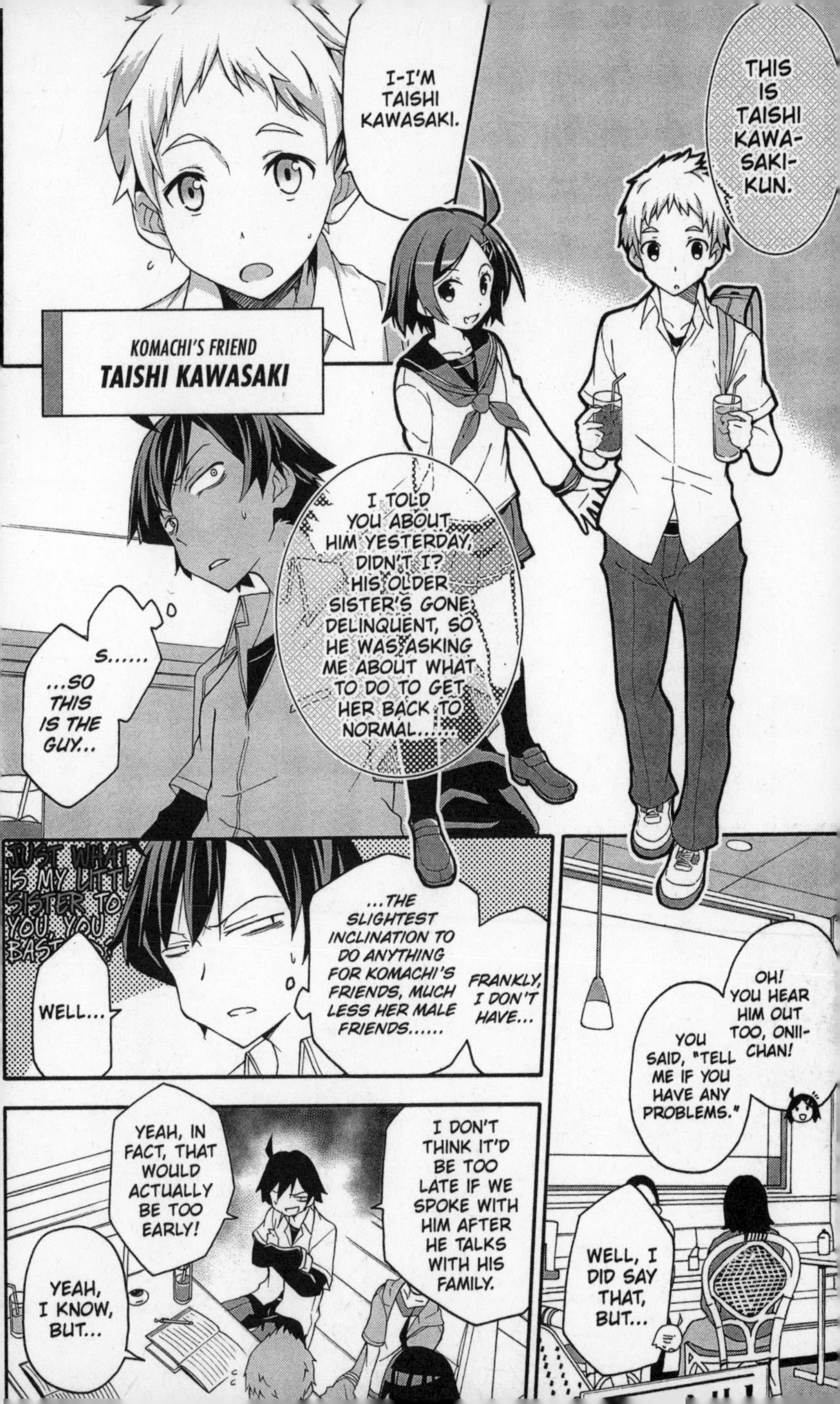
THIS IS TAISHI KAWASAKI-KUN.
I-I'M TAISHI KAWASAKI.
KOMACHI'S FRIEND
TAISHI KAWASAKI
I TOLD YOU ABOUT HIM YESTERDAY, DIDN'T I? HIS OLDER SISTER'S GONE DELINQUENT, SO HE WAS ASKING ME ABOUT WHAT TO DO TO GET HER BACK TO NORMAL......
S...... ...SO THIS IS THE GUY...
OH! YOU HEAR HIM OUT TOO, ONII-CHAN!
YOU SAID, "TELL ME IF YOU HAVE ANY PROBLEMS."
FRANKLY, I DON'T HAVE...
...THE SLIGHTEST INCLINATION TO DO ANYTHING FOR KOMACHI'S FRIENDS, MUCH LESS HER MALE FRIENDS......
WELL...
JUST WHAT IS MY LITTL SISTER TO YOU, YOU BAST
WELL, I DID SAY THAT, BUT...
I DON'T THINK IT'D BE TOO LATE IF WE SPOKE WITH HIM AFTER HE TALKS WITH HIS FAMILY.
YEAH, IN FACT, THAT WOULD ACTUALLY BE TOO EARLY!
YEAH, I KNOW, BUT...

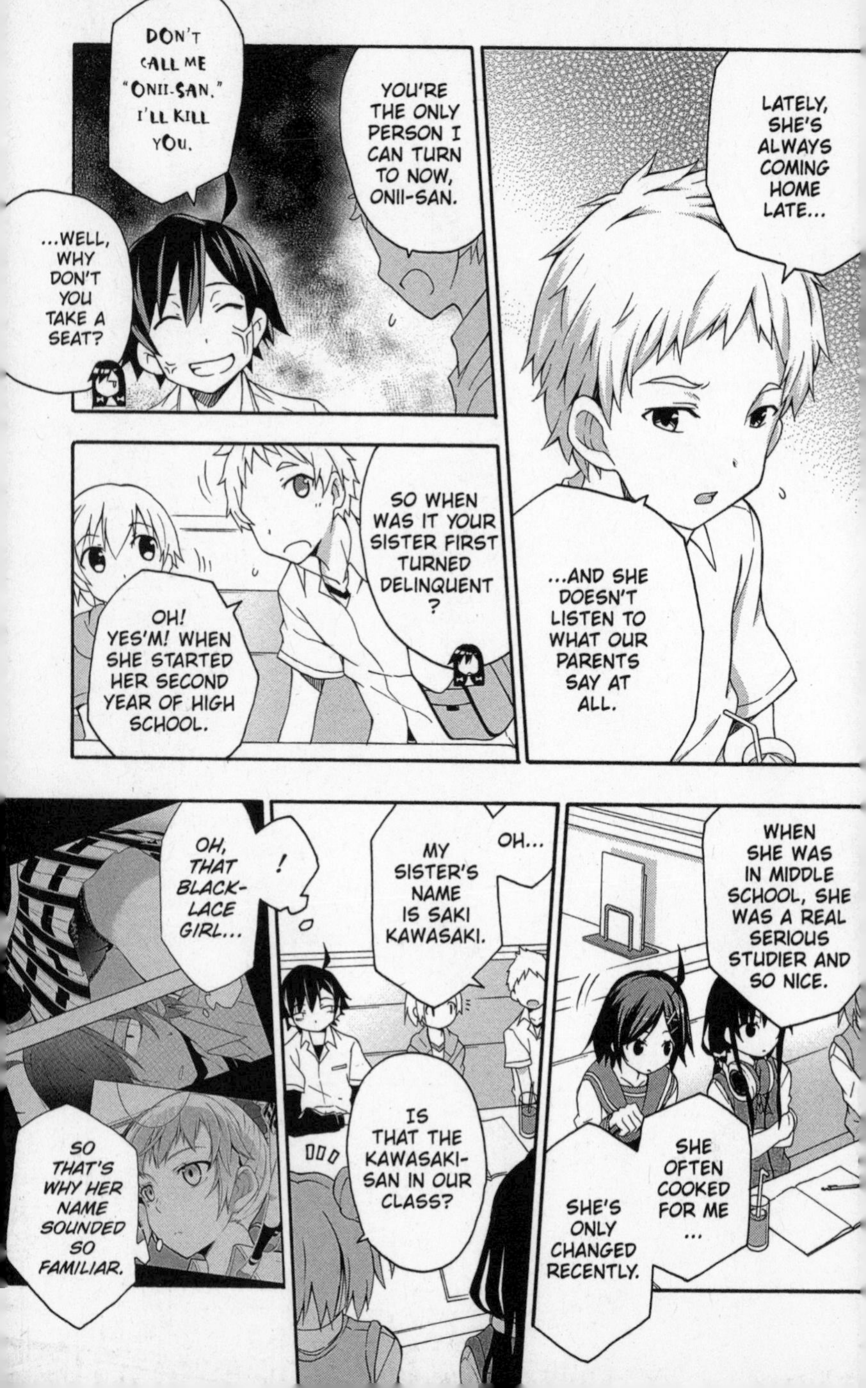
LATELY, SHE'S ALWAYS COMING HOME LATE...
...AND SHE DOESN'T LISTEN TO WHAT OUR PARENTS SAY AT ALL.
YOU'RE THE ONLY PERSON I CAN TURN TO NOW, ONII-SAN.
DON'T CALL ME "ONII-SAN." I'LL KILL YOU.
...WELL, WHY DON'T YOU TAKE A SEAT?
SO WHEN WAS IT YOUR SISTER FIRST TURNED DELINQUENT ?
OH! YES'M! WHEN SHE STARTED HER SECOND YEAR OF HIGH SCHOOL.
WHEN SHE WAS IN MIDDLE SCHOOL, SHE WAS A REAL SERIOUS STUDIER AND SO NICE.
SHE OFTEN COOKED FOR ME ...
SHE'S ONLY CHANGED RECENTLY.
OH...
MY SISTER'S NAME IS SAKI KAWASAKI.
!
IS THAT THE KAWASAKI-SAN IN OUR CLASS?
OH, THAT BLACK-LACE GIRL...
SO THAT'S WHY HER NAME SOUNDED SO FAMILIAR.

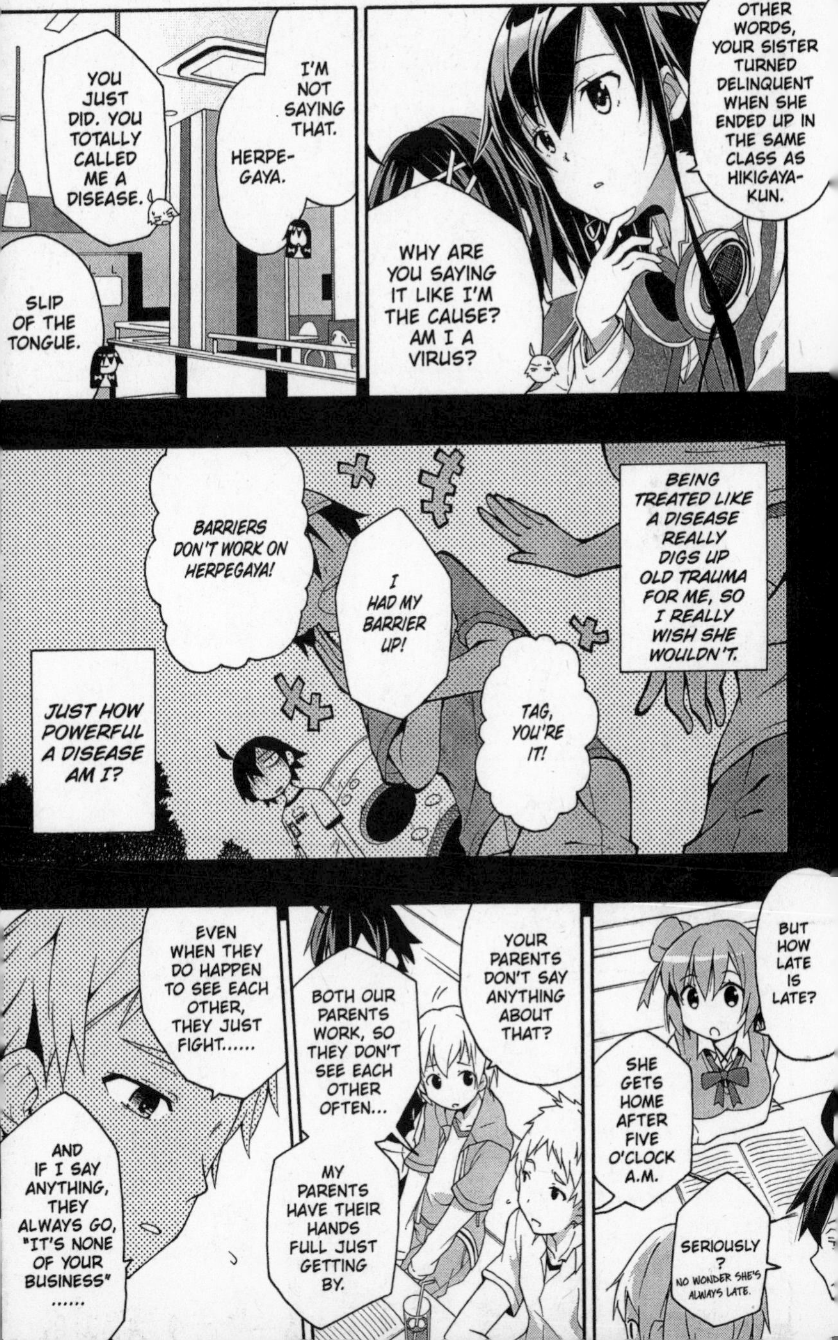
IN OTHER WORDS, YOUR SISTER TURNED DELINQUENT WHEN SHE ENDED UP IN THE SAME CLASS AS HIKIGAYA-KUN.
WHY ARE YOU SAYING IT LIKE I'M THE CAUSE? AM I A VIRUS?
I'M NOT SAYING THAT.
HERPE-GAYA.
YOU JUST DID. YOU TOTALLY CALLED ME A DISEASE.
SLIP OF THE TONGUE.
BEING TREATED LIKE A DISEASE REALLY DIGS UP OLD TRAUMA FOR ME, SO I REALLY WISH SHE WOULDN'T.
TAG, YOU'RE IT!
I HAD MY BARRIER UP!
BARRIERS DON'T WORK ON HERPEGAYA!
JUST HOW POWERFUL A DISEASE AM I?
BUT HOW LATE IS LATE?
SHE GETS HOME AFTER FIVE O'CLOCK A.M.
SERIOUSLY? NO WONDER SHE'S ALWAYS LATE.
YOUR PARENTS DON'T SAY ANYTHING ABOUT THAT?
BOTH OUR PARENTS WORK, SO THEY DON'T SEE EACH OTHER OFTEN...
MY PARENTS HAVE THEIR HANDS FULL JUST GETTING BY.
EVEN WHEN THEY DO HAPPEN TO SEE EACH OTHER, THEY JUST FIGHT......
AND IF I SAY ANYTHING, THEY ALWAYS GO, "IT'S NONE OF YOUR BUSINESS"......

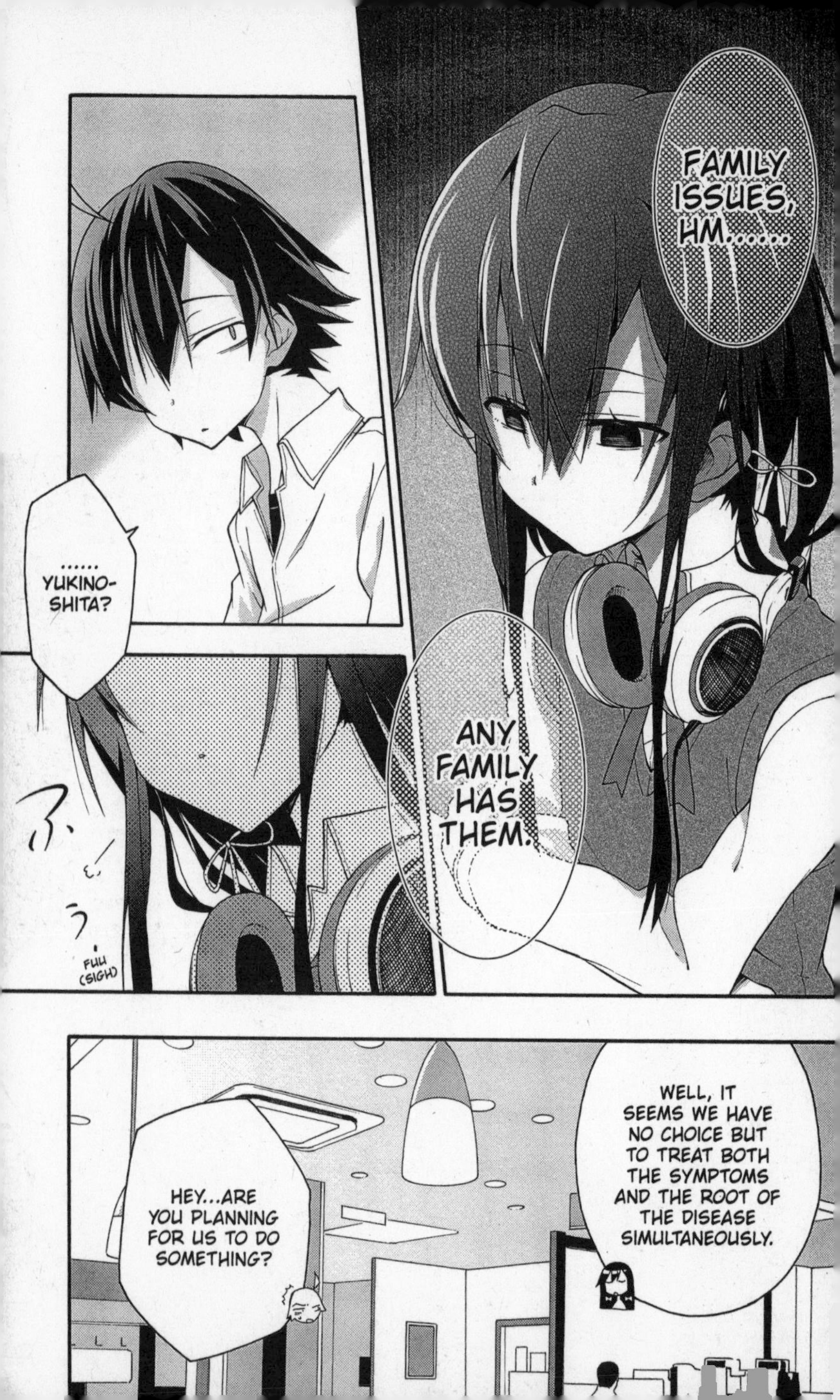
FAMILY ISSUES, HM......
ANY FAMILY HAS THEM.
......YUKINO-SHITA?
ふぅ
FUU (SIGH)
WELL, IT SEEMS WE HAVE NO CHOICE BUT TO TREAT BOTH THE SYMPTOMS AND THE ROOT OF THE DISEASE SIMULTANEOUSLY.
HEY...ARE YOU PLANNING FOR US TO DO SOMETHING?

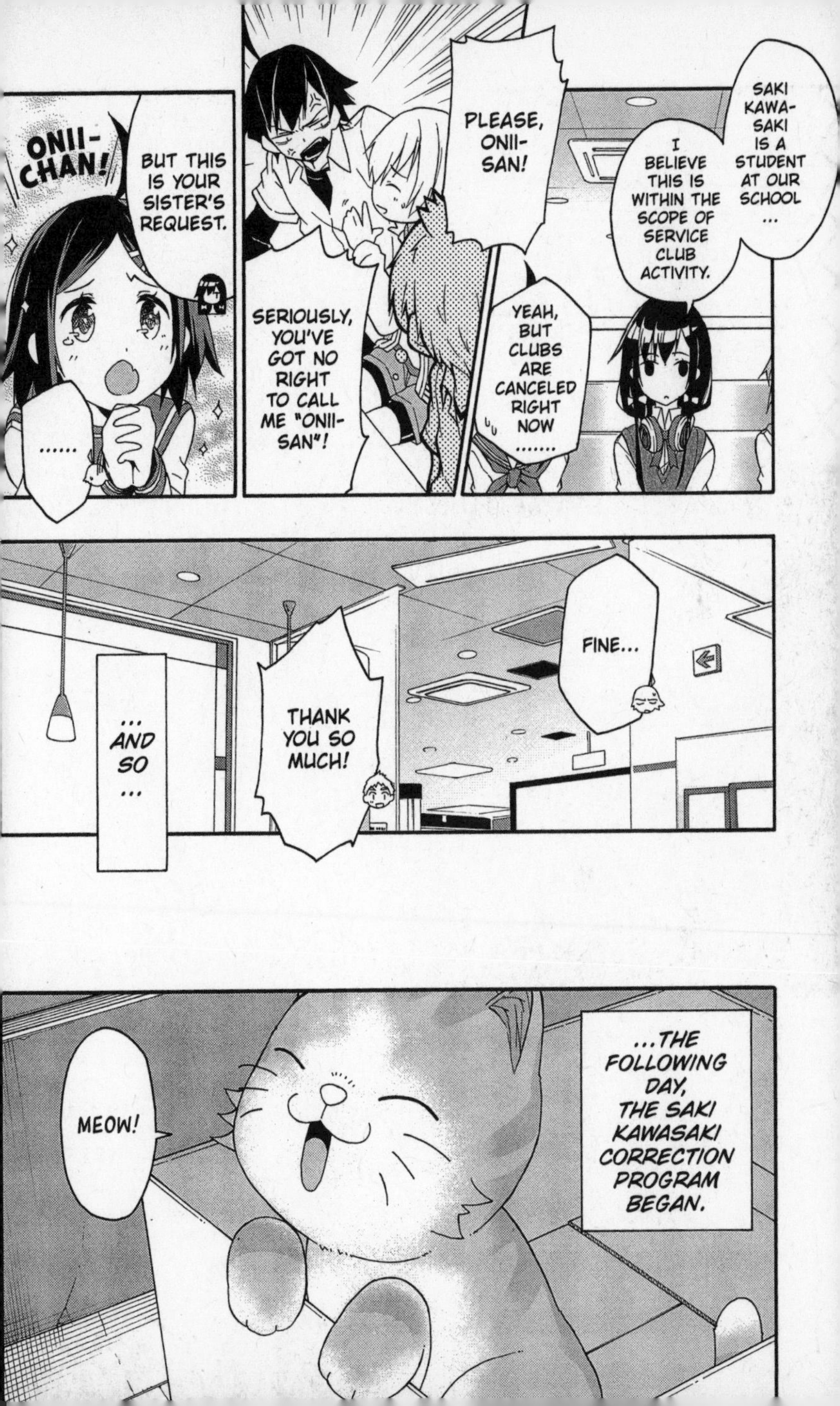
SAKI KAWASAKI IS A STUDENT AT OUR SCHOOL ...
I BELIEVE THIS IS WITHIN THE SCOPE OF SERVICE CLUB ACTIVITY.
YEAH, BUT CLUBS ARE CANCELED RIGHT NOW ....
PLEASE, ONII-SAN!
SERIOUSLY, YOU'VE GOT NO RIGHT TO CALL ME "ONII-SAN"!
ONII-CHAN!
BUT THIS IS YOUR SISTER'S REQUEST.
......
FINE...
THANK YOU SO MUCH!
... AND SO ...
...THE FOLLOWING DAY, THE SAKI KAWASAKI CORRECTION PROGRAM BEGAN.
MEOW!

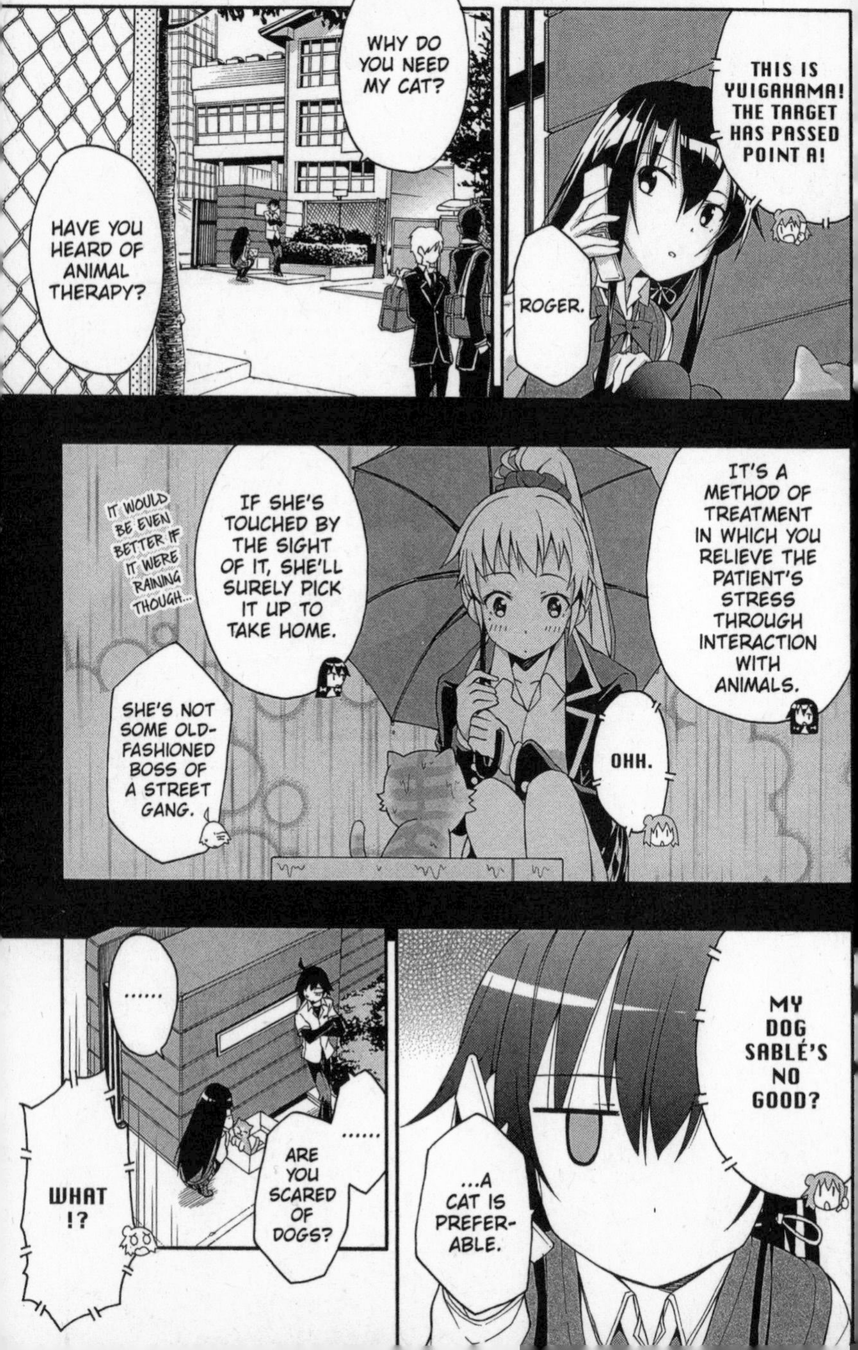
THIS IS YUIGAHAMA! THE TARGET HAS PASSED POINT A!
ROGER.
WHY DO YOU NEED MY CAT?
HAVE YOU HEARD OF ANIMAL THERAPY?
IT'S A METHOD OF TREATMENT IN WHICH YOU RELIEVE THE PATIENT'S STRESS THROUGH INTERACTION WITH ANIMALS.
OHH.
IF SHE'S TOUCHED BY THE SIGHT OF IT, SHE'LL SURELY PICK IT UP TO TAKE HOME.
IT WOULD BE EVEN BETTER IF IT WERE RAINING THOUGH...
SHE'S NOT SOME OLD-FASHIONED BOSS OF A STREET GANG.
MY DOG SABLÉ'S NO GOOD?
...A CAT IS PREFER-ABLE.
......
......
ARE YOU SCARED OF DOGS?
WHAT!?

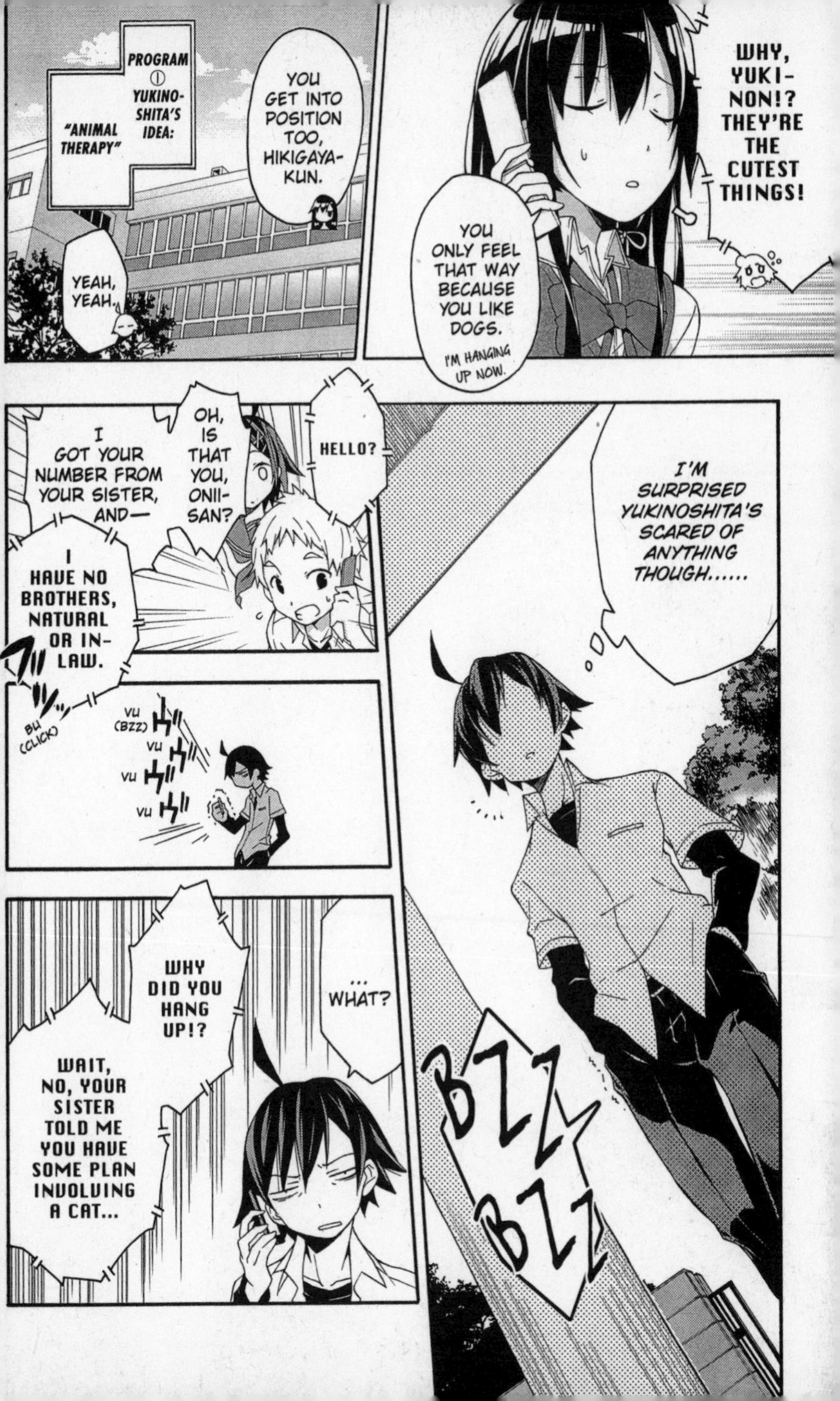
WHY, YUKI-NON!? THEY'RE THE CUTEST THINGS!
YOU ONLY FEEL THAT WAY BECAUSE YOU LIKE DOGS.
I'M HANGING UP NOW.
PROGRAM ① YUKINOSHITA'S IDEA: "ANIMAL THERAPY"
YOU GET INTO POSITION TOO, HIKIGAYA-KUN.
YEAH, YEAH.
I'M SURPRISED YUKINOSHITA'S SCARED OF ANYTHING THOUGH......
BZZ BZZ
HELLO?
OH, IS THAT YOU, ONII-SAN?
I GOT YOUR NUMBER FROM YOUR SISTER, AND—
I HAVE NO BROTHERS, NATURAL OR IN-LAW.
BU (CLICK)
VU (BZZ)
VU
VU
VU
... WHAT?
WHY DID YOU HANG UP!?
WAIT, NO, YOUR SISTER TOLD ME YOU HAVE SOME PLAN INVOLVING A CAT...

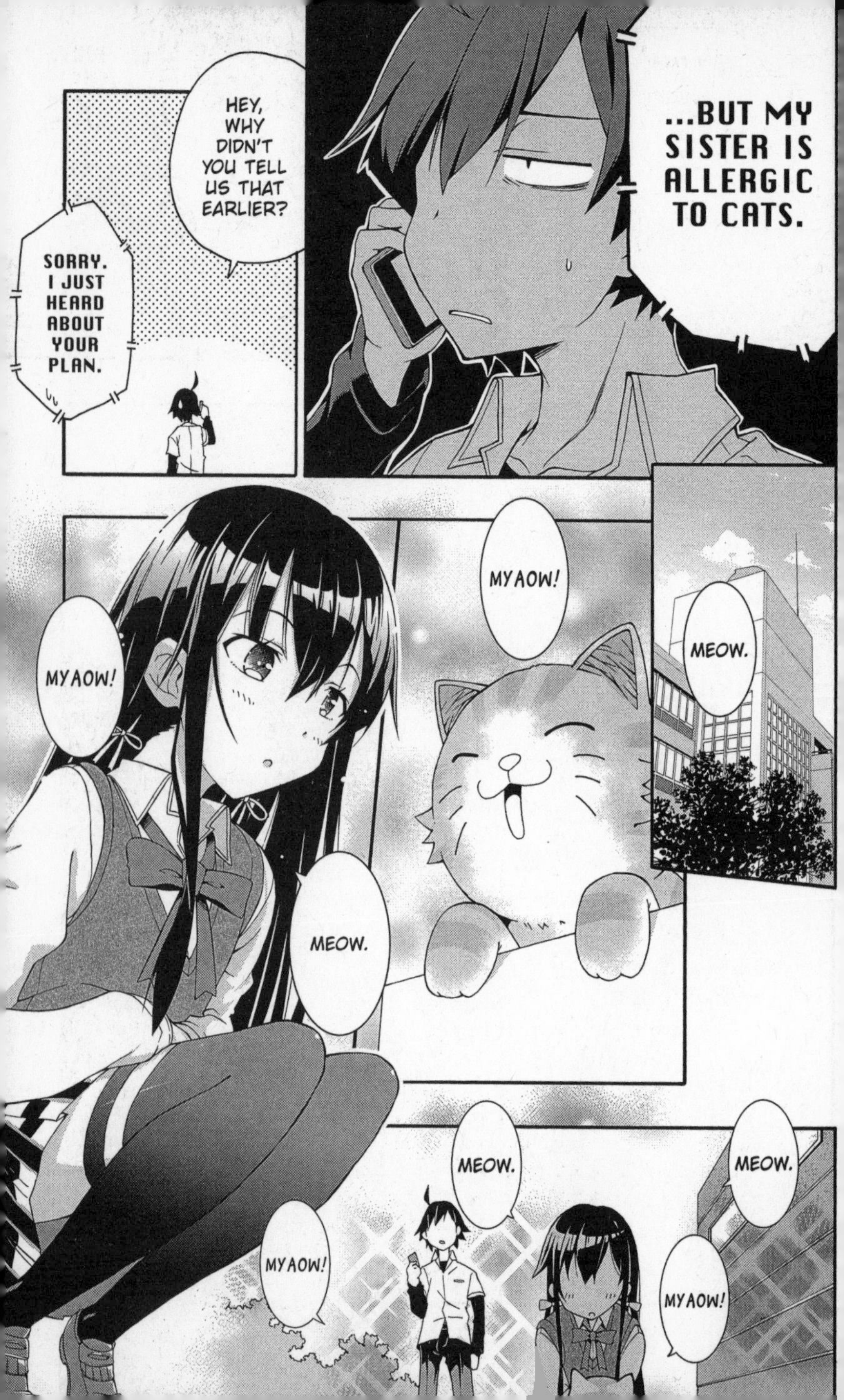
...BUT MY SISTER IS ALLERGIC TO CATS.
HEY, WHY DIDN'T YOU TELL US THAT EARLIER?
SORRY. I JUST HEARD ABOUT YOUR PLAN.
MEOW.
MYAOW!
MYAOW!
MEOW.
MEOW.
MEOW.
MYAOW!
MYAOW!

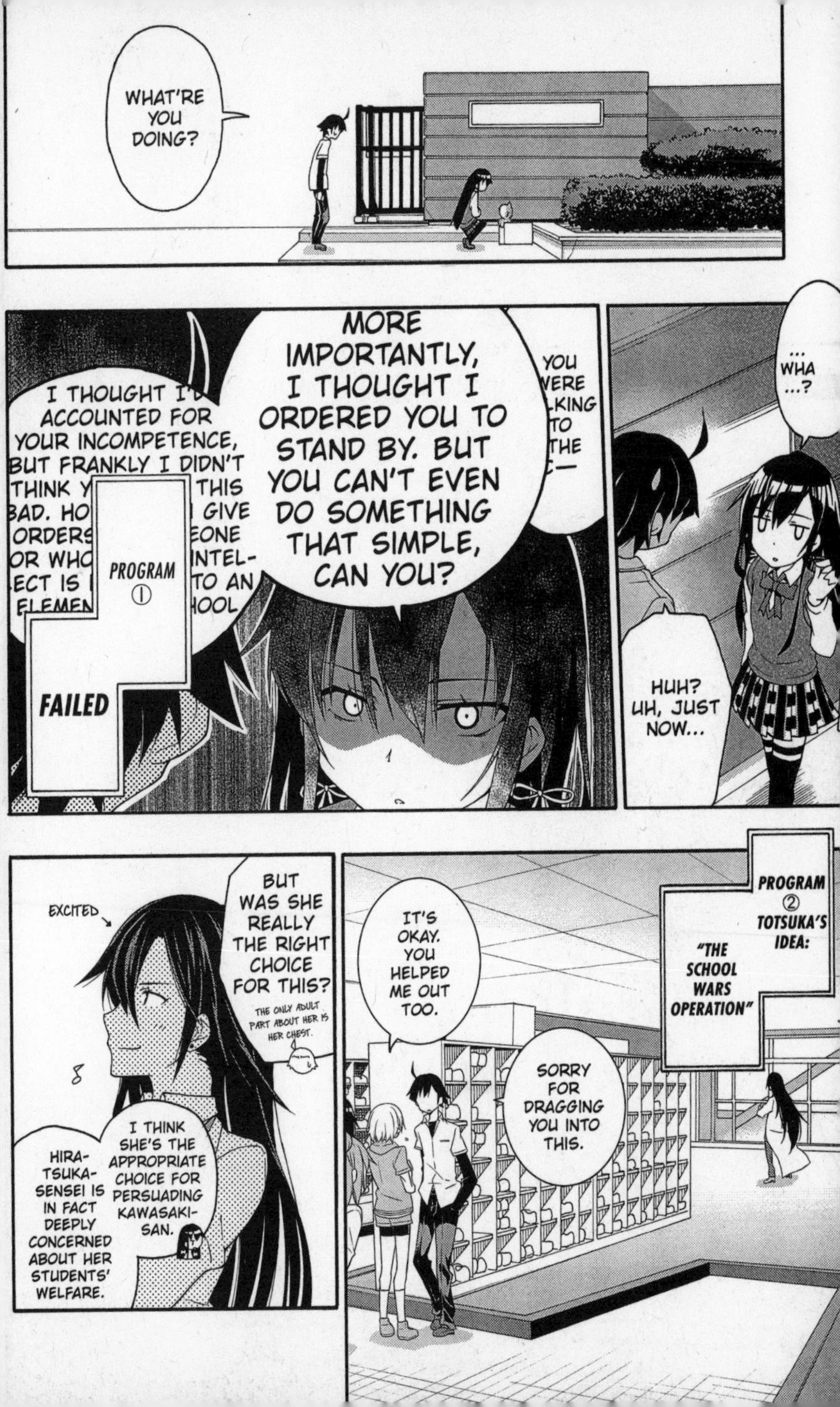
WHAT'RE YOU DOING?
...WHA ...?
HUH? UH, JUST NOW...
MORE IMPORTANTLY, I THOUGHT I ORDERED YOU TO STAND BY. BUT YOU CAN'T EVEN DO SOMETHING THAT SIMPLE, CAN YOU?
I THOUGHT I'D ACCOUNTED FOR YOUR INCOMPETENCE, BUT FRANKLY I DIDN'T
PROGRAM ① FAILED
PROGRAM ② TOTSUKA'S IDEA: "THE SCHOOL WARS OPERATION"
SORRY FOR DRAGGING YOU INTO THIS.
IT'S OKAY. YOU HELPED ME OUT TOO.
BUT WAS SHE REALLY THE RIGHT CHOICE FOR THIS?
THE ONLY ADULT PART ABOUT HER IS HER CHEST.
EXCITED
I THINK SHE'S THE APPROPRIATE CHOICE FOR PERSUADING KAWASAKI-SAN.
HIRA-TSUKA-SENSEI IS IN FACT DEEPLY CONCERNED ABOUT HER STUDENTS' WELFARE.

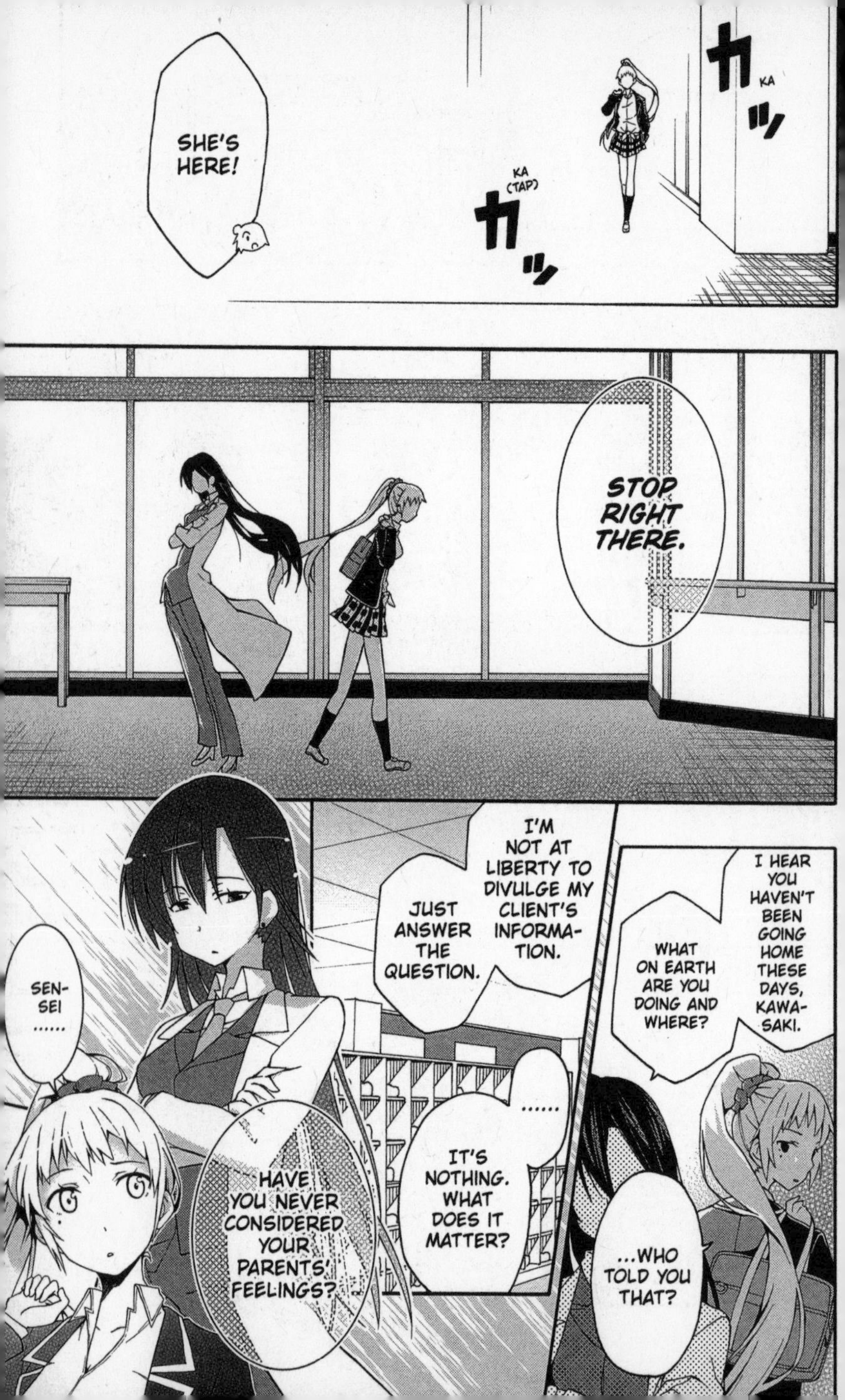

カッ
KA
KA (TAP)
カッ
SHE'S HERE!
STOP RIGHT THERE.
I HEAR YOU HAVEN'T BEEN GOING HOME THESE DAYS, KAWASAKI.
WHAT ON EARTH ARE YOU DOING AND WHERE?
...WHO TOLD YOU THAT?
I'M NOT AT LIBERTY TO DIVULGE MY CLIENT'S INFORMATION.
JUST ANSWER THE QUESTION.
......
IT'S NOTHING. WHAT DOES IT MATTER?
HAVE YOU NEVER CONSIDERED YOUR PARENTS' FEELINGS?
SENSEI......

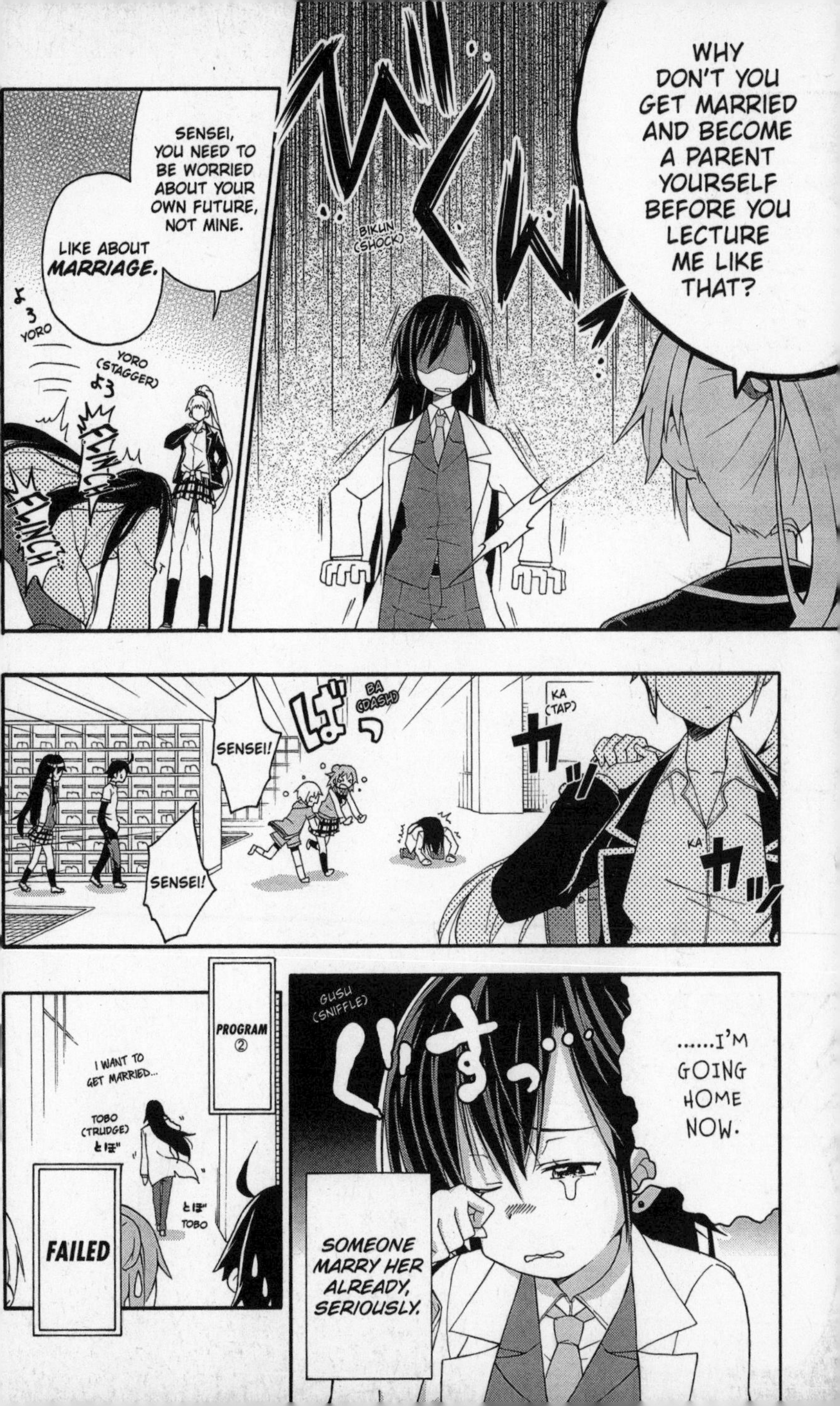
WHY DON'T YOU GET MARRIED AND BECOME A PARENT YOURSELF BEFORE YOU LECTURE ME LIKE THAT?
BIKUN (SHOCK)
SENSEI, YOU NEED TO BE WORRIED ABOUT YOUR OWN FUTURE, NOT MINE.
LIKE ABOUT **MARRIAGE.**
よろ
YORO
YORO (STAGGER)
よろ
FLINCH
FLINCH
KA (TAP)
KA
BA (DASH)
ばっ
SENSEI!
SENSEI!
GUSU (SNIFFLE)
ぐすっ
......I'M GOING HOME NOW.
SOMEONE MARRY HER ALREADY, SERIOUSLY.
PROGRAM ②
I WANT TO GET MARRIED...
TOBO (TRUDGE)
とぼ
とぼ
TOBO
FAILED

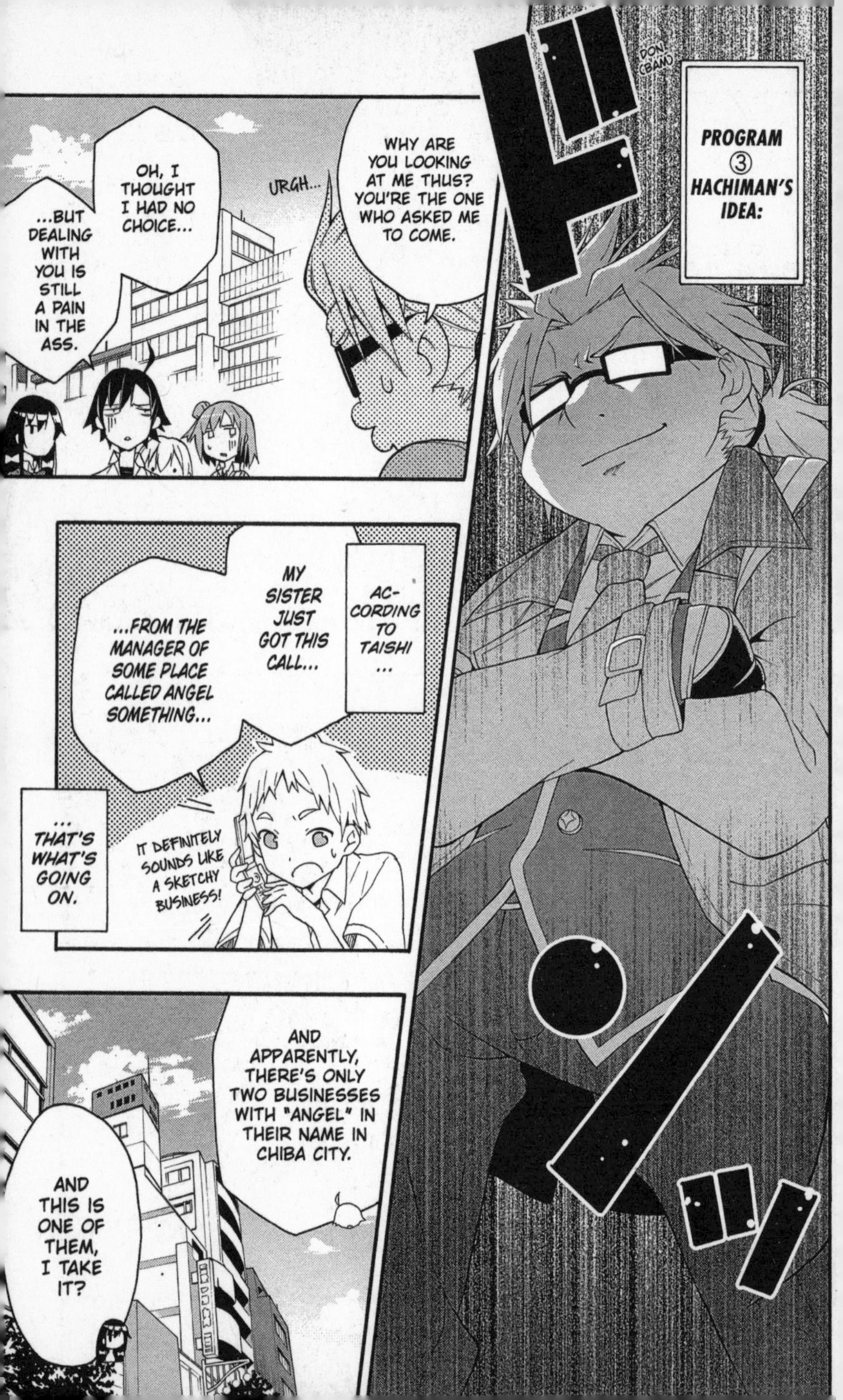
PROGRAM ③ HACHIMAN'S IDEA:
DON (BAM)
WHY ARE YOU LOOKING AT ME THUS? YOU'RE THE ONE WHO ASKED ME TO COME.
URGH...
OH, I THOUGHT I HAD NO CHOICE...
...BUT DEALING WITH YOU IS STILL A PAIN IN THE ASS.
AC-CORDING TO TAISHI...
MY SISTER JUST GOT THIS CALL...
...FROM THE MANAGER OF SOME PLACE CALLED ANGEL SOMETHING...
IT DEFINITELY SOUNDS LIKE A SKETCHY BUSINESS!
...THAT'S WHAT'S GOING ON.
AND APPARENTLY, THERE'S ONLY TWO BUSINESSES WITH "ANGEL" IN THEIR NAME IN CHIBA CITY.
AND THIS IS ONE OF THEM, I TAKE IT?

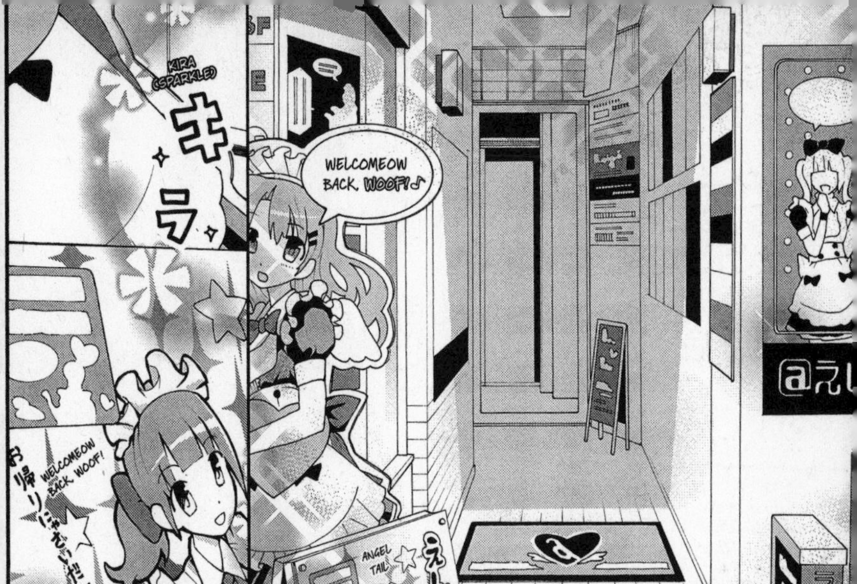
WELCOMEOW BACK, WOOF!♪
キラ
KIRA (SPARKLED)
WELCOMEOW BACK, WOOF!
ANGEL TAIL
キラ
KIRA (SPARKLED)

PHOTOGRAPHED WITH THE COOPERATION OF @HOME CAFÉ, MAIN BRANCH (AKIHABARA)

SIGNS: ANGEL TAIL / WELCOMEOW BACK, WOOF!

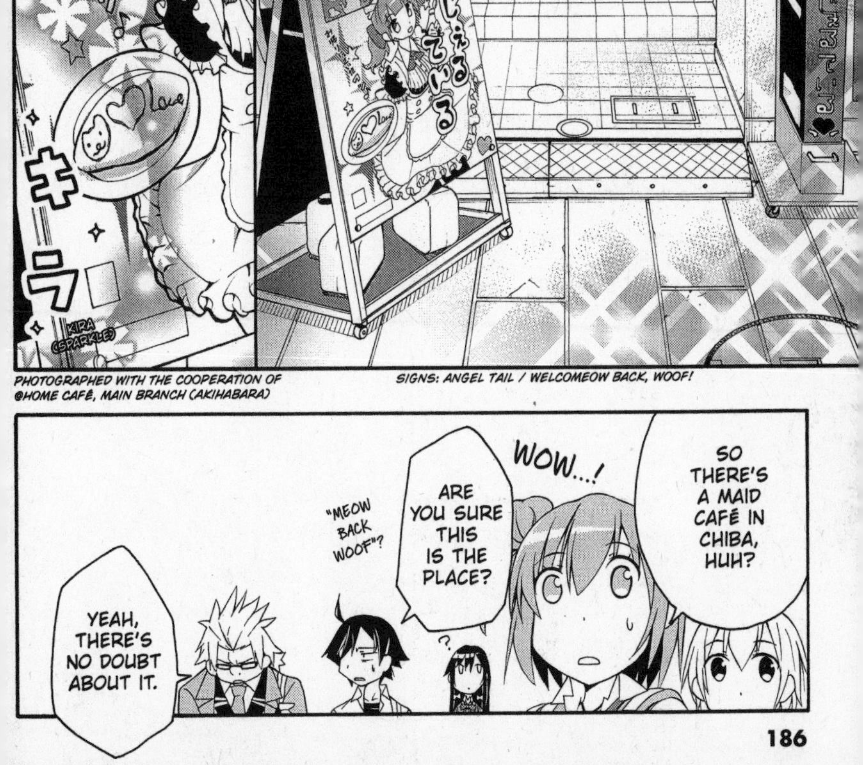
SO THERE'S A MAID CAFÉ IN CHIBA, HUH?
WOW...!
ARE YOU SURE THIS IS THE PLACE?
"MEOW BACK WOOF"?
?
YEAH, THERE'S NO DOUBT ABOUT IT.

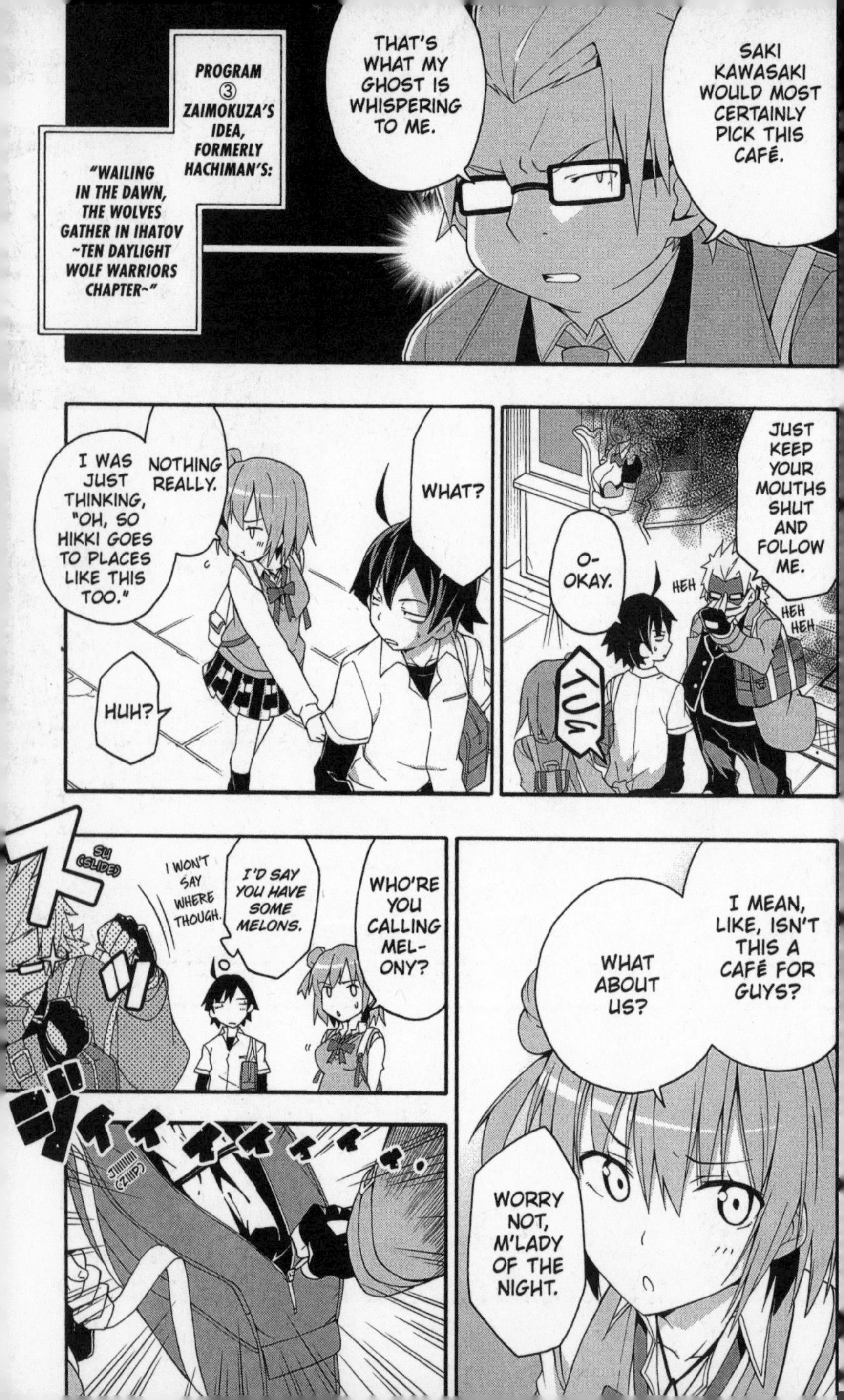
SAKI KAWASAKI WOULD MOST CERTAINLY PICK THIS CAFÉ.
THAT'S WHAT MY GHOST IS WHISPERING TO ME.
PROGRAM ③ ZAIMOKUZA'S IDEA, FORMERLY HACHIMAN'S:
“WAILING IN THE DAWN, THE WOLVES GATHER IN IHATOV ~TEN DAYLIGHT WOLF WARRIORS CHAPTER~”
JUST KEEP YOUR MOUTHS SHUT AND FOLLOW ME.
HEH
HEH HEH
O-OKAY.
TUG
WHAT?
NOTHING REALLY.
I WAS JUST THINKING, “OH, SO HIKKI GOES TO PLACES LIKE THIS TOO.”
HUH?
I MEAN, LIKE, ISN'T THIS A CAFÉ FOR GUYS?
WHAT ABOUT US?
WORRY NOT, M'LADY OF THE NIGHT.
WHO'RE YOU CALLING MELONY?
I'D SAY YOU HAVE SOME MELONS.
I WON'T SAY WHERE THOUGH.
SU (SLIDE)
JIIIIIII (ZIIIP)

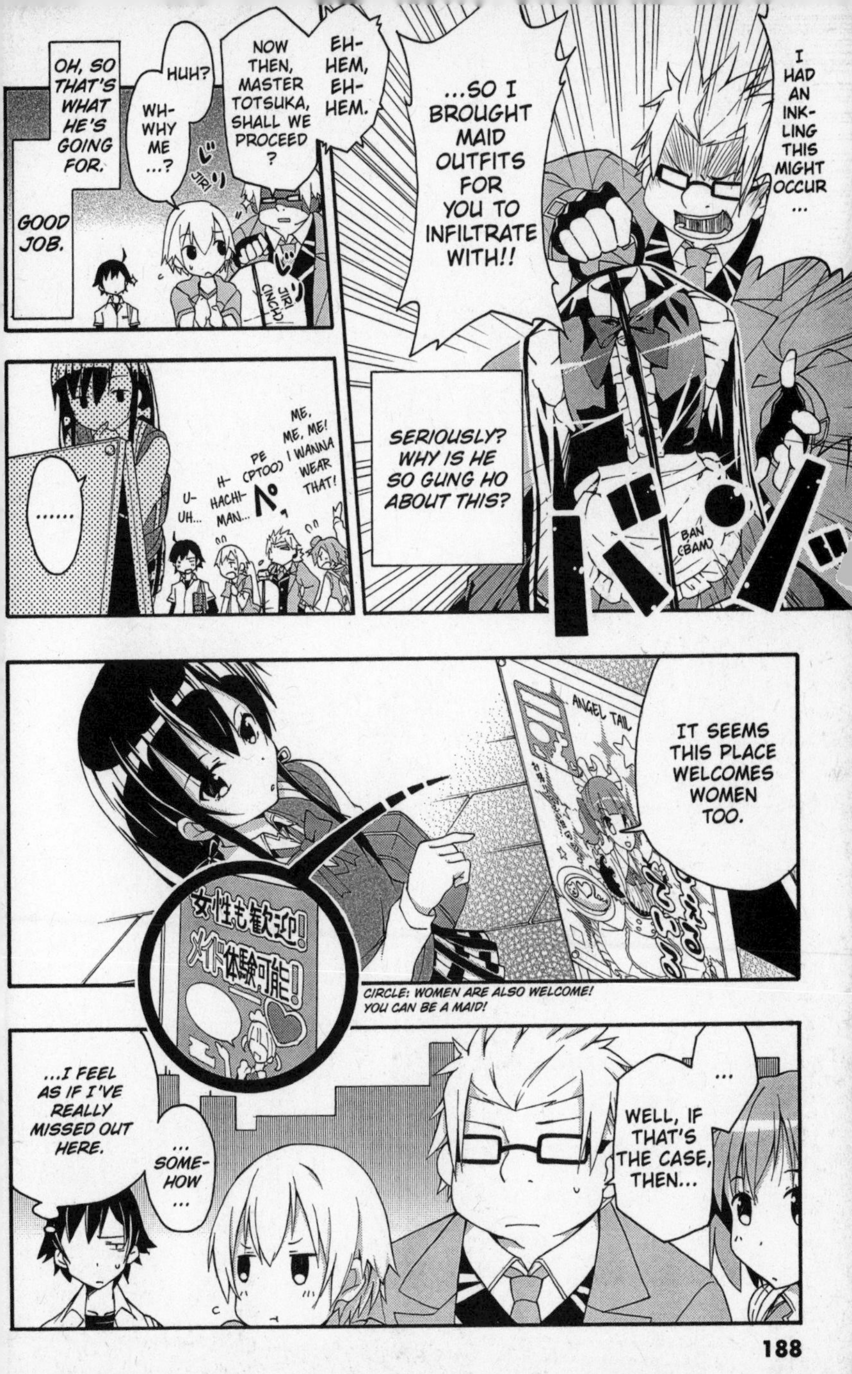
I HAD AN INKLING THIS MIGHT OCCUR...
...SO I BROUGHT MAID OUTFITS FOR YOU TO INFILTRATE WITH!!
BAN (BAM)
SERIOUSLY? WHY IS HE SO GUNG HO ABOUT THIS?
EH-HEM, EH-HEM.
NOW THEN, MASTER TOTSUKA, SHALL WE PROCEED?
JIRI
JIRI (CINCH)
HUH?
WH-WHY ME ...?
OH, SO THAT'S WHAT HE'S GOING FOR.
GOOD JOB.
ME, ME, ME! I WANNA WEAR THAT!
PE (PTOO)
H-HACHIMAN...
U-UH...
......
IT SEEMS THIS PLACE WELCOMES WOMEN TOO.
ANGEL TAIL
女性も歓迎!
メイド体験可能!
CIRCLE: WOMEN ARE ALSO WELCOME! YOU CAN BE A MAID!
...
WELL, IF THAT'S THE CASE, THEN...
...SOMEHOW...
...I FEEL AS IF I'VE REALLY MISSED OUT HERE.

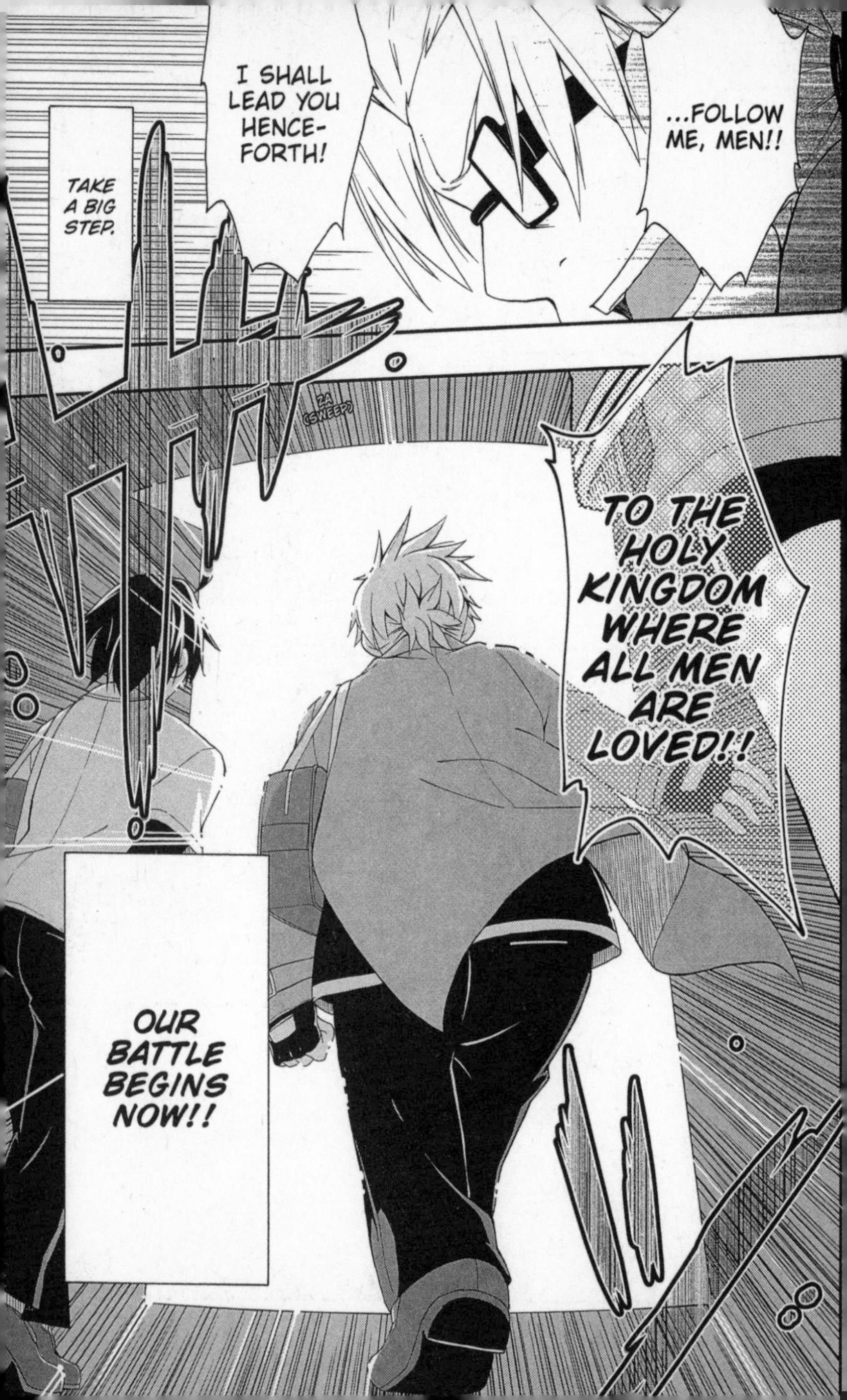
...FOLLOW ME, MEN!!
I SHALL LEAD YOU HENCE-FORTH!
TAKE A BIG STEP.
ZA (SWEEP)
TO THE HOLY KINGDOM WHERE ALL MEN ARE LOVED!!
OUR BATTLE BEGINS NOW!!

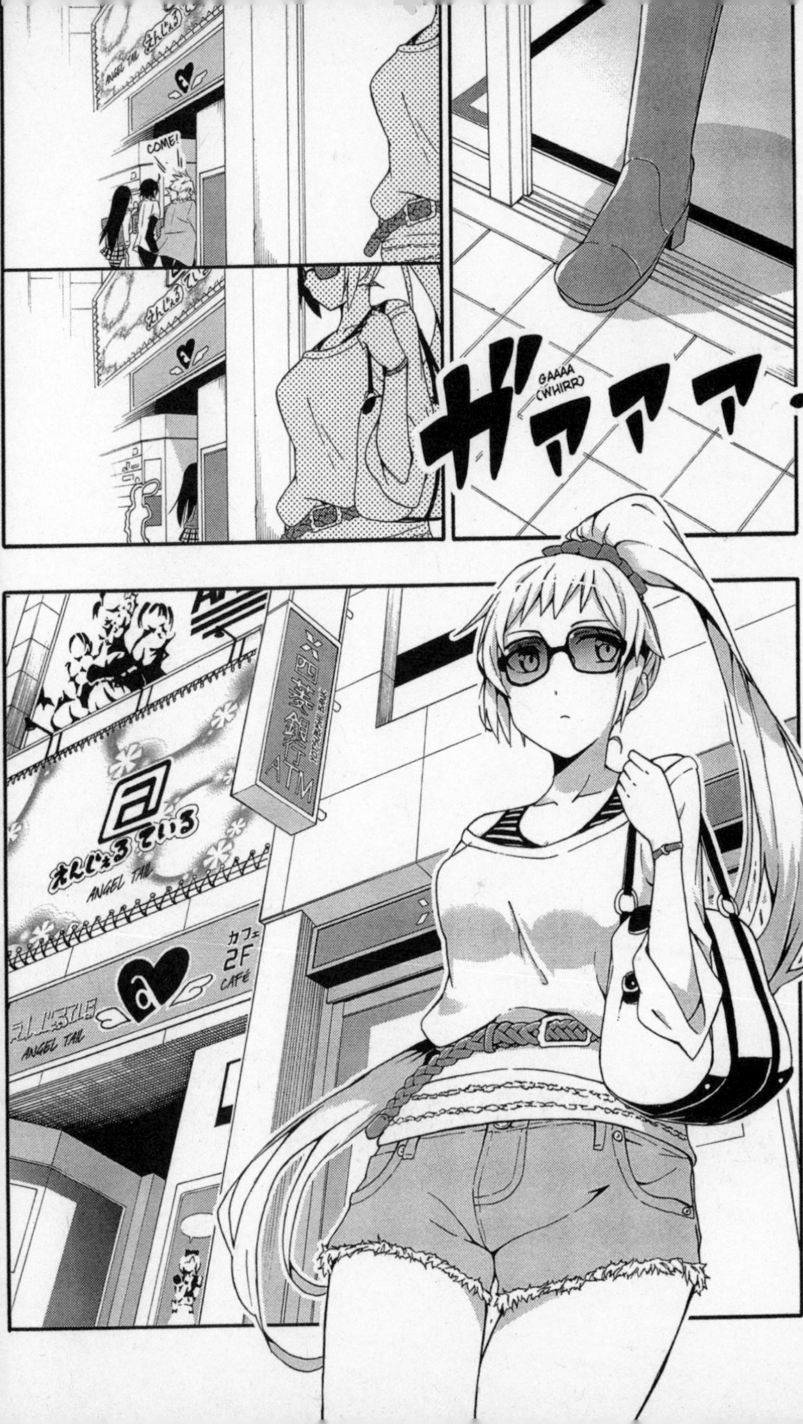
ガァアア
GAAAA (WHIRR)
ANGEL TAIL えんじぇる
COME!
えんじぇる
えんじぇるている
ANGEL TAIL
四菱銀行
YOTSUBISHI BANK
ATM
カフェ
2F
CAFÉ
ANGEL TAIL

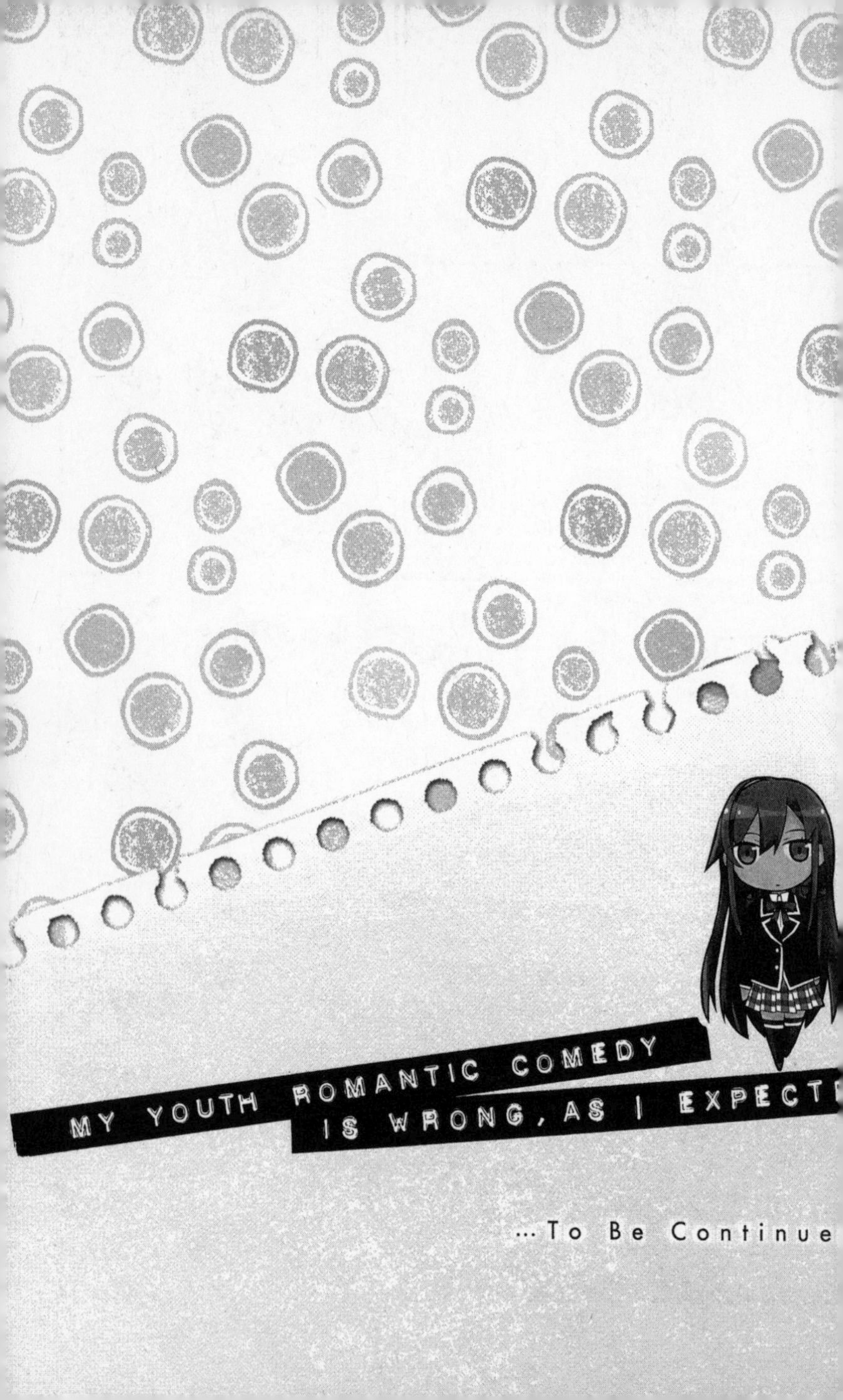
MY YOUTH ROMANTIC COMEDY
IS WRONG, AS I EXPECT
...To Be Continue

アトガキ。

AFTERWORD

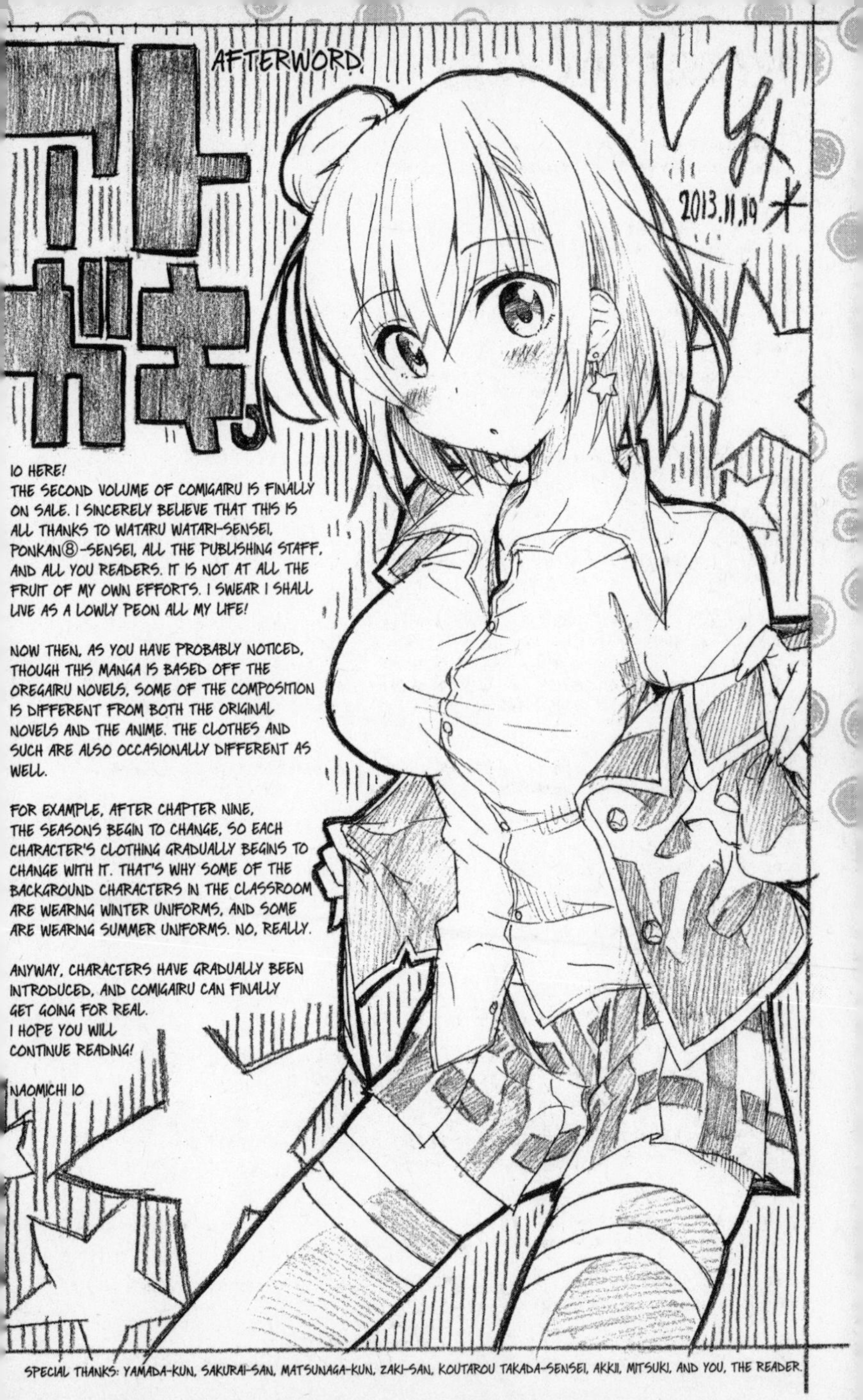
2013.11.19

IO HERE!
THE SECOND VOLUME OF COMIGAIRU IS FINALLY ON SALE. I SINCERELY BELIEVE THAT THIS IS ALL THANKS TO WATARU WATARI-SENSEI, PONKAN⑧-SENSEI, ALL THE PUBLISHING STAFF, AND ALL YOU READERS. IT IS NOT AT ALL THE FRUIT OF MY OWN EFFORTS. I SWEAR I SHALL LIVE AS A LOWLY PEON ALL MY LIFE!

NOW THEN, AS YOU HAVE PROBABLY NOTICED, THOUGH THIS MANGA IS BASED OFF THE OREGAIRU NOVELS, SOME OF THE COMPOSITION IS DIFFERENT FROM BOTH THE ORIGINAL NOVELS AND THE ANIME. THE CLOTHES AND SUCH ARE ALSO OCCASIONALLY DIFFERENT AS WELL.

FOR EXAMPLE, AFTER CHAPTER NINE, THE SEASONS BEGIN TO CHANGE, SO EACH CHARACTER'S CLOTHING GRADUALLY BEGINS TO CHANGE WITH IT. THAT'S WHY SOME OF THE BACKGROUND CHARACTERS IN THE CLASSROOM ARE WEARING WINTER UNIFORMS, AND SOME ARE WEARING SUMMER UNIFORMS. NO, REALLY.

ANYWAY, CHARACTERS HAVE GRADUALLY BEEN INTRODUCED, AND COMIGAIRU CAN FINALLY GET GOING FOR REAL.
I HOPE YOU WILL CONTINUE READING!

NAOMICHI IO

SPECIAL THANKS: YAMADA-KUN, SAKURAI-SAN, MATSUNAGA-KUN, ZAKI-SAN, KOUTAROU TAKADA-SENSEI, AKKII, MITSUKI, AND YOU, THE READER.

TRANSLATION NOTES

Page 2
"Perfect Superwoman": *Kanpeki Choujin*, or "Perfect Superhuman," is a reference to a class of Choujin in the *Kinnikuman* manga by the creator duo Yudetamago. The Kanpeki Choujin were so powerful, they were exiled to the heavens.

Page 16
Hikitani: The second kanji character in Hachiman Hikigaya's name means "valley" and can be read as "tani." Tobe is therefore misreading his name as "Hikitani."

Page 19
Hadoukyuu is a technique used by Tetsu Ishida from Fudoumine Middle School in the manga *Prince of Tennis* by Takeshi Konomi.

Page 48
"So those sausage curls of hers...are not just for show, huh?" This is a reference to Madame Butterfly, a voluminously coiffed character in *Ace wo Nerae!* ("Aim for the Ace!"), a famous seventies *shoujo* manga about tennis.

Page 102-103
Shocking First Bullet, Annihilating Second Bullet: These skills are special attacks of Kazuma Torisuna, the main character in the *shounen* anime and manga *s-CRY-ed*.

Page 104
Yutori education: *Yutori Kyouiku*, or "relaxed education," is the general tendency of government policy to reduce classroom time and contents while adding things like extracurriculars. This began in the seventies. It's constantly under criticism in the vein of "students these days don't learn anything anymore, and school is too easy."

"Make me miso soup every morning." This is an old-fashioned way to propose marriage. A man would not ask a woman to marry him directly by getting down on one knee, Western-style. Rather, he would just casually ask one day, "So when are you quitting your job?" or "I'd like to eat your meals every day." The growth in popularity of Western-style proposals and weddings as well as greater participation of women in the workforce has turned this into a rather quaint and old-fashioned thing to say, and many young people (like Totsuka) might not even be sure what it means.

Page 121
Saize in Plena: Saize is short for Saizeriya, a famous family-style restaurant chain. Plena is short for the Plena Makuhari mall, a popular hangout spot in Chiba that's a short train ride away from Tokyo.

Page 132
The Zone: The steamroller in the artwork is a reference to the iconic fight in the Stardust Crusaders arc of *Jojo's Bizarre Adventure*, where villain Dio Brando drops a steamroller on protagonist Jotaro. Dio's power during that incarnation is The World, said in English in the same way The Zone is in English here.

Star Driver: Hayama is dressed as Takuto from the anime *Star Driver* (2010–2011), a magical boy/*mecha* anime.

Page 142
Fujoshi literally means "rotten woman" and refers to women who enjoy BL manga and fantasizing about sexual or romantic relationships between men. The Japanese counterpart of the slash fangirl.

Seme and *uke* are used by *fujoshi* to describe sexual roles of characters in BL manga: *Seme* is the top, and *uke* is the bottom. It's notable that gay men do not use these terms—that would be *tachi* and *neko*, respectively.

Page 182
"The School Wars Operation." This is a reference to *School Wars*, a Japanese TV drama from 1984 about a high school rugby coach who helps to reform delinquent students.

Page 187
"That's what my ghost is whispering to me." This is a quote from the film and anime series *Ghost in the Shell*. Motoko Kusanagi, the protagonist, tends to say it when she has a hunch about something.

Ihatov is a term made up by the author Kenji Miyazawa (1896–1933) to describe a sort of idyllic scenic beauty. It's thought to allude to Iwate prefecture, Miyazawa's native province.

Page 189
"Our battle begins now!!" This is a phrase commonly seen on the final page of battle manga that have been canceled early.

MY YOUTH ROMANTIC COMEDY IS WRONG, AS I EXPECTED @COMIC ②

Original Story: Wataru Watari
Art: Naomichi Io
Character Design: Ponkan⑧
ORIGINAL COVER DESIGN/Hiroyuki KAWASOME (Graphio)

Translation: Jennifer Ward

Lettering: Bianca Pistillo

This book is a work of fiction. Names, characters, places, and incidents are the product of the author's imagination or are used fictitiously. Any resemblance to actual events, locales, or persons, living or dead, is coincidental.

YAHARI ORE NO SEISHUN LOVE COME WA MACHIGATTEIRU.
@COMIC Vol. 2 by Wataru WATARI, Naomichi IO, PONKAN⑧
© 2013 Wataru WATARI, Naomichi IO, PONKAN⑧
All rights reserved.
Original Japanese edition published by SHOGAKUKAN.
English translation rights arranged with SHOGAKUKAN through Tuttle-Mori Agency, Inc., Tokyo.

English translation © 2016 by Yen Press, LLC

Yen Press
1290 Avenue of the Americas
New York, NY 10104

Visit us at yenpress.com
facebook.com/yenpress
twitter.com/yenpress
yenpress.tumblr.com

First Yen Press Edition: September 2016

Yen Press is an imprint of Yen Press, LLC.
The Yen Press name and logo are trademarks of Yen Press, LLC.

The publisher is not responsible for websites (or their content) that are not owned by the publisher.

Library of Congress Control Number: 2016931004

ISBN: 978-0-316-31810-5

10 9 8 7 6 5 4 3 2 1

BVG

Printed in the United States of America